The Grass
Is
Always Greener
Over
The Septic Tank

Erma Bombeck

FAWCETT CREST • NEW YORK

For Marianna, Helen, Charmaine, Marie, Lil,
Mary Ellen, and Annie, who when I was drowning
in a car pool threw me a line . . . always a funny one

Contents

Foreword

Soon after the West was settled, Americans became restless and began to look for new frontiers.

Bored with the conveniences of running water, electricity, central heating, rapid communication, and public transportation, they turned to a new challenge . . . the suburbs.

The suburbs were discovered quite by accident one day in the early 1940's by a Welcome-Wagon lady who was lost. As she stood in a mushy marshland, her sturdy Red Cross shoes sinking into the mire, she looked down, and exclaimed, "It's a septic tank. I've discovered the suburbs!"

News of the discovery of a septic tank spread and within weeks thirty million city dwellers readied their station wagons and began the long journey to the edge of town in search of a bath and a half and a tree.

It wasn't easy for the first settlers. They planted trees and crabgrass came up. They planted schools and taxes came up. Surveyors planted stakes and they disintegrated.

The first winter, more than half of the original settlers perished. Some lost their way in cul-de-sacs and winding streets with the same name trying to find their way home.

Other poor devils died of old age trying to merge onto the freeway to the city. One was attacked by a fast-growing evergreen that the builder planted near his front door. (They named a high school after him.)

There wasn't a day that went by that they weren't threatened by forces from the city: salesmen of storm doors, Tupperware and Avon ladies, traffic lights, encyclopedia salesmen, Girl Scout cookie pushers, and Golden Arches everywhere.

The survival by at least one family of PTA's, garage sales, car pools, horse privileges, Sunday drivers, Little Leagues, and lights from the shopping center is what this book is all about.

It traces the migration of the Bombeck family from their modest—but pathetic—apartment in the heart of the city to a plat house (one original and 216 carbons) just outside the city limits.

They make the trip with a son who has spoken

four words in five years ("I get the window"), their daughter who sleeps with a baton, and a toddler who has never known anything but apartment living and consequently does not own a pair of hard shoes.

It took a week to load their station wagon and after the good-byes they settled back to enjoy their new adventure.

"Look, honey, sit down on the seat. Daddy cannot drive with scissors in his ear. No, I don't know how long it has been since I cut the hairs in my ears! Erma, for God's sake, find something for him to do."

"Are we there yet?"

"It's my window and I say when it goes down and when it goes up. Mom! Isn't it *my* window?"

"You did not see a cow and if you mark it down I'm going to mark down a chariot on my list. A chariot gives me fifty points."

"I'm hungry."

"Start the motor. They'll be better when we get moving."

"Erma, do you smell something? Check the dog."

"The dog checks out."

"Check the feet of the kids."

"They all check."

"Check your own."

"You check yours first."

"Mom! I'm gonna be sick."

"You are not going to be sick and that's my final word!"

"Boys! Get your hands in this car or they'll blow off."

"How many kids had their hands blown off last year?"

"Too many to count."

"Did you ever see a hand that blew off on your windshield, Dad?"

"Erma, for God's sake find something for the kids to do."

"Mom! Andy took a bite out of a cookie and put it back. I'm telling."

"You tell about the cookies and I'm telling about your chicken bone collection."

"Stop the car! That's what we smell."

"Dad, when you get mad the veins in your nose swell up."

"I thought you were going to give them a sedative. How much farther?"

"We've got a hairpin, a thumbnail and a breath-mint to go, according to this map."

"Can't you interpret a simple road map?"

"Don't shout at me, Bill, I can't handle shouting today."

"I'm not shouting, I'm just suggesting that you are a high-school graduate and are capable of interpreting a simple scale on a map."

"Hey, Dad, I just saw a hand fly by."

"What day is it?" I asked. "I don't know how much longer I can stand the driving, the confinement, the loneliness. Not being able to talk to anyone. Bill, maybe we shouldn't have come."

"It won't be long now!" he said.

The Bombecks made it to the suburbs in their station wagon on June 9th. It was the longest fifty-five-minute drive any of them had ever endured.

CHAPTER ONE

Station Wagons . . . Ho!

Staking Out a Claim

It was either Thomas Jefferson—or maybe it was John Wayne—who once said, "Your foot will never get well as long as there is a horse standing on it."

It was logic like this that attracted thirty million settlers to the suburbs following World War II.

The suburbs were a wilderness with nothing to offer but wide, open spaces, virgin forests, and a cool breeze at night that made you breathe deep, close your eyes and sigh, "My God! Who's fertilizing with sheep dip?"

My husband held out against migration for as long as he could. Then one day we heard from our good friends, Marge and Ralph, who, together with their two children, set out in one of the first station wagons to a housing development thirty miles south of the city.

As Marge wrote, "We reached the suburbs on the 14th. There was no water and no electricity in our house so we had to hole up in a Holiday Motel for three days. The pool wasn't even heated.

"The yard is barren and there are no sidewalks. Mud is everywhere. There is no garbage pickup, our old stove won't fit in the new hole, and the general store has never heard of Oregano.

"We have aluminum foil at the windows to keep the sun from fading the children. I feel like a turkey. We have to claim our mail at the post office a mile and a half away. There is no super. We have our own washer and dryer which don't require quarters. I understand, however, that at the end of the month, there is something called a utility bill that is presented to us.

"There are some bright spots. We have a bath and a half. It is wonderful not to have to take numbers any more. Tomorrow, we are going to visit our first tree. It is situated on the only 'wooded' lot in the subdivision and is owned by the builder's daughter. Pray for us. . . . Affectionately, Marge."

"Doesn't that sound exciting?" I said, jumping to my feet.

"You say the same thing when your soup is hot."

"Where's your adventurous spirit?" I asked. "It's a new world out there—full of challenges. We're young yet. We could survive."

He put down his paper and swept his arms around to encompass the entire apartment. "What! Move and give up all of this?"

I looked around. I had to iron in the playpen. The kids were stacked in a triple bunk at night like they were awaiting burial at sea. If the phone rang, I had to stand on my husband's face to answer it. The dog slept under the oven, next to the crackers. And one day I yawned, stretched my arms and someone stored the complete works of Dr. Seuss and a pot of African violets on them.

"You'd never survive," he predicted. "It's a raw frontier—no schools, no churches, and only three registered Republicans. Frankly, I don't think you have the stamina or the threshold of pain for it."

"Stamina!" I shouted. "Are you telling me I have no stamina? A woman who has lived on the fourth floor of this apartment building for five years with the stairs out of order has no stamina? I have legs like a discus thrower. As for pain, I have been known to go without support stockings for as long as two hours."

"Do you honestly think you could move to a land where your mother is a 35-cent toll charge for the first three minutes?"

I hesitated, then squared my shoulders and said, "Yes!"

It was probably my imagination, but I thought I heard a whip crack and a voice shout, "Station Wagons . . . Ho!"

The selling of the suburbs made the coronation of Queen Elizabeth look like an impulse.

On a Sunday afternoon you could tour Cinderella's Red Coach Farms, Mortgage Mañana, Saul Lieberman's Bonsai Gardens, or Bonaparte's Retreat ("Live the Rest of Your Life Like a Weak King").

Every development had its gimmick: flags flying, billboards, free rain bonnets, balloons for the kiddies, and pom pom girls that spelled out LOW INTEREST RATES in script.

My husband spread out the newspaper and together we went over the plats we had visited.

"What did you think of Tahitian Village?" he asked.

"Cute," I said, "but a little overdone. I mean dropping the kids into a volcano to play each morning just . . ."

"What about Chateau on Waldren's Pond?"

"Call it a woman's intuition, but I've never trusted a lake that had a sudsing problem on Monday mornings."

"Wanta check out Sherwood Forest?"

"Why not?"

The sales office of Sherwood Forest was a tree stump surrounded by five or six salesmen dressed in tunics. Nearby was a plastic campfire that held a plastic pig on a spit and beyond that were 800 plastic houses.

"Welcome to Sherwood Forest," said a salesman schlepping along in a brown frock, a rope, and a pair of sandals. "I'm Friar Tuck and if you have any questions, feel free to ask them."

"If this is Sherwood Forest," I asked, "where are the trees?"

"You're standing over it," he said, staring at my knees.

My husband picked up the price list.

"You'll find that it is in keeping with the Robin Hood philosophy," he smiled.

We bolted toward the car, pursued by six Merry Men.

The adventure of moving to the suburbs had nearly worn off when we stumbled into Suburbian Gems.

"How much are the houses?" asked my husband.

"We have one standard price in Suburbian Gems," said the salesman. "$15,000."

We couldn't believe it. "Could we see the tracts?" we asked. He pulled down a giant map behind him solid with blocks representing houses. "I'm afraid we're pretty well sold out," he said. "The Diamond section went before we even advertised. Jade went fast. So did Ruby. And Pearl. I see even Zircon is blocked off."

"What's left?" we asked.

"Frankly Fake," he said. "Climb in the car and I'll drive you over to the sites so you can get the feel of the development."

When we pulled up in front of the house, I couldn't believe it. I got out of the car and ran through the two-story iron gates, up the half mile of driveway to the veranda porch, touched the massive white pillars and ran my fingers over the large carved door. "It's Tara!" I said, my eyes misting, "I've come home to Tara."

"You understand, this is only the model home," said the salesman.

I buried my face in the wisteria that crept along

the windows. "We understand. Could we see the rest of it?"

The double doors opened and our voices echoed our pleasure in the house, from the huge foyer to the curved stairway leading to the second floor.

Then, inside the living room, I saw it—the fireplace. A warmth came over me. I could see my husband standing against it in a sports coat with leather patches on the elbows holding a brandy and a copy of Emerson's essays.

I visualized me hanging a della Robbia wreath over it at Christmas and laughing children basking in its reflection after a snow. "We'll take it," I said suddenly.

As my husband lifted his hand to touch my face in a gesture of love, he was amazed to find a pen in it.

"If you will just sign the purchase agreement," said the salesman, " we can get on with the details of your new home in Frankly Fake."

I squeezed my husband's arm as he signed the agreement.

"We've never had a fireplace before."

"Oh, then you want the model with the fireplace?" asked the salesman.

We nodded.

"Well, now, is there anything else about the Williamsburg model that you like?"

"We like everything," I said.

"Oh, then you want the second floor, the extra baths, the tiled foyer, the stairway, the veranda porch, the larger lot . . . ?"

"Are you saying all those things are extra?"

"The Williamsburg is our best home," he said stiffly. "Our basic $15,000 is much the same only on a smaller scale."

"How small?" asked my husband.

"Let's see," he said, checking his price list. "The Pee Wee has three bedrooms and a one-car garage, spouting to protect your porch from the sun, full landscaping, and 850 luxurious square feet."

"Does it have a family room?"

"Two of them—both in white fixtures."

"But the Pee Wee does have the pillars and the porch . . ." I asked anxiously.

"I told you, it has everything except a second story, stairway, entranceway, and extra lot. Now, that covers about everything except what you want to do about the garage."

"What about the garage?" asked my husband.

"Do you plan on putting your car in it?"

"It crossed our minds."

"I see. I only mention it because a lot of people

like to have a driveway leading to it. You don't have to, you understand, but it does get a little muddy and it's worth the extra cost to some people to have it filled in."

"But everything else is included in the original price?" asked my husband.

"Absolutely. All you have to do is make some decisions regarding the quality of materials. For example, all wiring is borderline standard unless you want to pay extra and have it pass inspection. (We nodded.) I think that's wise. Now, about your tub. Do you want it hooked up under your shower?"

We nodded numbly.

"I assumed you did because you already said you wanted to put a car in your garage and that's where we usually store the tub until the owner tells us otherwise. Speaking of storage, you are aware that without the second story, there is a crawl space over your entire house for storage?"

We smiled happily.

"Do you have some way of getting up there or do you want us to install a pull-down stairway as an extra? Let's see—apart from the paint, floor covering, spouting, storm windows, kitchen hardware, countertops, lighting fixtures, and keys, which are all extra, I think that does it."

His fingers fairly raced across the keys of the

27

tabulator as the extras mounted. Finally, he smiled and said, "The final tab is $29,500. Welcome to Frankly Fake!"

As my husband handed back the pen, he smiled, waved it aside, and said, "Keep it. As a token of our mutual faith in one another."

Out of the corner of my eye, I saw him add, "Pen @ 59 cents" bringing the total to $29,500.59.

Lot No. 15436 . . . Where Are You?

We must have driven two and a half hours before we found our house.

"Are you sure this is it?" asked my husband.

"I'm sure," I said tiredly. "This is the eighth house from the corner and the builder always staggers his styles so they won't all look alike. I counted them. There were the Williamsburg, the Richmond, the Shenandoah, and the Pee Wee, a Williamsburg, a Richmond, a Shenandoah, and this is our Pee Wee."

"I thought it was supposed to look like Mt. Vernon," whined our daughter, "with big pillars."

"But it does have pillars," I said, pointing toward the four supports that looked like filter-tip cigarettes.

"Will they grow?" asked our son.

"Children, please!" said my husband. Then, turning to me he asked, "Happy?"

I looked at the packing boxes stacked at the curb, the mail box on the ground, chunks of plaster embedded in the mud, windows dusty and spackled with paint and said, "I wish I could tell you—in front of the children."

"Well, let's go in and get settled," he said. "And take your muddy boots on the porch inside."

"What muddy boots?" I said. "Aren't they yours?"

"They're mine," said a woman coming out of one of the bedrooms.

"Who are you?" asked my husband.

"I live here," she said.

"Isn't this 5425 Ho Hum Lane?" he asked.

"Yes, but it's 5425 Ho Hum Lane Northeast. It used to be 18 Bluebird of Happiness Drive, but then the other street came through and changed it. When we bought it, it was 157 Squirrel Road, but Ho Hum Lane is on a circle and the even numbers change to the odd numbers at the house where the door is on backwards. You know the one?"

"Right. That's two down from the chuckhole in the road where your car falls through."

"That's the one. Besides, 5425 isn't going to be

your permanent number. That's a lot number and will change when the post office assigns you your new one."

"Oh? Where's the post office? We haven't been able to find it."

"No one is quite sure yet. You notice how everything blends with the surroundings out here?"

"I've noticed. We went to a furniture store today and there was a bread card in the window. We almost passed it by."

"I know," she said. "The gas station on the corner blends in so well, I feel guilty if I pull in after dinner when he's cutting the grass. It was the council who decided they didn't want commercial businesses to look like commercial businesses. We had enough of that in the city. They wanted them to have that residential feeling."

"That makes a lot of sense," I said.

"I suppose so," she said, "but the other night it was embarrassing. My husband and I went out to dinner and there was a huge line so Russell (my husband) slipped the maître d' $2 and said, 'I think if you'll check your reservations, you'll find we're next. You came personally recommended.'

" 'By whom?' asked the man in the black suit. 'This is a funeral home.' "

As we continued the search for our new home, I

expressed some concern that every time we left the house we'd have to leave a kid on the front porch for a landmark.

"Things will be different," said my husband, "when the builder puts in the shrubbery."

"How much landscaping comes with the house?" I asked.

He tilted his head and recited from memory, "Let's see, we're down for five maples, eight taxus, six evergreens, two ash, four locust, 109 living rose hedge plants, two flowering mother-in-law tongues, and a grove of fifteen assorted, colorful fruit trees."

"Hey, I think this is it," I said, as he pulled into a driveway. "We are officially home!"

We turned the key in the door. My husband and I raced through the house to the backyard to get a glimpse of the flatbed truck and the lift that would turn our barren patch of mud into a jungle. The yard was empty.

"Where's the shrubbery?" asked my husband.

One of the children called from the house, "Mommy! Daddy! The shrubbery is here!"

"Where?" asked my husband.

"On the dining room table with the mail." We stood around the table. No one spoke as we viewed the envelope holding five maples, eight taxus, six evergreens, two ash, four locust, 109 living rose hedge plants, two flowering mother-in-law tongues, and a grove of fifteen assorted, colorful fruit trees.

My son had more foliage than that growing under his bed.

"Gather it up," said my husband, "and put it in the garage and for God's sake watch the dog. He has eight assorted fruit trees stuck in his tail."

By noon the next day we had planted the entire package.

"Whatya think?" asked my husband.

"It looks like a missile site," I grumbled.

"I think everything will survive the transplanting with the exception of the maple tree. The dog . . ."

"He didn't."

"Yep. His tail brushed against it and the trunk snapped in half."

"I'm worried about the flowering mother-in-law's tongues."

Why?"

"They just spoke to me. They said, 'Help.' "

The Original Settlers

The triumph of man over the suburbs was made possible by the sheer guts of a band of original settlers.

Later, other fringe businesses would sprout up:

a water supply, hospitals, grocery stores, post offices and schools; scouting programs and Good Humor trucks, but at the beginning, these scouts welcomed the newcomers from the city with hands out-stretched—and palms upward.

The Telephone Representative

"Do you want a phone?" asked the lady at the door.

"What kind of a joke is that?" I asked irritably. "Does John Wayne salute the flag? Does Dean Martin drink? Does the Pope work Sundays? Of course I want a phone," I said, literally dragging her into the living room. "Where do I sign?"

"My goodness," she smiled. "Not so fast. We have some decisions to make. First, let me introduce my-self. I am Miss Turtletaub, your telephone repre-sentative, and I'll be handling your application. Now, to begin with, what type of service do you want?"

"The one where the phone is in the house."

"You're teasing," she said. "Do you want the party line that is quaint, but a drag, the two-party line where you share your phone with an informer, or the popular private service?"

"Private. Now when . . ."

"I assume you want more than one phone in a house of this size. Where is your family room?"

"Down the hall, first door to the left and lock it or the kids will bust in on you."

"Oh. Then what about a phone in your bedroom? After all, there is nothing more frightening than the insistent ring of the phone after midnight when your loved ones need you the most and you are busy breaking your leg in a dark hallway."

"The bedroom sounds great. Could you . . ."

"Three phones. That's smart. Now, what about a jack? After all, basking out of doors is the reason you moved to this cornfield in the first place. Just say you are standing out in the backyard talking to your neighbors. Without a phone nearby, you'll never know when some disc jockey is trying to give away $10,000. Look at it this way—a jackpot like that would pay for the jack in one phone call's time."

"Terrific. One jack. Now could we talk about . . ."

"Color? I knew you were discerning the moment I walked in. I brought along some color chips and I think you'll find coordinated phones for every room in your house. There's God's green, barnyard brown, brothel red, and of course boring black."

"One barnyard, one God's, and one boring."

"Wise choice. Now, have you thought about which model you prefer? We have a great one that hangs from the wall for the kitchen that doesn't take up valuable counter space. Then we have the cradle type with the traditional dial, and we have the collector's gallery: the conversation-piece types in the French provincial, the Early American ones shaped like a pump, and here's a cutesie shaped like an ear trumpet."

"Ah . . . traditional is fine," I said, fidgeting, "now, would you be able to tell me . . ."

"You have to live with it. Now about the listing. I know you have youngsters in the family and most of our sophisticated clientele such as yourself want their children listed so they might reap the entire benefits of a phone."

"That's fine," I said.

"Now, unless you have any questions, I think that does it," she said, smiling and snapping her book shut.

"Just one," I said excitedly. "When can you install the phones?"

She shuffled through her papers and came out with a schedule. Then, tracing down with her fingernail, she paused and said, "A year and a half."

"*A year and a half!*"

"You sound shocked," she smiled. "Have you any

idea how much money is involved in cables and poles and electronics to bring phone service all the way out to Suburbian Gems? Why it takes an Act of Congress just to clear the land. We can't perform miracles, can we? Excuse me," she said, "I must dash. There's a couple moving in today down the street. What would they think if the phone company wasn't there to offer their services?"

The Insurance Salesman

Biff Rah said, "You look familiar. Didn't we go to school together?"

It was a funny thing for a man to say over the telephone.

But that's the way neighborhood insurance men in the suburbs were. They clutched at any straw to establish some common basis for your trust and your signature on an endowment. "Listen," he said, "I know you are busy getting settled. Don't I know it? I'm ten years—and I'm still unpacking, right?"

"The children are a little . . ."

"Hey, kids. Do I know kids?" he said. "Got five of them myself so I understand your problem. All I want to do is to come over and review what you've got in the way of protection, and leave, okay?"

We agreed.

Biff grabbed my hand at the door, pumped it and said, "You look familiar. Didn't we go to school together?"

"Not unless you wore a plaid jumper and knee socks. It was an all-girls' school."

"I was the one with the knobby knees who never shaved!" he grinned, punching me in the arm and knocking me into the bookcases. "But seriously folks," he said, whipping open his briefcase. "I didn't come here to make jokes. I simply dropped by to spell out a few facts of life. You've just moved into a new house, your kids are in their jammies watching TV, you're employed (nodding to my husband), you've got a car, and you (nodding at me) stay home and bake bread. You gotta be like this family here in the picture, right?"

We looked down to a page in his notebook at a picture depicting what had to be the All-American family with straight teeth, healthy gums, yellow hair, tennis sweaters, and a house behind them that looked like the Williamsburg.

"Now, what if this happened?" he asked dramatically and with a small brush that took no longer than fifteen seconds removed my husband from the picture.

"How did you do that?" I asked.

"You're missing the point," he said irritably. "Now what happens to that happy family if Daddy is gone. They're repossessing the car. They're taking the house away. They're taking the furniture away. The children are crying. Mommy doesn't know which way to turn. Now, do you know what that means?"

"It means I get custody of the kids," I snapped.

"It means Daddy didn't make plans."

"It wouldn't be the first time," I snapped.

"Lucky," interrupted Biff, "it's not too late. There is still time to protect your loved ones with this twenty-year-pay life. While you are young, the premiums aren't too bad, but in a few years when you develop those heart problems, circulatory disorders, high blood pressure, and an aneurysm, it may not be available to you at any price."

My husband signed the agreement in mid-air. As I squeezed his hand in appreciation, Biff leaned down and addressed himself to our children. "I can tell by looking at you that Mommy has done a wonderful job. And you're not to blame her when she leaves and you are left alone to shift for yourselves."

"Where am I going?" I asked.

"Face it. It's inevitable that someday you'll be going to that big utility room in the sky. May I ask you something? How much insurance do you carry on yourself?"

"I don't know," I stammered, "my husband takes care of that."

"I don't like to make trouble," he said, "but usually a man will cover his wife with a policy which he considers to be her value to him."

"How much am I covered for?" I asked.

"You have the basic $96-no-frill-no-fault-burial-policy," he mumbled.

"*Ninety-six bucks!* That wouldn't bury a bird in a shoebox!"

"That's right," said Biff. "Basically what this means is that when you go, they prop you up in a Christian Science reading room, play a record of Perry Como singing 'Don't Fence Me In,' put you on a public bus, and God knows what happens to you."

We signed another policy.

As Biff got up to go he said, "You're such bright people I'm almost embarrassed to ask, but I have a responsibility to you. You are putting aside $50 a week for each child's education aren't you? Don't bother to answer. Of course you are."

"As a matter of fact," said my husband, "we aren't."

Biff shrugged, "Forget I mentioned it. I mean the chances are they'll never need it. Depressed and disappointed at the lack of opportunity, they will drop out of high school, pick up with another drop-out who pumps gas, marry, and live in one room until the baby comes . . ."

"*Stop!*" I shouted. "Tell us what to do."

"Well, there are endowments. They're expensive, but it all depends on what your children are worth to you."

"They're worth everything we own."

"That'll about cover it," he smiled. "Well, you are wonderful people and a great little family and if, by some act of God, the house should burn to the ground, don't fail to call me and I'll try to work something out—contributions from neighbors, a phone call to an agency . . ."

"You mean we're not covered?"

"It's so simple to be covered, it's hardly worth mentioning, but if you'll sign here, it's done." My husband scribbled his signature.

"Listen," said Biff, "I've overstayed my visit. I must be running along. And don't worry about the coverage on your car. Parents are great for pitching in when bad luck strikes. According to statistics, two out of every three cars will be involved in an accident this year, but who knows, you could be the lucky one. Anyway, welcome to Surburbian Gems—and don't you feel better now?"

The Antique Dealer

Some say the antique syndrome surfaced to offset the newness of the land, the homes, and the settlers.

Some say the interest was initiated by a desire to return to the roots of yesterday.

I contend the entire movement to acquire antiques was born out of sheer respect of things that lasted longer than fifteen minutes.

Whatever the reason, in Suburbian Gems, there was an Eagle over every sofa, a slop jar of geraniums in every bathroom, and a deacon's bench in every hallway.

The weekends found every husband in the neighborhood sanding, sawing, staining, restoring, or stalking every antique dealer and show in the area.

My husband became an antique nut. I never saw a man become so possessed. He brought home white SuppHose, reputedly worn by Thomas Jefferson, a moose's head that had personally witnessed the Battle of Appomattox, and a primitive machine for storing water during the cattle drives west. (I didn't have the heart to tell him he bought the water cooler in the church hallway where they were holding the sale.)

It's hard to single out any one antique dealer for this documentary. They all had a different "style." Some were "story tellers." My husband loved the "story tellers." They were the ones who if you bought a button would relate how this button was from the uniform of a Confederate soldier who had scratched the name JAY on the back. His brother, who had been visiting north, joined the Union forces and he too had their family name, Jay, scratched on the back of one of his buttons. The two buttons would bring a price of $150. Unfortunately, he had only one, but if we would leave our phone number, when he came across the other one, he would give a call. In less than a week (isn't that unbelievable!) he called to say the other button had been found and was available.

There were the scavenger dealers who were like ambulance chasers. They watched the death notices and anyone over the age of forty-three got a visit from them to appraise and buy goodies from the estate. Scavenger dealers knew only one phrase, "Do you have any idea what we could have gotten for this pitcher/glass/bowl/tumbler/plate/mirror/ etc., had it not been cracked?" My husband loved the "scavenger dealers." He always felt he was getting a real buy under the table from them.

There were also the "hustlers in bib overalls." These were the little farmers who feigned surprise that someone would want to buy boards from a barn that was ready to fall down.

My husband loved the "barnyard hustlers." He would stop the car, introduce himself, chew on a piece of hay, and talk about how the rains or drought had affected the crops. Then he would venture, "Hey, how much would you want for a couple of those old two-by-fours over there on your barn?"

The farmers would give a little crooked smile and say, "You kiddin' me, mister? You mean those old faded, weathered boards, wormy with termites on that barn that a good wind would knock over?"

"Those are the ones," said my husband.

"Oh, I suppose $50 would put 'em in your trunk."

We were dealing with pros.

If I had to name one original settler who was known by everyone, it would have to be Miss Emma. Miss Emma was a sweet, little old lady whose farmhouse in the suburbs stuck out like a birth-control clinic in a retirement community.

There was no quaint sign flapping from her lamppost proclaiming, "ANTIQUES." She never advertised. Never brought her wares to a show at the church. The word just got around that if Miss Emma answered the door on that particular day and was in a good mood, she "might" sell you some of her precious heirlooms right out from under her.

In truth, Miss Emma should have been voted by the Academy of Arts and Sciences as the year's Best Actress of any year.

Responding to your knock, she would open the door a crack and say, "Today isn't a good day. Come back—say tomorrow?" which only made you more determined to somehow smuggle a checkbook into that house and cart away half of its furnishings.

Once inside, if you expressed an interest in, say a desk, she would throw her body in front of it protectively and say, "Oh no, this is the one thing I couldn't possibly sell. Martin (her late husband) would come right out of his grave. You see, it belonged to his great-grandmother who got it from a General Washburn."

"Are you sure it was Washburn? Could it have been Washington?"

"Could be. Great-grandma Tucker was a little hard of hearing."

Five minutes later, the desk would be in the back of someone's trunk and on its way to a place of prominence to be treated as a member of the family.

My husband and I begged her to let us come in

one Saturday. "Only if you don't stay too long," she agreed. Then my husband spotted it. One of the most enormous wooden bowls we had ever seen. "How much would you sell this bowl for, Miss Emma?" asked my husband.

She jumped between the bowl and my husband. "This bowl is not for sale. You may buy anything in this house, but not this bowl."

At that moment I knew that if I didn't have that bowl, I would not continue breathing. "Please, Miss Emma, we'd give it a good home and cherish it as you have cherished it."

"It's been in our family for generations," she said sadly. "I can remember my grandmother bathing the babies in it (my throat hurt and I wanted to cry). My mother used to bake bread in it—ten loaves at a time—and I just keep it around to store apples in it for the little children who visit."

"I know," I sobbed, "I know and I will do likewise."

A few minutes and a substantial check later, we were headed home with the bowl. "Do you know what I'm going to do with that bowl?" asked my husband. "I'm going to sand it down and then varnish it with a clear varnish and keep it in a natural state. We can put it on our divider and keep bright, shiny apples in it all the time."

He must have put in 184 man hours on that bowl. Every night in the garage I heard him sanding away. Then one night he came into the bedroom from the garage and said, "I don't believe it. I sanded all the way down through the stain and do you know what I found? (I shook my head.) MADE IN JAPAN. That can only mean one thing."

"What?" I asked excitedly.

"That Great-grandmother Tucker was Japanese. We've got an oriental antique on our hands."

We were elated, of course, and spared no time in telling our antique enthusiasts about our "find."

"Is it a huge wooden bowl with a crack down the middle?" asked the Martins.

"Yes! You've heard of it!"

"Heard of it? We got one too," said the Martins. "So have the Palmers and the Judsons."

"You're kidding! Where did they get theirs?"

"Miss Emma's."

During the next few years Miss Emma's family heirlooms became as standard in Surburbian Gems as doorknobs.

It's funny. In the five or six years everyone bought furniture out of Miss Emma's house, the house always was filled and always looked the same. You'd have thought someone would have noticed.

CHAPTER TWO

Major Battles Fought
in the Suburbs

Finding the Builder Who Built the House (1945-1954)

Edward C. Phlegg, the builder of Suburbian Gems, made Howard Hughes look like an exhibitionist.

No one had ever seen him. His phone number was a candy store that took messages. The billboards bearing his picture showed only the back of his head.

"If it's an emergency," said my husband, "I suppose I could track him down."

"Well, every time I push down the toaster, the garage door goes up. The hot-water heater is hooked up to the garden hose and I am sautéeing the lawn. The sliding-glass doors don't slide. The wall heats up when I turn on the porch light. The hall toilet does not accept tissue. Half of our driveway is on our neighbor's property, the grapes on the kitchen wallpaper are growing upside down, and I have a sign on our front door reading, 'OUT OF ORDER! PLEASE USE HOUSE NEXT DOOR.' "

"I think our best bet is to try and pin down the contractors," said my husband. "I'll see what I can do."

Two months later, we had tracked down our plumber. He had defected to a small country behind the iron curtain taking with him the last of the 1/15-inch pipe used in our bathrooms. Delivery was guaranteed in three years.

Our electrician was facing charges of involuntary arson of a large office building where political corruption was suspect. (He contended his bid was the lowest offered—a case of Coors.)

Our building foreman had returned to high school. He explained it had only been a temporary summer job to earn enough for a bicycle.

Our furnace man was living under an assumed name in Yuma, Arizona.

Our painter was drying out in a Sanitorium in upper New York State.

And our concrete man was studying contract law at the University of Cincinnati.

"I don't want to panic you," said my husband, "but I think we're stuck with our own repairs."

"Why should I panic? Just because when our water pipes sweat you prescribed an anti-perspirant?"

"Oh c'mon."

"Just because you were too embarrassed to ask for a male or a female plug at the hardware store and I had to write you a note."

"You made your point."

"Just because we have the only toilet in the block reseated with Play Doh . . ."

"Look," he said, "did you marry for love or did you marry to have your toilet fixed?"

When I didn't answer he said, "I'll get my toolbox and we can talk about what has to be done."

He set down a small fishing tackle box that had been originally inscribed "FIRST AID." This had been crossed out and "TOLS" was misspelled across the top in pencil.

Inside was a cork, five feet of pink, plastic clothesline, a small hammer, a flashlight with no batteries, a curler, a poker chip, and a book of rain-soaked matches.

"This is it?"

"This is it. What do you need first?" he asked.

"Storm windows for the entire house."

"Are you crazy?" he gasped. "I'll need a miter box."

"I thought we sprayed for them."

"Couldn't I start with something easy—like a revolving door?"

"As a matter of fact, you could make one of those little doors for the dog that saves you from letting them in and out all the time. You know, the one with the little hinges that flap in and out?"

"Right," he said. "No problem. You just saw a little hole in the door, attach the hinges and you're in business."

When I left him he was standing the dog against the wall with a tape measure and saying, "Let's see how much you've grown today."

A few hours later I felt a draft in the bedrooms and went to check. You could have slung a herd of buffalo through the little hole in the door.

"Don't worry," he cautioned, "the door on it will eliminate the wind whistling through."

"Now what are you doing?" I asked, as he dropped to his hands and knees.

"Showing the dog how to go through it. Dogs have to be taught, you know. But they're great little mimics." He twisted and groaned until his body was halfway through the door.

"What's wrong?" I asked.

"I'm stuck."

"Which end do you want me to save?"

"Will you knock it off with the jokes? Here I am with half of my body on the front porch and the other half in the hallway and . . ."

"Would you be terribly upset if I opened the door right now?"

"Why?"

"The dog has to go out."

"Well, hurry up. When I'm finished here, I want to start on the storm windows."

The search for Edward C. Phlegg continued for nine years. Someone thought they spotted the back of his head at an Arthur Fiedler concert. Another neighbor heard he was involved in selling beachfront property in Fargo, North Dakota.

Whatever, we never saw the builder of Suburbian Gems face to face.

Then one day we opened our newspaper and saw where Edward C. Phlegg had died. His funeral was one of the biggest the city had ever known. Mourners from Suburbian Gems alone filled the church. (Contractors who hadn't been paid couldn't even get inside.)

There wasn't a dry eye in the church.

We were saying good-bye to the only man who knew where in Hong Kong our furnace was made. Who alone knew the secret ingredients of our patios that bubbled when the sun hit them. Who would take with him his reasons for slanting the roof toward the center of the house and burying the septic tank under the living room floor.

As we stood in the cemetery mourning our loss, there was a flash of lightning and a rumble of thunder as before our very eyes, the large stone bearing the name Edward C. Phlegg sunk to one side and remained at a 40-degree angle.

There was no doubt in our minds. God was trying to tell us that Mr. Phlegg had gone to that big Escrow in the sky.

The Second-Car Ten-Day War

We had talked about the isolation of the suburbs and the expense of a second car before moving there and I thought I had made my position very clear.

I did not want a car. Did not need a car. And would not take a car if it were offered me.

I lied.

"I've got to have wheels," I said to my husband one night after dinner.

"We've talked about this before," he said, "and we agreed that the reason we migrated was to explore all the adventures the suburbs has to offer."

"I've explored both of them. Now I need a car. A car will put me in touch with the outside world. It will be my link with another culture, another civilization, another world of trade."

"Aren't you being a little dramatic?" he suggested.

"Let me lay it on you, Cleavie, the high spot in my day is taking knots out of shoestrings—with my teeth—that a kid has wet on all day long. I'm beginning to have feelings for my shower-massage pik. Yesterday, I etched a dirty word on the leaf of my philodendron."

"And you think a car is going to help you?"

"Of course it will help. I'll be able to go to the store, join a bowling league, have lunch downtown with the girls, volunteer, go to the dentist, take long drives in the country. I want to see the big, outside world from atop a lube rack. I want to whirl dizzily in a cloud of exhaust, rotate my tires with the rest of the girls. Don't you understand? I want to *honk* if I love Jesus!"

For a reason I was soon to understand, *all* of us

went to the showroom to pick out *my* car. Within minutes, I saw it. It was a bright yellow sports number—a one-seater that puts you three inches off the ground and sounds like a volcano when the motor turns over. Near to ecstasy, I closed my eyes and imagined myself at a traffic light, my large sunglasses on top of my head like Marlo Thomas, and as I quickly brushed lip gloss on my lips from a small pot, a dark stranger from the car next to me shouted, "Could we meet and talk?" And I laughed cruelly, "Don't be a fool! I'm a homeroom mother!" and sped off.

The rest of the family was gathered around a four-wheel-drive station wagon with a spare tire on top, space for extra gas cans along the back and fold-down seats giving you room to transport the Cleveland Symphony and all their instruments.

"Hey, is this a car?" asked my husband, his eyes shining.

"That was *my* next question," I said. "Look, I don't want transportation to a war, I just want a car to take me to the store and back."

"Of course you do," he said, "and this is the no-nonsense car that can get the job done."

Oh, I tried all right to hide my disappointment. I put glasses on top of my head, touched up my lip gloss at traffic lights, and even occasionally ran my tongue over my lips like Jennifer O'Neill, but I never climbed behind the wheel of that orthopedic vehicle without feeling like I was following General Patton into Belgium.

Besides, I was the only woman in the neighborhood with a big wagon. All the others tooled around in small, sleek, sports cars that had previously belonged to their husbands.

By the end of the first week, the newness of owning my own car had begun to wear off. I had transported six kids a day to school, a power mower to the repair shop, a porch swing for a garage sale, and the neighbor's dog to the vet who would not fit into a Volkswagen, Nova, Pontiac, Plymouth, Oldsmobile, Tank, or Global Van Lines.

The second week things picked up. I transported thirty-five sleeping bags and supplies for a week at camp, paneling from a lumber yard which wouldn't make delivery until the following week, a missile launch for a science fair, eight baseball bats, four base bags and twelve Little-League players, eight bags of fertilizer for the lawn and six surly homeroom mothers who arrived at a tea smelling like fertilizer.

It was of no comfort to me whatsoever knowing that I would make U-Haul Mother of the Year. I had to unload that car. Things came to a head one afternoon when I stopped for a traffic light and a huge transport truck pulled alongside me. The ones that travel all night to get your bread fresh to you in the morning. While waiting for the light to change, a burly driver looked over and shouted, "Hey, Mac, where's a good place to eat and get some sack time?"

I knew then I had to make my move and trade up—to my husband's car.

"You don't suppose we could switch cars?" I asked that night after dinner.

"Why would we want to do a thing like that?" he asked.

I hesitated dramatically, "I didn't want to tell you but the children get drowsy in the back seat. I think something is leaking in."

"Then, by all means, take it to the garage and have it fixed." (STRIKE ONE.)

"I'm in the garage so often now, I have my own key to the restroom. What would you say if I told you I only get seven miles to the gallon and I'm costing you $1.50 every time I wait for a light to turn green?"

"We knew the car would be an added expense when we bought it." (STRIKE TWO.)

"It's really a shame for your new, small, compact, car to sit out all day in the harsh sun and the rain and the cold when it could sit in a nice, warm garage."

"There's something to that, but how would you transport all those children every day?" (BALL ONE.)

"I just read a survey that a smaller car is safer because the children are packed together and do not have room to swing around and argue about who gets a window."

"That makes sense (BALL TWO) but what would I do with a big car that eats gas and attracts burly truck drivers?" (BALL THREE.)

It was three and two and I wound up for the big one.

"In a way it's a shame you don't have the station wagon. That way you could pick up some paying riders who would love transportation to the city. The extra money would pay for your gas."

HOME RUN!

"It's funny you should mention that," he said. "The Osborn's daughter, Fluffy, asked me just the other day if I had room in my car for her to ride to the city."

"You mean the girl in the next block who always looks like she's wearing a life preserver?"

"What a thing to say. She just has good posture."

"That's inflatable—I mean debatable."

"Then it's settled. We trade cars. You can drive mine and I'll take the wagon."

I never knew victory could make you feel so rotten.

Getting Sex Out of the Schools and Back into the Gutter Where It Belongs

My son was five years old when his teacher sent home a note informing me he was sexually immature.

I confronted her the next day after school and said, "What is this supposed to mean, Mrs. Kravitz?"

"It means we had a little quiz the other day on reproductive organs and he defined every one of them as an Askyourfather. You are sending a child into the world, Mrs. Bombeck, who thinks Masters and Johnson is a golf tournament and fertilization is something you do in the fall to make the lawns green."

"That's true," I nodded.

"Have you ever discussed sex in your home?" she asked.

"No, but once he caught Barbie and Ken together in a cardboard car in their underwear."

"Have you ever discussed with him the parts of his body?"

"Only those that showed dirt."

"You have to do better than that. This is a new day, Mrs. Bombeck. We don't hide our heads in the sand any more. Suburban schools are taking the lead in informing our young people about sex at an early age. For example, I am expecting a baby and I told the class about it."

"You told them you had something in the oven?" I asked incredulously.

"I told them I was pregnant!" she said.

I bit my finger. "Good Lord, Mrs. Kravitz. I didn't know why my husband gasped every time Lassie cleared the fence until I was twenty-six."

"Then you had better get used to it," she said. "Your son is about to be informed."

The suburbs didn't invent sex—it only gave it a wider distribution. No one could have known the ramifications sex education could have had in the community. Little boys wrote dirty sayings on the sidewalks with chalk as they always did, but adults didn't protest. They didn't understand what they meant.

Parents who tried to deal directly with their children by saying, "Look, Brucie, there seems to be some confusion between sexual and asexual reproduction," were only to be interrupted with, "Look, Dad, you should have come to me sooner. What do you need to know?"

Eavesdropping (among young people) dropped off 75 percent but increased 86 percent among adults. And one second grader confronted his parents one night with, "You little devils, you. And you told me I was conceived without sin."

Things had clearly gotten out of hand and we knew it. So, a meeting was called at the school to discuss the future of sex education.

"Frankly," said the librarian, "I'm worried. Do you realize the new *National Geographic* has been in for three weeks and has not been checked out once by a third grader?"

We gasped. "The youngsters don't want to play Doctor and Nursie any more," said a distraught father. "My son wants to open up his own office."

"I'm afraid," said Ken Kinsey, "that the impact of sex education goes even deeper. We now have before us the problem of dress code. It seems with the laxity of certain rules and the casualness with which we are regarding the human body, some youngsters are coming to school in various attire.

Tonight, we have been asked to consider the outcome of displaying—(he swallowed hard)—the navel."

The librarian sucked in her breath. The co-chairman cleared his throat and I grabbed for my son's sex manual to see if it had a double meaning.

"It seems," continued Ken, "that many of our little girls have been wearing jeans that fit around the hips and shirts that hang just below the rib cage and there is a bare area in between that needs some clarification. Anyone have any ideas?"

"Well, I have always felt if the Good Lord had meant for people to go nude He would never have invented the wicker chair," said one mother.

"That is a good point," said Ken. "Anyone else?"

"Have we established what a navel is?" asked a teacher.

"I think it is safe to assume that most of us are familiar with the navel . . ."

"Wait a minute," said a mother, "there are navels and there are navels. I mean some are 'outies' and some are 'innies.' I personally find the outies disgusting."

"That's strange," said her husband, "I find them sexy."

"You don't know how strange," said his wife. "I

have an 'innie' and demand to know where you've seen an 'outie.' "

"Please people. Let's get back to the issue here. Should we permit the navel to be displayed in a classroom atmosphere?"

"Today the navel, tomorrow the buttock," grumbled the math teacher.

"It seems to me," said a parent, "that if lax dress codes are allowed to continue, we may be in for something that only the National Guard can handle."

"I worry," said a mother who had been sitting quietly, "that it will blow the lid off a whole can of emotions. I mean, how do you expect a six-year-old to stay in the lines when he colors if he is distracted by a bared navel sitting at the desk next to his."

"That's a good point, Ethel," said Ken.

"I see nothing wrong with navels," said a militant in the rear. "Why are all of you so hung up over something as normal as a navel?"

"Navels are not on trial here," interrupted Ken. "It's simply we must draw the line somewhere with the relaxing of morals among our young people."

"So, if you're ashamed of your navel," persisted the militant, "I'll put a Band-Aid over it."

"What does the U.S. government say about navels?" asked a businessman.

"To my knowledge, there is no department at the moment that is conducting any sort of findings on the subject," said Ken. "If we could just get back to the subject . . ."

"If you ask me," said a concerned mother, "I think by our condoning navels in a public-school building, we are lowering the age of puberty. Next thing you know, we will permit them to have acne before they are ten and lower their voices at nine. I say they are growing up too fast. Let's save the navels for later when they can handle them and enjoy them like adults."

There was a round of applause and a few in the back stood up and said, "Here, here."

"Should we put it to a vote?" asked Ken. "Okay, all of you in favor of issuing a dress code in which navels must be covered, signify by saying, 'Aye' (a roar). Opposed? (One, 'You bet your sweet umbilical cord!')

"Now, the next thing on the agenda," said Ken nervously, "is Miss Barker, who teaches the third-graders human sexuality, would like to have a lab . . ."

I slipped out the back door. I wanted time to consider the ramifications, the objectives, the impact of bringing such a program within my child's learning processes. Also, to have my six-year-old explain to me what human sexuality is.

Saving the Recession from a Depression

Following World War II, when the nation began its migration to the suburbs, there was fear that the economy would give way to a period of depression.

There entered upon the scene three commodities destined to bring the country to its economic feet again: The Picture Window, the Green-Lawn Syndrome, and two teenage dolls, Barbie and Ken.

No one could have imagined the impact these three items had on the spending habits of the settlers. In retrospect, it was simply a matter of figuring the odds. Thirty-million suburbanites, all supporting and maintaining a picture window, green grass, and two naked dolls—it would have brought any nation out of the darkness of despair and into prosperity once more.

The Picture Window

To build a house in the suburbs without at least one picture window was considered un-American.

I personally knew my heart would stop beating if I did not have one.

As I said to my husband, "Imagine! A window with nine feet of glass that would invite the sunshine in during the day and reflect the stars at night. That would reveal neighbors waving a friendly 'hello.' That would allow the gentle breezes of a summer night to come indoors and hold the snow of winter at bay with its frosty patterns on the glass. Who would need any form of entertainment with nature's panorama changing with the seasons. Who would need rewards in this life other than viewing happy children at play?"

"You got the picture window," he said helplessly.

Two days later, I said, "The man is coming today to cover the picture window. It will cost $500."

"Cover the window!" he gasped. "What about your 'inviting the sunshine in during the day and reflecting the stars at night?' "

"That sun is blinding me. I can't get away from it. And the dog is beginning to tan. As for stars, forget it. The only thing that window attracts at night are window peepers."

A month later I informed my husband, "The furniture has to be covered. It will cost $800."

"But it's always been good enough for us."

"Exactly, but is it good enough for the 'neighbors

waving a friendly hello' through our picture window?"

"But I thought we got the windows covered."

"You can't keep the curtains drawn on a picture window all of the time or people will think you have something to hide."

Four months to the day, I casually mentioned the picture window would need storm covering and screen. They would run about $400.

"Wait a minute," he charged, "is this the same woman who said she 'was going to allow the gentle breezes of a summer night to come indoors and hold the snow of winter at bay with its frosty patterns on the glass'?"

"That's before I realized the summer breezes harbor mosquitoes that suck your blood. Besides, I've had it with those 'frosty patterns on the glass.' The window is causing frosty patterns on the children's lungs and our walls look like a waterfall."

We were two weeks into summer when I informed my husband, "We are getting a liner to block out the light of our window so we can watch TV during the daytime. It will cost $150."

His head jerked up sharply, "What happened to 'nature's panorama changing with the seasons before your eyes'?"

"Nature's panorama has deteriorated into a view

of old Mr. Hudson framed in his picture window in his underwear scratching his stomach and picking his teeth with a matchbook cover."

One night I met my husband at the door. "We are getting Picture Window insurance. It will cost $28 a year."

"I don't believe this," he said. "When did you become disenchanted with the 'rewards of viewing happy children at play'?"

"When Michael Ormstead's baseball came crashing through our picture window. Meanwhile, we will have to have this one replaced. It will cost $160."

I had never seen my husband bite his necktie in half before.

The Suburban Lawn

Never, in the history of the world, have so many men sacrificed so much, so often, at such a price, for so little.

The green grass is what lured settlers to the wilderness in the first place. They wanted to cultivate a little patch of greenery that would tickle the feet of their barefooted babies, cushion their falls, and cradle them in the bosom of the soil.

It seemed incongruous in the quiet of an evening to hear a father pull his son close to him and say, "*You cut across that lawn one more time, Gilbert, and I'm going to break every bone in your body.*"

The suburban lawn not only became an obsession with the suburban husband, it became the very symbol of manhood. Not to have a lawn was like admitting you turned off the Super Bowl to take a nap, used deodorant shields in your T-shirts, or had training wheels on your Harley-Davidson. Every casual greeting opened with: "How's the lawn, Buddy?" "Hey, Frank, see you got your crabgrass on the run." Or "Set your blade down an inch, Buck. We all did."

Keeping up with a couple of hundred lawn enthusiasts was not only back-breaking, it was downright expensive. No one knew it any better than one poor devil in Suburban Gems who divorced his wife. His name was Lyle Link. The settlement was rumored to be the stiffest decision ever handed down in a court of law.

Lyle's wife received no alimony, no support whatsoever for the children, and she assumed payments on the house, the car, and the furniture.

Lyle got custody of the lawn.

It was like being on parole. He couldn't leave

the state. He couldn't afford to remarry and there wasn't time to drink.

There were fertilizers, weed killers, maintenance, and keeping up with his neighbors. Lyle was spending more time at home than he ever did when he was married.

There wasn't a night he was not hauling bags of manure and nitrogen, trimming around walks and trees on his hands and knees, watering, mulching, and clipping.

Lyle started out with a hand mower, but eventually bowed to neighborhood pressure and got a rotary mower. This led to a lawn sweeper to pick up the grass, and an electric lawn trimmer to get close to the walk, and a spreader to evenly distribute new seed and fertilizer.

Every week there was some new gimmick to buy that sent everyone racing to the garden center. One evening as Lyle was tooling around in his riding mower with the reclining bucket seats and the console dashboard—his automatic sprinkler creeping along silently over the green carpet, his hedges topped perfectly with his electric hedge clipper, his trees being fed automatically just the right amounts of iron and nitrogen—his neighbor dropped by and said, "Too bad about your lawn, Lyle."

Lyle shut off his motor and paled slightly. "What do you mean, 'Too bad about my lawn'?"

"The whole neighborhood is talking about it. I thought you knew."

"Knew what? For God's sake tell me."

"Your lawn has root rot nematode."

Lyle's eyes misted. "Are you sure?"

"Didn't you see the little brown spots that never seemed to get better when you watered them?"

"And it's such a young lawn," said Lyle. "How long does it have?"

"With no bicycles, sleds, or kids running over it, I give it about a year."

"Well, we're not going to give up," said Lyle, squaring his shoulders, "they come up with new things every day. We're going to fight!" he said, heading out toward the garden center.

"Hey," yelled his neighbor, "maybe this isn't the time to bring it up, but I heard your wife is getting remarried."

Lyle turned slowly, disgust written plainly on his face. "What kind of an animal are you?" he asked, his voice quavering with emotion. "First you come here and tell me my lawn has root rot nematode and there's nothing anyone can do to save it and at best it only has a year to live, and then you babble on about my wife remarrying.

Who cares? Don't you understand? If my lawn dies, I don't want to go on living any more. Leave me alone."

As his neighbor retreated, Lyle got down on his hands and knees and sobbed, "We'll travel. That's what we'll do—just you and me. We'll visit the White House lawn, the grounds at Mt. Vernon, maybe upper New York State where the grass is green most of the time and you can make new friends . . ."

Barbie and Ken

The real lifesaver of the economy was a pair of teenage dolls who appeared ironically one Christmas stacked (excuse the expression) among the baby dolls who burped, ate, cried, wet, walked, and were as sexless as a stick of gum.

My daughter picked Barbie up off the counter and exclaimed, "Look, Mommy, here is a doll that looks just like you."

I checked out the two-and-a-half-inch bust, the three-inch hips, and the legs that looked like two filter tips without tobacco and said, "She looks like she just whipped through puberty in fifteen minutes."

"I want her," my daughter whined.

Barbie cost $5.98 in the buff, so we purchased a little dress, a pair of pumps, a bra, and a pair of briefs that came to $6.95.

"Aren't we going to buy her a girdle?" asked my daughter.

"Let's wait until she eats and see if she needs one," I said.

If any of us believed for a moment that Barbie was going to be happy as a simple housewife, we were in for a surprise. Barbie was a swinger and she needed the wardrobe to do it.

Within a week, she had three lounge outfits ($5.95 each), an entire pool ensemble ($4.95), two formals ($7.95 each), a traveling suit ($6.95), and skating outfit ($5.00).

One afternoon as I was on my hands and knees fishing Barbie's beach ball out of the sweeper bag, my daughter announced, "Barbie's lonely."

"Terrific!" I said. "Why don't you mail her to Camp Pendleton. And send her satin sheets with her."

"I think we ought to buy Ken."

There was something weird about Ken, but I couldn't put my finger on it. He was a taller version of Barbie who came wearing a jock strap and an insincere smile. He cost $5.98. Within a week, his wardrobe consisted of tennis attire ($7.95), jump suit ($4.95), white tuxedo ($10.95), and a terry cloth robe ($3.95), plus a cardboard car ($12.95). As I explained to my husband, "You don't expect them to sit around night after night passing a beach ball back and forth, do you?"

The little freaks were draining our budget, but I bought some of the patterns and was able to satisfy their clothing appetite by sitting at the sewing machine day and night.

Then one day my daughter announced, "Ken and Barbie are getting married."

It seemed reasonable. After all, they were thrown together day after day in a shoe box under the bed and they were only human.

"What exactly does this mean to me?" I asked.

"Barbie has to have a wedding dress ($10.95) and a trousseau ($36.50) and Ken has to have a tuxedo."

"What's wrong with his white one?" I asked.

"That's for dancing—not marrying," she said.

"Anything else?"

"A wedding party."

"A what!"

"We have to buy Midge and some more people so they'll have people at their wedding."

"Can't you invite some of your other dolls?"

"Would you want someone at your wedding with bowed legs and diapers?"

The wedding was the social event of the year. Our gift to them was a cardboard house that looked like the Hilton.

It was months before all the bills were in but I figured the worst was over. Some families on the block were just starting with their first doll. All that was behind us now.

Then one afternoon in the kitchen, my daughter said excitedly, "Guess what? Barbie's going to have a baby. You're going to be a grandmother."

My eyes welled with self-pity as I ticked off the needs—one naked doctor (who played golf on Wednesdays), two naked nurses (who snorkeled on weekends), one ambulance driver in the buff who skied, an unclothed intern who . . .

CHAPTER THREE

The Great Plastic Rush

"You Will Come to My Home Party"

One day, a typical suburban housewife was storing a left-over in a small, plastic bowl. As she pushed down the center of the lid with her thumb, a whooshing sound came out and her neighbor, who was having coffee, said, "Did you just belch?"

"Of course not," she smiled, "I am burping my Suckerware."

"Burping your Suckerware?"

"Right. I find when you force all the air out of your plastic bowl, your cantaloupe will keep for days in your refrigerator."

This was the beginning of the Great Plastic Rush. Within weeks, news had spread throughout the country and the city and women were coming on buses, cars, and bicycles to witness this religious experience.

They did not go home empty handed. The Home Party was born and there was no stopping its growth.

This is how it worked. A housewife, motivated by the promise of a leftover tote bag, would invite twenty of her dearest friends to a party in her home.

Once inside, a professional pitchman would guide the guests to a dining room table laden with wares, and then oil his way through the group with an order form and a ballpoint pen.

No one was forced to go to a home party.

You went out of pure fellowship, need, and unsolicited fear. Fear that when you were tapped to host a party, no one would show up if you didn't go to theirs.

For an added incentive, you played games like "Dessert Bingo" to see how many words you could make out of the word "Leftover."

The plastics were the first to arrive on the suburban scene, but not for long. They were followed by the discovery of Whatever Cookware,

Sarah Covet-thy-neighbor Jewelry, One-Size-Fits-All Sportswear, Bow-Wow Cosmetics, and many more.

Probably the most boring party I ever attended was hosted by the Whatever Cookware company. The Burley brothers (two manufacturer's representatives) came to our house early to cook the entire dinner in their pots that locked in flavor and held captive all the natural juices.

The natural juices weren't the only thing held captive. As we sat around drinking celery cocktails I turned to my husband and asked, "So, whatya wanta do now?"

"We could check the expiration dates on our driver's licenses."

"I want to go home," I said stubbornly.

"You *are* home," he said. "What time do these birds serve dinner? I don't smell anything cooking."

"Of course you can't smell anything. The food is wallowing in its own juices which are locked in under the flavor-sealed lids."

Finally, one of the Burley brothers announced, "Dinner is served." That was only the beginning of the pitch. The Burleys were everywhere. At our elbows grinning, "Is that the most delicious roast you have ever put into your mouth? You have permission to talk with your mouth full."

"How's it going over here, guy? Here, give me your fork. Do you see how I can press it against this Brussels sprout and the juices continue to flow?"

"Don't get up. What do you need? No salt, guy, please. Learn to eat au naturel. The taste buds will adjust to it in time."

"Do you detect just a hint of mint? Ahh, you are discerning."

"Eat the jackets!" he commanded one guest who was scooping out his potatoes. "Look at this folks. He's leaving all the nutrition on his plate."

Following the dinner, we arranged our chairs into rows and watched a double feature: "The Birth of Grease" and "An Enzyme Visits New York."

One Thursday night as I was preparing to go to a home hair-coloring party, I got a call from Dollie Sullivan.

"Guess what?" she said excitedly. "I am giving a plant party. Can you come?"

"What is a plant party?" I asked.

"It's where you bring your sick plants to be healed and to buy new ones. It's really different," she said and hung up.

I figured, why not?

The plant party attracted a group of people I had never seen before. I had been there only five minutes when someone wanted to go halvsies on a 100-pound bag of manure and a perfect stranger showed me her aphids.

"Girls! Girls!" said the plant representative, "I hate to break this up, but we've got a lot of ground to cover this evening. No pun intended. First, I want to introduce you to my friends." Gathered around her on little chairs were a half dozen or so potted plants. She began to introduce them one by one. "This is Florence Floribunda, Polly Pothus, Ginny Geranium, Irene Iris, Dorothy Daffodil, and Phyllis Potbound—we'll talk more about Phyllis later.

"Now, before we get to the sickies, I want each of you to answer roll call with your favorite insecticide.

"Very good," she said when we had finished. "Now you all have an opportunity to find out about how to deal with your sick plants, so if you'll bring them up one at a time, we'll talk about them."

The first was a woman who was near tears.

"What seems to be the problem?" asked the leader.

"They have icky boo boo on the leaves," she sobbed.

"You're not being too scientific, but I know what boo boo in the back? In Latin, it's called *primus* you mean," she smiled. "Can all of you see the icky *blosis*. Its common name is dust. When a leaf is covered with five or six years of dust, it can't breathe. It suffocates."

"What should I do?" asked the woman.

"Let's do something gutsy," she said. "Let's wash it." (The crowd cheered.)

Next up was a woman whose plant was in the final stages of deterioration. The leaves were ashen and crumpled limply to the floor. The leader studied it carefully. "Do you talk to your plant? Give it encouragement? The will to live? The incentive to grow?"

"I talked to it yesterday," she said, "but I didn't talk very nice to it. I called it something."

"What did you call it?" asked the plant lady.

The owner whispered the word in the leader's ear. She too turned ashen and crumpled limply to the floor.

Toward the end of the evening, we were given the opportunity to buy fresh, new plants to refurbish the ones in our homes. I chose a beautiful split-leaf philodendron with shiny, green leaves in a pot of mulch fluffed up at its feet like a pillow. That night as I paced the floor with the plant over my shoulder I patted it gently and thought, "What the heck. It beats burping Suckerware."

CHAPTER FOUR

Hazards of Suburban Living

The Car Pool Crouch

A lot of my neighbors suffered from the Car Pool Crouch. It was one of those dreaded diseases you say can never happen to you.

Then one afternoon when you are attending a tea, someone will point out that your knees are apart and your right foot is extended out in an accelerator position. Your elbows are bent slightly and you are holding your purse in front of you like a steering wheel. When a woman leans forward next to you, your arm automatically goes out to catch her when she hits the windshield that isn't there.

You've got it. The Car Pool Crouch.

I have seen perfectly healthy, young, upright women climb into a car in September. By spring, they walked like Groucho Marx.

Out of this malady came the invention of the drive-in. A lot of people think the drive-in was born out of convenience. That's not true. It was born out of desperation of a community of women who could no longer get in and out of their cars.

I once went for an entire week behind the wheel of the car and never missed a beat running my house.

I drove the children to school, idling my motor as they tumbled out of the back seat.

Then it was on to the bank where I pulled in to within inches of the window, slid my check under a bean bag in the drawer, and massaged my legs as I waited.

With money by my side, I next pulled into the cleaners where I left off a bundle and was rewarded with hangers full of clean ones.

At the film service drive-in, I barely had to slow down the car. Just make a hook shot and promise to be back by tomorrow.

At the service station, I sat numbly while he checked my oil, my water, and cleaned off my glasses.

Then it was lunchtime and into a drive-in eatery for a quick bite.

Positioning my wheels on the pulley, I sat in my car while I went through the car wash, feeling just a little uncomfortable with the numbness that was causing shooting back pains.

But there was the post office that had to be driven through and then it was time to pick up the children.

Naturally, we drove to a drive-in for a slushee treat and as dusk was approaching, we hit for a drive-in movie.

On the seventh day, my husband said, "Look, you've been in that car all week. You're pale. You need fresh air. You are also very short. Let's go to that new church everyone is talking about over on Rural Road."

I dressed carefully. And painfully. It had been a long time.

Hesitating, I climbed into the car. It was a drive-in church.

As I sat listening to the voice of the minister on the speaker, I heard him say, "This is the time to pray for any special favors you might wish from God."

I opened my door and with great effort, pushed my legs out. Steadying myself, I grabbed onto the car with my hands and pulled myself up to my feet. I was standing.

From the other cars, I heard the applause, the voices raised in awe. Some blew their horns. "It's a miracle . . . a miracle!"

The Neighborhood Nomad

My husband put down his paper at breakfast one morning and said, "How many children do we have?"

"Three," I answered quickly.

"Then how come we have four children at breakfast every morning and at dinner each evening?"

I put down the cereal box and studied each one carefully. There was no mistaking the one boy. He had my husband's eyes and the girl definitely had my coloring. But the other two could have been phoned in.

"There's only one way to settle it," said my husband. "Will the real Bombecks please stand up."

They exchanged sheepish glances, a chair scraped, one started to get up, then sat down and finally, three got to their feet.

We all looked at Kenny who sat there staring at a piece of dry toast.

"Son of a gun," said my husband, "I didn't know Kenny wasn't ours. And I just apologized to him yesterday for not spending more time with him."

"How do you think I feel?" I snarled. "I just got him toilet trained!"

When we pressed for details, it seems a little over a year ago, Kenny had wandered into our house to use the bathroom, liked it, and sorta hung around.

"How did you know where our bathroom was?" I asked.

"You have the Pee Wee model just like ours— only with a fireplace. I like a fireplace."

"Doesn't your mother worry about you?" I asked.

"She knows where I am."

"I think I met her. We both went to your parent-teacher conference. At the time I thought she was being a little pushy when she wanted to see your attendance record."

I went to the phone and dialed Kenny's mother. "Mrs. Wick," I said, "I am bringing Kenny home."

"Who?" she asked.

"Kenny, your son."

"Has he been acting up?" she asked.

"No, I just feel Kenny has been with us too long."

"Why do you say that?"

"Because my husband and I just realized we postponed our vacation because we couldn't get anyone to sit with Kenny."

"I understand," she said.

Kenny was right. Their house plan was identical to ours with the exception of a driveway lamp (extra) and colored bathroom fixtures (also extra).

I couldn't help but feel a twinge of guilt as I watched Mrs. Wick bustle around with her brood. No wonder she hadn't missed Kenny. The house was crawling with children.

"Joey, you turn off that garden hose this minute. It's making spots on the TV picture tube."

"Leroy did *what* in the swimming pool?"

"Celia! Get your sister off that sofa in that wet diaper."

"Who wanted the peanut butter and catsup sandwich? It's ready."

"Ann, get the phone and tell whoever it is I've run away from home."

"Shut the door!"

"Now you've done it. You've swallowed your space maintainer in your bubble gum."

"When you put meal worms in the refrigerator,

Dan, kindly mark them 'meal worms.' Labeling them 'cole slaw' is not funny."

"Roger. I want to talk with you. Sit down. I've had it with you. You tease the younger kids. You hog all the toys. You refuse to take naps. Mr. Wick and I had a talk about you just last night. If you don't shape up, we're going to send you home to live, do you understand?"

I breathed a sigh of relief, "Thank goodness. Do you realize that for a moment, I thought all of these children were yours?"

Mrs. Wick looked at me numbly, "None of them are mine. Kenny is an only child. Some of these children are lost, strayed, or just plain bored at home. They wander in and just sorta blend with the surroundings. Kenny just said to me one day, 'I hate crowds' and wandered off to your house."

"How did you know where he was?" I asked.

She shrugged, "Saw him pictured with your family on your Christmas card."

"How do things get so confused?" I mused.

"I don't know," she said tiredly, "you just wake up in the morning and mechanically feed anyone who's at the table and you get so busy with the door opening and shutting and little people wandering in and out and water fights and—excuse me (she leaned over to hear a toddler whisper something in her ear). It seems your son, Bruce, just locked himself in my bathroom. Do you want to talk to him?"

"My son, Bruce? What's he doing here?"

"He's been coming every day since Christmas. It seems Kenny got a fleet of heavy-duty trucks and Bruce is crazy for them. If you want to leave him here, we could use the exemption on our income tax."

"No, I'll take him home," I said.

Later, I lifted the phone to call my husband. "Hey, guess who's coming to dinner? Remember the little kid who looks like your mother?"

The Elusive Washer Repairman

Every woman in the suburbs had a picture of a washer repairman in her billfold and a telephone number.

If, at any time, she spotted one, she was to report it to a central office where they recorded the sighting and tried to track him down. The fast-talking-elusive-repairman was an endangered species. Only five had been sighted in the suburbs during a five-year period.

We had all heard their voices. They said essentially the same thing, "I have you down for Tuesday." What we didn't know was (a) Who was I? (b) Where is down? and (c) What Tuesday?

But like fools, we waited. Every Tuesday, the streets were barren. Cars stood idle in the driveway. Doors were ajar. Some housewives sat on the curb in anticipation of the arrival of the washer repairman.

My washer had been broken for three weeks when I could stand it no longer. I called the washer repair service and said, "I demand you send me a washer repairman."

"Where do you live?" he asked mechanically.

"In Suburban Gems."

"Our serviceman is probably lost. The houses all look alike to us. He'll get to you."

"When?"

"Look, lady, some people have been waiting longer than you and are desperate."

"Do you know what desperate is?" I asked evenly. "Desperate is sending your kids to school in underwear made from broiler foil. Desperate is washing sheets in a double boiler. Don't you understand? I need a repairman."

"I have you down for Tuesday," he said.

On Tuesday, I was talking in the yard with

Helen when suddenly, a few streets away I got a glimpse of a black leather bow tie.

"It's him," I shouted excitedly.

"What are you talking about?" asked Helen.

"A washer repairman. I saw my first washer repairman." I ran to the house to get the picture. "That's him all right," I said smugly. "Blue shirt, black leather bow tie, dark trousers, and a cap with a bill on it. You phone it in. I'm going over and collar him.

"I can't believe it," I said. "A real, live washer repairman right here in my kitchen. Would you mind if I called my neighbor, Helen? She's never seen a washer repairman and she wouldn't spread it around, honest."

"What's wrong with the machine?" he asked gruffly.

"It won't work."

"Anything else?"

"That's it."

"And for that you called me?" He removed the front panel and at that moment started to speak in tongues.

"Your rump bump is nad. Can't pft the snock without trickin the snear."

"That's easy for you to say," I said, "but what's wrong with it?"

"I sad the roughing won't nit sowse you can't snapf the lig if the ffag won't chort."

"That bad?"

"Bad enough to need a raunch ring sloop."

"Is that why it won't spin?" I asked.

"No, the krincop broke and mital values stoffed to the weil ham made it groin."

I felt like I was talking to Professor Corey with a lip full of Novocaine.

"Could you speak a bit more slowly?"

"How old is the zoinc spring?"

"Oh, the machine is three years old."

His eyes rolled back in his head and he shrugged his shoulders, "Whatya smag?"

"Will it live?"

"With a new thircon tube and a blowfest."

"Sir, could you possibly translate all that for me in a simple sentence that I could tell my husband?"

He stood up, wiped grease off his hands and in a voice that would have put Rex Harrison out of work announced, "Seventy-four dollars and thirty-four cents."

"Well, I suppose it will have to be fixed," I shrugged.

"Can't. Your fasack box is a 19689 model."

"Is that bad?"

"It's a discontinued fasack box. Used 'em only

two months. When the smlax csble ghotend the galopian tube, it congested the tubular laxenspiel and the overflowed hose kinked and someone screwed up and FIRE!"

"Let me get this straight. Are you telling me my fasack box catches fire?"

"What's a fasack box?" he asked.

"Whatever my 19689 model is. Are you telling me it's unsafe and I'll have to get a new machine? Well, I won't pay for it."

"Rapf your warranty, lady," he shrugged.

"Where is my warranty?"

"Printed on the bottom side of the washer."

After the washer repairman left, I discovered I had become an instant celebrity. Women all over the neighborhood piled in to ask questions about what a washer repairman looked like.

"I don't see why you didn't just lock the door and keep him here," said Helen.

"Some things are meant to be free," I said.

Trick or Treat . . . Sweetheart

Halloween was my sixteenth favorite holiday.

It rated somewhere between the April 15th Income Tax deadline, and a New Year's eve without a baby sitter.

My husband and I readied for Beggar's Night a full week before. We stored the lawn furniture, brought the garden hose indoors, hid the clothesline and clothes posts, and dragged the Junglegym set into the garage for safe-keeping.

When we lived in the city, Halloween had been a night for little people to dress up as witches and little clowns, knock timidly at your door, and wait to be identified before you dropped a gingersnap into their little bags.

In the suburbs, Halloween wasn't a holiday. It was a full-scale invasion. Car pools transported herds of children from one plat to another (planes and buses deposited children from as far as three counties away). Greed stations were set up where loot could be emptied and they could start out "fresh." And the beggars themselves were so intimidating that if your "treat" wasn't acceptable you could conceivably lose your health through pain.

The small children usually came between 5 and 5:30 P.M. while it was still daylight. After that the beggars got bigger, the costumes less colorful, and the demands more aggressive.

Opening the door, I confronted a lad over six

feet tall, wearing a mustache, and carrying a shopping bag.

"My goodness," I cooed, "and what's your name?"

"*¿Qué?*" he shrugged.

"Do I know you?" I asked reaching up to tweak his mustache. The mustache was connected to his face by his own hair.

His partner nudged him. "*¿Cuál es su nombre?*"

"Manuel," he answered hesitantly. (Good grief, these had come all the way across the border for a bag of caramel corn.)

Next at the door was a twenty-seven-year-old or so wearing a dirty T-shirt, a leather band across his forehead, carrying a pillow case filled with ten-cent candy bars.

"Let's see," I mused, "you are too old for my insurance man and too big for King Kong. I give up."

He blew a giant bubble in my face and juggled his bag impatiently, "I'm Tonto."

"All right, Tonto," I said, "Here's a bright, shiny penny for you."

"Cripes lady," he said, "can you spare this?" (Later, I was to discover Tonto very strong. Tonto bent TV antenna after I gave him his shiny new penny.)

Mentally, I began to draw up a list of rules and

regulations that would give Halloween back to the little children. How do you know when you are too old to go "begging"?

1. You're too old to go begging when your mask tickles your mustache.

2. You're too old when you've figured out the only thing a penny will buy is your weight and you're watching it.

3. You're too old when you drive yourself to the subdivisions.

4. You're too old when you say "thank-you" and your voice is changing.

5. You're too old when you are rapping on the doors and Johnny Carson is signing off.

6. You're too old when you reach over to close your bag and your cigarettes fall out of your pocket.

7. You're too old when you have a sign on your bag that reads, "Personal Checks Accepted."

8. You're too old when the lady of the house turns you on more than the candy apple she just gave you.

Around eleven o'clock I refused to answer the door.

"Why?" asked my husband.

"Because we have run out of treats and when I told the last guy all I had left to give was a bruised orange, he moistened his lips and said, 'That's what you think, baby.' "

Seconds later, my husband returned from the door, "Quick! Give me some treats."

"I told you I don't have anything left. The refrigerator is cleaned out. So are the snacks. What do you think they would do if you offered them a raw potato?"

He peeked through the curtain and viewed two motorcycle freaks wearing sleeveless leather vests with no shirt and a helmet with a horn coming out of either side. "I think they would turn my nose inside out."

Crawling into the children's bedroom, we felt around in the darkness until we found their little orange trick or treat bags. We grabbed a few handfuls of taffy to appease the motorcycle gang.

Later, crouched in the hallway, the children's bags between us, my husband looked at his watch. "It's 11:30," he said. "Do we dare turn off the porch light?"

"I don't think so," I said tiredly. "It's too risky. The Mintons turned their lights off early last year and a group stole their garage. How much longer do you think we can hold out?"

"I don't know. How much ammunition do we have left?"

My fingers deftly counted out the bubble gum, the miniature candy bars, an apple with a bite out of it, and a few loose pieces of Halloween corn. "With luck, two or three hours."

We both sat up stiffly as the doorbell rang.

"I love you," I said simply without emotion.

"I know," he whispered.

The Identity Crisis

You would have thought with five thousand people living in Suburban Gems that we would have had an identity problem. This was just not true.

As I told my husband, "All you have to do is to reach out to people and the warmth is there."

"I don't have time to socialize," he said. "I work. I cut grass. I watch a little TV and I go to bed so I can get up tomorrow and start all over again."

"And you're missing the entire concept of rural living," I said. "That of getting to know one another on a personal basis. Today is Saturday. Why don't you go down and borrow Lawnsweeper no. 1's charcoal starter for the party we are having this evening?"

"Is he the one next to the pot-bellied stove on the porch?"

"That's Lawnsweeper no. 2 and you know it. Besides, the stove was stolen last Halloween. No, Lawnsweeper no. 1 lives next to the faulty muffler."

"Oh *him*."

"I know, but his wife's nice."

"What's her name?"

"She's the size 18½ with five garbage cans."

"Why didn't you say so. Incidentally, did you invite the guy who saves his anti-freeze each year?"

"Had to. I invited the people with the air conditioner in their bedroom window and they live right next door to one another."

"That would be awkward."

"I only hope they get along with the super liberals."

"What super liberals?"

"The ones who live two blocks over next to the kid who sets fires."

"How do you know they are super liberals?"

"You know that little black jockey statue that has a ring in it to hitch a horse to? They painted him white."

"I remember that. The rhubarb grower had a fit."

"I've never trusted anyone who grows rhubarb."

"Before I go, do we have anything we've borrowed from Lawnsweeper no. 1 and never re-

turned? I'd feel like a fool asking to borrow something that's never been returned."

"You should feel like a fool. He's the one who
borrowed our plunger and loaned it to the people
with CATS FOR SALE."

"They've had CATS FOR SALE since we lived here.
Do you suppose it's the same cat?"

"I feel sorry for the new people who just moved
in next door."

"Who are they?"

"The Airstream people. What that little beauty
doesn't have in it, they'll never need."

"They must have money."

"Wait until they find out they're wedged in between CATS FOR SALE and the people who let the
plastic pool kill their grass."

"I remember him. Met him at a party at the
house with the nut who flew the flag on John
Wayne's birthday."

"How could you forget them? They own that
big Doberman who hides his head in your crotch
and you're afraid to move. Speaking of weirdos,
got a card from the two-car garage people."

"How did they ever fit a two-car garage on that
lot is what I'll never know."

"If you met them personally, you would know.
They're pushy."

"I thought so. Where did they go?"

"Went camping with the people with the built-in appliances."

"It figures."

"You'd better get going."

"Hey, I just remembered. You know how you always accuse me of not meeting new people? I met a newcomer last night when I was looking for our newspaper."

"Who is he?"

"Name is Alan Cornwall."

"I'll never remember that. Who is he?"

"The Porsche with the kid who spits on our tires."

"The one who just sprayed the bagworms?"

"That's him."

"Why didn't you say so? I hate name droppers."

CHAPTER FIVE

The Heartbreak
of Psuburbaniasis

The Seven-Inch Plague

In 1946, the suburbs suffered its first plague.

It struck with little warning and attacked the weak, the bored, the vulnerable seeking relief from the monotony. Its name was television and by 1966, it would enslave sixty-two million families.

We fell victims just before Christmas when my husband carried it home to us from the city.

The disease looked harmless enough—a seven-inch screen that looked like a hand mirror. We put it on the bookcase in the living room, got a vanity bench from the bedroom and positioned our eyeballs 16 inches from the screen where we became mesmerized as a full-grown woman carried on a conversation with two puppets.

Television was a terminal disease that was to spread and worsen, driving people from acute withdrawal to chip-dip attacks.

Because I am basically a strong person, I was able to resist the disease better than most, but my husband's addiction to television grew steadily worse. He became a sports addict who was in a catatonic state twelve months out of every year.

No one would have guessed that his condition would become so hopeless that I would approach a lawyer to have him considered legally dead. The lawyer advised me that due to the legalities this was not an easy thing to do. Just because a man sits in front of a TV set with eyes fixed and no pulse is not enough. He said I would have to keep a log of my husband's behavior over a year's period of time. I began to keep a diary in August.

AUGUST

The fifteenth of this month was visiting day for the children. Waiting for a beer commercial, I lined them up and said stiffly, "Children, this is your father." He offered them a pretzel at the same time watching a beer can dancing with a hot dog. When we insisted he stand up, the children gasped. They remembered him as a much shorter man.

SEPTEMBER

The set went out today during the Dallas–Los Angeles game. "It could be a tube," I said.

"Shhh . . . and get out of the way. The Cowboys are ready to score."

"No one is ready to score," I said. "You don't understand. The tube is black."

"That's ridiculous. Look at that lateral . . . my God, they've fumbled."

"Just relax. It could be only this channel experiencing temporary . . ."

"Lady, you are going to be temporary if you don't get out of this room and let me watch my game in peace."

I left him sitting in front of the black screen screaming and cheering. Maybe I can talk some sense to him when he is watching the commercial that isn't there.

OCTOBER

Today, our living room was named the first recycling center to be served by a mobile unit. My husband was so engrossed in watching the World Series, he was quite unaware of what was going on.

Television cameras ground away while cub scouts gathered together eight barrels of cans, six barrels of bottles, and 500 pounds of paper.

I pecked my husband on the cheek as I left. He swatted at me and grumbled, "How did that fly get in here?"

NOVEMBER

I am really worried about my husband. On Sunday, he sat in front of the TV set from noon until 10:30 P.M. There was no evidence of breathing. I called our doctor who wheeled in an EKG machine to check the blood supply to his heart.

My husband rallied for a moment when the machine was placed directly in front of him. He bolted upright in his chair, blinked a few times, started fiddling with the knobs and said, "All right, whose been messing around with the antenna?"

DECEMBER

We have found it easier to decorate Daddy than to move him away from the television set.

First, we covered his feet with a simple felt skirt dotted with sequins. Then we hung a candy cane from each ear, and a string of lights around his head. Tonight, we are going to string popcorn and tinsel around his chest.

It's wonderful being a family again.

JANUARY

I'm terribly concerned about what's-his-name. He has watched more bowls this month than the rest-room attendant at Kennedy Airport.

He does not eat well. I poked my head through the door today and said, "Have I got a bowl for you!"

"What is it?" he asked, dipping his spoon into it.

"I call it 'Instant Replay.' In it are shredded sports pages, a dozen or so flip tops from beer cans, a few cigarette butts, and a lock of Howard Cosell's hair."

His eyes never left the set as he chewed mechanically. "It needs salt."

FEBRUARY

I read somewhere man does not live by Curt Gowdy alone.

Tonight, I slid into a nightgown made of Astro-Turf, and sat on the arm of his chair.

"I have a surprise for you," I said huskily.

"Keep it down. Fess Parker is trying to tree a coon."

"What would you say if I told you I had just bought a water bed?"

At first, I thought he didn't hear me. Then he turned slowly. "Are you serious?"

He bounded from his chair, ran to the bedroom and a smile crept across his face. "Are you thinking what I'm thinking?" he asked.

"I hope so," I breathed.

"Now I can stock my own trout."

MARCH

All the green things are coming out this month, except my husband. He is alive (if you call this living) and is being fed intravenously on a diet of basketball, baseball, golf, and hockey.

It has become a game with the family trying to think of ways to get Daddy out of his chair. We have tried, "Your sweater is on fire," "Watching hockey can cause bleeding gums," and "I am leaving. You get custody of the kids."

There is something very unnatural about a man who has a niche in the wall and every day puts fresh flowers under a picture of George Blanda.

APRIL

The baseball strike postponed the opening game thirteen days. Through conscientious throat massage and stuffing his mouth with pebbles, we were able to get my husband up to four words a day during this period.

The first day he said, "Wha . . ."

The second day he said, "What."

The third day he was up to, "Whhhat is yyyour naaaame?"

The players settled their differences soon after and he has regressed once more to clearing his throat.

MAY

We put his mother in knee socks, shin guards, and a hockey face mask and shoved her in front of his chair for Mother's Day.

My husband was watching a ping-pong game and granted her an audience for only a few seconds. Then he punched her playfully on the arm and said, "Hang in there, kid."

JUNE

In an attempt to clean out all of the old things we never use any more, I realized that I had inadvertently set my husband at the curb on top of a rusted bicycle.

The driver of the truck led him to the house and said, "It's cute, but what's it for?"

"It does a lot of things," I said. "It eats leftovers, contributes body heat to a room, and can quote more statistics than the *Sports Almanac*. We use him for a doorstop."

"What's he doing with a candy cane over each ear?"

"He looked so great at Christmas, we hated to take him down."

JULY

"I am leaving you," I said calmly. "I can't stand it any more—the loneliness, the boredom, the roller derbies, the golf tournaments, the snacks. I'm young. I have all my own teeth. I want to see a movie besides the Frazier-Ali fight. I want to dance and drink champagne from a slipper. Do you understand?"

"Shh," he said, "there's a commercial coming up. The one where the beer can dances with the hot dog."

The Suburban Myth

There was a rumor going through the city that the suburban housewife drank her breakfast, accepted obscene phone calls—collect—played musical beds with her neighbors, and rewrote the book on Show and Tell.

The rumor was started by Edward C. Phlegg, the builder of Suburbian Gems who was smart enough to know that when virtue moves in, there goes the neighborhood. And if anything could sell the suburbs, sin could.

Everyone who lived there had the feeling that everyone was "swinging" except them. In fact, one evening in the paper there was a story about a "local" young mother who put her children under sedation every afternoon and engaged in an affair.

The idea intrigued us and we devoted our entire coffee klatsch to it. "Okay, who's the little temptress who is spiking the peanut butter with Sominex and carrying on in the daylight?"

We all sat there stunned.

"Marci?"

"What!" she sputtered. "And give up my nap?"

"Helen?"

"If you find my car in the driveway and my front door locked, call the police. I have my head in the oven."

"Linda?"

"Get serious. The last time I was in my bathrobe at noon, I had a baby in the morning and was dressed in time to get dinner that evening."

The plain and simple truth is the suburbs were not conducive to affairs. Bus service was lousy and in the winter you couldn't depend on it at all. The house numbers were all fouled up and it was difficult to find your way through the rows of houses in the plat.

The neighborhood was crawling with pre-schoolers who insisted on coming into their houses to use the bathroom. The floor plan was clumsy. There were too many traffic areas—too much glass —and besides, there were no alleys for a Plan B alternate exit.

Everything was against us from the beginning, including the domestic rut we had fallen into.

As Marci pointed out, "I think we're fighting a losing battle. We wouldn't recognize a pitch if we heard it. Take me. Please. My vocabulary has been reduced to five sentences which I mumble like a robot every day of my life. They never change.

1. Close the door.

2. Don't talk with food in your mouth.

3. Check out the clothes hamper.

4. I saw you playing with the dog so go wash your hands.

5. You should have gone before you left home.

"The responses never vary—not in ten years of child raising. One night at a party," she related, "I drifted into the kitchen in search of an ice cube when a devastating man leaned over my shoulder and said, 'Hello there, beautiful.'

" 'Close the door,' I said mechanically.

" 'I don't believe we've met,' he progressed. 'My name is Jim and you are ????'

" 'Don't talk with food in your mouth.'

" 'Hey, you're cute. I like a sense of humor. What say we freshen up your drinkypoo and find a nice, quiet spot all to ourselves.'

" 'Check out the clothes hamper,' I said brusquely.

"He hesitated, looking around cautiously, 'Are you putting me on? I mean we aren't on Candid Camera or anything are we?' He slipped his arm around my waist.

" 'I saw you playing with the dog so go wash your hands.'

"His arm dropped and he edged his way to the door. 'Listen, you just stay put,' he said, 'I've got something to attend to.' "

"Tell me you didn't," said Helen.

"I yelled after him, 'You should have gone before you left home.' "

"Did you ever see him again?"

"Never," said Marci sadly.

"Well, someone is having a good time out there," said Linda. "Who could it be?"

"What about that slim blonde in the cul-de-sac, Leslie?"

"What about her?"

"I think she drinks," said Linda.

"What makes you think that?"

"Her curtains are drawn all day, the dog is never out, the car is always there, and she's pale."

We all exchanged glances. "You don't know about Leslie?"

Linda shrugged her shoulders. "She doesn't drink?"

"Not a drop," I said. "She's a Daytime Soap Operaholic."

"You're kidding."

"No, she has a fifteen-serial-a-day habit. Just sits there day in and day out with the curtains drawn and cries."

"Just because you watch a lot of soap operas doesn't mean you're addicted," defended Linda.

"Haven't you seen the literature from SO (Soap Operaholics)? Here, if you have any one of these symptoms, you're in trouble."

Helen handed Linda the SO Handbook.

1. Do you watch a soap opera at seven in the morning just to get you going?

2. Do you watch soap operas alone?

3. Do you hide *TV Guide* so your family won't know how many serials you are watching?

4. Do you lie about how many shows you watch a day?

5. Do you contend you can turn off "As the World Turns" and "Love of Life" any time you want to?

6. When you are "Guiding Light"–ed are you an embarrassment?

7. Do you refuse to admit you're a Soap Opera-holic even though you refused to miss "The Secret Storm" to have your baby?

"If that isn't a kick in the head," said Linda. "The Suburban Orgy is a myth!"

Helen clapped her hand over her mouth. "Lower your voice, you fool. What do you think would be the resale value of these houses if that got out?"

Hosting a Famine

Fat just never caught on in the suburbs like I thought it would. I used to sit around and think how this is the year for the Obese Olympics, or the Pillsbury Eatoff or Bert Parks warbling, "There she goes, Miss North, South, and Central Americas," but it never happened.

Fat just never made it big. No one championed thin more than the women in Suburbian Gems. Some dedicated their entire lives searching for a lettuce that tasted like lasagne.

They exercised. They counted calories. They

121

attended Diet Seminars. Their entire conversation centered around how wonderful it felt to starve to death.

Ever since the babies came I had noticed a deterioration in my own body. My neck became extended, my waist filled in, the hips ballooned, the stomach crested, and my knees grew together.

One day my husband looked at me and said, "Good heavens. Are you aware that you are shaped like a gourd?"

At that moment, I converted to the suburban religion called Cottage Cheese. I ate so much cottage cheese my teeth curdled.

That wasn't the worst of it. Once you were an ordained cottage cheese disciple, you were committed to total understanding of the entire diet community.

I don't think I will ever forget the first luncheon I gave for my neighbors in Suburbian Gems. They were all on a different diet. It was like hosting a famine.

Helen was on the Stillman diet which means eight glasses of water, lean meat, and a bathroom of her own. (What does it profit a woman to look thin if you have to wear a nose plug for the rest of your life?)

Ceil was on the Atkins diet for which I cooked

an egg swimming in butter served on a table in the corner due to her acute bad breath. (No diet is perfect.)

Marge was still on the drinking man's diet. She required a bottle, a little ice, and a clean glass. (Marge hadn't lost a pound, but it didn't seem to make any difference to her.)

Ethel was on the Vinegar-Kelp diet. (She worried us. She kept drifting toward the ocean.)

Wilma was enjoying maintenance on her Weight Watchers program. Before dinner was served, she ate the centerpiece (a candle and a plastic banana) and mumbled, "Bless me Jean Nidetch for I have sinned."

I, of course, had my cottage cheese.

Why do women do it?

You're talking to a pro. There was a time when I derived some comfort out of the knowledge that one out of every three Americans is overweight. But I never saw the one. Everywhere I went I was flanked on either side by the two chart-perfect women.

I was surrounded by women whose pleats never separate when they sit down, who wear suspenders to hold up their underwear, who have concave stomachs and the gall to say to me, "I'm cutting down. Do you want my dessert, honey?"

Every dieter has her moment of truth when she faces up to the fact that she is overweight. Sometimes, it's just a little thing like seeing a $50 bill on the sidewalk and not being able to pick it up, or accusing the car wash of shrinking your seat belt, or having shortness of breath when you chew gum. With me, it was a photograph taken on the beach. You couldn't see the blanket I was sitting on, or the sand, and only a small part of the ocean.

My husband said, "The best diet in the world is to put that picture of yourself on the refrigerator door."

He was right. The picture was delicious and actually contained few calories, but with the picture gone I fell into my old eating habits.

The Fat-Picture-on-the-Door diet is just one of many that have swept the country during the past decade, each one promising you more food than you can eat, instant results, and strangers on the bus coming up and asking you to dance.

There was one diet that wasn't publicized, but I think had great merit. It was called the Tall Rat Experiment X-70, or as it was popularly called, "Grow Up—Not Out."

The program was perfected by a scientist named Bert Briarcuff whose basic philosophy was, "There is no such thing as a fat girl. They're only too short." Of course; why hadn't anyone thought of that! Women weren't overweight. They were undertall.

He gathered together several cages of obese rats and went to work to make them look taller.

The results were astounding. Rats in wedgies looked five pounds thinner than those in loafers. The rats in jump suits with vertical stripes gave the illusion of being thin while those in polka dots looked grossly overweight.

Then he employed the old photographic trick. When a rat was talking with someone in the gutter, the rat placed himself on the curb. If his companion was on the curb, he stood on the steps. If his partner jumped on the steps, he would leap to a spouting above.

Briarcuff found that by teasing the rat's hair, his cheekbones would stand out like Katharine Hepburn's. Women didn't have to starve to death any more. They would just have to learn to create an illusion of tallness.

The Tall Rat Experiment X-70 spread like wildfire in our neighborhood. We shopped at tall girl shops to get the waistlines to hang around our hips. We volunteered to take off our hats at movies. I personally made no new friends over five foot two.

At a dance one night I vowed to dance with no

one taller than I. I bet I danced with every ten-year-old boy there.

After six months, however, the Tall Rat Experiment X-70 began to bore me. I was sick of stacking pillows in the car to make me look like my head was coming through the roof.

Besides, I had a new toy. The kids chipped in and bought me a Flab-Control belt. As they explained it to me, there was no dieting. All I had to do was put the adjustable belt, which was equipped with a small electronic buzzer, around my waist. When my stomach muscles became slack, the buzzer would sound. It was a case of chronic flab. The noise drove me crazy. I went back to cottage cheese.

Desperate, I enrolled in one of the Gastric Show and Tell classes offered at the high school in the evenings.

Their program seemed quite revolutionary to me. Foods that I had always considered decorations for the mantel like carrots, cucumbers, squash, and chard were touted as edibles. Following interesting lectures on nutrition and how certain foods were needed for the body, our instructor, Miss Feeney, asked, "Are there any questions?"

"What if I go through all of this and discover the life after this one is all fat people?"

"Don't make trouble," she said softly. "Just try the foods."

By the end of three weeks when I had not dropped an ounce, Miss Feeney took me aside and said, "You promised you would try to stick to our diet. What happened?"

"Miss Feeney," I said, "you have to face up to what you are dealing with. Dieters are basically nice people. I have a snout full of integrity. I don't throw chewing gum on the sidewalk. I don't put less postage on my letter than I know it takes. And I don't lie about my age. But when it comes to diets, you can't believe a word I say."

"You will live to eat those words," she said.

My face brightened. "Are they fattening?"

Oh, there were others. The denture-adhesive diet where you cement your teeth together and the one-size-fits-all pantyhose worn to the table, but I always came back to cottage cheese.

It's not so bad—a little gravy over it once in awhile, a cottage cheese sandwich between two warm slices of homemade bread, a cottage cheese sundae with a glob of chocolate. . . .

CHAPTER SIX

Ya Got Trouble

NEWS ITEM: Plans for a proposed drive-in movie will be submitted to members of the Suburbian Gems Plat Council at Wednesday night's meeting.

The theater, to be known as The Last Roundup, would be erected on the patch of ground between "CLEAN FILL DIRT WANTED. CALL AFTER 5 P.M. at 959-8800" and Ned Stems' Car Wash. Estimated to occupy about thirty acres, it will feature a western motif, 350 speakers, a refreshment stand, and permanent personal facilities. Prof. Harold Swill, vocal band director of Suburbian Gems High School, is heading a group of dissidents opposing The Last

Roundup and is expected to speak out against the proposal.

"A drive-in movie!"

"Don't you understand? Friends, either you are closing your eyes to a situation you do not wish to acknowledge or you are not aware of the caliber of disaster indicated by the presence of a drive-in movie in your community.

"Well, ya got trouble, my friends, right here, I say trouble right here in Suburban Gems. Sure, I'm a lover of the arts and certainly mighty proud, I say mighty proud to say it.

"I consider the hours I've spent with Sousa and Romberg are golden, helps you cultivate timing, discipline, a natural ear, and a way to get girls.

"Did you ever take a pocket comb, covered with toilet paper on a picnic and improvise with Tiger Rag—hah! I say any boob can fake a few bars of the "Beer Barrel Polka," but I call that tacky—the first big step on the road to the depths of degrada . . . I say first the Rape of Mozart, then a near-beer six-pack.

"And the next thing you know your son is marching with hair right down to his knees, listening to some stoned-out hippie talking about pot.

"Not a shiny cooking pot with Mom's ham and beans, no siree, but a pot where they freak out of their skulls, makes you sick I should say, now friends let me tell you what I mean, you got R (restricted), X (nothing censored) and a GP where Flipper gets a hickey—movies that make the difference between a pervert and a bum with a capital B that rhymes with D that stands for drive-in.

"And all week long your Suburban Gems youth'll be goofing off—I say your young men will be goofing—goofing away their noontime, suppertime, choretime too, hook the speaker to the car, never mind getting the lawn fertilized, the sand in the litter box, sitting little sister and never bother delivering the Sunday paper till the supervisor calls on a Sunday afternoon and that's trouble, my friend —lots of trouble—I'm thinking of the kids in the back seat, kissing till their braces spark, cold popcorn, melted ice balls and that's trouble, right here in Suburban Gems with a capital T which rhymes with D which stands for drive-in.

"Now I know all you folks are the right kind of parents. I'm gonna be perfectly frank. Would you like to know what kind of conversation goes on while they're watchin' those outdoor flicks? They'll be talkin' about Gatorade, trying out filter tips, popping in breath mints like pill-popping fiends, and bragging all about how they read *Valley of the Dolls* in one swell evening.

"One fine night as they leave the drive-in, headed for the malt shop, you'll find your son, your daughter in the arms of an over-sexed sophomore, mattress-minded—all systems go, parental guidance . . .

"Friends! The idle motor is the devil's playground!

"Trouble, oh ya got trouble, trouble right here in Suburbian Gems, trouble with a capital T that rhymes with D that stands for drive-in. We surely got trouble—gotta figure out a way to stamp out puberty.

"Trouble—trouble—trouble.

"Mothers of Suburbian Gems. Heed the warnings and the telltale signs of corruption before it's too late.

"The minute your son leaves the house, does he stuff his 4-H bylaws in the glove compartment?

"Does he take a blanket on a date and tell you the heater in the car isn't working and it's August?

"Does he have a copy of *Playboy* hidden between the pages of *Boy's Life?*

"Has he ever refused to finish a knock-knock joke in your presence?

"Are certain words creeping into his conversation—words like 'far out' and 'Linda Lovelace' and 'Ma, where's your purse?'

"Well, my friends, you got trouble, trouble with a capital T that rhymes with D that stands for drive-in.

"You surely got trouble, right here in Suburban Gems, remember God, Motherhood, Flag—and Paul Harvey.

"Oh, oh you got trouble, terrible, terrible trouble that field of passion under a sky of stars is the flag of sin.

"You got trouble, trouble, trouble, oh great big trouble right here in Suburban Gems with a T that rhymes with D that stands for drive-in."

NEWS ITEM: Plans for a proposed drive-in movie were approved last night when members of the Suburban Gems Plat Council reached a compromise.

Originally, council members complained that the speakers might contribute to noise pollution in the area. Approximately 140 students, representing Suburban Gems High School, volunteered as a group to turn the sound off completely during the showing of movies.

Prof. Harold Swill, band director of Suburbian Gems High School, said, "It is maturity like this that restores my faith in young people."

CHAPTER SEVEN

It Comes with the Territory

Loneliness

No one talked about it a lot, but everyone knew what it was.

It was the day you alphabetized your spices on the spice rack.

Then you dressed all the naked dolls in the house and arranged them on the bed according to size.

You talked to your plants and they fell asleep on you.

It was a condition, and it came with the territory.

I tried to explain it to my neighbor, Helen.

"I'm depressed, Helen," I said, "and I think I

know what it is. (Excuse me) '*Lonnie!* I see you sneaking out of the house with my mixer and I know what you are going to do with it. Put it back!' "

"More coffee?" asked Helen.

"Just a half a cup. I've seen this coming for a long time. The symptoms are all there."

"What symptoms?" asked Helen.

"Helen, I'm so bored. I went to the food locker yesterday to visit my meat."

"You're kidding."

"No. And the other day I flushed a Twinkie down the toilet just to please Jack Lalanne. (Just a minute) 'Is anyone going to get the phone? Never mind. Hello. Yes. What do you want? I'm in therapy with Helen. You'll be home late and don't wait dinner. Right.' Now, where was I, Helen? Oh yes, my behavior. It's bizarre. Remember when a man came out to clean the septic tank? I dropped everything, ran out, and sat on the edge of the hole and asked, 'So, what's new with you?' "

Helen nodded silently.

"I called my mother long distance the other day just to tell her I found a green stamp in my sweeper bag."

Helen stirred her coffee slowly. "Did you ever put up your hair to answer the door?"

"Yes. Oh yes," I said with relief. "Excuse me, Helen, someone's at the door. (Later) It was Joan. She just dropped off her two and she'll be back for lunch. Where was I? Oh yes, my problem. I find myself doing odd things I've never done before. Remember when Dr. Joyce Brothers was on a local talk show and they invited questions from the audience? I called in, Helen. I really did. And I announced to the entire English-speaking world that I wanted her psychological opinion of a man who insisted on sleeping next to the wall. Did I ever tell you that, Helen? Bill refuses to sleep on the outside of a bed. He's positively paranoid about the inside track. Didn't it ever occur to him that just once I might like to sleep next to the wall?"

"Your phone is ringing again," said Helen.

"It was the school nurse. Wanted permission to give my son an aspirin. What he really needs is an enema. I wonder how many people are wandering the streets today in glasses who only need an enema. More coffee?"

"No, I can't stay long," said Helen.

"I've thought about my problem ever since we moved out here and I think I've finally put my finger on it. Every morning, we see the men driving out of paradise onto the freeway and into the city. Leaving us to what? Did I tell you I spent an hour and a half the other morning putting together a cannon out of balsa wood that I found in the cereal box only to discover one of the kids swallowed the wheel and we couldn't play with it? Wouldn't you know if you had a wheel in your mouth?"

Helen sighed. "You going to the Frisbee recital at the school Friday?"

"I suppose so. Hang on a minute. There goes Nancy and I still wanted to talk with her about Wednesday. 'Hey Nancy! We going to that 1-cent tree sale Friday after the store? Let's go early. It's a mob scene.' Sometimes, Helen, I wonder why we moved to the suburbs. As I told the girls at Trim Gym class last week, I never thought I'd see the day when I'd want my own apartment before the kids did."

"You're just restless," said Helen.

"No! I'm not restless. That's not the word," I said vehemently. "Restless is having lunch with your wigs and having a good time with them. It's a temporary condition that goes away. I'm talking about old, Helen. I'm old. Don't protest. I know what I am. I'm old and fighting for my identity in a young society. Everyone around me is under twenty. My doctor carries a gym bag. Our lawyer is still in braces. And I swear to you my dentist had a string on his mittens last winter. Do you know what it is to go into a confessional and have your priest reeking of Clearasil?"

"It's not your imagination?"

"It's not my imagination. I don't know what is wrong with me. I'm . . . I'm so desperate. I purposely picked a fight with the hamster yesterday. I stood in front of the hall mirror and said, 'So, who did you expect? Snow White?' "

"There's nothing wrong with the way you look," comforted Helen.

"I'm a mental midget, Helen. My husband is growing professionally every hour and I didn't even know penguins got barnacles on their feet until Pearl Bailey missed it on Hollywood Squares. It's hard to talk to a man who has a meaningful relationship with the TV set."

"Well," said Helen, "I've got to be going."

"Say it! I'm boring, aren't I?"

"Of course you're not boring."

"Do you know that if I had continued my night school classes I would have graduated from college this June. That's right. If I had just found my car keys I could have picked up my B.A. and could be one of those women who only wash on Saturdays and freeze their bread."

Helen looked at me squarely. "Do you know what you are?"

For a moment, there was only the silence of a toilet being flushed consecutively, two dogs chasing one another through the living room, a horn honking in the driveway, a telephone ringing insistently, a neighbor calling her children, the theme of "Gilligan's Island" blaring on the TV set, a competing stereo of John Denver, one child at my feet chewing a hole in the brown-sugar bag, and a loud voice from somewhere screaming, "I'm telling."

"I'm lonely," I said softly.

"Tell your husband," said Helen.

Tell my husband.

I once read a poll of what husbands think their wives do all day long.

The results were rather what you would expect.

Thirty-three percent said women spent five hours out of each day putting lint on their husband's socks.

Twenty-seven percent said they spent four hours daily pouring grease down the sink and watching it harden to give their husbands something to do when they got home.

Ten percent swore their wives held the door open all day to make sure all the warm/cool air (depending on the season) got out of the house.

A walloping 58 percent said women divided their time between hiding from the children, watching soap operas, drinking coffee, shrinking shirt collars, discarding one sock from every pair in the drawer, lugging power tools out to the sandbox for the kids to play with, and trying to get the chenille creases out of their faces before their husbands came home.

I was dialing Mrs. Craig's number when my husband came home one night after my conversation with Helen.

"Who are you calling?" he asked.

"Mrs. Craig. I thought she could sit with the children for a few days while I ran into the city to visit Mother."

My husband leaned over and gently replaced the receiver. "Do you honestly believe that I can't handle things around here without you? I'll do double time between here and the office and fill in until you get back."

"You've never been a strong man," I said.

"What kind of a crack is that?"

"I'm only suggesting that any man who has to have a spinal block to trim his toenails doesn't have the greatest threshold of pain in the world."

"And who went to bed for three days when she had her ears pierced?"

"That's not true. Look, I was only trying to spare you. Are you sure you can handle things around here? The kids? The cooking? The laundry? The routine?"

"Does Dean Martin know how to handle a martini?" he grinned. "Of course I can handle this stuff. Don't worry about it. You just go off and do what you have to do and don't give us another thought."

I didn't give them a thought until I let myself into Mother's house in the city. "Call home," she said.

"One quick question," said my husband, "what does 'Bwee, no nah noo' mean?"

"Who said it?"

"Whatya mean who said it? Your baby just said it and looked kinda desperate."

"It means, 'I have to go to the bathroom.' "

"Thanks, that's all I needed to know. Have a good . . ."

"It also means, 'I want a cookie. Where are my coloring books? The dog just crawled into the dryer. There's a policeman at the door. I am floating my $20 orthopedic shoes in the john.' The kid has a limited vocabulary and has to double up."

"I can handle this. It's just that she looks so miserable."

"It also means, 'It's too late for the bathroom.' "

As I readied for bed, the phone rang again.

"What's up?" I asked.

"No problem," he said cheerfully. "It's just that Maxine Miltshire just called and can't drive the car pool tomorrow because she's subbing for Janice Winerob on the bowling team. She can pick up— unless it rains. Her convertible top won't go up. However, if the weather is decent she can pick up and trade with Jo Caldwell who is pregnant and three weeks overdue, but who had a doctor who was weak in math. That means I will drive Thursday unless Jo Caldwell's doctor lucks out. In that case I'll have to call Caroline Seale because I have an early meeting and it might rain. Do you understand any of this?"

"No."

"I'll call you tomorrow night."

The next night I answered the phone. There was a brief silence. Then, "Well, I hope you're happy, Missy. I am now the only thirty-eight-year-old child in my office who has been exposed to Roseola. I was late for work because little Buster Smarts was eating chili off the dashboard of my car and spilled it all over the upholstery and my job is in jeopardy."

"Why is your job in jeopardy?" I asked.

"Because *your* son answered the phone this morning while I was putting catsup on sandwiches

147

and I heard him tell Mr. Weems, 'Daddy can't come to the phone now. He's hitting the bottle.' "

"Tomorrow is Saturday. It'll be better," I promised.

The phone rang early Saturday.

"Hello," I giggled. "This is Dial-a-Prayer."

"Oh, you're cute," he snarled, "real cute. Just a couple of questions here. First, where are the wheels off the sweeper?"

"On the back of the bicycle in the garage."

"Check. Where does the washer walk to when it walks?"

"It never gets any farther than the door."

"Check. When was the last time you were in the boys' bedroom?"

"When I was looking for eight place settings of my good china."

I arrived home much later from the city than I intended. Everyone was in bed. My husband staggered to the door.

"I'm home," I announced brightly. "Tell me, why is there an X chalked on the side of our house?"

He rubbed his eyes tiredly.

"A baby sitter put it there. I think we're marked for demolition."

I wandered through the house. The dog was drinking out of an ashtray. There was a pad of blank checks by the phone with messages scribbled on them. The blackboard had a single message on it, "I'm leaving and I'm not coming back." Signed, "Daddy."

"Why is the baby asleep in the bathtub?" I asked.

"She drank four glasses of water just before bedtime."

"There is a crease on your face shaped like a duck."

"I had to separate the boys so I slept in the baby's bed."

I opened up the refrigerator and a leftover reached for me and I slammed the door shut.

"What happened?" I asked, spreading my arms out to make a wide circle.

"Don't start up," he said. "It's all your fault. I had dinner so long in the oven that the bucket caught fire."

"What bucket?"

"The cardboard bucket holding the chicken."

"You're supposed . . ."

"Don't say anything. I mean it. While I was trying to put out the fire, *your* baby chose a rather inopportune time to get a penny stuck up her nose. I've got thirty-five boys in the bathroom watching movies. I tried to make a drink and there are no ice cubes, and besides, Maxine called to tell me I've been named homeroom mother! And all the while you are living it up at your mother's, drinking out of clean glasses."

"You'll feel better after a good night's sleep," I said as he crawled back into the crib.

I was right. The next morning he turned to me brightly and said, "Good-bye dear. You'll find everything in ship-shape order. Boys, kiss your father good-bye."

The boys turned away and one said flatly, "He murdered our guppies."

"We'll talk about it tonight," he said. Then he whispered, "By the way, could you call and let me know how Lisa makes out on 'As the World Turns'?"

The Pampered Dog

When the dogs in the city talked among themselves, the conversation always drifted to the suburbs.

It was the dream of every canine to someday live out where every dog had his own tree, where bad breath had been conquered, and where fleas had to register at the city limits and carry their I.D.'s at all times.

The suburban dog had it made. Owners pampered them to death with dietary dog food, dental appointments, knitted stoles to take off the evening chill, dog beds shaped like hearts, doggie bar nibbles, and car seats.

I personally felt I could live a fulfilled life without a live-in lawn fertilizer, but my husband convinced me the children would grow up to steal hubcaps without the security and affection of a dog.

In a weak moment, we bought Arlo.

The first day Arlo came home, his feet never touched the floor. In a single day he was fed eight times, burped five, danced on the TV set, slid down the banister, was given a bath, blown dry with my hair dryer, visited twelve homes, rode on a bicycle, and barked long distance on the phone to Grandma. He slept his first night under my dual-control thermal blanket.

On the second day, Arlo continued to reign. It took eight saucepans to warm his dinner, he watched a puppet show staged by the children for his benefit and as he headed for the door, one of the children slapped his brother while the third child leaped for the dog and opened the door . . . first.

On the third day, there were some complaints from the children that Arlo had kept them awake all night with his howling. When I suggested the dog be fed, one son said his brother did it, who vowed his sister did it, who said, "It's not my turn."

On the fourth day, my daughter took Arlo to Show and Tell. He blew it by showing too much and didn't have a finish, and a clean-up committee of one was delegated to do the honors. One of the children said if Arlo followed him to school one more time and he had to bring him home he was going to kick him.

On the fifth day I reminded all of them that the rule of the house was that the first one to spot a puddle, etc., automatically cleaned it up. The entire household fell victim to indoor blindness.

On the sixth day, I said, "Has anyone seen Arlo?"

One of the children yelled back, "Arlo who?"

So much for security and affection.

I began to become suspicious that Arlo was not a registered Irish Setter when his roots came in white, his nose was concave, and within six weeks he was eye level to the kitchen table.

This was confirmed as I sat in the vet's office one afternoon. I shifted uncomfortably as a woman read a magazine to a cat with running eyes, a pet raccoon ran around the playpen, and a small terrier mistook my leg for a forest.

Finally, a well-dressed man on my left with a small poodle ventured, "I am intrigued with your breed. What kind of a dog is that?"

"Irish Setter," I said.

He looked astounded, "You have papers?"

"All over the house." I got a firmer grip on the forty feet of pink plastic clothesline around Arlo's neck and ventured, "What's wrong with your dog?"

He looked soulfully at the poodle and patted it gently, "Jessamyn isn't sleeping well."

"Me either," I said.

"She's just been through a rather bad pregnancy."

"Me too," I said excitedly.

"Actually, Jessamyn is too highly bred and tense for motherhood."

"I know what you mean," I commiserated.

"We thought of aborting, but there was so much social pressure brought to bear, we finally consulted a psychiatrist who thought it best to go through with the births and then get them away from her as soon as possible so she could pull herself and her life together again and then exercise some measure of birth control. What's wrong with your . . . Setter?"

"Worms."

"How disgusting," he said, wrinkling his nose. "I

wonder what's keeping that vet?" he said. "I have some flowers in the car for Jessamyn's mother."

"Jessamyn's mother?" I asked, my eyes widening.

"She's (he leaned over and spelled slowly) P-A-S-S-E-D-O-V-E-R. Jessamyn and I go once a month to visit. They were very close. She's at the Bow Wow Cemetery. Beautiful grounds. Incidentally, if you ever go on a vacation and need a reliable shelter the K-9 Country Club is a marv. Restricted, you know. None of your tacky clientele. The ones with the new luggage. They have a chef there you wouldn't believe. Well," he said as he was summoned, "Nice meeting you and good luck to—what's-his-name?"

"Arlo."

"Oh my God," he said, touching his nose with his linen handkerchief and sniffing.

Because I am basically a "swift" person, it didn't take me long to realize that Arlo and I were to become an "item." Just the two of us. I fed him, kept his water bowl filled, got him shots, license, fought fleas, took out ticks, and let him in and out of the house, 2,672 times a day.

My husband came home one evening to view the dishes on the breakfast table with hardened egg, the unmade beds, the papers from the night before strewn all over the living room, the laundry spilling out over the clothes hamper onto the floor, and said, "Fess up! You've been playing with that dog all day long."

"Did anyone ever tell you you have a future in comedy . . . along with Jane Fonda and Eric Sevareid?"

"C'mon now," he teased, "look at the way that little dickens is jumping up and down."

"The little dickens is aiming for your throat. He wants out."

"Don't be ridiculous," he said. "He just came in when I did."

"So now he wants out. I go through this over two thousand times a day. The dog has a Door Wish. He can't go by one without scratching it until it opens. The other day he scratched, barked, and jumped for fifteen minutes. Finally, I opened the door and he ran in and two minutes later started scratching again. He realized he was under the sink."

"Why does he want out so much? Maybe something is wrong with his kidneys?"

"A dog with kidneys the size of a lentil could have better control than he has."

"I got it," said my husband, snapping his finger. "We'll go out when he goes in. That way we'll confuse him into not knowing if he's out or in."

Standing there huddled in the darkness on the cold porch scratching with our paws to get in, I tried to figure out where I went wrong. I think it was when my mother said to me, "You're not getting any younger."

"You are going to think this is a dumb question," I asked, "but why did we get a dog in the first place? I mean, if it was for the kids, forget it. All it has done for them is to keep them from looking down when they walk."

My husband took me by the shoulders and I saw shock written on his face. "Do you mean to tell me you really don't know?" he asked.

"No."

"We did it for you," he said.

"You bought a dog for me?" I asked numbly.

"But of course. For your protection. Maybe you don't realize the dangers of being by yourself out here in this wilderness. There are loonies and crazies running around all over the place."

"True, but we're all on a first-name basis."

"You may be as light about it as you like, but just wait until some day when I am at work in the city, and a wild-eyed stranger knocks at your door and wants to use your phone on some pretense and you'll be mighty thankful Arlo is around."

I looked at Arlo. He was lying on his back in

front of the fireplace with all four paws sticking up in the air—passing gas.

The mental picture of a sex pervert at my door and the only thing between us was Arlo, sent a shiver down my spine.

It was several weeks later that Arlo was to be put to the test. I answered the door to find two men standing there rubbing Arlo behind the ears.

"Pardon us," said one of the men, "but our truck broke down and we'd like to phone our company for help."

I grabbed Arlo by the collar and jerked him to his feet. "I must apologize for the dog," I said. "I'll try to hold him so he won't tear you to shreds. Down boy!"

The men looked at one another and shrugged as the dog blinked sleepily and slumped to the floor. "He looks pretty friendly to me," said one of them.

I knelt and pushed back Arlo's lip to show his teeth. When I released the lip, it fell back into a ripple as he licked my hand. "You may not believe this but I had to register this dog with the police as a deadly weapon. Just ask anyone around here and they'll tell you about Arlo."

"Arlo?" the men grinned.

"Steady boy!" I said, propping him up to get him

off my foot. "Just don't make any sudden moves," I cautioned.

One of the men came inside to use the phone while Arlo and I held the other man at bay at the door.

"Why, one of the kids was just playing around one day," I related nervously, "and inadvertently punched me on the arm. Arlo liked to have made raw meat out of him before we could pull him off."

"Is that right?" asked the stranger.

His friend returned and together they thanked me, playfully pushed Arlo over on his back, scratched his stomach, and left.

As they walked to the car I heard one say, "Boy, that was one terrifying experience."

"What, the dog?"

"No, the woman. She's a real whacko!"

They were probably right and I realized things weren't going to get any better when one afternoon I answered the phone. It was Mr. Wainscott.

"Remember me?" he asked. "I'm Jessamyn's father."

"Of course," I said, "from the vet's waiting room. Jessamyn is the one who had the same symptoms as I had. I've been dying to ask what the doctor prescribed."

"Lots of bed rest, time to herself, no major decisions, analysis, and a light social calendar."

"I guess one out of five isn't bad," I said. "So, how are things?"

"Fine. I was calling to ask if Arlo could attend Jessamyn's birthday party. Are you there?"

"Yes," I said. "A birthday party. Where?"

"This Saturday at two. We live two blocks north of the highway next to the golf course. You can't miss it. Oh, and it's informal."

When we arrived a dozen or so dogs romped around the room.

"So glad you could come," said Mr. Wainscott.

"I must apologize for the present," I said. "Arlo ate it on the way over."

"That's perfectly all right. Gang!" he shouted, "this is Arlo. Arlo is one of Jessamyn's neighbors. Don't be frightened," he said as Arlo stood at the sink and licked water out of the spigot. "He's big for nine months. Why don't you pick Arlo up in a few hours?"

I don't know what happened to Arlo at the party, but he was never the same dog after that. One day I caught him looking at his teeth in the bathroom mirror. (Jessamyn had her teeth capped). Another time, he hopped on the bathroom scale, gasped, and refused to eat table scraps any more. One afternoon, I begged Arlo for ten minutes to go outside. He was sitting in a chair watching David Susskind.

The only time he seemed happy was in his encounter group.

The Garage Sale

There are four things that are overrated in this country: hot chicken soup, sex, the FBI, and parking your car in your garage.

What's such a big deal about pulling your car into a garage if you have to exit by threading your body through an open window, hang from a lawn spreader, climb over the roof, and slide down a garden hose before reaching the door.

Our garage was a twilight zone for garbage, the dog, old papers, boxes, excess laundry, redeemable bottles, and "projects" too awkward (big, dirty, stinking) to have in the house. So was everyone else's. In fact, there was a garage clause in most of our accident polices that if we were folded, bent, spindled or mutilated while walking through our garage we could not file a claim.

Then one day something happened to change all of that. Helen came over so excited she could barely speak. "How would you like to go to a garage sale?" she asked.

"I have one."

"You don't buy the garage, you ninny," she said. "That's where the sale is. A woman over in the Dreamland Casita plat just advertised and I want to check it out."

A good fifteen blocks away from the sale, we saw the cars bumper to bumper. I had not seen such a mob since the fire drill at the Health Spa.

We parked the car and walked, slowly absorbing the carnival before our eyes. On the lawn, a woman was trying on a skirt over her slacks. "Do you do alterations?" she yelled to the woman who had sold it to her.

"Whatya want for 25 cents?" she yelled back, "an audience with Edith Head?"

Inside, mad, crazy, frenzied ladies fought over an empty anti-freeze can for $1.50 and an ice cube tray with a hole in the bottom of it for 55 cents.

One lady was lifting the snow tires off the family car and shouting, "How much?" Another was clutching a hula hoop over her shoulder and asking, "Are you sure this is an antique?" An older couple was haggling over a pole lamp insisting it would not fit into their car, and arrangements must be made for a suitable delivery date. It was marked 35 cents.

Outside, Helen and I leaned against a tree. "Can you believe this?" I asked. "I feel like I have just attended Alice's tea party."

"What did you buy?" asked Helen excitedly.

"Don't be ridiculous," I said. "It's all a bunch of junk no one wants. I didn't see anything in there I couldn't live without."

"What's that under your sweater?"

"Oh this. It's the only decent thing worth carrying out."

I held it up. A framed picture of the "Last Supper" done in bottle caps.

"Isn't that exquisite?" I asked.

"That is without a doubt the worst looking picture I have ever seen. Look how distorted the faces are and besides, Judas is rusting. How much did you pay for it?"

"Six dollars," I said defensively.

"*Six bucks!*" said Helen doubling over, "you've got to be kidding." As she laughed, an electric iron dropped from behind her handbag.

"What's that?" I asked.

"An iron. I really needed an extra one."

"It doesn't have a handle."

"So why do you think I got it for 75 cents?"

"Look," said a lady who had been standing at our elbow for ten minutes, "are you going to buy this tree or just stake it out so no one else can get to it?"

"No," I stammered . . . moving away.

She dug her shovel into the soil and began moving dirt.

Frankly, I didn't give the garage sale another thought until another neighbor, Grace, said to me one day, "Why don't you stage a garage sale?"

"Because spreading one's personal wares out in a garage for public exhibition is not only crass, it smacks of being tacky."

"Pauline Favor made eighteen bucks," she said.

"Get the card table," I snapped.

My husband was less than enthusiastic. "Those things are like a circus," he said. "Besides, we need all of this stuff."

"Hah!" I said, "that is all you know. This stuff is junk. One of these days we'll wake up and find the junk has taken over. We won't be able to move for boxes of rain-soaked Halloween masks, and stacks of boots with one missing from each pair, and a broken down potty chair. If you want to live like a pack rat, that's your business, but I've got to make a path through this junk—and soon."

In desperation, he gave in and the garage sale was scheduled for Thursday from 9 A.M. to 5 P.M.

At 6:30 A.M. a woman with a face like a ferret

pecked on my kitchen window and said, "I'll give you 30 cents for this door stop."

I informed her the doorstop was my husband who is not too swift in the mornings and if she didn't put him down this instant, I would summon the police.

By 7:30 there were fifteen cars parked in the driveway, nineteen on the lawn, two blocking traffic in the center of the street, and a Volkswagen trying to parallel park between the two andirons in my living room fireplace.

At 9 A.M. I opened the garage door and was immediately trampled to death. Grace said she had never seen anything like it.

They grabbed, pawed, sifted through, examined, and tried out anything that wasn't nailed down, but *they weren't buying.*

"What's the matter with them?" I asked.

"It's your junk. It's priced too high."

"Too high!" I exclaimed. "These heirlooms? Do you honestly think that $8 is too much for a box of candle stubs? And this stack of boots for $5 each. They don't make rubber like that any more. And besides, who is going to notice if you're wearing a pair that don't match? Dare to be different. And take this potty chair . . ."

"For twelve bucks, *you* take it," said a potential pigeon. "You can buy a new one for $15."

I wanted to hit her. "With training wheels? Why, this potty chair can take a kid right into football season. When collapsed, it will fit snugly in an Army duffle bag. It's not for everybody. Only the discerning shopper."

"You are going to have to lower your prices," whispered Grace.

Grace was right. Of course, but she should have prepared me for the personality change I was about to experience when I sold my first piece of junk.

I became a woman possessed. As one by one the items disappeared from the card tables and the nails on the side of the garage, I could not stand to see the people leave.

They bought the boots with a hole in the sole, electric toothbrushes with a short in them, a phonograph that turned counter-clockwise, and an underground booklet listing the grades of Harvard Medical School graduates 1927–1949.

The junk began to clear out and I knew what I must do to keep them there. Running into the house, I grabbed dishes out of the cupboards, clothes out of the closets, and books off the shelves.

I snatched my husband's new electric drill and marked it $3. I ripped the phone off the wall and sold it for $1.75. When my son came home from school, I yanked him off his bicycle and sold it for $5.

I grabbed a woman by the throat and said, "Want to buy a fur coat for $1? I was going to give it to my sister, but she looks like a tub in it."

"I am your sister," she said dryly.

To be perfectly honest, I lost control. Grace had to physically restrain me from pricing the baby who was being admired by a customer who cooed, "I'd like to take you home with me."

It was seven o'clock before the last car left the driveway. I was exhausted mentally and physically.

"Did I do all right?" I asked Grace.

She hesitated, "In a year or two, when you are well again, we'll talk about today."

"I don't know what happened to me," I said.

"You were a little excited."

"Are you trying to tell me I went crazy?"

"I am trying to tell you it was wrong to sell your garbage for 40 cents."

"But she insisted," I said.

"By the way," said Grace, "what's that under your arm? You bought something."

"It's nothing," I hedged.

She snatched the package and opened it. "It's your laundry!" she said, "that you keep in a plastic bag in the refrigerator. How much did you pay for this?"

"Two dollars," I said, "but some of it still fits."

CHAPTER EIGHT

Law and Order

Florence Sykes
Alias: The Pied Piper
Leads a trail of hopefuls
around in search of her
lost car

Phyllis Hardhat
Woman who makes a sharp left
turn into your parking place
and pretends she doesn't see
you.

Ruby Wynette
Alias (See Postal Clerk)
Woman with packages you
follow for three hours who
drops off packages and
returns to shop

Pat Pill
Woman who drives an
emergency vehicle to
the store to take
advantage of parking

Marietta Busch
Woman with "Jesus Saves"
bumper sticker with a pedestrian
clutching the hood of her car

Who's Watching the
Vacant House? Everyone.

I had only met Officer Beekman on two occasions.

The first time was when I inadvertently rammed into my husband's car when I backed out of the driveway and he was summoned by my husband. (The case is still pending.)

The second time was when he helped me over a rather bad spot in my driver's test by chalking a B on the brake pedal and an A on the accelerator.

"I suppose you are wondering why I have summoned you," I said as I let him in the front door.

"Yes Ma'am," he said, removing his crash helmet and his dark glasses.

"My husband and I are going on vacation and . . ."

He held up his hand for silence and looked around him anxiously. "Are we alone?"

"I think so."

"Fine. That is the first rule. Never tell anyone you are leaving."

"I understand."

"We handle hundreds of house-watching assignments each year and the key word is: *secrecy*."

"Don't people become sorta suspicious when they see a police cruiser in front of the house every night?"

"I don't park in front of the house every night," he explained, "I just sorta cruise by and give it this." (His head jerked like he was having a neck spasm.) "Now, the second key word is *lived in*. Make your potential burglar believe you are home by leaving on a light or a radio playing. If you'll just tell me where you are going, when you'll be back, and give me a number where you can be reached, we'll take care of everything."

"That's wonderful," I said, seeing him to the door. As he climbed into the car I shouted, "See you in two weeks!"

He touched his finger to his lips and said, "Remember, secrecy is the key word."

Helen was the first one over after he pulled away. "Why was the police cruiser in your driveway?"

"Shhh," I said, looking around. "We're all going to Yuuck Village for two weeks and Officer Beekman is going to watch our house to see that no one burglarizes it. Don't tell anyone. He said the key word is secrecy."

For a change, my husband agreed. "That is the smartest thing you have ever done," he said. "Who are you calling?"

"Officer Beekman's second suggestion was that the house look 'lived-in.' I'm calling Margo to tell her when we are leaving so she can come in every night and turn on a different light. Then I have to call the paper boys and the dry cleaner—and the postman."

"What about discontinuing the milkman?"

"Discontinue the milkman? Why don't you just stand out in front of the house in your underwear and hold up a sign reading, 'COME IN AND BROWSE.' Thieves follow milkmen like flies follow a garbage truck. Let me handle this. I'll just have him deliver four quarts every other day like he's always done."

"Won't the crooks get suspicious when he drinks

all four quarts and takes the empties back to his truck?"

"He'll just rattle a few bottles and pretend he's delivering," I sighed. "Now, where was I? Oh yes, I have to tell Mike we're leaving so he can come over and cut the grass, and Mark so he can plant garbage in our cans and put them at the curb on garbage day and . . ."

"I don't believe this," said my husband.

"You'd believe Maybelle Martin, wouldn't you? She and Dave were going to Disneyland for a few days. She dressed up her sewing form in a pants suit and a wig and propped it against the mantel with a drink in its hand. Her house was robbed the next morning. They took almost everything but the form. Do you know what gave her away?"

"Someone noticed she had a pole for legs?"

"The ice cubes in her drink melted and even crooks know no one stands around with a warm drink in his hand."

"You have told seven people already that we are leaving. How many more are you going to tell?"

"Well, I have to tell Charmaine to bring her children over to play in the yard, and Frederika said to call when we leave so she can bring her dog over on a weekend to bark. Naturally, I'll have to call my hairdresser, my cleaning lady, my insurance agent, my car pool girls . . ."

"That's sixteen."

"My Avon lady, AAA, the soft-water man, the utility meter reader, the Cub pack . . ."

"That's thirty-three."

"Of course our family vet and the check-out girls at Willard's market, my foot doctor, the guys at Bufford's service station, our minister and Miss Baker, who does that chatty column in the *Tattler* . . ."

"Roughly, how many people are you telling we are leaving town?"

"About 683."

"Why don't you just take an ad in *The New York Times?*"

"Glad you reminded me. Grace said a great way to get phones calls while you are gone is to put an ad in the paper selling a toaster or something.

"Or you might even let a dozen insurance agents think you are in need of a good liability policy. There is nothing like a ringing telephone to scare robbers away from an empty house."

"I think you are overreacting to the entire situation," said my husband. "All these elaborate measures to make the house look lived-in are insane. If you get any more people running in and out of here, we'll have to stay home and park cars."

We both dropped the subject until a few days ago when my husband came into the kitchen where I was preparing dinner. "I met an interesting fellow today in the garage where I park my car," he said. "He arrived here two days ago from Chicago. When I introduced myself he said, 'Oh, you're the fellow who is going to Yuuck Village for ten days beginning the fifteenth of next month.'"

"How could he have known that?" I asked, my mouth falling open.

"It seems his wife's nephew had a corn removed by a foot doctor who attended a cookout the other night at the home of our meter reader."

"Gas, electric, water, or taxi?" I asked carefully.

"It's not that important," he continued. "What was rather interesting was a story he told me regarding their vacation last summer. He said they were only gone a matter of hours when their house was ransacked. Picked clean."

"Didn't I tell you!" I shouted triumphantly. "Let me guess. They forgot to leave a radio playing low so burglars would hear sound. Or they didn't hire a cat to sit in their window. I got it. They didn't plan a party in their house while they were gone or leave bicycles lying around the driveway."

"They did all of those things," my husband said softly.

"Then what did they forget?" I shouted.

"To lock the front door."

Suburbian Gems Police Blotter

- Stolen grocery cart spotted

- Dog complaint

- Fire hydrant buried by snow

- Officer requested for women of the moose law enforcement appreciation dinner

- Summons issued for DWI, driving with 0.10 percent or more alcohol in bloodstream and illegally parking in lobby of drive-in bank

- Woman having trouble with neighbors

- Rescue unit answered call of cat in dryer

- Went to gas up police car and pump went dry

- Report of strange-acting car. It was running well

- Call from supermarket that young male trying to purchase beer for his sister to shampoo hair

- Found door open at town hall. Nothing missing

- Woman reports harassing telephone calls from ex-husband

- Owner of dog in heat demands thirty dogs be evicted from his property

- Had brakes and drums replaced on police car

- Young boy hitchhiking claims he was running away from home. Sought assistance in crossing highway

- Bread delivery tipped over on sidewalk. Notified store manager. Restacked bread

- Report of septic tank odors

- Checked out burgled car wash coin box

- Got police car washed

- Woman reported car lights in cemetery. All three cruisers responded to call

- Women reported large dog from next door deposited a mound the size of Mt. Olympus on their lawn each morning. Requests gun permit

- Man reports having trouble with house builder. Thinks wife may have been harassed. His attorney working on problem

- Bicycle stolen while chained to bike rack

- Supermarket reports bike rack stolen

- Restaurant files missing report for twelve steaks and five bottles of booze. Possibly party in progress

- Flat tire on police car fixed at garage

- Illegal burning of leaves at 8486 N. Platinum Lane

- Bad check returned to woman who thought her husband had made deposit

- Fire gutted Suburbian Gems library. Loss estimated at $143.95

- Subject observed urinating in parking lot

- Man reports kid plugging flow of creek

- Principal holding suspected drug user. Subject revealed pills to be breath mints

- Private citizen complains churchgoers blocking his driveway every Sunday. Warned of legalities in letting air out of tires

- Officer requested to speak to Rotary Club on "Crime! It's a jungle out there!"

- Officer called to investigate dirty word scratched on exit ramp freeway sign. Sign out of jurisdiction. Also misspelled

- Expectant mother requested assistance in getting out of compact car

CHAPTER NINE

Put Your Winnebagos into a Circle and Fight!

You couldn't help but envy the Merediths.

Every weekend, they left their all-electric, three-bedroom, two-bath, w/w carpeted home with the refrigeration and enclosed patio and headed for Trailer City.

Here, these thrill-seekers parked their trailer between a tent holding thirty-five people, and a public toilet. They did their laundry in a double boiler, cooked over an inverted coffee can, killed mosquitoes that had their own air force, and watched the sun set over a line of wet sleeping bags.

We never dreamt that someday we too could escape all of our conveniences and head beyond the suburbs where the air smelled like kerosene and the streams were paved with discarded beer cans.

Then one day my husband pulled into the driveway with a twenty-one-foot trailer hooked behind the car.

It was the biggest thing that had happened in the neighborhood since home milk deliveries. The entire neighborhood turned out to inspect it.

Standing in the middle of the trailer, I felt like Tom Thumb. It looked like a miniature doll house. Those dear little cupboards. The little beds. The little stove. The miniature doors and windows. The tiny closets. What fun it would be keeping house. Of course, there would have to be a place for everything and everything would have to be in its place, but I could hardly wait to hit the open road.

"You know," said my husband, "it might be even more fun if we went with another family."

"You're right," I said. "Things are much better when they are shared."

"Are you thinking about the same couple as I am thinking?"

"Get serious," I said. "Who else would I be thinking of but Eunice and Lester?"

Eunice and Lester had moved to Suburbian Gems

the same time as we. Their two children were between our three agewise and there had never been a cross word between us.

"Lester is a prince," said my husband. "Why I'd use Lester's wet toothbrush."

"And I've never had a sister closer to me than Eunice," I mused. "If Eunice was pregnant, I'd volunteer to carry it for her."

We called Eunice and Lester that night and together we planned a two-week vacation. Originally, we talked about the first of June but Lester had an appointment to have his teeth cleaned and he needed a few days to get back on his feet and Eunice's horoscope forbade her to travel until her sign got off the cusp, so we juggled the schedule around and came up with the first two weeks of July.

The *Mayflower* never had a bigger send-off. The four of us packed provisions for three months. There were Eunice's astrology charts and her wok ("I never go anywhere without my wok"), and Lester's pills and ointments and of course the gear brought by their children Beezie and Wendyo: a four-by-six baseball return net and an inflated walrus (which when we tried to deflate threw Wendyo into terminal paranoia), the food and the extra linens, and the motor for the boat—but it was fun.

Then we all waved good-bye and climbed into the wagon and were off. "Isn't this going to be fun?" I said, clasping Eunice around the waist.

"Watch it!" she winced. "My kidneys."

"What's wrong with your kidneys?" I asked.

"Nothing, now that your son has his guitar out of them."

"Maybe we should trade," I giggled. "I'll take my son's guitar out of your kidneys if you take your son's bubble gum out of my left eyelash."

We both laughed so hard we almost fell out of the car.

Several miles out of town a pattern began to form. Our two families and our little travel trailer were only part of a caravan of campers which snaked in a thin line all the way across the United States.

At one point, we tried to pass a motorcycle, which was attached to a U-Haul, which was pulled by a trailer, which was hooked to a boat, which was hitched to a Volkswagen, which was being towed by a station wagon laden with vacationers.

They were all winding around the highways looking for the same thing—a picnic table. Hours passed and everywhere we went it was the same story. Someone had gotten there first. I looked at the children. Their faces were white with dust, one was coughing from exhaust fumes, and the others were staring silently with hollow, vacant eyes out of the rear window.

"Maybe," I said, touching my husband's arm gently, "we should turn back. We should never have left the suburbs to come to this God-forsaken scenic route. It's not for myself, I'm begging, but —for the children. Soon they are going to need fresh air . . . fresh fruit . . . restrooms . . ."

"Just hang on a little longer," said my husband. "I heard at the last pit stop there was a picnic area about eight miles down the road."

"Do you suppose it would have a shade tree nearby?" I asked. "Don't get your hopes built up," he said. "It was just a rumor."

We bumped along another ten miles when Eunice spotted it. "Look! A picnic table!"

Tears welled in my eyes. "All right, children, get ready. The moment the car slows down, you all jump out and run over and throw your bodies across the table until we can park and get there."

They poised their bodies at the door ready to spring when panic set in.

"There's an Airstream coming in at four o'clock," said Lester.

"There's also a four-wheel drive bearing down over the ridge," said my husband, shifting gears.

We all skidded in in a cloud of dust as the children spilled out of the cars and flung themselves on the table. When the dust had settled, we discovered we had all been too late. A dog was tied to the picnic table to stake it out for another camper.

We pulled our vehicles into a circle to plan our next strategy.

Somehow, after a dusty lunch standing around a gas pump, we all felt better and continued on toward the Ho Hum Campgrounds, arriving around dusk.

"Parking the trailer is a little tricky," said my husband. "I'd appreciate a little help."

"What are fellow-campers for?" said Lester. "I'll direct you from the front."

"And I'll stand near your left rear wheel," chirped Eunice.

"I'll stand near your right rear wheel," I said, saluting smartly, "and the children can relay any messages you can't hear."

My husband pulled up and started to back in.

"Turn your wheels," yelled Lester.

"Which way?" answered my husband.

"That way!" said Lester.

"What way is that way?" returned my husband.

"To the left," said Lester.

"Your left or my left."

"Your left."

"Hold it!" screamed Eunice.

"What's the matter?" yelled my husband, jamming on the brakes.

"Not you," yelled Eunice, "*him!*"

"Who me?" yelled Lester.

"No, Beezie. He's making those faces at Wendyo again and . . ."

"For crying out loud, Eunice," snapped Lester. "This is no time to yell at the kids."

"Okay, when Wendyo cries, I'll send her to you."

"What did I just hit?" yelled my husband.

"Just a tree limb," I shouted.

"I can't see. It's on my windshield."

"You should have been watching for him above," said Eunice.

"It wasn't my side, sweetie," I purred.

"Turn! Turn!" shouted Eunice.

"Which way?"

"The right way."

"Not right," yelled Lester. "She means left."

"Don't speak for me, Lester," said Eunice, "I can speak for myself."

"Are we level?" asked my husband.

"What's this little hole for?" I asked.

"Where is it?" asked my husband.

"Right here in front of me," I said.

"I mean *where* is it?"

"Under your tire."

"Good heavens, that's my hook-up."

"Straighten it up," said Lester.

"Pull forward," said Eunice, "you've only got this far."

"How far?" asked my husband.

"Look at my hands," said Eunice.

"I can't see your hands," said my husband.

"I can see them," said Lester, "and she's crazy. You got another three feet back there."

"Let's just leave it," said the driver, "until it stops raining."

"It's not raining," said Lester, "you just hit a water hook-up on the next trailer."

"My God," I groaned as the water hit me, "and me without a hairdresser for two weeks."

"Moooommmmmeeeee," whined Wendyo.

"Did I tell you, Lester?" (To Wendyo:) "Tell your father."

"What is she doing out of the car?" yelled Lester.

"If you get your foot run over don't come skipping to me, Missy."

"Dad! If Wendyo is out of the car, how come we can't get out?"

"I think we're in quicksand," I yelled. "The car and the trailer are sinking."

"It is not sinking," said Lester. "The tire is going flat."

My husband got out of the car. It had taken nine people and forty minutes to help him back into a spot that was a pull-in . . . accessible by two roads.

The next morning, we all felt better about our togetherness—so much so that I decided to keep a diary.

THE FIRST DAY: This is going to be such fun. All of us have a job on the duty roster. The children are in charge of firewood. Lester is the camp doctor. Bill is in charge of camp maintenance, and I am the house mother. Eunice is the social director and is picking out songs to sing around the campfire.

The men are having a wonderful time. As Bill said this morning, "That Lester is a prince. Do you know what he is doing? He is out there fixing the motor already."

"What's wrong with the motor?" I asked.

"The pin dropped out of it in 12 feet of water at the dock."

"Who dropped it?"

"Lester did, but it was an accident. He reached

191

back to swat a mosquito and lost his balance. Lester said he had a balancing problem."

I can believe that.

THE SECOND DAY: As Eunice was out on a nature hike with the children (they are labeling trees) Bill said, "What are you doing?"

"Washing out the public garbage cans," I said. "As Eunice pointed out, you don't know where they've been. She is so meticulous. You know, we are so lucky. Can you imagine spending two weeks with a couple of slobs? Yuuuck."

THE FIFTH DAY: Didn't mean to miss so many entries in my diary, but I've been so busy. Isn't it funny, the things you worry about never happen. I was wondering how two cooks could occupy this little kitchen. Eunice hasn't been in the kitchen but once since the night we got here. It's not her fault. Poor dear has been trying to find a store in the area that stocks bean curd cakes and lotus roots for the wok.

Lester is a klutz. I don't know how poor Eunice stands it. Always running around with a nasal spray hanging from his nostril. Right after he dropped the pin from our motor in the water, he dropped our flashlight down the only outdoor convenience. It's still down there lit. Now we can't see where we're going—only where we've been.

I have to tell myself fifteen times a day that Lester was wounded at Ft. Dix when he stapled his elbow to a private's request for transfer.

THE SIXTH DAY: What kind of animals leave hair in a brush on the kitchen table? At first, I thought it was little Beezie or Wendyo but neither of them has combed his hair in a week. It has to be their parents.

Tonight, just to break the monotony, we invited the Parkers over from the next trailer to spend the evening. Eunice told that amusing story she tells about the nun not knowing what to order in the bar and having a little booze in a coffee cup. I love the way she tells it. Eunice *is* funny. Her horoscope told her she was going to have an adventure on water. I hope so. I've carried every drop of it!

THE NINTH DAY: This trailer is driving me up the wall. There's more room in an oxygen tent and it's better arranged. The other day I took the cap off the toothpaste and had to open the window.

The refrigerator holds a three-hours' supply of meat, the oven makes one piece of toast at a time, the sink converts to a bed, the bucket doubles as a bar stool, and yesterday when Lester and Eunice slept late, we had breakfast on Lester's chest.

Tonight, Eunice sleeps with the wok!

THE ELEVENTH DAY: As I said to Bill when we

undressed for bed, "How long have we known Eunice and Lester?" He said, "About six years," and I said, "Isn't it strange that we never noticed that Lester snorts when he laughs. When Eunice told that ethnic slur about the nun again, he sounded like a '38 pickup truck with water in the fuel line."

"He's a prince though," said my husband. "I mean the oil slick wasn't really his fault. He was only trying to wash the dust from our car by backing it into the lake and just accidentally hit the crankcase with a rock. It would never have happened had he not had one of his blinding migraines."

THE TWELFTH DAY: Are you ready for this? King Lester said this evening. "Why didn't you tell us the mosquitoes were so bad this time of year?"

"If Eunice had gotten off her cusp in June, there wouldn't have been any mosquitoes," I said. "Besides, my kids have taken all they're going to take from Heckle and Jeckle or whatever you call your two weak chins with the overbite."

"It's not the season," said Eunice bitterly. "It's the fact that your children are on the threshold of puberty and still don't know how to close a door."

"Speaking of doors," I said, "when was the last time you opened an oven, refrigerator, or cupboard door?"

"I suppose my braised prawn sandwiches did not meet with your middle-class taste?" she snarled.

"I don't pretend to be a connoisseur of *bait!*"

"Just a second, Erma," interrupted Lester, "if it hadn't been for Eunice's wok, we'd have starved to death."

"Only because you used my only large cooking pan to store a snapping turtle for Sneezy."

"That's Beezie!"

"It's one of the seven dwarfs!"

"Someone had to play with the children," said Lester, "since Bill was too busy cleaning out his tackle box."

"Only after you spilled the suntan lotion all over the lures, Fat Fingers."

"Hold it!" I said. "We are all exhausted from having such a good time. Let's sleep on it."

THE THIRTEENTH DAY: Tomorrow we go home. No more marshmallows catching fire and burning black. No more sand in the butter. No more bathing suits that smell like fish. No more soggy crackers.

All that is left is a stack of postcards no one mailed.

You know something? Now that I've read them, I didn't realize we had such a good time.

I wonder if Eunice and Lester could get off her cusp for a couple of weeks next year. . . .

SUPER MOM

★ AWARD

PRESENTED TO: *Estelle*

YOU ARE AWARDED THIS SUPER MOM
CERTIFICATE

1. Because: you have a pencil by
The telephone.
2. you see the DENTIST twice a year.
3. you grow your own HERBS.
4. you make the CHILDRENS' clothes.

CHAPTER TEN

Super Mom!

A group of first-graders at Ruby Elementary school were asked by their teacher to draw a portrait of their mother as they saw her.

The art was displayed at an open house.

Some mothers were depicted standing on a sailboat. Others were hauling groceries, cutting grass, or talking on the telephone.

All the mothers had one thing in common. They were pregnant.

In the suburbs, pregnancy wasn't a condition, it was the current style. Everyone was wearing a stomach in various stages of development—whether you looked good in one or not.

I frankly felt I was too short for pregnancy and told my husband so. A lot of women looked great when they were expecting. I was always the one with the hem that reached down to the ankle in the back and up to the knees in front and I forever dribbled things down my stomach. Usually, I went into maternity clothes at two weeks and by the ninth or tenth or eleventh month my drawstrings wouldn't draw and my mirror talked back to me.

Sometimes, I'd sink into a chair in my fifth month and couldn't get out until the ninth month of labor/or the chair caught fire—whichever came first.

The preoccupation with motherhood was the only thing we had in common. From then on, mothers were divided into two distinct groups: the Super Moms and the Interim Mothers.

The Super Moms were faster than a speeding bullet, more powerful than a harsh laxative, and able to leap six shopping carts on double stamp day. She was a drag for all seasons.

Super Mom was the product of isolation, a husband who was rarely home, Helen Gurley Brown, and a clean-oven wish. There was a waiting list for canonization.

The Interim Mothers were just biding their time until the children were grown. They never gave their right name at PTA meetings, hid candy under the dish towel so the kids would never find it, had newspapers lining the cupboard shelves that read, "MALARIA STOPS WORK ON THE CANAL," and secretly believed that someday they would be kissed by an ugly meter reader and turned into Joey Heatherton.

There were no restrictions in Suburban Gems. Super Moms were free to integrate at any time they wished and when one moved in across the street, I felt the only decent thing to do was welcome her to the neighborhood.

The moving van hadn't been gone a minute when we saw her in the yard waxing her garden hose. I walked over with my nine-bean "trash" salad and knocked on the door. Her name was Estelle. I could not believe the inside of her house. The furniture was shining and in place, the mirrors and pictures were hung, there was not a cardboard box in sight, the books were on the shelves, there were fresh flowers on the kitchen table, and she had an iron tablet in her hand ready to pop into her mouth.

"I know things are an absolute mess on moving day," I fumbled.

"Are people ever settled?" she asked, picking a piece of lint off the refrigerator.

Then she waltzed in the children and seeing one lock of hair in her son's eyes, grimaced and said, "Boys will be boys!"

If my kids looked that good I'd have sold them.

"Hey, if you need anything from the store, I go every three hours," I offered.

"I shop once a month," she said. "I find I save money that way by buying in quantity and by planning my meals. Besides, I'm a miser with my time. I read voraciously—right now I'm into Cather and I try to go three or four places a week with the children. They're very aware of contemporary art. Now they're starting the romantics. Could I get you something?" she asked softly. "I just baked a chiffon cake."

I felt my face break out.

"The doctor said I have to put on some weight and I try desperately . . . I really do."

I wanted to smack her right across the mouth.

Frankly, what it boiled down to was this: Could a woman who dyed all her household linens black to save time, find happiness with a woman who actually had a baby picture of her last child?

The Interim Mothers tried to get along with Estelle, but it wasn't easy. There was just no getting ahead of her. If the Blessed Mother had called

Estelle and said, "Guess what, Estelle, I'm expecting a savior," Estelle would have said, "Me too."

She cut the grass, baked her own bread, shoveled the driveway, grew her own herbs, made the children's clothes, altered her husband's suits, played the organ at church, planned the vacation, paid the bills, was on three telephone committees, five car pools, two boards, took her garden hose in during the winter, took her ironing board down every week, stocked the freezer with sides of beef, made her own Christmas cards, voted in every election, saw her dentist twice a year, assisted in the delivery of her dog's puppies, melted down old candles, saved the anti-freeze, and had a pencil by her telephone.

"Where is Estelle?" asked Helen as she dropped by one day.

"Who knows? Probably painting her varicose veins with crayolas to make them look like textured stockings. I tell you that woman gets on my nerves."

"She is a bit much," said Helen.

"A bit much! Would you trust a woman who always knows where her car keys are?"

"I think she'd like to be your friend."

"It wouldn't work."

"You could try."

"You don't know what you are saying. She's

so . . . so organized. They're the only house on the block that has fire drills. Take the other day, the school called to tell her Kevin had been hurt. Do you remember what happened when the school called me when my son flunked his eye test?"

"You became hysterical and had to be put under sedation."

"Right. Not Estelle. She calmly got her car keys off the hook, threw a coordinated sweater over her coordinated slacks, put the dinner in the oven on warm, picked up that pencil by the phone, wrote a note, went to school to pick up Kevin, and drove him to the emergency ward."

"So—you could have done that."

"I'm not finished. In the emergency ward, she deposited Kevin, remembered his birth date, his father's name, and recited their hospitalization number from *memory*."

"I remember when you took Andy to the hospital."

"I don't want to talk about it."

"What was it again the doctor said?"

"He wanted to treat my cracked heels."

"That's right. And you had to write a check for a dime to make a phone call."

"Okay. I remember."

Actually, Estelle didn't bother anyone. She

wasn't much more than a blur . . . whipping in and out of the driveway each day. I was surprised when she appeared at my mailbox. "Erma," she asked, "what's wrong with me?"

"Nothing," I hedged. "Why?"

"Be honest with me. I don't fit into the neighborhood. Why?"

"I don't know how to explain it," I faltered. "It's just that . . . you're the type of woman you'd call from the drugstore and ask what you use for your irregularities."

"All I want is to be someone's friend."

"I know you do, Estelle, and I'd like to help you, but first, you have to understand what a friend is."

"Tell me."

"It's sorta hard to understand. But a friend doesn't go on a diet when you are fat. A friend never defends a husband who gets his wife an electric skillet for her birthday by saying, 'At least, he's not one to carouse around at night.'

"A friend will tell you she saw your old boyfriend—and he's a priest.

"A friend will babysit your children when they are contagious.

"A friend when asked what you think of a home permanent will lie. A friend will threaten to kill anyone who tries to come into the fitting room when you are trying on bathing suits. But most of all, a friend will not make each minute of every day count and screw it up for the rest of us."

From then on, Estelle, neighborhood Super Mom, began to change. Not all at once. But week by week, we saw her learning how to compromise with herself. At first, it was little things like buying a deodorant that wasn't on sale and scraping the list of emergency numbers off the phone with her fingernail.

One morning, one of her children knocked on my door and asked to use our bathroom. He said his mommy locked him out.

The next week, Estelle ran out of gas while making the Girl Scout run. A few days later, she forgot to tie her garbage cans together and the dogs dragged TV dinner boxes all over her lawn for the world to see.

You could almost see her image beginning to crumble. She dropped in unexpectedly one afternoon and leaned over the divider to confide, "I have come to the conclusion there is an after-life."

"An after-life?"

"Right. I think life goes on after the children are grown."

"Who told you that?"

"I read it on a vitamin label."

"What are you trying to say, Estelle?"

"I am trying to tell you that I am going to run away from home. Back to the city. There's a life for me back there."

"Don't talk crazy," I said.

"I've tried to be so perfect," she sobbed.

"I know. I know."

At that moment, one of Estelle's children ran excitedly into the room. "Mommy! Mommy!" she said wildly, "I was on the side using a toothpaste with fluoride and I only have one cavity."

Estelle looked at her silently for a full minute then said, "Who cares?"

She was one of us.

CHAPTER ELEVEN

The Volunteer Brigade

Crossword Puzzle

ACROSS

14　nine-letter word syn. with frozen dinners, pin in children's underwear, laundry in refrigerator, five-hour meetings, no pay, no health benefits, causing head to hurt a lot.

DOWN

3　six-letter word meaning same as nine across

ANSWER

P
I
G
VOLUNTEER
O
N

"I Am Your Playground Supervisor"

One evening, the phone rang and a voice said simply, "We have not received your response to the mimeographed request that we sent home with your son."

"What request is that?"

"We need you for playground duty at the school."

"Please," I begged, "don't ask."

"Is this the woman who protested paid potties in airport restrooms by throwing her body across the coin slot?"

"You don't understand," I said.

"The woman who made Christmas tree center-pieces out of toilet tissue spindles and macaroni?"

"Don't . . ." I sobbed.

"Is this the freedom fighter who kept them from building a dairy bar in front of the pet cemetery with a flashing sign that read, CUSTARD'S LAST STAND UNTIL THE FREEWAY?"

"I'm only human," I sobbed. "I'll report Monday to talk about it."

On Monday, I met with Mrs. Rush, the home-room mother. "Mrs. Rush," I began, "there are several reasons why I cannot volunteer for playground duty, not the least being I have not had my shots."

"Your old ones are good for three years," she said mechanically.

"I see. Then I must tell you the truth. I am expecting a baby."

"When?"

"As soon as my husband gets home."

"Do you have any more excuses?" she asked dryly.

"Yes. I'm a registered pacifist."

She shook her head.

"How about, 'I'm a typhoid carrier'?"

"I'm afraid all those excuses have been used before," she said. "Do you realize that only four mothers returned their mimeographed bottoms?"

"That many?" I asked incredulously.

"One mother is unlisted, one had a transportation problem, and the third one was a bleeder. We couldn't take the chance. That left you. Here is a mimeographed page of instructions. You will report Monday and good luck."

Slowly, I unfolded the yellow, mimeographed sheet. It had a picture of a mother with the countenance of St. Francis of Assisi. At her feet were a group of little adoring children. A bird was perched on her shoulder. I smiled hesitantly. Maybe playground duty wasn't the hazard the women rumored it to be.

The first day I opened up my mimeographed page of instructions:

"PLAYGROUND DUTY CONSISTS OF STROLLING AMONG THE CHILDREN AND WATCHING OUT FOR FAIR PLAY."

A group of boys parted and I began to stroll. I felt like a stoolie strolling through San Quentin between Edward G. Robinson and Humphrey Bogart.

"What are we playing today?" I asked cheerfully.

"Keepaway," they chanted, as they tossed an object over my head.

"Boys! Boys!" I admonished. "Put Miss Manieson down. She's only a sub and doesn't understand how rough little boys can play. If you want to play keepaway, I suggest you use a ball. Come on now, I mean it. I'll give you two minutes to find her glasses and return her to her classroom."

"We don't have a ball," they whined.

"Perhaps these nice boys here could share," I suggested.

"You touch that ball," said a boy who looked thirty-five years old, "and you'll wish you hadn't."

"Look," I said, returning to the boys, "why don't all of you play a quiet game. Let's ask this little fella over here what he's playing. He's sitting there so quiet."

"He's quiet because an eighth-grader just tied his hands behind his back and took his lunch money!" said a small, blond kid. "Who wants to play Rip-off?"

On Tuesday, I went to the principal, unfolded my mimeographed sheet and said, "I should like to talk about rule no. 2: Here, A FIRST-AID CLINIC IS MAINTAINED IN THE SCHOOL FOR CUTS, BRUISES AND OTHER MINOR ACCIDENTS."

"What seems to be the problem?" she asked.

"I feel they really should have some provisions for the kids too."

"We'll discuss it," she said coldly.

Wednesday was one of the coldest days in the

year and I figured there would be few children on the playground. I was wrong. "Boys! Boys!" I shouted, "you must not push or shove. It says right here on my mimeographed sheet, 'SHOVING AND UNDUE PUSHING IS NOT PERMITTED.'"

"We're not shoving and pushing," they said, "we are keeping warm."

"If you keep any warmer, I will have to suspend you from the playground for three days."

"Who says?"

"My mimeographed orders say, that's who. Read this: 'A PLAYGROUND SUPERVISOR'S ORDERS ARE TO BE OBEYED THE SAME AS THE TEACHER'S.'"

He wiped his brow. "You had me worried there for a minute."

"Is it my imagination," I said, "or do I sense you have done something with Miss Manieson?"

"She's only a sub," they grinned.

"Today's sub is tomorrow's birth-control militant," I reminded.

"So, who are you to tell us what to do?"

"I am your playground supervisor," I said, squaring my shoulders.

"So?"

"So, how would you like to go to a nice school where they make license plates?"

"And how would you like to go . . ."

I grabbed my mimeographed sheet out of my pocket, and read, "A PLAYGROUND SUPERVISOR SHOULD DRESS SENSIBLY. SHE NEVER KNOWS WHICH AREA SHE WILL BE ASSIGNED NEXT."

As I read the lips of the class bully, I had the feeling I was dressed too warmly for where I had been ordered to go.

Wanda Wentworth; Schoolbus Driver

Wanda Wentworth has been retired for about ten years now, but they talk about her still.

No one commanded the entire respect of the suburban populace more than Wanda Wentworth who held the record for driving a schoolbus longer than any other woman in the entire school district . . . six weeks.

Every morning, fearless Wanda crawled into a schoolbus and dared do what few other adults would attempt: turn her back on eighty school children.

In the beginning, it had been a job for men only. Strong men who could drive with one hand and pull a kid in off the rearview mirror with the other. Who knew that Robbie Farnsworth could disguise his voice as a siren and liked to kill a little time by pulling the bus over to the side of the road. Who could break up a fight between two kids with bad bananas.

And then, along came Wanda. She had read an ad for drivers in the *Tattler:*

WANTED

DRIVERS FOR SCHOOLBUS

SEE MAGNIFICENT SUNRISES AND SUNSETS

ENJOY THE LAUGHTER OF CHILDREN AT PLAY

BE A FULFILLED VOLUNTEER

ORPHANS PREFERRED

Few of us saw much of Wanda after she took the job. I saw her only twice: one day in the dentist's office (she had fallen asleep in the chair) and another time in the supermarket when I got a bad wheel and she whipped out her tool kit and fixed it.

"How are things going on the bus?" I asked.

"Terrific!" she said. "There's nothing to it. You just have to be strict. Let them know you mean business."

I looked at Wanda closely. Her right eye rolled around in her head—independently of her left one.

"I don't allow no cooking on the bus," she said, "even when they have a note from home. Now, I know a lot of drivers who don't mind small fires, but I say if you want a hot meal, put it in a thermos."

"I think you are absolutely right," I said slowly.

"Another thing," she said, spitting on her hair and trying to get a curl to stay in the middle of her forehead, "all notes from home have to be legit. They come up with all kinds of stuff. 'Please let Debbie off at the malt shop. Eric is spending the night at Mark's house. Wait for Lillie. She has to get Marci's nail polish out of her locker.' Any time I see a note written on stationery with a pencil or a pen, I know it's a fake. Mothers only write with yellow crayons on napkins."

"You are very wise."

"They're not dealing with any dummy," she said. "Like games. I don't allow any games on the bus."

"You mean they're not allowed to play count the cow or whip out an Old Maid deck?"

"Nope. They get too excited. We tried playing Blind Man's Bluff one day and those little devils spun me around so fast I nearly hit a tree with my bus. I just laid it on them after that. Absolutely no more blindfolding me while the bus was in motion. Actually, the time goes pretty fast," she said, folding her lower lip into a crescent and biting on it with her teeth until it bled. "By the time I pick them up and they punch everyone on the bus, and open their lunches and eat them, and make their homework into gliders and sail them out of the window, and open the emergency exit in traffic, and take off their boots and leave them under the seats, and unravel the mittens their mothers put on them, and yell obscenities at the motorists passing by, we are at school."

"It sounds like it really has its rewards," I smiled nervously.

"Oh it does. Did you hear that Tim Galloway won first prize in the science fair? He rides my bus. As a matter of fact he constructed a weather station using parts he stole off my dashboard while I was having the bus 'gassed up.' "

"That's wonderful," I smiled, "but I still don't know how you hung on for six weeks. That's longer than any other person in the history of the school. How did you do it?"

"These little gems," she said, patting a bottle of pills in her coat pocket.

"Tranquilizers?" I asked.

"Birth control," she smiled, swatting at a fly that wasn't there.

Ralph Corlis, The Coach Who Played to Lose

In the annals of Little League baseball, there was only one man who made it to the Baseball Hall of Shame five seasons in a row. That was Ralph Corlis.

Ralph was an enigma in suburban sports. He brought his two sons to a housing development two years after his wife died, and together they hacked out a life for themselves. They planted a little garden, built a little racing car in the garage, and on a summer evening would go over to the ballfield and watch the kids play ball under the lights.

It was after the third or fourth game that Ralph began to take note of the thirty or forty kids on the bench who wore the uniform, but who rarely played the game.

"What do those kids do?" Ralph asked his sons.

"They watch the team play ball."

"For that they have to get dressed up in full uniform?"

"Oh no," said his son, "they go to all the practices, work out, run, field, catch, pitch, and do everything the team does . . . except play."

Ralph thought a lot about the bench warmers and

221

one day he approached several of them and said, "How would you like to join my team?"

When Ralph was finished, he had enough for five teams and sixteen benches. The first night they met on a piece of farmland donated by a farmer.

"This is first base," said Coach Corlis, dropping his car seat cushion on the ground, "and this is second," he continued, dropping his jacket, "and I see there's already a third base."

"But . . . it's a pile of dung," said one of his players.

"So, don't slide," said Ralph.

"Do you want to see me pitch?" asked a tall, lean, athletic boy.

"No," said Ralph. Then turning to a kid two feet tall who could scarcely hold the ball in his hand, he said, "You pitch today."

At random he assigned a catcher, basemen, infield and outfield, and said, "The rest of you—relax. On this team, everyone plays."

You cannot imagine what an impact a team where "everyone plays" had on the community. Word spread like a brush fire.

One night Coach Corlis answered his door to discover a visit from three other coaches.

"Hey, what a surprise," said Ralph. "Come in."

"What's your game?" asked one of the coaches.

"Baseball," said Ralph.

"You know what we mean," said one of the other men. "What are you trying to prove? Playing every boy who goes out for the team. How many games have you won?"

"I haven't won any," said Ralph. "I didn't think that was very important."

"What are you, some kind of a loonie? Why would you play a game, if not to win?"

"To have a good time," grinned Ralph. "You should have been there the other night when Todd Milhaus slid into third."

"Unfortunately, losers don't draw crowds," smirked the third coach.

"Oh, we don't want crowds," said Ralph. "Adults just mess things up for the kids. I heard at one of your games that a mother threw a pop bottle at her own son."

"And he deserved it," said the first coach. "He should have had his eye on second base. That kid has the brain of a dead sponge."

"He's pitching for me tomorrow," said Ralph.

"Look," said the second coach, "why don't you let the boys go? What do you want with them? They're not even winning."

Ralph thought a minute then said, "It's hard to explain, but kids go all through their lives learning how to win, but no one ever teaches them how to lose."

"Let's get out of here, Bert," said the third coach.

"Wait a minute," said Ralph. "Just think about it. Most kids don't know how to handle defeat. They fall apart. It's important to know how to lose because you do a lot of it when you grow up. You have to have perspective—how to know what is important to lose and what isn't important."

"And that's why you lose?"

"Oh no. We lose because we're too busy having a good time to play good ball."

"You can't talk sense to a man who won't even sell hotdogs at a game and make 13 cents off each dog."

Ralph Corlis's team racked up an 0-38 record the very first season. The next year, it was an even better 0-43. Parents would have given their right arms to watch the team play, but they were not permitted to view a game.

All eighty of the players used to congregate at a drive-in root beer stand and giggle about their contest. When there was criticism it was from themselves. The important thing was that *everyone was sweating*.

In the annals of sandlot baseball, there had never been another team like it. They had lost every game they played and they did it without uniforms, hotdogs, parents, practice, cheerleaders, lighted scoreboards, and press coverage.

Then one afternoon something happened. Ralph had a little nervous bedwetter on the mound who had never played anything but electric football. He wore glasses two inches thick and refused to take the bicycle clamp off his pantleg.

The kid pitched out of his mind, throwing them out at first, catching an infield pop-up and pitching curves like he invented them.

Ralph's team (it had no name) won the game 9-0.

The boys were strangely quiet as they walked slowly off the field. Defeat they could handle—winning was something else. Ralph sat in his car a long time before putting his key into the ignition. He wanted time to think.

"See you next week, Coach," yelled a couple of the boys.

But Ralph Corlis never went near the cornfield or a baseball game again. As he explained to his sons, "I couldn't stand the pressure."

Confessions of an Officer in the Girl Scout Cookie Corps

No one was more surprised than I at being named Girl Scout Cookie Captain.

I had been in the restroom at the time of the promotion.

The moment following the announcement was rather exhilarating. Mothers crowding around me patting me on the back and whispering in my ear, "If you need anything, I'm in the book," and assuring me, "This is going to be the best year ever."

Then they were gone.

And there were twenty-five little girls looking at me to lead them into door-to-door combat.

"At ease," I said, "you may chew gum if you like."

One girl blew a bubble the size of a pink gall bladder. Another one looked at her watch and shifted her weight to the other foot. The others just stared.

"Now then," I said, "I think this is going to be a great experience for all of us. I'll help you and you can help me. I have only one question before you leave today. What's a Girl Scout Cookie Captain?"

"She sells cookies," said the girl with the gum.

"And where does she get the cookies?" I asked.

She shrugged, "From her own living room."

I nodded. "I see, and how do they get to her living room?"

"A big truck dumps them there," said another scout.

"Okay, girls, I'll get it all together and be in touch."

At home, I grabbed the phone book and began calling all of those wonderful people who had volunteered to help.

Frankly, I didn't realize there were so many of life's losers in one neighborhood.

"I'd love to help, but I'm allergic to children."

"We're only a one-phone family."

"Give me a break! I'm on a diet and I'm in remission."

"I'm volunteering so much now my husband reported me missing."

"Do I know you? Oh, *that* sister!"

The first meeting of the Girl Scout cookie army went well. We discussed on what day we would take orders and on what day they must report their sales to me. I, in turn, would process the order for the entire troop and then there was nothing left to do but sit around and wait for C-Day to arrive.

It was about five weeks later when my husband nudged me out of a sound sleep one morning and said, "Do you hear something?"

"Ummm. What's it sound like?"

"Like a truck in our driveway."

We staggered to the window. By the headlights I saw them: full-grown men unloading carton after carton of cookies. "Where do you want them, lady?" they shouted.

I pointed to the living room.

When I told the girls the cookies were in they did a fantastic job of holding their emotions in restraint.

One cried, "There goes the skating party."

Another one slammed down her purse and said, "I wish I were dead."

And another one declared, "If it rains, I'm not delivering."

"It's all right, girls," I smiled, "don't hold back. You can show your excitement if you want to. Frankly, I'm just as choked up as you are. As I was telling my husband this morning as we breakfasted over 250 cartons of vanilla creams, 'This will show me to go to the restroom before I leave home.' "

The delivery of the cookies was a lot slower than I had anticipated. Hardly a day went by that I wasn't on the phone trying to contact one of the girls to pick up their cookies and deliver them.

"Hello, Marcia? I have the eighty-six boxes of cookies you ordered and . . ."

"My grandmother died."

"I'm sorry about that Marcia, but there are still the cookies."

"She was down for twenty-eight boxes."

"I see. Do you happen to know where I can get in touch with Debbie?"

"She moved."

"Where?"

"I promised I wouldn't tell you."

"What about Joanne?"

"She's dropped scouting. She's selling peanut brittle for the band now."

"Marcia! You tell the girls I'm up to my Girl Scout motto in cookies and I want them out of my living room by this weekend, do you hear?"

"Have you tried freezing them?" she asked mechanically.

"Freezing them! Sara Lee should have such a freezer!"

Stripping a captain of his rank in the cookie crops is not a pretty sight. I ripped off my armband, turned in the sign from my window that read "COOKIE HEADQUARTERS" and laid my golden badge on top of my yellow scarf.

"Do you have your records book?" asked the leader.

"I do," I said smartly. "It's all there. There are

143 cartons of cookies unaccounted for and $234 or $12.08 outstanding. It's hard to tell."

"Do you have anything to say."

"Yes," I said, my voice faltering. "I want the record to show that I tried. When twenty-five girls literally vanished from the earth, I tried to dispose of the cookies myself. I sprinkled cookie crumbs on my salads, rolled them into pie crusts, coated pork chops in them, and packed them in lunches. I made paste out of them and mended books, rubbed them on my callouses and rough elbows, and wedged them under the door to keep it open.

"I sent them out with my bills each month, wore two of them as earrings, gave them as wedding gifts, and set glasses on them and pretended they were coasters.

"I put them under my pillow for good luck, made an abstract for the living room, dumped a canful over my compost and crumbled some of them up for kitty litter. I have a cookie rash on 97 percent of my body."

"Is that all?" asked the leader somberly.

"Yes, I'm finished."

As I started to leave the room, I could hear nominations being presented for next year's cookie captain.

I turned suddenly and took a front row seat. I couldn't take the chance of leaving the room again.

CHAPTER TWELVE

"By God, We're Going to Be a Close-knit Family If I Have to Chain You to the Bed!"

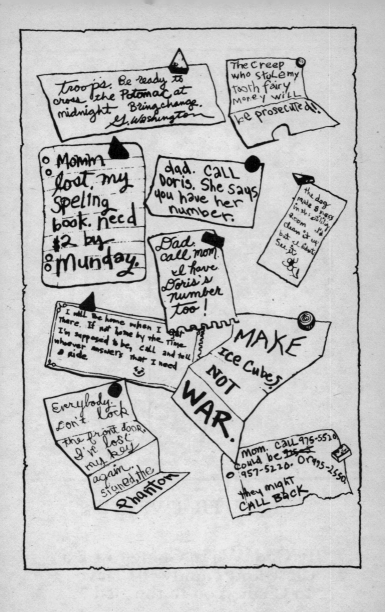

The Frozen Kiosk

When historians poke through the rubble of the suburban civilization, they will undoubtedly ponder the refrigerator mystique.

For no apparent reason, other than its functional value, the refrigerator became the meeting place of the American suburban family. It also became a frozen message center whereby anyone could drop by anytime of the day or night.

The rules of communications via refrigerator were simple: Don't write with food in your hand. If phone numbers were illegible, be a sport. Messages left unclaimed over seven years would be destroyed.

This, then, is how the suburban family communicated:

THE LANGUAGE OF REFRIGERATOR DOOR

"*Momm. Lost my spelling book. Need $2 by Munday.*"

"*Dad. Call Doris. She says you have her number.*"

"*Dad. Call Mom. I have Doris's number too!*"

"*I will be home when I get there. If not home by the time I'm supposed to be, call and tell whoever answers that I need a ride.*" Unsigned.

"*Everybody. Don't lock the front door. I've lost my key again. Signed, the Phantom.*"

"MAKE ICE CUBES. NOT WAR."

"*The dog made a mess in the utility room. I'd clean it up but I didn't see it.*"

"*Mom. Call 975-5520. Could be 957-5220. Or 975-2550. They might call back.*"

"*The creep who stole my tooth fairy money will be prosecuted!*"

"Troops. Be ready to cross the Potomac at midnight. Bring change. G. Washington."

"Mom and Dad: How much is it worth to you for me to lose the notice of PTA Open House?"

Starving to Death at the Spiritual Family Feast

I got the idea from a sermon.

In church one Sunday, the Reverend said, "The dinner table each evening should have all the elements of a service . . . a spiritual family feast whereby each one can share his day and his love with one another.

"Wasn't that beautiful?" I said in the car on the way home.

"Mom! Guess who stole the sponge out of the Holy Water font?"

"I'm telling. You know when we're supposed to shake hands in a sign of peace? Guess who pressed a dirty nose tissue in my hands then wouldn't take it back?"

"If one of you kids doesn't stop kicking the back of my seat," said their father, "I'm going to clear the car."

"Will you knock it off?" I said. "Didn't anyone hear the sermon?"

"Yeah, it was something about sharing pizza."

"It was not about sharing pizza. It was sharing your spiritual love at a family feast."

"Same thing."

"Do you know when was the last time this family ate a meal together?"

No one spoke.

"It was four years ago at Grandma's birthday."

"I remember," said our son, "I did the dishes that night."

"You did not," said his sister, "I did them because I remember we had lasagna that stuck to the pan and I had to soak it."

"Yeah, for three weeks!"

"Well, I'm not like some people who put a giant bowl in the refrigerator with a peach pit in it."

"Only because you eat everything in sight . . . including the pits."

"Look," I said, "we are long overdue. Tomorrow night, this entire family is going to sit down together and eat a meal. Only a certificate of death —a recent one—will be acceptable for a no-show."

The voices in the car became hysterical.

"I was going to practice cheers with Linda after school and then go to the library."

"You know I have ball practice until 7."

"It seems to me I have a five o'clock dental appointment and traffic on the expressway is murder. Maybe Tuesday would be a better day."

"Well, if we're not finished loving one another by 6:30, I'm going to split."

I remained firm. "Dinner on Monday. Together."

On Monday at 6 P.M. the scene was set for the Great Spiritual banquet.

It held all the giddiness of the "Last Supper."

My husband had a mouthful of Novocaine and couldn't get his lips to cover his teeth.

One son appeared in stereo—a transistor in one ear and the phone in the other.

Our daughter had Linda waiting for her behind her chair.

And the other son dressed his arm in a sling to dispel the possibility of having to do dishes.

"Well now," I said, "now that we are all together, each one of us should think about sharing our day with one another. That should be an enriching experience."

"Do you know what Ramsey Phillips said were the seven words you can't use on TV?"

"Not that enriched," I said, clapping my hand over his mouth. "Dear," I said to my husband, "what would you like to talk about?"

That was a mistake.

Over the years, my husband has composed and committed to memory five standard dinner-table lectures that are as familiar to all of us as the Pledge of Allegiance. They include:

1. "WHY DON'T YOU WANT YOUR FATHER TO HAVE A LAWN?" (two minutes, forty seconds). This is a real heart-tugger in which Dad recaps his failure to triumph over bikes, sleds, plastic pools, football games, cars, wagons, dogs, and all the little perverts who cut across his lawn just to make him paranoid.

When his eyes begin to mist, he is ready to go for options. Donate the front yard to the government for nuclear testing. Put a sentry at the driveway with a loaded rifle. Or perhaps (and this is drastic) have the kids take an interest in mowing, fertilizing, and trimming the yard so they can appreciate what he is trying to do. His zinger is, "My compost is in your hands."

2. "DO I LOOK LIKE A MAN WHO OWNS THE WATER WORKS?" (one minute, forty-eight seconds).

This is a table favorite that is brought on when Dad is overcome by steam and requires oxygen when he tries to enter the bathroom. In his mind, he is convinced that he cannot afford the child who is trying to break into the Guinness Book of Records for using forty gallons of hot water to wash off a ninety-six-pound body.

This is the lecture in which he uses visuals: prunes to show feet of child exposed to too many showers, and a broom illustrating how hair dries out and cracks from overshampooing. It's a two-parter, the second half taking place immediately following dinner when he takes the group to the bathroom and demonstrates how to turn off the faucet all the way.

3. "CAPTAIN QUEEG AND THE ICE CUBES" (one minute, thirty-four seconds). The children can always tell when Daddy is going for the Ice Cube number. He appears at the table with two steel balls in his hands and for five minutes does nothing but rotate them. Then he relates with a slight smile how he has trapped the culprit who put the ice cube tray in the freezer—*empty*. When he made his drink, there were nine ice cubes in the tray. By crouching unnoticed in the broom closet, he noted four of them were used by our daughter to make a malt, three were used by Mother for a glass of iced tea, and the younger son used one to suck on and he was the culprit.

When the younger son protested there was one left, his father's face lit up and he said. "Wrong! You dropped one on the floor to melt because I slipped on it and nearly broke my back." The entire table is left to meditate on the consequences.

4. "I'M PAYING YOU KIDS AN ALLOWANCE TO BREATHE." (two minutes). This is a fun presentation because it's a group participation lecture.

"Do you know how much money I made when I was a child?" asks Daddy.

"Five cents a month," they yell in unison.

"Five cents a month," he says as if he hasn't heard them. "And do you know how old I was when I got my first car?"

"Twenty-three years old," they sigh.

"Twenty-three years old and do you know who bought it for me?"

"You did."

"I did," he says, "and have you any idea how much I had to buy with five cents a month?"

"You had to buy all your own clothes, books, tuition, medical expenses, rent, and pay for your entertainment."

"I had to buy all my own clothes, books, tuition, medical expenses, rent, and pay for my entertainment," he said. "And can you imagine what I did for entertainment?"

"Changed your underwear."

"Don't ad lib," he warns. "We really knew how to squeeze a buffalo in those days."

When three fourths of the table asks, "What's a buffalo, Daddy?" the lecture begins to deteriorate.

5. "I DON'T WANT TO TALK ABOUT IT" (thirty minutes). This is the lecture we have all come to dread. It's the I-Don't-Want-to-Talk-About-It lecture that he talks about all during dinner.

Dad appears at the table morose, depressed, and preoccupied, picking at his food—a picture of utter despair.

Finally, one of the kids will volunteer, "If it's about the duck in the utility room."

"I don't want to talk about it," he says.

"I'm going to empty all the garbage on the back porch tonight," promises another.

"Forget it," he says.

"Hey, just because your shorts came out pink doesn't mean we can't wash them again and put a little bleach . . ."

"It doesn't matter," he says tiredly.

By the end of the dinner hour, we have all confessed to every crime to date and he is still sullen.

Finally, in desperation, I say, "If it's about the dent in the car . . ."

"That's what I want to talk about," he says.

This Monday evening, however, my husband surprised us all by introducing a new lecture. It was called, "BY GOD, WE'RE GOING TO BE A CLOSE-

241

KNIT FAMILY IF I HAVE TO CHAIN YOU TO THE BED!"
He began:

"It certainly is wonderful sitting down to a table together for a change."

"Is that it?" asked our daughter, pushing back her chair. "Can I go now?"

"No!" he shouted. "We are going to sit here and get to know one another. I am your father."

"We thought you were taller," said the son with the sling on his arm.

"I'm sorry if I haven't seen as much of you as I would have liked. It isn't easy commuting to and from the city every day. Now, we are going to go around the table and each one of you can tell me something about yourself." He looked at our daughter.

"I'm the token girl in the family. I like birthday cards with money in them, bathroom doors that can't be unlocked from the outside by releasing it with a pin, and I want to be a professional cheerleader when I grow up. Can I go now or does it have to be longer?"

"Stay put," said her father. "Next," he said, turning to our son with his arm in a sling. "I'm the middle child in the family and am bored, depressed, neurotic, unfulfilled, and subject to pressures which will eventually drive me to my own apartment."

"Why not?" I said dryly. "You have to be driven everywhere else."

"Now, Mother," said Daddy, "it's not your turn."

"It's never my turn," I sulked. "Do you know what I think? I think you stopped loving me the day my upper arms became too big for puffed sleeves. Admit it?"

"Come now, let the boy talk."

"I have to do everything in this house," he continued. "Even though I was freed legally in 1860 by Lincoln. Take out the garbage. Let the dog out. Answer the phone. Get the paper. Change the channel on TV. Get Mom a drink of water."

"Drinking water wasn't my idea," I said wistfully.

"Hey, don't I get to say anything again?" asked the youngest. "Do you realize because I'm the baby of this family I never get to open my mouth. I've been trying to tell a joke at this table for the last three years."

Dad held up his hand for silence. "The boy is right. Take those wires out of your ears and tell us your joke."

"Well," he began, "there was this guy who stuttered a lot."

"I've heard it," said his brother, pushing away from the table.

243

"How do you know you've heard it? There are a lot of guys who stutter."

"I happen to know that of all the guys who stutter, only one of them made a joke out of it. Mom! Don't let him tell it. It's sick."

"It is not sick," persisted the youngest, "and was your stutterer from the South?"

"How long is this joke?" asked Linda, leaning over our daughter's shoulder. "If it's going to be much longer, I have to call home."

"You are excused to call your mother," said Dad. "Now continue with the joke."

"Well," he giggled, "this guy from the North said to the guy from the South, 'What are you doing up North?' And the stutterer said, 'Llllloooooook-kinnnng for a jjjob.' "

"Didn't I tell you it was sick? said his brother.

"Then," he continued, "his friend said, 'What sort of work are you looking for?' He said, 'Rrrrrrraaaaadddiooo aaannnnouuunnnciing.' Then his friend asked, 'Any luck?' And this guy said (he held his sides with laughter as he blurted it out), 'Nnnnooo, whhhaaat chance does a stttttuutttteerer have?' "

We all sat there in silence.

"That is the dumbest joke I've ever heard," said his sister.

"It's sick," said his brother.

"Are you sure you got the tagline right?" I asked.

"I've heard the joke," said his dad, "and the tagline is 'Whhat chaance hhhas a Sooooutheeerner?'"

"Why is this family down on Southerners?" asked our daughter, leaving the table.

"I don't like your ending," said our youngest son.

"It's not *my* ending," said his father, "it's the way the joke goes."

"If you heard it before, you should have stopped me," he said, rushing to his room in tears.

"It's not my turn to do dishes," announced the last child, slipping out of his chair.

My husband turned to me. "When was the last spiritual family feast we shared together?"

"Four years ago at Grandma's birthday," I said numbly.

"Time flies when you're healing," he mused.

CHAPTER THIRTEEN

POSTSCRIPT TO
SUBURBIAN GEMS

It was either Isaac Newton—or maybe it was Wayne Newton—who once said, "A septic tank does not last forever." He was right.

Suburbian Gems was a real community.

So were most of the characters in this book.

Certainly, the frustrations, the loneliness, the laughter, the challenges, and especially the analogy were for real. We were like pioneers, in a sense, leaving what we knew in search of our American dream.

Some settlers found Xanadu waiting in the suburbs. For others, it was an exile at San Clemente.

For me, it was one of the most exciting times of my life: a time when my children were young, my husband ambitious, and happiness for me was having a cake that didn't split in the middle and have to be rebuilt with toothpicks.

In the beginning, it was as we thought it would be: the smell of new wood (why not, it was green), doors that stuck permanently, and the weekend battle cry that shook the countryside, "Why pay someone to do it when we can do it ourselves."

The supermarket chains hadn't arrived yet with their frozen conveniences, express lines, and red lights over the pot roast.

There was only the country store where the owner was confused by the newcomers who insisted he bag the vegetables and ran him to his grain elevators for 15 cents' worth of pellets for a pet hamster.

I remember one Thanksgiving asking the kid at the gas pump in front of the store, "Do you have Mums?" he wiped his nose on his sleeve and said, "Yeah, but she's up at the house."

I never looked at the schools that I didn't imagine John Wayne saying to Beulah Bondi, "Someday this town is going to have a real school, and a school marm, and the children will learn to read and write their sums, etc. etc."

Our kids in the beginning got choked up when Spot chased a stick and Mommy put on a new apron. (Well, what did you expect from a twenty-year-old teacher who earned $1200 a year, taught five spelling classes, two history sessions, supervised the cafeteria during lunch, was class advisor for the Future Homemakers of America, and was in charge of the Senior class play and the drill team's peanut brittle candy sale.)

Later, that too changed when children would duly report to their parents, "I'm part of an innovative enrichment program that is structurally developed to stimulate my mental attitude with muscular development, combined with a language pattern design that is highly comprehensible and sensory." (One mother advised, "Keep your coat on, Durwood, and no one will notice.")

One book on the suburbs referred to it as "Creeping Suburbia." It sounded like a disease. ("This creeping suburbia has got me climbing the wall, Margaret.") Critics credit it with weakening the family structure, becoming overorganized, isolating people of like incomes, race, social levels, politics, religion, and attitudes from the rest of the world.

It probably did all of those things and some more that haven't been dissected and labeled yet.

But no one can quarrel with the unique sense of

belonging that got the suburban settlers involved in their communities.

In a few short years, it became one of the most powerful forces in this country. How they voted. How they ran their schools. How they designated their land. How they incorporated around them what they wanted and needed. How they were governed.

I only know that one morning I looked longingly beyond the suburbs to the city and said to my husband, "Got a letter from Marge and Ralph yesterday."

"When did they leave Pleasure Plantation for Crown City?"

"A week ago," I said. "Marge wrote, 'We reached the Downtown complex on the 15th. There are 17,500 units in our section, contained on 83 acres of land. There is rubble everywhere (they're still laying carpets in the hallways) and some of the elevators don't stop at our floor. None of the gift shops is open yet in the mall.'"

"The sheer guts of it," said my husband.

"'The bus service to Ralph's office building in the suburbs is horrendous—sometimes every hour—sometimes an hour and fifteen minutes between buses. It's lonely and desolate here on the fifty-fifth floor. It's like floating in an atmosphere with no trees, no birds . . . only the wind and an occasional jet.

" 'The children have to walk to school. It will take some getting used to after busing it in the suburbs, but they're becoming used to hardships. The mail deliveries, garbage pickups, fire and police protection are nonexistent, but the strike is expected to be settled as soon as the city is solvent again.

" 'There are some bright spots. No more getting in the car to go shopping. There is a store in the building that delivers and we are fortunate enough to have our own cloverleaf exit that comes directly into the building garage.

" 'Also, it is quiet. On a summer night we can walk and breathe clean air and feel no one else is around. Tomorrow, we are going to visit a tree. It is being planted in the mall in our building. Come visit us. You can't miss us. We have a lamp in the picture window.' "

I put the letter down. "Doesn't that sound exciting? Living in a city eighty stories high. That is where the next frontier is."

"What!" shouted my husband. "And give up all of this?"

I looked around. Our "wilderness" had grown to 100,000 people, fifteen traffic lights, five shopping centers, six elementary schools, two high schools, fifteen churches, four drive-ins, a daily newspaper, and street lights on every corner.

Report cards were computerized, horses were "boarded," lube jobs on the car were "by appointment only" and there were three, sometimes four cars in every driveway.

Our garage bulged at the seams with lawn spreaders, leaf sweepers, automatic mowers, snow plows, golf carts, bob sleds, skis, ice skates, boats, and camping gear.

Our all-electric kitchen crackled with the efficiency of micro-ovens, dishwashers, ice cube crushers, slow-cooking pots, electric knife sharpeners, brooms, sanders, waxers, blenders, mixers, irons, and electric ice cream freezers and yogurt makers.

The once-silent streets had been replaced by motor and trail bikes, transistors, and piped-in music in the shopping-center parking lot and the air was thick with charcoal.

As we weighed our decision, I couldn't help but speculate how future historians would assess the suburbs—the ghost cities of tomorrow.

Poking through the rubble of that unique civilization, would they be able to figure out what 1200 bleacher seats and two goalposts were doing in the middle of a cornfield?

Would they be able to break the code of the neon signs that flapped in the wind: " GO-GO," "CARRY-OUT," "DRIVE-IN," or a sign that instructed, "SPEAK CLEARLY AND DIRECT YOUR ORDER INTO THE CLOWN'S MOUTH?"

Would they be dismayed by the impermanence of a Nova camper with a sign in the window, "SUNSET BANK. Hours: 8 A.M.–2 P.M. weekdays. CLOSED SATURDAYS AND SUNDAYS"?

Would they probe the sandboxes and come up with a Barbie and Ken form, and figure we got sick?

Or would they piece together scraps of PTA notices, home parties, church bazaars, and little Green Stamps (thirty to a page) and ponder, "How did they survive?"

At that moment the ghosts of 100 million settlers are bound to echo, "We drank!"

About the Author

A former obituary writer and homeroom mother, Erma Bombeck is the author of three bestselling books, a syndicated newspaper column, and is co-author with her husband, Bill, of three children. Her column "At Wit's End" is syndicated throughout the world in 542 newspapers. Her books include *At Wit's End*, *"Just Wait Till You Have Children of Your Own!"* and *I Lost Everything in the Post-Natal Depression*. The Bombecks live in Paradise Valley, Arizona.

THE QE 2 IS MISSING

"What could have happened to her?" The search pilot asked, as he had been asking for days now.

"Someone said maybe a sudden tidal wave," the copilot offered.

"Nothing like that has been reported. No tidal waves, no collisions. Just *nothing*, that's the damnable part of it!"

"Bermuda Triangle?" the copilot asked. The pilot just sniffed loudly. "I know. Just a lot of nonsense. But nevertheless, Lieutenant, she appears to have vanished . . . ."

A Thriller by
Harry Harrison
author of **SKYFALL**

THE QE2 IS MISSING

BY HARRY HARRISON

TOR

A TOM DOHERTY ASSOCIATES BOOK
Distributed by Pinnacle Books, New York

The QE2 Is Missing

Copyright © 1980 by Harry Harrison

A Tor Book

Published by Tom Doherty Associates
8-10 W. 36th St.
New York City, N.Y. 10018

First printing, April 1982

ISBN: 0-523-48031-8

Printed in the United States of America

Distributed by Pinnacle Books
1430 Broadway
New York, N.Y. 10018

For Anthony Cheetham—
who started the ship's engine

1

The wide-winged bulk of the United States Navy Hawk-eye plane broke out of the low-hanging cloud, barely a hundred feet above the surging waves of the Pacific Ocean. Tropical rain lashed the glass in front of the pilots, rain so heavy that the wipers had almost no effect on it. The ocean swells were gigantic, reaching up higher and higher towards the early-warning aircraft as though about to engulf it. The copilot's knuckles were white where he gripped the edges of his seat.

"Christ, Lieutenant," he said. "You're going to have us swimming in that stuff in a minute. Those clouds go right down to the deck — I swear the waves are break-ing against the bottom of the clouds. And there's noth-ing to see, nothing at all."

Lieutenant Leroy Palmer nodded reluctantly. The visibility was almost zero, what with the lashing rain and flying scud torn from the waves. There was a real danger that a sudden gust might put them down in the drink. He pulled slowly back on the wheel and the big turboprop plane lifted back up into the clouds. He felt the same relief as Corker the copilot did, though he tried not to show it.

"For a minute there I was sure we had had it," Corker said, aware that the sweat on his forehead had more cause than just the tropical heat. "And there's nothing we could do down there. Visibility still zero, that goes in the report. We are still going to have to rely on radar."

"Well, don't go blaming me because the screen ain't showing nothing but shit!" the radar operator said, not disguising his belligerence. He had been hauled out of his nice warm sack in San Diego, away from his nice round wife, and flown south without sleep and pushed aboard this search plane, and he was just not happy about it. "All I get on the screen is wave-echo and crud like that, and the goddamned *QE2* could be down there and I couldn't see it."

"You redneck moron," Corker said, his temper barely under control — he had been flying for two days with almost no sleep, "that's just what is down there somewhere. What the hell do you think we're doing up here going around in circles . . . . "

"Hold it," the pilot said, "I'm getting a news broadcast in English." Palmer was a good officer; he tried to stop trouble before it developed. "Sounds like a limey, BBC or something. There . . . . "

There was the continuous crackle of atmospherics in their earphones, but the calm voice of the announcer still came through clearly enough.

" . . . search still goes on. Ships and flying craft from more than twenty nations are now actively involved in the search in one capacity or another, while at least two space satellites are scanning the area. It is known that the American military satellites can detect objects as small as two meters in length, but even this precise ability is of no use when a tropical storm completely covers the area of search. For almost three days now, since the *Queen Elizabeth the Second* did not respond to attempts at radio contact, the search has gone on. Though the ocean is wide it still seems impossible that the *QE2,* the largest liner afloat, could remain undetected for this length of time. Even if this great ship has been sunk — horrifying as that thought may be, it must still be considered — there should be some debris, lifeboats, ship's launches, something. But there is nothing. It is as though the liner has vanished from the face of the globe. No warning given, a sudden cessation of radio contact. Then silence . . . . ''

''That's a big help,'' Corker said, and the pilot nodded agreement and switched the radio off. ''Same old story rehashed just one more time. Let's do a navigational check.''

The Hawkeye was an early-warning aircraft, easily identified by the giant parasol-shaped radar dome mounted above the wings. It had been pressed into service for this search because of the sophisticated inertial and satellite navigation equipment it carried. They were flying long legs out and back in a carefully worked-out search pattern, in conjunction with many other aircraft, most of them from the carrier *Kitty Hawk*. This particular area of the Pacific Ocean where they were searching was off the normal shipping routes and far enough from the coast so that the sea was empty even of offshore fishermen. It was a boring — but very necessary — routine.

''I think I'm getting something,'' the radar operator said suddenly. ''Harder than goddamn to pick out a blip from all the shit out there — but, sure — there it is again!''

Before the operator had finished speaking, the copilot had unbuckled and was standing behind him, squinting at the hash of white flecks on the screen. The operator tapped with his finger. ''There,'' he said, and Corker nodded.

''There sure as hell is something down there, Lieutenant. Comes and goes, but it is big and it stays in the same place. Too solid for a ghost.''

''I'm taking her down,'' Palmer said. ''Strap in.''

The turbulence inside the clouds rocked the plane, sending sudden shudders through her frame. The two pilots looked out grimly at the ceaseless rain, while the altimeter unwound. Lower and lower.

"On course. Dead ahead, ten miles," the radar operator called out.

They dropped. Down and down. When they finally burst out beneath the clouds it was as though a physical pressure had been relieved. The cloud base was a good three hundred feet above the ocean here, so the towering waves were well beneath them.

"There!" the copilot called out. "Saw it for a moment. A ship, just a glimpse. Big."

"It could be her," Palmer said, trying not to be too hopeful, yet at the same time clutching his hands tightly on the wheel. "We're crossing her plotted course, the one the *QE2* should have taken. She might have gotten this far . . . ."

They plunged through the sheets of rain, closer and closer, until they could see the vessel clearly.

The low bulk of a supertanker appeared before them, waves crashing across her bow and water running the immense length of her decks.

"I'm taking her back up," the pilot said, suddenly weary. The others did not speak. The craft climbed steadily to cruising altitude and they went on in silence. The copilot logged the tanker, then worked on his fuel consumption figures. They flew another leg far out into the ocean, made a careful turn and searched another stretch of empty sea. The copilot checked his calculations twice before he spoke.

"When we finish this leg we better head for home," he said. "We'll be bucking headwinds on the way back and we'll need the fuel reserve."

"What could have happened to her?" the pilot asked,

as they had been asking aloud for days now.

"God knows," Corker said, rubbing at his red-rim-med eyes, "I certainly don't."

"There were heavy seas when she stopped reporting, but nothing that could have any effect on a ship as big as the *QE2*. And they had been in constant radio contact without reporting trouble of any kind."

"On course, just a normal cruise . . . ."

"Then . . . nothing. It doesn't make sense."

"Someone said maybe a sudden tidal wave."

"No way, Corker. Nothing like that has been reported. No tidal waves, no underwater volcanoes, no collisions, plenty of other ships in the same area and none of them reported anything more dangerous than rain and heavy seas. Just *nothing,* that's the damnable part of it. Okay, small ships without radios can get into trouble, even sink, without anyone knowing about it. But not a liner—not the biggest liner in the world. She has safety doors, multiple alarm systems, automatic sprinklers for fire, plenty of boats and launches. Sure she could be sunk — but the world would damn well know if she was hurt and going down. But not this, not a complete absence of news of any kind. It's as though she had vanished from the face of the earth . . . ."

"Bermuda Triangle?" the copilot asked. The pilot just sniffed loudly and looked at him out of the corners of his eyes. Corker smiled. "I know. Just a lot of nonsense. Dreamed up by hacks who want to get rich writing about the mysteries of the seven seas. But never-theless, Lieutenant, she appears to have vanished, at least vanished as far as anyone can tell. And we've cer-tainly been looking hard enough . . . ."

"Got another blip," the radar operator said. "Doesn't look very big but it's persistent. Something down there all right."

"Another tanker probably," the pilot said. "We're over the north-south routes now. We'll take a look."

Once more they plunged down through the clouds and out beneath them. The rain had ceased here and they flew between two slate-gray masses, the sea below, the clouds above. A dark speck appeared on the surface of the ocean ahead and the pilot banked that way. The ship had been obscured by a line squall which blew suddenly away.

"Jesus . . . , " the pilot said, breathing out the word.

There, silent and unmoving on the heaving seas, was the *QE2*.

They came in low, just above mast height, roaring over the decks, then going back in a wide turn.

"All the boats . . . they're gone," the pilot said. "Not a lifeboat left. And no one aboard. I could look into the Bridge and there was no one there."

His eyes met those of the copilot and he saw his own horrified image mirrored in the other's face. He fumbled for the radio.

2

The Peruvian Coast Guard ship, *Huascaran,* crashed headlong through the mountainous waves, plunging her bow deep into the green sea, shuddering as the foaming water tore along the length of her decks. It had been many years since she had been subject to this kind of punishment — she had originally been a British mine-sweeper — and her ancient plates and ribs groaned at the harsh treatment. This did not disturb her Commanding Officer in the slightest. Captain Borras had great faith in his ship. As long as the pumps were working and the turbines spinning at top speed, he would press on. He had received a gift, perhaps from God — he crossed himself quickly in case it were — but it was a gift in any case.

Eighty-three degrees West Longitude, fifteen and a half degrees South Latitude, that's what the voice on the radio had said. On the emergency frequency. It had been the report of a sighting that the entire world had been waiting for for three days. A sighting off the Peruvian coast, barely outside territorial waters. In his mind's eye, Captain Borras could see the exact spot in the Pacific, knew just how close they were to it — and knew almost to the minute just how long it would take to reach it. He had been ringing the engine room for top speed even as the position had been spoken.

The *Huascaran* would be there first — pray God she would be first! What the little ship could do, what was awaiting them, he had no idea. But they would be there first and the entire world would know it. His charge shuddered and lurched heavily in the violent sea; water thudded with great force against the glass port before him, obscuring all vision completely while the helmsman struggled to hold her steady. The Captain did not move. When the water drained away he looked out impassively at the waves rushing towards them, most of them taller than the mast-head of his small vessel.

"Position," he called over his shoulder to the navigator who had propped himself tightly against the wall of the tiny chart-room so he would not be hurled to the deck by the ship's frenzied rolling and pitching.

"Four, five kilometers, no more. We are now roughly at the position given by the airplane who sighted her. Radar cannot help, the aerial has been torn away. . . ."

His voice was drowned out by the sudden roar of engines as a dark form swept over the ship like an immense bird of prey. It appeared to hover for an instant, then swept on; a stubby body with a strange circular structure above the wing. Coming from astern of them and across their bow. Heading ten points south of their course. The radioed voice burst loudly from the speaker, so close was the source.

"Rescue ship below, this is Navy Hawkeye. You are off course for *QE2*. Alter course in my direction. I am now overflying target. You are within a mile of her, repeat one mile ahead on this course."

"Alter course to one hundred and two," the Captain ordered, then picked up the Bridge microphone and ordered the radio operator to silence. Captain Borras prided himself on his knowledge of the English Language.

"*Huascaran* to U.S. aircraft. Am altering course as

directed. Are there any other ships in this area? Over.''

"None we can see. But plenty on the way. Over."

"Please inform them that Peruvian Coast Guard ship *Huascaran* is . . . . ''

"There, Captain, ahead! I saw her! Like an island in the sea!" The helmsman shouted the words, altering course slightly at the same time.

"The *Huascaran* is in sight of the *QE2* and will make contact. Stand by for further reports. Out."

Captain Borras hammered his fist on the wooden rack before him with unspoken pleasure. They were first! The rain was slacking now, blown away like an unwanted curtain. Another wave broke over the bridge and when it had washed away a dark form was clearly visible ahead. The *QE2*!

"Reduce revolutions," he ordered. He didn't want anything to carry away — not now. As their headway slowed, the ship no longer buried her bow in the waves but rode easily up and over them.

Not only had the rain stopped but clear patches were showing on the horizon, patches of blue sky where there had been only solid cloud for over five days. As though the storm, having concealed the great liner from an anxious world for all this time, had now relented, with the quarry found. The blue patches widened, merged, and golden sunlight poured down the great, silent length of the ship.

"*Madre de Dios* . . . . " someone breathed aloud. Speaking for all of them.

Unmoving in the sea, to the casual eye apparently unharmed by the recent storm, the *QE2* lay dead in the ocean. Her accommodation ladders stowed; all of her loading doors closed. No one was visible on deck or on her bridge, which could be clearly seen through powerful binoculars. The only sign of anything out of the norm was the absence of all her lifeboats and launches. Yet the davits, the metal arches that swung out from the hull to lower the boats, were still in their upright position. There was something frightening about her immobility, her silence.

"Shall I signal to her, Captain?" the radio operator asked, his strained voice breaking the silence.

"Yes — but not with the radio. They've been trying that for three days. Use the lamp. See if anyone is on the bridge."

A gust of moist, hot air blew across the bridge as the operator struggled the wing door open and forced his way out. He had to hold onto the lamp with his free hand as he worked the handle up and down, over and over. The shutters clacked and the signal went out. And there was no response.

"We'll go around her stern," the Captain said. "See if there is anything more to be seen on her port side."

With just enough revolutions to give her way, the *Huascaran* moved slowly to the stern of the liner, the towering black hull slipping by beside them like a great wall. Row after row of portholes and windows dotted the metal. All sealed. There were lights behind many of them — but no sign of motion. Nor did anyone come to the rails high above to wave down at the passing of the tiny ship.

They reached the stern and turned behind the bulk of her towering sternpost. The seas were still high and as they passed the stern of the liner it sank down — then surged up far above them. The portside propeller rose up out of the foam-flecked sea, streaming water like a surfacing sea creature. The bronze blades were still, unmoving, hanging there for an instant before sinking back beneath the surface.

The port side of the *QE2* was no different from the

starboard. The boats and launches were gone, all entrances sealed. From the deck of the coast guard ship, the metal wall of the hull rose up a hundred feet above them. The sailors, who were now coming out on deck, had to strain their necks back to see the railings above.

"We must get aboard," Captain Borras said. "Break out the line gun."

The sailors worked swiftly and efficiently, for this was something they had been well trained to do. There was no need for the Petty Officers to shout their commands; they did so in any case. There was a relief in the familiar voices, something to temper the dark menace of the silent ship beside them. The keg of coiled rope was hauled into position below the mouth of the gun, the steel shaft of the grapple slid down the barrel. The shell, with the charge of explosive that would send it hurtling out, slammed into the breach and locked home.

"Too close," the Bo'sun said. It was his task to aim and fire the gun. "Can't raise it high enough."

The gun was already at maximum elevation and was pointing at the liner's side. It had been designed to hurl a line across another ship, not a floating island like this one.

"We'll move away," the Captain said. "Fire when we roll."

They waited in expectant silence while the Bo'sun aimed the gun at the stern deck, the lowest accessible part of the ship. Waiting, holding their breath, as they rolled — but not far enough to suit the gunner. He released the handles, spat on his palms, then seized his grip again. This time a large sea surged beneath them, the coast guard ship rolled heavily — and the gun fired with a sudden sharp crack.

Almost leisurely, the tonged grapple soared up and out in an arc, towing the thin strand of rope behind it.

High up and over the rail, to vanish from sight.

"Haul in the line," the Captain ordered.

The sailors pulled mightly until the line grew suddenly tight.

"Secure, sir," the Bo'sun said. "Caught firm on something."

The Captain looked up at the thin arc of line, curving up and away from the deck, almost vanishing from sight above. Presenting a very large problem, he suddenly realized. Normally this light line would be simply used to connect the two ships together, a first simple contact. Then a heavier line, then perhaps a cable would be bent to the end, each one thicker and stronger than the one before, each hauled across in turn. By sailors at the other end. Not this time. No one had appeared on the deck of the other ship. The grapple had anchored itself and that was the end of it. What next?

With the question came the answer. A possible answer; the one man on board who might possibly be able to help. "Basilio," Captain Borras ordered. "Get him up on deck."

The message was passed and the Captain waited in silence, looking up at the cliff of a ship that bulked high above them. The *Huascaran* moved back and forth in the heavy seas under the helmsman's skilled touch as he worked to keep them from crashing into the liner, or moving away from it so far that the line parted. It took two minutes for Basilio to reach the deck; he was a stoker and labored deep in the engine room. He came out, blinking in the harsh sunlight, gaping up at the liner beside them.

"Can you do it?" Captain Borras asked. "Can you climb up that rope?"

Basilio frowned as he thought about the question; frowned even harder as he followed the arc of line with his eyes. He reached up and seized the thin line and put his weight on it, testing to see if it was thick enough to grasp and climb. It was. He nodded solemnly and flexed his biceps and fingers, the tendons in his arms standing out like cables. He was stupid — but he was strong — the strongest man on the ship. The only who who might possibly climb that thin rope. He reached up over his head, seized it in both hands, waited until a surge of the ship lifted him clear of the deck. Then began to climb.

Hand over hand. He made no attempt to throw his feet over the line to ease the weight on his arms. He simply climbed. Like a machine. Swing, release. Swing, release. Upwards with a steady rhythm. Higher and higher. He appeared to slow, but perhaps that was only a trick of distance. Then he was at the rail, resting for a moment before swinging an arm up to hook his hand over the wooden rail. Then the other hand, a kick of his legs and he was up and over. There was a spontaneous cheer from the men on the deck; silenced instantly by a growled command from the Captain.

"Bend the rope ladder to the line," he said. "Have him haul it up and secure it."

While this was being done, Captain Borras went to his cabin and pulled on a pair of leather gloves. He hesitated an instant as he passed his desk — then slid the top drawer open and took out the holstered .38 revolver. Why? He asked himself that even as he buckled it onto his belt. There was no simple answer. Fear of the unknown, perhaps. He had no idea of what he might find aboard the liner. Certainly this popgun would be of little avail against any forces that might have caused the liner's disappearance. He still felt better wearing it.

Basilio was just securing the ladder to the rail above when the Captain came back on deck, waving his arms to show that the job was done. Captain Borras was walking towards the ladder when the loud roar of an engine caused him to stop and look up.

A helicopter with a white star on its side floated overhead, hovering over his ship. An American carrier must have been close enough to hear the sighting radio call.

"Send a radio message at once," the Captain shouted, jumping for the ladder. "Notify the Americans that this is a matter for the Peruvian Coast Guard. Tell them that I am boarding now and will make a report as soon as I can." He climbed the ladder, quickly, panting for breath, but not slowing or stopping. He was first aboard; the newspapers would report it that way. First.

"Nobody here, Captain. I can't see nobody."

"Shut up . . . and give me . . . a hand . . . , " Captain Borras gasped.

The sailor reached down and lifted the Captain easily over the rail. Borras pushed the man's hands away and brushed his jacket straight. "Follow me," he ordered, and turned and walked across the deck.

It was as empty as the sailor had said. The folding chairs and lounges were neatly stacked and secured in place with tight-knotted lines. Dark windows stared at him and he felt a prickling of fear on his neck. Where were the people? He would never find out standing here. Hitching up his belt so the pistol was close to hand he walked across the deck, somehow reassured by the heavy tread of the sailor close behind him. The door opened easily to his touch and he stepped into the compartment beyond.

The bottles were ranked thickly behind the bar, illuminated by softly glowing lights, ready for service. Glasses were arranged neatly below them. The bar was air conditioned and comfortable; recorded music was playing, the chairs were set expectantly before the tables, ashtrays neatly centered on the tables — the nearest one of them held an empty cigarette packet. Everything was ready.

Except there were no people.

"Nobody here," Basilio said in a hushed voice. The Captain started to reprimand the sailor for speaking, but he didn't. The sound of a human voice was unexpectedly reassuring. He led the way towards the door at the far end of the bar. At the last table he noticed a cigarette in the ashtray there. Long, expensive. Just lit, then grubbed out quickly and broken. Dark lipstick on the filter. Did it mean anything? He couldn't tell.

The lounge beyond was as empty as the bar. Magazines lay on the tables, the chairs were there waiting. But something was wrong.

"The life jackets, Captain, they're all gone," the sailor said, pointing at the empty lockers.

"Obviously," Captain Borras said, heading towards the stairway. He wanted to go to the bridge; the solution to this unnerving mystery might be there. He climbed the stairs, then pushed open the doorway leading to the boat deck and stepped through it.

Face to face with the blank-eyed goggled man dressed in thick-padded clothing.

"*Dios!*" he gasped, fumbling for his revolver. The man drew back, waving his hand before him.

"Not the shooter, for Christ's sake!" he said. "This is the U.S. Navy!"

Even as the man spoke the Captain was aware of engine sounds from above. The helicopter, of course. He rested his hand on his belt, as though that was what he had meant to do all along.

"Captain Borras, Peruvian Coast Guard."

"Chief Nicolas. We got the message about finding the

Queen. I just winched aboard. I was heading for the bridge."

"As was I, Chief. Shall we go there now?"

"On the way. Have you seen anyone?"

"No. No one at all. But the life jackets are missing."

"Lifeboats, too. That's all I could see."

They walked the great length of the boat deck in silence, then up the companionway to the bridge deck. Captain Borras hesitated for a moment with his hand on the door — then threw it open.

"Deserted," Chief Nicolas said, so quietly his words could barely be heard. "Underway at sea, crew and passengers aboard. It's impossible . . . ."

Captain Borras could only nod in agreement. Impossible, yes. But it had happened. The lights were all turned on, as were the instruments. That meant that at least standby power was being generated. The log — that's what he must see!

He hurried to it, looked at it, at the last entry.

"It's for June thirteenth," he said.

"The day she vanished," Nicolas said. "And look here, at the chart."

There was evidence here as well. A ruled course with a neatly pencilled notation beside it. Position as of midnight, 13 June. Just at the time the last radio message had been received.

"What the hell happened here?"

Chief Nicolas almost shouted the words, shouted with puzzlement and fear. "This can't happen. I mean not today, with radio and satellites to look at the sea traffic and everything. This is no sailing ship like the goddamn *Marie Celeste*. This is the world's biggest liner with a couple of thousand passengers and crew aboard. They don't just vanish into thin air . . . ."

"*Capitano! Ven' aqui . . . !*"

As the connecting door burst open Captain Borras realized that the sailor, Basilio, had not been with them when they had entered the bridge. But he was here now, gasping, his face white with shock. Or was it fear? Waving wordlessly down the passageway.

"He has found something," the Captain called out. "Come with me."

They had to hurry to follow the man. Down the companionway to the deck below, to stare uncomprehendingly at a black circle burnt into the carpet. Why — how? But the sailor was calling to them urgently. They followed him, aware now of the acrid smell of smoke still heavy on the air. Something was wrong. Very, very wrong.

This was the signal deck where the luxury suites were located. The door to the first one was open and they stopped in front of it. Staring in.

A disaster. It was burned, destroyed, consumed. Fire had eaten away the carpets so that the charred decking showed, had burned the furniture and even charred the ceiling black. The walls were blackened and blistered — and punched full of ragged holes. The automatic extinguishers had been tripped and had sprayed water over everything, turning it into a blackened soggy mess.

"What happened — what the hell happened to this ship?"

Chief Nicolas shouted the words aloud. Shouted the question without an answer.

What *had* happened to the *QE2*?

3

Some Months Earlier

There was a raw wind blowing in from the Solent, moist
Atlantic air that drove the thick banks of cloud before
it. Although it was mid-afternoon it was as dark as evening, so that the burst of lightning lit up the wet streets
and drab buildings of Southampton like a monstrous
flashbulb. Instants after the lightning, the crash and roll
of thunder burst down upon the city as well, echoing
away with an angry muttering rumble. It was as though
the lightning had pierced the sky, for the rain started
then, a continuous downpour that hammered onto the
already wet streets, sending quick runnels of water
along the pavement.

Rafael Viar held tightly to the brim of his cap as he
made his way across Town Quay, trying to avoid the
deepest puddles, hurrying ahead of a heavy lorry on its
way to the docks. His shoulders were wet where the rain
had soaked through the thin raincoat and he could feel
the water squelch in his shoes with every step. This was
no day to go sightseeing in England.

It was also no day to stay aboard the ship. Because
the S.S. *Polar Star* was a seagoing slum. A piece of rusty
filth that disgusted him when he so much as thought
about it. The freighter was Liberian registered and cap-
tained by a Greek pederast. The First Officer and the
Chief Engineer were alcoholics who spent most of their
time locked into the cabin with their cases of cheap gin.

With this sort of leadership, the underpaid crew did the minimum amount of work with the maximum amount of complaining. Since Rafael worked in the kitchen he received most of the insults. He couldn't blame them, the food was terrible, but he still did not enjoy it. Now that they were in port he braved the unbelievable English weather to escape for a while from the stench and dirt of the kitchen. He knew that he carried the smell of it with him on his clothes, so there was no real escape. But he still had to leave, if only for a few hours. Even though there was no decent wine in this harsh country, and he really did not like the beer. Yet he was no longer aboard the *Polar Star*. That was enough for him.

There was a large green square ahead of him now, with shops and buildings on the far side. One of them was a café with lights glowing beckoningly through the misted windows. Good. A hot cup of tea would be very much in order. Perhaps some food, the famous English bacon and egg. He waited for a gap in the heavy, one-way traffic, then hurried across, stepping up onto the pavement in front of a large office building. There were steps leading up to the entrance where a man sheltered from the driving rain, a well-dressed man in a heavy coat and black hat. Rafael was facing in his direction when lightning crashed across the sky again. Rafael could see his face clearly, no more than two meters away.

As the thunder rumbled and rolled, Rafael fell against the stone wall of the building, clutching to it, pressing his face to the rough wet surface.

That face! He knew that face — how he knew it. But not here, certainly not in Southampton. Far across the Atlantic in a warmer, Latin country. Could it really be him?

Rafael turned slowly, still leaning against the building for support. The man remained in the doorway, looking out at the road, ignorant of the sailor nearby.

There could be no doubt. That profile, too familiar by far. The beak of a nose with the filthy little hairline moustache below. It was him.

Rafael started forward just as the man moved. He walked quickly in order to stay dry, just the short distance down the steps and into the open black door of the waiting limousine. The door slammed shut even as Rafael stumbled towards it. He looked in, impotently, through the rain-speckled glass. Staring at Major José de Laiglesia sitting in warm comfort and looking at a brochure of some kind, a red and yellow folder.

And then he was gone. The car pulled swiftly out into a gap in the traffic and disappeared from sight. Rafael stood staring numbly after it, unaware of the rain soaking him, aware of nothing except the detested face of the man in the car.

What was he doing here? Where was he going? Why wasn't he still working at his dirty business back in Paraguay? Oh, how he would like to know the answers to these questions.

Had de Laiglesia come out of this building? There was a good possibility that he had, because he had been standing in the doorway waiting for his car. Rafael looked up at the heavy lettering. SOUTH WESTERN HOUSE, it read, with CUNARD under that. The shipping company? Of course, this was a seaport, perhaps the home port of the line. He walked up the steps and into the lobby. The first thing that he saw was a large advertising display with an immense color photograph of an ocean liner. QUEEN ELIZABETH II it said.

Ranked beside the display were racks of advertising brochures.

One of them was red and yellow.

They were free for the taking. Rafael walked slowly towards the rack, suddenly aware of how wet he was, how hard his heart was pounding in his chest. This wasn't good. The doctor in Barcelona had told him about the strain that had been placed on his heart, how he should not overexert himself, should not place himself in stressful situations. The hammering within his body frightened him and he walked slowly and carefully as though he were treading on eggs. He took one of the red and yellow folders from the rack and stuffed it into his pocket, then turned and headed still more slowly towards the door.

There was a pub, just a few doors away. He shuffled towards it, clutching fearfully at his chest as though to hold the offended organ in place. The barman drew a pint of beer for him and he fumbled coins onto the stained wood and carried the mug to an empty table near the fire. The pill box was in an inside pocket and he took it out and shook three of them into his palm, then washed them down with the beer. Then rested with his eyes closed until the terrible hammering had slowed.

Only then did he take the paper folder from his pocket and spread it out on the table before him.

WORLD CRUISE QE2 it read. Inside were photographs of distant places and copy in English that he did not try to read. What did it mean? Was that piece of filth de Laiglesia going on a cruise around the world? Impossible. He was just a hireling, a jackal, a creature that obeyed. Then had he been sent here? And if so by whom? Rafael wanted very much to know. He wanted to know anything that had to do with Major José de Laiglesia who had come to his father's house in the middle of the night with his soldiers. They had clubbed the old man down, struck down Rafael as well when he had tried to stop them, tore his screaming mother from her bed and dragged her into the street in her night-clothes, in front of everyone, and thrown her brutally into the open truck. That was all that Rafael remembered, because he had lost consciousness then.

He had never seen his parents again. They were gone, vanished as though they had never been. His father had been the best known lawyer in Villarrica, which was of course why they had taken him. Rafael was of no importance. Major de Laiglesia had enjoyed beating him with a heavy pole, then had personally attached the electric leads to Rafael's testicles, had laughed until he had cried at Rafael's antics when they turned the current on. In a few months the Major had tired of this fun and they had released him because he was unimportant and of no danger to the state.

Perhaps that had been their mistake. Perhaps what he had seen now was important. Perhaps something could be done about it. He didn't know what, but he did know someone who might be interested. A man he had met at a rally in London who had promised to see if anything could be discovered about Rafael's parents. Nothing could be found out, but he still reported to Rafael that they were trying. His name was Leandro Diaz and his phone number was on a piece of paper in Rafael's wallet. He dug it out, took all of the change from his pocket and made his way to the public telephone in the rear near the toilet. It might mean nothing at all, but he felt still that Diaz should know.

Diaz seemed interested, but he was in a hurry and wanted to call back. Rafael gave him the number of the phone, then went back to his table. He finished the beer and had a second one. Then a cold sausage from the bar, because he was hungry, which he regretted as soon as he had eaten it. The British had some strange tastes in food. Almost an hour passed before the phone rang. The barman answered it, then put the hand-piece down and looked around.

"Call here for a Rafael Beer."

"For me, thank you, thank you a much."

Leandro Diaz spoke quickly in Spanish.

"Can you come to London? Now, this evening?"

"Of course, that is why I phoned you. Where do you want me to go?"

"There is a public house called the Blue Posts. It is very easy to find. Go down Rupert Street from Shaftesbury Avenue, it is there on the corner of a small passage named Rupert Court. Do you understand?"

"Yes. No trouble. I will take the next train."

"Good. I'll be waiting for you."

Once he was in the warmth of the railway compartment, Rafael found himself dozing off, exhausted by the strain of the past hours. It was not a restful sleep, for he dreamt that he was back in the prison in Emboscada where he was beaten with *el sargento,* the cat-o'-nine-tails with lead balls on the tip of each thong. He had never been whipped with this cruel invention but had seen others torn to pieces by its flails. It was always his terrible secret fear that it would be used on him as well. It was there, often, in his dreams, especially when he was very tired. When the crashing of doors in Victoria Station woke him up, Rafael was soaked with sweat. He was the last one to leave the train.

The queue of people waiting at the taxi stand was a short one, as was the journey. They passed Buckingham Palace and went through a park, then the driver went through Piccadilly Circus and up Shaftesbury Avenue, stopping at the corner where he pointed out the bar that Rafael was looking for. Rafael paid the sum on the meter, added a careful ten percent tip since the driver had been courteous, then pushed through the door of the Blue Posts. Leandro Diaz was waiting in an alcoved booth to the rear.

They shook hands and Diaz looked him up and down.

"You don't look so good, my friend," he said.

"Unhappily, I feel just as I look."

"You will have a drink then, an Irish coffee, specialty of the house. Very warm and nourishing, with alcohol in it as well."

They waited until the drinks had been brought before they talked. Then Diaz said, "Please tell me exactly what you have seen."

Leandro Diaz sipped at his drink while Rafael talked, the fresh cream leaving a white line on the dark skin of his upper lip which he carefully licked off. He was a handsome man in his middle thirties, taller than most of his countrymen — the heritage of his Spanish ancestors — dark-skinned and strong like his Indian forbears. This strength had permitted him to live through four years of confinement in the despicable National Penitentiary of Tacumba. Four years that had nurtured his hatred for General Alfredo Stroessner and his followers. He wore his straight black hair quite long to cover the scars on his neck; the invisible scars within were hidden behind his set and passive expression. He nodded silently and listened as Rafael talked. When the sailor was finished he remained quiet, thinking for a moment, while Rafael gulped at his drink.

"You saw no one else in the car?" Diaz asked.

"No one in the back with de Laiglesia. A driver, of course, but just a glimpse of a uniform hat."

"Did the Major carry anything?"

"Yes, of course! I had forgotten until you asked. A leather briefcase, dark brown or black."

"This is all very interesting," Diaz said. He took a

packet of dark, thin cigars from his pocket and extracted one. Rafael waved them away when they were offered to him. Diaz struck a match, waited until the chemicals had burned away, then carefully lit the cigar. Only then did he speak.

"We have been keeping a close eye on your sadistic Major, who now enjoys the rank of military attaché at the Paraguayan embassy here. He is a running dog, nothing but a messenger boy who does their dirty errands for them. Small fry — but small fry are the easiest to watch. He drinks a lot, gambles, goes with Spanish whores in Soho — while he weeps a lot about his mother while they whip him. A dirty piece of work, our Major."

"I would like to kill him," Rafael said vehemently.

"So would a lot of other people. But he is of more value to us alive for the time being. Something is happening in Paraguay, something big. We have had reports from Asunción. There have been couriers coming here and a lot of stirring about. We do not have enough people to watch them all of the time so we missed de Laiglesia's little motoring journey. Our thanks for pointing it out to us. I have checked and he was seen leaving the embassy around noon. So this is a quick round trip to Southampton. For what reason?"

"To do something that he did not wish to be seen doing in London?" Rafael asked, hesitantly.

"My reasoning exactly. They know they are being watched; they're not complete fools. So a flying visit to Cunard in Southampton, with a briefcase that can hold papers, money . . . . "

"Or it could hold tickets."

"Quite possibly. But whatever it held it was something that they didn't want us to know about — which means we are now very interested in it. A briefcase with something they are very concerned about in it.''

"And a brochure about a world cruise on the *QE2*. Is there a connection?''

"I don't know — but I do know that we are going to find out. Our thanks, Rafael, for your help.''

"I want no thanks — I will do anything to combat these filth, these vermin . . . . ''

Rafael started to cough, deeply and strongly, and Diaz rested his hand on the other man's arm, lightly. There was little else he could do for him or any of the other victims of the régime. "We have had no more word about your parents,'' he said.

Rafael nodded and wiped his hand across his lips. "I know . . . you would have told me right away if you had.''

"There is still hope —.''

"I doubt it. I have stopped hoping. It does no good. I have no family, I have faced that. I am a stinking dishwasher aboard a filthy tub. Some day, God willing, I will be able to go home again. It is you and your people, Diaz, who will make that possible. Perhaps I will be able to go back to the university. I don't know. Meanwhile stay alive . . . . ''

"Old friend; do you need some money? Is there anything we can do for you?''

Rafael shook his head in a slow *no*. "I have nothing to spend money on. I'm all right. Just do what you are doing. Now I will finish this drink and go back to the station. There is a late train I can get so I will be back to the ship tonight. There is less trouble that way.''

They shook hands and Rafael departed in silence. Diaz looked after him as he left and seemed unaware of the man who came in through the side door of the pub and joined him in the booth.

"He has gone out for the evening,'' the newcomer said.

"Apparently on the way to his whores again. Victorio is following him."

"And Victorio has a radio?"

"Yes."

"Good. Then he can warn us in time if the pig is returning to his quarters. We will be looking for a briefcase that could be of immense interest. Come then Luis, I'll tell you about it on the way."

Charles Street in Mayfair is not far from Park Lane and most of the top hotels in London. The area is well lit, clean, well-policed, and reeks of gentility and money. The two Paraguayans parked their car in Berkeley Square and strolled slowly in the direction of the park. If they were noticed, they were accepted, for they were neatly dressed and groomed; the thin attaché case Diaz carried could have held papers rather than the tools of the criminal trade.

Without slowing or looking about, they turned into the doorway of the building where de Laiglesia lived. There were other apartments here and Diaz had enquired about a vacancy some months earlier; taking the opportunity to make an impression of the estate agent's key at the time. They saw no one as he unlocked the front door and made their way up the stairs to the second floor. Diaz had the lockpick ready in his fingers as they approached the door in the front of the building. Diaz knocked on the door, waited a few moments, then knocked again.

"He's out," Luis said, "you know that."

"Of course I know that. But perhaps he left a visitor behind who doesn't know that. Always use care."

Luis shrugged expressively, saying as clearly as he could with words that he disagreed. When no one answered after the second knock, Diaz took out the pick and inserted it in the lock.

"What are you doing there?" a woman's voice asked

from down the hall.

Diaz calmly knocked on the door again, at the same time palming the lockpick.

"Can't you hear me? What do you want?"

Luis was standing stock still, not knowing what to do. But Diaz turned slowly, saw the sharp-faced woman in the open door down the hall, and tipped his hat politely.

"Excuse me, madam. I didn't realize that you were talking to us."

"Well, who else is in this hall? Well?"

"How charming of you to ask." Diaz smiled warmly. "We are here knocking on the door of our friend Mr. Penninck who pressed the button to release the catch on the ground floor door so we could enter the building. Does that answer your question, madam?"

The woman sniffed and withdrew her head — then almost smiled. "It is a very good answer. Except that you are on the wrong floor. Mr. Penninck is the floor above." She closed the door with a triumphant bang.

"So sorry," Diaz said, winking strongly at the befuddled Luis.

They walked heavily down the hall and up the stairs. Diaz leaned close to whisper.

"Do you see what I mean about taking care?"

"Yes . . . but who is this Penninck?"

"I have no idea. But I took the precaution of noting his name when I was last here. In case I should ever have to explain my presence in the building."

Luis was impressed. Even more so when Diaz knocked on the fire door, then opened it. "Ahh, hello, do come in," he said in a deep voice trying to disguise his own. Then he slammed the fire door shut and touched his fingers to his lips.

On the floor below they heard a door close.

"For a lawyer you make a pretty good thief," Luis whispered.

''Many people would say that they are the same thing. We'll wait a few minutes, then go down as quietly as we can. No noise. If she sees us again we'll have to leave.''

Diaz forced himself to wait a full three minutes. They slipped down the stairs and tiptoed to the apartment door below. Diaz had the lockpick ready in his fingers and he quickly inserted it and probed for the combination. Luis looked worriedly towards the entrance of the woman's apartment. When the door finally opened they pushed in as quickly as they could and closed it silently behind them.

Inside the dark apartment Luis used his pencil flashlight. It threw only a small spot of light onto the floor, just enough for him to see his way across the room to close the curtains.

''All right,'' he said.

Diaz turned on the lights and they looked about the room. ''There's the briefcase,'' he said.

''And if you look you will see that there is a wall safe right above it. I hope that I am wrong.''

''Unhappily you are correct,'' Diaz said gloomily, poking about inside the empty case. ''Whatever he brought back is undoubtedly in the safe now.''

''Can you open it?''

''I am a better lawyer than a thief, Luis, still learning my new trade. We could get someone who could break into it without leaving any marks. But not before tomorrow. By that time the Major will be through with his whores and will have taken the contents of the safe to the Embassy.''

Diaz was looking about the room as he talked, at the pretentious and gawdy furniture, the vulgar prints on the walls. A sideboard was covered with bottles of expensive liquor mixed with flasks of cheap *aguardiente;* the Major had low tastes. On the floor next to the sideboard was a wastebasket shaped like a drum. Diaz went to it, kneeled and took out a crumpled red and yellow folder.

"It's marked by drops of water," he said. "As though it has been out in the rain. An advertisement for a world cruise on the fabulous *QE2*." He laid it out flat on the desk and opened it. On the inner page was a list of fares and schedules, with accommodation varying from 'Duplex Suite with Private Veranda' and 'Two-Room Duplex with Bath, Shower and Toilet' to 'Quad, Two Beds & Two Uppers' right down at the bottom of the list.

Someone had been doodling on the brochure with a red felt-tip pen. Marking little crosses and circles and hatching in the white spaces that surrounded the printing. The sort of doodling that someone might do during a boring ride to London in heavy traffic.

The doodler had done some marking on the printed copy as well. Diaz laid his fingertip on the two inked circles and looked up into Luis's eyes.

"Does it mean anything?" Luis asked.

"It might. And we're going to find out, aren't we?"

Luis nodded slow agreement.

The circles red-ringed the listing for the two duplex suites.

The Trafalgar Suite and the Queen Anne Suite. The best accommodation on the world's most luxurious liner.

4

The two men shook hands briefly, then parted just around the corner from the Cunard ticket office, Diaz staying and watching for a moment as the other casually opened the Cunard door and walked in.

As the man entered, the clerk looked up, then nudged the girl next to him.

"Now, just look at this fine specimen that's just come in from the lobby," Willy Mahon said. "Look closely, Heather, and tell me just what you think of him."

Heather was an executive trainee at Cunard, destined for greater things in the offices of the company. That was her future. However, right now she was serving as a sales assistant in the booking office in London. Willy Mahon was her training officer, and after the first weeks of getting to know him she was finally beginning to appreciate his better qualities. Not his personal qualities, a quick grope and an even quicker slap had established that relationship quite early. It was his sales ability she admired, his knowledge of the complicated fare structure of all the Cunard ships, linked with a talent for always selling a cruise or accommodations costing that little bit more than the customer thought he could really afford. She followed his instructions now and looked closely at the young man who was examining the rack of sales brochures. She tried to sum him up.

"Young, late twenties, not too well dressed, probably

can't afford a cruise, and will probably ask us where he can book on a tramp steamer. Right?''

''Wrong on all counts, ducks, except maybe his age. This chap is a gent and maybe the heir to millions. Notice how tightly rolled the umbrella is. Dead giveaway. And the clothes are old, but that's to show that he doesn't care about money. You shouldn't let that fool you. Take a look instead at the jacket he's wearing. It's hand-woven thornproof tweed and it would set you back the best part of a hundred knicker if you wanted to buy one like it. Shoes polished to a dull glow — and handwoven thornproof tweed and it would set you monocle if they weren't out of style right now. And notice one hand in the bottom jacket pocket. That's to show he doesn't care if someone pinches his wallet or not — since there's plenty more where that came from.''

''My, aren't we being Sherlock Holmes today?''

''Listen, love, I could have taught that old junkie a thing or two — yes, sir, can I be of assistance?''

''Yes . . . ahh, perhaps. A cruise, that's the thing.''

Willy cast a glance of triumph towards his assistant as the nasal Oxbridge tones washed over them. Heather acknowledged his accuracy with a nod and a thumbs-up sign out of sight behind the counter. Then moved decorously away so that he could slip in for the hard sell and the kill.

''Could I interest you in a world cruise, sir? Since you have the brochure in your hand I thought . . . ?''

''Quite . . . ,'' the customer gaped slightly at the colorful brochure, as though seeing it for the first time, then dropped it onto the counter. ''*QE2.* A rather nice . . . .''

''Nice, sir — why that's like calling the Mona Lisa a fair painting. She's the flagship of the British fleet, sir, the queen of the oceans so to speak. There's nothing like her sailing the seven seas, nothing.'' As he talked Willy produced a glossy pamphlet adorned with a large colored photograph of the *QE2* sailing one of these seas.

''She's one of a kind, sir, and you've never seen her like before nor will you ever again. I won't bore you with the details of her standard accommodation — five hundred and forty-one rooms in all there — but just look here at the three hundred and twenty deluxe rooms, all outside and all with bath and shower, twenty of them deluxe suites with outside verandahs . . . . ''

''I know. I've sailed on her,'' the customer said with great weariness. ''Stilton wasn't quite ripe.''

Willy was indestructible and he loved a challenge. His smile was a sincere one as he instantly produced another elaborate brochure and spread it out over the first one.

''Of course, you know the vessel, sir, so I want to outline this world cruise, the first of its kind, a rest, a relaxation, holiday, call it what you will, but it's the sort of thing that happens but once in a lifetime. We leave Southampton on the fifth of April and awaken in the warm sunlight on the way to Capetown. From there to Australia, on to Hawaii and . . . . ''

''Yes, I can see that in the itinerary. It's the accommodation that I really care about.''

''As well you might, sir.'' Another quick rustle of paper. ''And right here on this deck plan you can see the rooms that are available on the signal and sports decks.''

The customer dropped an unerring finger onto the most expensive accommodation and Willy, knowing the thrill of the chase, closed in for the kill.

''This,'' the customer said, ''it is a suite, isn't it? Seems all right.''

''And that it is, sir. The Queen Anne Suite. Equalled

but not bettered by the Trafalgar Suite opposite.''

"Available?"

"Very possible, sir. Just a moment to check. The price . . . . ''

"Unimportant."

"Of course, sir. I'll just be a tick."

Willy was humming as he went to the computer terminal, at peace with the world, happy enough to bestow a conspiratorial wink upon Heather. He punched in the request for accommodation — then gaped at the screen. He cleared it, some mistake, surely it was, but the same details were displayed yet again. He tapped the keys for more information then scribbled some notes on a pad. He returned to the counter, a far less exuberant man than the one who had left it moments ago.

"I'm very unhappy to say this, Mister . . . ?"

"Hunt-Palmer."

"I'm most sorry to report, Mr. Hunt-Palmer, that those suites have both been booked, by the same party it seems."

"Both of them! Anyone I know?"

"Can't say, Mr. Hunt-Palmer. Party by the name of Van der Leiden. But out of Capetown only. The whole cruise has been paid for but there is a note saying that the Southampton to Capetown leg is available if you are interested . . . . ''

"Certainly not. Are there other suites?"

"Not suites, sir. But excellent deluxe accommodation, connecting doors . . . .''

"Thank you for your time. Good day."

Hunt-Palmer nodded politely and turned and was gone before Willy could think of anything more to say.

"Not interested?" Heather asked, ever so sweetly.

"Damn well interested — and sold too! Except someone already flogged the suites to some sodding Afrikaaner. There should be a rule about where they sell the tickets first.''

Willy slammed his fist down on the counter just once, then shrugged. He folded the brochures neatly and put them away. Can't win them all. The world of shipping was forgotten for the moment and his thoughts instantly returned to his current full-time preoccupation. How to get into the knickers of sweet little Heather.

Hunt-Palmer was obviously in no hurry when he left the Cunard office. The air was crisp but the day sunny, and he whistled lightly as he walked to the corner and looked about for a taxi. A number passed, all with passengers, until one with the illuminated *Taxi* sign appeared. Being a gentleman, he did not indulge in any of the whistling or arm-waving so enjoyed by the tourists, but instead pointed his umbrella outward from the curb at an angle of approximately twenty-two degrees. The taxi swerved towards him and came to a stop.

''Earl's Court tube station,'' he said through the front window, then opened the rear door and climbed in.

A parked gray Cortina pulled away from the curb when they passed and swung into the traffic behind them. Possibly a coincidence. Hunt-Palmer paid it no heed. He relaxed during the cab ride, jingling the coins in his pocket.

When they reached the Earl's Court Road he paid for the cab and entered the Underground station. He had the coins ready in his hand so he could slip them into the ticket dispensing machine as he came up to it. One ten, one five pence piece. The machine chunked and delivered a piece of yellow-sided pasteboard into his hand. He put it into the automatic turnstile which also chunked loudly, admitting him and returning the ticket at the same time. He pushed through quickly — then fell to examining the Underground route-map posted by the entrance. It was so fascinating that he stayed there looking at it for almost five minutes. It was not by chance that he also had a fine view of everyone entering the station. He abandoned his scrutiny when he heard a west-bound train rumbling towards the station, then hurried down the steps to reach it just before the doors closed.

He did not board it. Instead he waited until the disembarking passengers had all left the station. Only then did he climb back up the stairs, alone, and hand his ticket to the collector. Who raised his eyebrows slightly at the thought of a fifteen pence trip from Earl's Court to Earl's Court, but said nothing.

No one followed him into the street, and as far as he could tell he was alone when he crossed the square and rang the doorbell of the large block of apartments on the south side. The door buzzed and unlocked and he pushed his way in, ignoring the elevator and quickly climbing to the third floor. The door was open and he walked into the apartment and heard it close behind him.

"Were you followed here?" Leandro Diaz asked him in fast Spanish.

"No. I'm sure of that. I took precautions," he answered in Spanish, just as fast and just as perfect.

"What happened?"

"I'll be happy to tell you after I sit down and after you give me a glass of wine from that fine-looking bottle of Sangre de Toro I see on the table."

There were four other men present; they all seemed to know each other as there were no introductions. One of them poured the wine and brought it to Hunt-Palmer who sipped carefully from it, then sighed.

"Were there any suspicions?" Diaz asked. "Did they take you for an Englishman?"

"How could they not, dear boy? All those terrible school dinners, all the years of freezing — as well as all my father's money spent on Eton — all wasted if I couldn't pass as one of the chosen. As far as Cunard knows a gentleman by the name of Hunt-Palmer . . ."

"Like the biscuits!" Diaz cried.

"Close, but not too close to cause suspicion. If the functionary who served me had known that my name was really Rivelles would he have been so helpful? As I said, a proper gentleman made inquiries and that is the end of it. There is no possible way they can connect the inquiries with your group. But I've found out about your suites. They have been booked for the entire cruise by a gentleman by the name of Van der Leiden."

"Both suites?"

"Yes. And here is the interesting part. Although they are completely paid for — no one will be in them until the ship arrives in Capetown."

"Capetown!" Diaz was astonished. "What in the world has South Africa to do with South America — much less Paraguay?"

"I can only guess, my friend. And my guess is that the Afrikaaners who board there might be speaking Spanish."

Diaz nodded, frowning. "It is my guess that your guess is right. If Major de Laiglesia did buy those tickets — then this cruise of the *QE2* is somehow linked with the affairs that are stirring at home."

"Any idea yet what is happening?" Rivelles asked.

"No, nothing definite. Just that it is big. We have a good man on the inside but it is hard for him to pass on messages. We'll find out in time, don't worry about that. Meanwhile we must do what we can at this end, find out what we can about the mysterious passengers on this cruise. Have you ever been in South Africa, Rivelles?''

''Don't ask me that!'' He raised his free hand in a pushing-away gesture. ''I am in the export-import business and I can take a few hours off, OK, but my uncle would slit my throat if I left the country . . . . ''

''Rivelles,'' Diaz said, kindly but firmly. ''You will find a way. Get sick, go into a nursing home, something. But everyone in this room is well known to the thugs in the *Colorados*. If they spot us they will know that we are onto them. While you, you are a respectable Argentinian businessman. They can have no idea what happened to your cousin or that you approached us and offered to help. We are taking up that offer now. Besides, we are a poor organization and the air ticket to Capetown must be very expensive.''

''Leave my work, pretend I'm sick, chase murderers to South Africa — and pay for it myself!'' Rivelles sighed. ''You don't ask very much do you?''

''We ask a great deal,'' Diaz said in a low and intent voice.

Rivelles started to protest — then smiled instead. ''Of course you ask a lot. And of course I'll help. It is little enough to do.''

''It is a lot and we appreciate it. Now drink your wine while Antonio calls up the travel agent and finds out about your ticket. Give him your American Express Card number like a good fellow, will you? It will make things easier.''

5

Rivelles felt like death. He had been in the South African Airways 747 for the best part of twenty-four hours before they had touched down in Johannesburg. The flight had left late because of a strike at Heathrow, so, of course, he had missed his connecting flight to Cape Town. Sitting in the lounge had been torture — was there an international sadist who designed the uncomfortable furniture for airports? — and the two-hour flight to Cape Town no more enjoyable. At least the Mount Nelson hotel had saved his room for him, despite the delay, and a hot bath followed by a cold shower had restored him slightly. Yes, the view of Table Mountain was just as fine as they had said it would be. Washed, shaved, dressed, he collapsed in the chair and admired the view. And still felt like death.

He put the dexadrine tablet into his mouth and washed it down with a large gulp of whisky and soda. This should do the trick. He would just rest for a bit while it took effect . . . .

Rivelles woke with a start, shaking his head. Like a simple fool he had fallen asleep. He blinked at his watch. Just ten minutes. But ten minutes wasted. The QE2 would be docking in a matter of hours, so he did not have the ten minutes to waste. With a groan he hauled himself to his feet and went and dug the classified section of the phone book out of the stand by the bed. Then ran his finger through the listing of photographers. They were all either British or Dutch names and that was no good. They were sure to know more than he did about the local situation and might be suspicious of his cover story. Yes, here was a possibility. Nino Rossino. He marked a line under the number and went to the phone.

Nino was a freelance photographer, yes, and sure, he did newspaper work. No problem — except not today. A portrait assignment, impossible to break the appointment. The appointment was broken when a cash payment of two hundred rands was offered in advance against fee. Yes, he could be at the Cunard office within the hour. A pleasure.

Cunard was even easier to convince than the photographer had been. Someone in Leandro Diaz's organization had discovered that *Newsweek* magazine was doing an in-depth report on cruise liners, with a good-sized section on Cunard. Rivelles had very good reason to feel that his authentic-looking *Newsweek* press card and documentation were all forged. The Cape Town Cunard executive did not think so, however, which was all that counted. Yes, happy to oblige, no trouble getting aboard, yes, the well-known popular novelist Sheila Conrad was on board the *QE2* and would undoubtedly love to grant him an interview. Passes would be instantly supplied for him and his photographer and would he be able to have drinks afterward with the Captain? It was all very straightforward. Rivelles, once again Hunt-Palmer, shook hands for a second time and allowed himself to be shown out of the office. A swarthy man, hung with camera bags, was waiting in the reception room, moodily nibbling on the remains of a well-chewed fingernail.

"Mr. Rossino?"

The photographer jumped to his feet, wiping his

fingers against his pants-leg before he extended his hand to Rivelles.

"Nino, if you don't mind. You're Hunt-Palmer then, *Newsweek*. My pleasure. I've never worked with your people before, going to be great, take some great shots."

"You're not Italian then? This is for you." He passed over the envelope with the two hundred rands. Nino took a quick glimpse inside then jammed it into his pocket.

"Italian-American. I guess you can tell. I've got plenty of experience in the States, count on that. But, well, more opportunity over here, you might say."

Rivelles was listening more to the tone of the man's voice than his words and he jumped to a sudden conclusion. Maybe it was a wrong one — but he lost nothing by trying.

"Ever do any divorce work, Nino? Or work with investigation agencies?"

Nino's eyes slitted and his voice changed. Cold, suspicious.

"I done a lot of work, here and there. Why do you want to know?"

Jumped-to conclusion confirmed, Rivelles thought to himself. Little Nino had been around. He lowered his own voice almost to a whisper when he spoke.

"Well, you might say I have interests other than *Newsweek*. A matter of litigation, some photographs of people who might not want to have their photographs taken. Well-paid, of course."

As he spoke, the suspicion faded from Nino's face and was slowly replaced with a broad smile.

"Hunt-Palmer," he said, patting his camera case, "You may not realize it yet but you have come to the right man. I was the best, the absolute best in the city.

Too good. A couple of pix got into the wrong hands and now I'm sort of sitting it out in the boonies until things cool down. What's the deal?''

''We'll talk about it in the cab, if you don't mind. The ship will be docking soon and I want us aboard before the passengers.''

Nino was a find. Rivelles had a cover story planned, which he quickly abandoned. Nino did not want to know any of the details. He just wanted to know what or who he had to shoot, he would do the job and earn his fee.

''I gotta look at the setup first,'' he said. ''I'm not saying that your idea is a bad one, but it looks too obvious just standing around clicking off shots. We need a good cover. The thing is to appear to be doing one thing while all of the time you're doing something else. Who is this broad you gotta talk to? Is she on the boat now?''

''Sheila Conrad? Yes, she boarded at Southampton. But I don't really have to talk to her at all.''

''But I want you to, Mr. Hunt-Palmer . . . . ''

''John.''

''Right, John. Let me look at the lay of the land first and then we figure out what to do. It's gonna be a piece of cake! And a helluva lot better than doing all the fucking dago weddings!''

As the cab pulled into the street beside the dock, Rivelles had a shock that jarred his system to life faster than the dexadrine had done.

The *QE2* was already tied up at the pier.

Had all of the time and effort been wasted? He was shamed; how could he face the Paraguayan resistance people after this? He stumbled from the cab and after a half-look at the meter pushed banknotes into the driver's hand. Then walked, fast, towards the entrance.

There was a crowd here and above their heads he could see that the covered gangways were in position.

"Sorry, sir. Passengers only here. Do you have a ticket?"

The guard at the entrance blocked Rivelles's way with firm insistence.

"Press," he said, fumbling for his papers. "Have they started to board yet?"

"Not to worry, sir. Health and Customs officers just gone aboard. It will be a while yet before they let anyone else through. Right this way, sir, if you will go through that door. Is this gentleman with you?"

"Yes, of course."

"In you go then."

They joined the small group of press and officials in the VIP suite and were offered coffee while they waited. Rivelles would have preferred something a good deal stronger, but he took the coffee and sipped at it. They did not have long to wait. Within a few minutes one of the ship's officers appeared and led the way aboard.

Despite what Rivelles had said in the Cunard office he had never been aboard the *QE2* before. He was a man in a hurry and could not bear to travel by trains, much less ships. The airplane, for him, was the only means of conveyance that was at all civilized. He had been convinced, by a woman, of course, to take a cruise. Just once. The daily boredom, despite the heavenly passion of the evenings, had been excruciating. He had abandoned both liner and girl at their first port of call and had flown home at a pleasurable six hundred miles an hour. Therefore the *QE2* came as more than a little surprise to him.

Firstly, he had no feeling at all of being aboard a ship. This was more like a first-class hotel; the sort that he always enjoyed. But this was no hotel, he realized, when he came out on deck. He could see that it was a ship with rails, lifeboats, portholes — but it did not have the feel of a ship. It was too big. The deck stretched away from him like a city street. The scale was something that was hard to accept. Intellectually he knew that this was the largest liner in the world. The reality was something else altogether. Rivelles, a man who was very hard to impress, was very impressed indeed. He shook his head. Back to work; that's what he was here for. He pushed through the nearest door and back into a world of soft carpeting, unobtrusive lighting and seductive panelling. When he explained his needs to the Bureau, they were catered to at once. A quick phone call determined that Ms. Sheila Conrad was in her cabin and was indeed expecting him. An attendant appeared to lead the way.

"Pretty ritzy," Nino said as they followed their guide down the corridor and into the elevator.

"Not exactly the phrase I would use, but an accurate summation."

"You talk to this tomato a bit, alone. I want to look around. I won't be long. Tell her how great she is or something, but don't start the interview until I get

"To tell you the truth I never heard of her before I got this assignment. Do you perhaps know what she does?"

Nino raised his eyebrows and shook his head in disbelief. "Where do you live, John? Under a barrel? This broad must have made a million bucks writing tit books. Even I read them, and I don't read much usually. Real horny stuff. Maybe you can make out."

"Not really what I had in mind."

"This is the cabin, sir," the attendant said, accepting the proferred banknote with the assuredness of one who had done it many times before. Nino vanished as

Rivelles knocked on the door.

"It's open. Come on in," a woman's voice called from the other side.

He turned the handle and entered and was treated to the sight of Sheila Conrad — who had obviously prepared herself for his visit. She was sitting on the couch with her back to the window, the warm antipodean light pouring over her. Rivelles's first reaction was that there was a lot of girl there, and a good deal of it was exposed for his consideration. She wore an expensive-looking black dress; with diamonds so ostentatious that they had to be real. Her arms were resting lightly on the back of the couch, her legs crossed so that the short dress rode well up onto her thighs.

"You're from *Newsweek*, right?"

"Correct. My pleasure, Ms. Conrad."

"Call me Sheila. That's what your crummy book reviewer did when he laid into my last novel. Just plain Sheila. Never bothered to mention I had a last name. Nothing but dirty digs and insults. A creep. The highbrows never like my stuff. I hope you do better."

"I adore your work . . . Sheila." He adored her inescapable cleavage too, rising up to him with pink exuberance. "I have been looking forward to this interview with a great deal of pleasure."

"I hope it's a shared pleasure —" she squinted at a note she held, "— John. I wouldn't be talking to you except that my agent made me promise to give interviews to any magazine with circulation over a million. What's your latest A.B.C.?"

He had no idea of what the term even meant, but before he could fumble out an answer he was saved by a knock on the door.

"You expecting someone?" she asked.

"My photographer."

"Better and better. Let him in."

"Hiya, boss," Nino said, maneuvering his bulky cases through the door. "My pleasure, Ms. Conrad. I thought your last one, *Come Quick, My Love,* was the best damn book I read in the last hundred years."

"I love you, baby, not only for your literary taste but your neat turn of phrase. You have a name?"

"Nino Rossino."

"And from Brooklyn, too!"

"You can sure read them."

"I ought to, I grew up in Greenpoint."

"Please," Rivelles begged, glancing at his watch. "I want to interview Ms. Conrad, take some photographs. . . ."

"No sweat, boss. No one's come aboard yet, so if it's OK I want to get some shots outside in this kinda lounge. A real luxurious setting for a real luxurious lady."

"You're a breath of fresh air, Nino darling," she said, blowing him a kiss from glossy, painted lips. "Let's get your pix and come back here and open some champagne. This trip has been the kind of bore you can't imagine."

Nino led the way to a junction in the corridor where it widened into a lobby. There were chairs here and end tables, the area decorously lit and elaborately decorated, with soft leather lounges and fresh flowers set before the mirrors. Nino pointed out where he wanted them to sit.

"You there, please, Ms. Conrad. Boss, you can start the interview while I set the cameras up. I want this to look real natural. Get a couple of shots of you together, then the lady alone, if that's OK. Would you hold this while I open the tripod?"

When he bent over the camera bag Nino had a chance

for a quiet word in Rivelles's ear.

"Right down that corridor behind you, the first two doors, they're the two suites you're interested in. Whoever goes into them has to pass me or come the other way. I'll get them. Plenty of light, fast film, wide-angle lens. It'll look like I'm shooting the sex queen but I'll have the doors in sharp focus."

"You're a genius, Nino."

"I know. Now get to work — here come the first passengers!"

"Sit right here, John," Sheila said, patting the cushion.

"If I sit that close I'll wrinkle your dress."

"Silk. It doesn't wrinkle. So fire away."

This close, Rivelles was aware that Sheila wasn't the youth she once had been; fine wrinkles were visible around her eyes. But she still had plenty of mileage left in her; this close, the cleavage threatened to swell out and engulf him. He fumbled for his pocket tape recorder and switched it on.

"Interview with Sheila Conrad." She smiled expactantly and his mind emptied completely of all thought. He had never done this sort of thing before, had no idea of what to say. He groped desperately for an idea and dredged one up from his subconscious. "What ever made you take up writing, Sheila?" he asked.

"Christ! Not that old chestnut again. Don't you people ever have any new questions? The answer, for your millions of readers, is that I can make more money at the typewriter than I can on my back."

An elegant and elderly couple, she was wearing floor-length mink, were passing as she snapped out the answer in penetrating tones. The sound of eyebrows shooting up could be clearly heard. The woman took one quick sideways look and hurried on.

"Next question," Sheila said complacently.

"Would you look at me, please?" Nino said.

He had the 35 millimeter single-lens reflex mounted on the tripod; a long cable release ran from it. The camera was equipped with a power-driven film advance and it clicked and whirred three times in as many seconds.

"That's really great, great shots. If you would stand for a second, boss, I want some singles. Smile, you adorable creature, that's it, really great. Would you look up a bit now?"

More and more passengers were passing, most of them looking on with interest. Nino had a second camera out now and the sudden flash of an electronic blitz lit up the hallway.

"Can we get on with the interview," Sheila said. "It's not like we have all day."

Rivelles had taken advantage of the reprieve to remember all the talk shows he had seen on television and had scribbled down some obvious questions on a piece of paper. Sheila liked the sound of her own voice and was soon going ahead with little prompting. He only half-listened, nodding insincerely from time to time, trying to notice the people who passed by. There were fewer and fewer of them. And Sheila had obviously had enough.

"If that doesn't satisfy your editor, nothing will," she finally said. "And Brooklyn here has shot twenty rolls of film at least."

"Just a last couple, winding up," Nino said. "That wraps it up for me. What about you, boss?"

"Yes, fine."

"About time." Sheila stood and smoothed her dress and led the way down the corridor. "The champagne is cold by now.''

It took over half an hour to get away. Rivelles sipped the champagne and made light talk while Nino finished off all of the sandwiches that the waiter brought with the second bottle. Sheila did most of the drinking with an enthusiasm that showed years of experience. Nino finally wiped his lips and stood.

''Gotta get the film to the lab, boss. Too much of this high life is bad for a working stiff.''

''You'll have to excuse us, Sheila.''

''Wish you were sailing with me,'' she said, squeezing his hand. ''So far this trip has been old-fartsville. We could have some fun.''

''We could, I'm sure, I know. My pleasure.''

He finally extricated his moist hand and fled.

''That's a lot of good old girl there,'' Nino said as they went down the corridor.

''Quite. Of slightly greater importance are the photographs. How did it go? I couldn't see a thing.''

''I did, which is what counts, and I got the pix, which is what counts more. No broads, but five guys went into the two suites. A couple of old ones and three punks. Look like heavies. You'll see in the pix.''

''I will indeed. That's something I'm looking forward to.''

They went into Nino's darkroom, which had formerly been the bathroom of his flat. This was located in a run-down building located in the seamier part of the city. Nino opened a bottle of South African brandy, very sweet and very nasty, Rivelles realized when he took a sip, then set to work. He was a professional who knew just what he was doing.

''Got to do a bit of forcing,'' he said, loading the film into the developing tank. ''Could have used some more light or faster film, but I wanted fine grain so we could blow up the detail. I was shooting at a thousand, so we should be OK.''

He developed and dried the rolls of film, then spread the negatives out on a light box and examined them with a magnifying glass, muttering happily to himself.

''Great, really great, if I say so myself. I'll make you a blow-up of this one and you'll see what I mean.''

The projected image had Rivelles and Sheila large in the foreground, which Nino ignored. He moved the print frame until they were completely out of it, and concentrated on the figures in the corridor behind them.

When the print came out of the drier he took it into the front room and thumbtacked it proudly to the well-scarred wall and focussed a spotlight on it. ''Those the guys you're looking for?'' he asked.

''If they went into those suites, they are.''

''Went in and never came out.''

Rivelles looked closely at the photograph, then examined it even more closely with a magnifying glass. It meant nothing to him. All five of the men were unknown to him. Three young, two old, just as Nino had said. They did not look like Latin Americans, certainly the young ones weren't. The mystery was still a mystery. The people in London might be able to identify them.

''They OK?'' Nino asked.

''They're just perfect. You're an artist, Nino, just like you said. There's a plane I can take in just three hours time. Will they be ready by then?''

''A piece of cake. You make the reservations while I finish off the prints. Help yourself to the brandy — you're paying for it.''

6

There were three of them around the dining room table. The table was spread with old newspapers in place of a cloth, papers that were stained and marked and ragged. Diaz sipped at a cup of black coffee while the other two stared into space. The flat was large, old, shabbily furnished and drab. There was an air of impermanence about it as though the men had only stopped temporarily, were just passing through. Yet they had been here for years and might stay for many more. But their hearts, their thoughts, were far across the Atlantic in a small tropical country that most people had never heard of. Though they lived out their existence in these cold rooms, the echoing hallway and the grubby kitchen, they lived with an air of impermanence. Their home was far, far away indeed.

The tapping on the hallway door was very light, but all three men around the table heard it, turning together towards the sound. One of them started to pull a gun from his pocket but Diaz shook his head in a silent no. He stood and walked down the dank hallway and stood next to the door.

"Who is it?"

"The wanderer returned," a voice said. "And I'll collapse if you leave me out here an instant longer."

Diaz quickly unlatched the door and opened it wide, looking out quizzically at the man who was standing there.

"You know, my friend," he leaned against the wall while the door was closed and locked, "there have been times when I have felt a good deal better. I've spent two out of the last three days on planes. Not only haven't I slept, but my stomach is being ruined by the fresh frozen filth they serve for food."

"There's some black beans and rice in the kitchen."

"I'll sell my soul to the man who brings me a plate of them. Here are the pictures."

He passed over the envelope which was instantly seized and opened. "Do you know who they are? In the photographs," Diaz asked.

"Sorry, no. I hope you do."

Rivelles dug into the food with a happy sigh while Diaz, and two others, spread the pictures on the table and examined them closely. There were loud comments and differences of opinion and one of them went to fetch a magnifying glass. Rivelles had a beaker of Spanish wine to hold down the food and was resting comatosely when Diaz turned from the table.

"Unhappily, they are unknown to us as well. Did you speak with them or hear them talk at all?"

"No. I was with this unusual woman the entire time. I didn't even see them go by. Why?"

"Just a guess. Come look through the glass. At this picture here, the man looking into the camera with the frown."

"The photographer was pretty good. He set off the flash to draw their attention so he could photograph them full in the face as well as profile. I see him, ugly devil — what about it?"

"Look at his cheek, there. Could that be a scar?"

Rivelles looked close and grunted agreement. "Could be. Why do you ask?"

"Because he could be German. That could be a saber

scar. He's old enough to have gone to school in the twenties when saber scars were almost a requirement for graduation. They had these fencing clubs in the universities where they used sharpened sabers and masks that only covered part of their faces. Apparently the idea was to cut the other man up and get cut a bit yourself."

"That sounds sort of stupid. What did it prove?"

"That one had plenty of macho. We don't have a monopoly on machismo, you know."

"No, I'm sure we don't. Stupid ideas travel widely. But looking at him, at the others, they all could be German. But what does that prove."

"For the young ones, nothing. But the old ones, scars, the military, more than old enough to have fought in World War II . . . . "

"Nazis!"

Diaz nodded. "Very possibly. But how do we find out?"

"We have some in Argentina, but small fry for the most part. You have them in Paraguay, don't you?"

"A few. Military advisors they call them. But as far as we know small fry like yours. But — wait! — not too far down the river is . . . . "

"Uruguay! Where they all are! The concentration camp commanders, the SS bullies, the mass murderers. They are everywhere there, in the government and out, like filthy roaches."

"Just a few kilometers down the river," Diaz said quietly. "If what we think is true, we may have established the link we are looking for. But we must find out who these men are."

"The Tupamaros might know. Do you have contacts with them?"

Diaz shook his head. "Not any more. Most of them

were killed in 1974, then the movement collapsed. But I
can make enquiries. But that will take time. The *QE2*
has left Cape Town and will be in Australia in a few
days. We must find out at once who those men are.
Who would know?''

"The Jews!" Rivelles said. "The Israelis must know
who and where the escaped Nazis are. They could identify them. But how do we contact them? You can't just
walk into the Israeli Embassy and ask for help.''

"Why not?" Diaz said, putting the photographs back
into the envelope. "If we have information they want,
they'll talk to us. And we have nothing to lose by
trying.''

"It sounds a wild idea — but it might work. But for
God's sake call a taxi so I can take it too and go home
and fall into bed. And get ready to face my uncle in the
morning.''

"Did you tell him you were ill?''

"No, he wouldn't believe a simple story like that.
He's a most suspicious man — he would want a letter
from the doctor. I'm going to keep it simple. I'll tell him
I'm in love and went away with the woman to
Brighton.''

"Why should he believe that?''

"I'll tell him it's a married woman. He's so afraid of
scandal that he'll worry about that and not my taking
off the time. I can also use the idea again if there is an
emergency and I need the time.''

"I'll get the taxi. Someone look in the phone book
and get me the address of the Israeli Embassy.''

Diaz got out of the taxi on Bayswater Road and walked
down Kensington Palace Gardens. One of the last
private roads in London — with a guard at both ends.
Discreet, quiet, a good place for the Israelis. The Arab

terrorists wouldn't find it easy to get in here. A policeman at the front door looked him over closely as he
went in and a very solid young man stopped him as he
stepped inside.

"Would you mind opening your coat please, just a
formality." He frisked Diaz quickly and efficiently,
then moved away. "Thank you. Reception is right
through there, please."

Diaz had difficulties at once with the steely-eyed
young lady behind the desk.

"Just who would you like to see?"

"I'm not sure. Perhaps your military attaché."

"Would you state your business, please?"

"I would like to tell him."

"I'm afraid we don't have a military attaché. If you
would tell me what you wanted I am sure I could find
someone to help."

Diaz was aware of the people sitting around the room
behind him, could almost feel their ears twitch in his
direction. He was beginning to feel slightly foolish.

"I'll be happy to tell someone when they help me."

She gave him a withering look that would have
burned a hole in sheet steel. "The Vice-Consul is free
now. Perhaps he will be able to understand your problem."

"You're very kind," he said, trying to sound as
though he meant it. She was not convinced. Nor was the
Vice-Consul.

"Mr. Diaz, I can understand what you are saying, but
I'm afraid that I cannot help you." He was as young
and soberly determined as the girl.

"If I could talk to someone in your military — or
your intelligence service . . . . "

"Mr. Diaz! Do you realize what you are saying? We
are the official representatives of our nation in Great

Britain. A friendly country. You don't think for a moment we would have an intelligence service operating here?''

Diaz, knowing the ways of international politics, was certain that they had intelligence people here. As did every other embassy in London. But, of course, this man could not admit it. Diaz could be anyone as far as they were concerned; spy, provocateur, anything. He made his mind up. He dropped the envelope with the photographs on the desk then scribbled his phone number on it.

"You're right, of course, and I'm sorry to bother you. I have some photographs here that I was hoping your intelligence people might have been able to identify. We think at least one of them is a German. The photographs were taken just a day ago. No — please don't say anything. I'm going to leave these photographs with you and pick them up at this time tomorrow. Meanwhile, if anyone wants to get in touch with me I can be reached at this number. Thank you for your time.''

"I'm afraid that we cannot help you," the Vice-Consul said as Diaz left. "This is most irregular and there is nothing that we can do.''

Yet even as he said this he did not touch the photographs or insist that Diaz take them away with him.

Outside, the sky had clouded over and there was the smell of rain in the air. Diaz walked to the bus stop, taxis were a luxury they could not normally afford, and stood at the end of the queue. And by taking a bus he would know if he was being followed or not. Security becomes a reflex when most of your friends are dead.

It was an hour before he reached the apartment and let himself in.

"What have you been doing?" Alvaro asked.

"What do you mean?"

"The phone. It has been ringing steadily for the past thirty minutes. Always the same voice, asking for you. Hangs up at once when he finds out you're not here . . . ."

He was cut off by the strident ringing of the telephone bell.

"It must be him again. You take it this time," Alvaro said.

"Leandro Diaz speaking," he said into the phone.

"Are you the gentleman who recently left some photographs with your name and phone number on the envelope?" a man asked. A neutral, mid-Atlantic voice with no trace of a recognizable accent.

"I left the photographs, yes."

"Would you please tell me where they were taken . . . ."

"No. I want to meet someone and then I will be happy to supply all the details about the photographs. Understood?"

"I understand. Can you be in Oxford Street within the hour?"

"Yes."

"Go to the Centrepoint building at the corner of Charing Cross Road. You want the twenty-first floor, room 20135. Understood?"

"Of course . . . ."

The line went dead as he spoke the words and the dial tone hummed in his ear. Diaz dropped the receiver back into the cradle and smiled. "They're interested, very interested. Alvaro, get the cash box — and no complaints this time, if you please. With the car being repaired again I'll need a taxi to get there in time."

Outside the Centrepoint building, the splatter of the ornamental fountains was half drowned in the continuous roar of traffic. But once inside the doors the air-conditioned silence was broken only by the ubiquitous sound of muzak. The lulling music played in the elevator as well and all the way down the corridor of the twenty-first floor. The entrance to 20135 was suitably impressive with its two large mahogany doors. On one of them, conservatively spelled out in small bronze letters, was the legend *Cabot, Lowell, Smith & Greenstein.* Diaz went into an equally impressive waiting room where the receptionist, blonde and very attractive, gave him a toothpaste commercial smile.

"May I help you, sir?" she said in accents of purest Roedean.

"Yes, please. My name is Diaz and . . . ."

"Thank you, Mr. Diaz, you are expected. If you will go down the hallway to your right, it is the third doorway on the left, if you please."

The hall had subtle indirect lighting and soft carpeting underfoot. One wall was covered floor to ceiling with bookshelves and Diaz glanced at one of the titles on a ponderous tome as he passed. *Yearbook of Revisions In Riparian Rights — 1957* it read. A law firm, at least he knew that much now. He knocked lightly on the door, opened it and entered.

"Mr. Diaz," the man said, rising from behind the large desk. "I'm Hank Greenstein."

They sized each other up as they shook hands. Greenstein was in his mid-twenties, tanned, over six feet tall, with pale blue eyes peering through the dark-rimmed spectacles. He was either an athlete, or had been one so recently that the muscle had not yet turned to fat.

"Please take that chair," he said, pointing. "It's the most comfortable." He dropped into his own chair, resting comfortably on the end of his spine and hooking one foot over the corner of the desk. "Now, before we have our discussion, I want to tell you a few things. Firstly, this business is just what it looks like, a respectable international law firm with branches around the world. It has no connection whatsoever with the Israeli government. In fact if my father — or any of his partners — found out what I was doing they would skin me alive. I'm helping the Israelis in a strictly private capacity."

"You work for them?"

"Call me a volunteer. I'm a Jew, Mr. Diaz, and I feel quite strongly about the existence of the national homeland. So you see you can't blackmail me or threaten me or anything like that. I'm sorry to have to phrase it that way. But precautions must be taken."

"I am not an Arab, Mr. Greenstein."

"Neither were the Japanese who shot up Lod Airport. But don't get me wrong. I want to talk to you about these photographs." He tapped the envelope on his desk. "Perhaps we can help each other. Please try to understand that."

"I do. No offense taken. Do you know who the men are in the pictures?"

"Two of them have been identified. Where and when were the pictures taken?"

"In South Africa, less than forty-eight hours ago."

"Do you know where the men are now?" He spoke the question easily, but there was a sudden feeling of tension in the air.

"Yes. We know exactly where they are — and where they will be for the next few weeks."

Greenstein's feet crashed to the floor and he jumped up, fists clenched on the desk before him. "That's great, really great! We can't thank you enough, Mr. Diaz."

"Yes, you can. You can tell me who they are. We

thought they might be Germans.''

"You're right, at least about the two older men. The young ones haven't been identified yet. But the first two are Nazis, two very important sons of bitches who dropped from sight a few years ago. Look, please, can you tell me just who you are and how you got onto this?''

Diaz shrugged. "I suppose I will have to. Are you recording this conversation?''

"No. Are you?''

"No. But we both could be, couldn't we? I will just have to trust you, Mr. Greenstein. But please understand — what I am going to tell you affects the lives of a number of people. What do you know about Paraguay?''

"I'm sorry to say — very little. South America, near Brazil as I remember, stable government. That's about it.''

"Unhappily, as far as the rest of the world knows, that *is* it. We are the Cinderella of South America and enjoy the blessing of the tightest little dictatorship in that continent. Since the army took over in 1954 they have ruled with an iron hand. Our lifetime President, Alfredo Stroessner, does not believe in competition. In the 1960s international pressure, mostly North American, forced him, for the first time, to allow an opposition party in politics. But as soon as they began getting votes he put all of the leaders in jail. He has winning ways, our President. He declared a state of emergency and repressed all individual rights until the emergency was over. Of course the emergency only lasted three months. Not too bad. But at the end of the emergency period he declared another emergency and then another — and this has been going on since 1954.''

"It doesn't sound a happy place.''

"It isn't. But why should the world care about this little land-locked country of a few million people? The military are very efficient in their security — they should be, since they were trained by escaped Nazis and SS guards who fled there after the war. So all of the opposition is either dead, in jail — or has fled the country. There are over six hundred thousand of us living in exile, well over a fifth of the population."

"These photos you gave me — are they of Paraguayan Nazis?"

"No, we are sure of that. Most of our Nazis are gone now. Your CIA has taken over the training in their place and has introduced sophisticated tortures such as psychological deprivement and mind-distorting drugs. . . ."

"Is that true?" Greenstein asked angrily, "Or are you just parroting the old anti-American line?"

Diaz spread his hands wide. "I have nothing against your country, please understand that. I am just speaking the truth. It was sources in America who revealed the CIA involvement."

"I'm sorry."

"Please don't be. We are not here to trade insults but to uncover some facts — perhaps to our mutual satisfaction. I personally am a friend of your country. I am a businessman, or rather I was until I went into politics. I ran for the state election as a member of the PLR, the *Partido Liberal Radical.* The party is quite conservative, I assure you. My mistake was in winning the election — so I, of course, went to jail. I eventually managed to make my way here to London where I am a member of a group of Paraguayans in exile. We do very little, really. Aid other refugees, write letters of protest to the newspapers. For the most part we just wait for that wonderful day that may come when we can return to our country. We are well known among the expatriates, so people bring us information. Which brings my long story up to the present. Something is stirring in official circles in Paraguay, something big — but we don't know what. Plenty of coming and going and troop movements. We recently connected all of this activity to a cruise of the *QE2* and to certain passenger accommodation aboard this ship. The two best suites. It appears that these suites were empty until a few days ago, when five men boarded the ship in Cape Town . . . . "

The five in these photographs!"

"Precisely. So now you know as much as we do. We have reached a dead end. Except that we had some slight reason to suspect that at least one of the men was a German. Which is why we approached the Israelis. Hoping they might be able to make the identification that we could not."

"They've been identified all right." Hank Greenstein slid the photographs out onto the desk and pointed to the man with the scar on his face.

"This is Colonel Manfred Hartig, former supervisor of the Polish extermination camps. He disappeared right after the war — the Poles tried him *in absentia* and he has a death sentence hanging over his head. He surfaced for a while in Argentina, but vanished completely about ten years ago. At the same time as this one, in the other photograph. Karl-Heinz Eitmann. Eitmann was a great organizer, the liaison man between the camps and the factories. He saw to it that there was a steady flow of slave labor at all times."

"Two nice guys."

"Yes. Aren't they. But the best is yet to come. There is no hard evidence, but it is pretty certain that there is a central committee of escaped Nazis who handle large sums of money. The Germans are a very organized people. Even when they become mass murderers they maintain their love of routine. And remember, immense sums were looted from the occupied countries. Millions, perhaps billions of dollars. You don't keep money like that buried in your back yard. Of course, a lot of them do, individuals who escaped with a bundle of their own. But we're talking about the big money now. And these two, Hartig and Eitmann, are reported to be right at the top of the money circle. In fact it is rumored that they are next in the pecking order right under the infamous Dr. Joachim Wielgus himself.''

"Wielgus? I don't think I know the name."

"Very few people do. Wielgus was the right-hand man of Albrecht Spier, the so-called economic genius who arranged the financing of the Third Reich. In the beginning this was easy enough to do since the big corporations like Krupp were interested only in maximizing their profits. They had no trouble looking the other way when slave labor was needed to keep the factories operational. But as the war went on, more and more funds were needed as the bombing raids knocked out German production. That is where the good Herr Doktor Wielgus came into the picture. He was the one who took care of the nasty part of the financing. Arranging for the gold teeth to be knocked out of the corpses' heads in the concentration camps, shaving these heads as well for the hair for mattress-stuffing, actually making soap from human fat — and all of this always for a good profit.''

"That's . . . disgusting," Diaz said. "I had no idea that people could sink that low. In my country torture and murder are commonplace but this . . . this is commercialization of evil."

"People forget," Hank said, the lines of his face set into a pattern of dark memory. "Or they are too young,

born after the war. It is just part of history to them, like
Ghenghis Khan and Napoleon. But it's not that, not yet.
People are still alive today with numbers on their arms
and endless dreams of those concentration camps. And
millions are dead who might be alive if the Germans had
not been so determined to found their thousand-year
Reich. Your South American dictators are very good at
torture and execution but thank God they'll never be
able to match the scale of the Nazis.''

There was just silence between them for a moment
before Diaz spoke.

"Tell me about the Nazis who still survive."

"As I said, the Germans are a notoriously organized
race,'' Hank said, coldly and grimly, trying to keep the
emotion out of his voice. "But all of these things are a
matter of public record. It all came out during the war
trials. But, of course, by that time Wielgus had
vanished. He was always a very invisible man. We have
only one picture of him, and that is very old. Since he
worked all over the map it has taken years to piece
together his operation. It turns out to be the biggest
financial one of all to take place during the decay of the
Third Reich. When the handwriting was clear on the
wall, some of the top people, like Goering, began to
look for ways to get away with their loot. Wielgus was
the man who arranged it for them. Swiss banks, sale of
art treasures, transport of bullion, Wielgus did it all.
Which is why there is still such a big interest in the man.
The war is long over, many of the war criminals dead of
old age and terminal syphilis. But the stolen money is
still out there. The trail has been followed for a number
of years, and all of the leads seem to come back to
Wielgus sooner or later. Which explains the present
interest in Hartig and Eitmann. They must be followed,
watched . . . . ''

THE QE2 IS MISSING

"In the hopes that they lead you to the big fish?"

"Exactly so."

"But in addition to maybe leading you to Wielgus, these men must be of interest in their own right. There is the possibility that they may be transferring funds?"

"It's a good possibility. I know that certain people are very interested in these men. Do you know anything about Israeli intelligence?"

"Nothing."

"Well, what I am going to tell you is no secret, but a matter of public record. The organization called Aman is basically a data-gathering group, they sort of coordinate all intelligence information no matter where it comes from. This is utilized by Shin Beth, primarily a counter-espionage organization, as well as the Mossad, the major and most important intelligence group of them all. The people from Aman were the ones who identified these two rotten apples — though they haven't dug out anything about the three others yet. No sooner had this happened than the Mossad stepped in. They won't say why they are interested, but we can make an educated guess. Something big is in the works. What and where I personally don't know."

Diaz smiled wryly. "You'll pardon my saying so, Mr. Greenstein, but if you personally don't know — then who does? You're the one who called me in here in such a great hurry . . . . "

"On the insistence of others. I have just mentioned the names of a few organizations to you. Some of them are more than very interested in these Nazis. I have been pressured to obtain information from you."

"Well, now you have it."

Hank Greenstein rubbed his jaw and sighed. "I have it — but that doesn't mean I can make any sense out of it. A South American dictator, a pair of aging Nazis who board a British ship in South Africa . . . . ''

"And an American Jewish lawyer along with a refugee Paraguayan politician, that really makes sense of the whole thing."

"What a mish-mash!" Hank Greenstein started to laugh. Leandro Diaz had to smile himself.

"I'm afraid I never learned that word in my English studies, Mr. Greenstein."

"Hank, if you please. And you didn't learn it because it's not English but Yiddish. It means something like a big mix-up, a screwed up situation of some kind."

"It certainly is all of that. We will just have to get more information, that is the long and short of it. I just wish we knew now where the infamous Major José de Laiglesia is. He was the one who booked the tickets on the *QE2*. He's the one who would have some answers to these questions that are puzzling us so."

"The word will be sent to my people to look out for him. We'll let you know if we find him."

"Please do that — and we'll do the same in return. Call me at this time tomorrow and we'll arrange another meeting, set up some sort of constant liaison."

"That is very good, thank you. Until tomorrow then. I'll let myself out."

They shook hands and Diaz left. Hank waited a moment after he had gone, then went to the door and opened it a crack to look out. The hall was empty. He closed and locked the door then dropped back into his chair, resting comfortably again on the end of his spine.

"OK," he said. "He's gone."

The connecting door to the next office opened and a thin, dark-skinned man with black hair and a hawk-like nose came in. He looked very much like an Arab, in fact he spoke such perfect Arabic that he had passed as an Arab many times. The name most people knew him by was Uzi Drezner. There was no reason to suppose that it was any more his real name than the many others he used. Even though he kept the lowest of profiles, made sure that the newspapers did not know of him or publish his photograph, his reputation was nevertheless known in certain circles. He worked very closely with Simon Wiesenthal in Vienna and was reputed to have master-minded the Eichmann kidnapping. His most recent suc-cess was in tracking Oberstsurmbannfuehrer Rauff to Punta Arenas in Chile. Rauff, who was responsible for the murder of 100,000 people had been a prime tar-get for years. His presence here, in Hank's office, was some measure of the importance attached to the photo-graphs.

"What do you think about this fellow Diaz?" Hank asked.

"He's all right. We know about his group, and have even had some contact with their members about Nazis in Paraguay. That was some years back, but I imagine we can re-open contacts, make investigations. I'm sure he is everything that he says he is — and we'll take that as read until we learn differently."

"Then what do we do next?"

"At this point we — meaning my organization — do our best to get more information about the people involved in this affair. That can be time consuming so we must start at once. We have no official status, so we must work through friends in different departments."

"What do you mean "no official status"? Everyone I have talked to speaks very highly of the work you are doing."

"That's it, they speak. But you won't see anything on paper. Nor will you even hear mentioned the name of the organization."

Hank chewed his cheek for a moment as he tried to

recall everything he had been told. In the end he nodded.

"You're right, people told me to see Uzi, he would
take care of it, his organization knows how to take care
of these people. But, yes — no names were ever mentioned."

"It has to be that way. My group is based in Vienna
and we have private sources of funds. We have no legal
standing any place in the world, and certainly no official
connection with the Israeli government. This is only because everything we do is completely illegal."

"That's a very good reason," Hank said.

"It is. Though I shouldn't say everything. Our
records section exchanges information continually with
Aman, since the simple collection of intelligence is not a
crime. Aman in turn exchanges information with other
governments. It's what we do with the information that
isn't exactly kosher."

"And that is . . . ?"

"We find Nazis. We see that they are returned to
Europe — or Israel — to stand trial. Many times we
must extract them from countries where they have a
legal status as citizens. We don't like doing this. And we
only do it when there is absolutely no doubt that the
person in question is a war criminal — and usually a
convicted war criminal. You might say that we are a
means of last resort. When all else has failed we step in.
Unofficially and usually quite illegally. To see to the
administration of justice that must cross international
boundaries."

"I'm sorry you told me this."

"I didn't. You just thought you heard it. You are
going to quite legally help in obtaining information
about some very wanted war criminals."

"What do you mean that I am going to help? What

more can I do?''

''You can act while we investigate. We cannot wait for more results before we move. There's not time enough. It's important to get someone aboard the *QE2* at once. Would you like a nice sea voyage,

''Don't say it! I can't, not now, my fiancée would kill me if we postponed the wedding again! It's been hard enough to arrange in any case.''

Uzi raised his hands in surrender and smiled. ''Wait — don't panic. I didn't say instantly. And you may not have to go. It's still just a maybe. I'll let you know as soon as we see about bookings on the *QE2*. That's one job. Another that I'm going to start at the same time is a tracer on Major de Laiglesia. He is at the heart of this affair and his whereabouts are surely related to it. Find him and we may find the answer to this mystery.''

7

Major José de Laiglesia looked out of the window of the Lear jet and covered a yawn with his fist. The plane tilted up on one wing as it turned, presenting him with a magnificent view of the lush green jungle, set against a starkly beautiful range of mountains in the background. The Major was totally indifferent to the view, was scarcely aware that it was there, and his drowsy thoughts were completely occupied with drink. Rum. Should he have another one? Would it wake him up or put him to sleep? He could not be sure. His deep cogitations were interrupted when the girl in the seat before him turned around to speak.

"That river down there, the wide one, do you know its name?"

The Major squinted at the river and the mountains, trying to get his bearings. "It is the Alto Paraná, I think. It marks the border between Paraguay and Argentina."

"Then we are almost there?"

"Almost. We'll be landing at Asunción soon. You have been there before?"

"Never. What's it like?"

"Very nice. I'm sure you will enjoy your visit."

"This is a business trip. I'm not here for pleasure," she said coldly and turned back in her seat.

You are a cold bitch, Aurelia Maria Hortiguela, the Major thought to himself. A strange one to be involved in this kind of business. Somewhere in her late thirties, he thought, still young enough to be good-looking, in a big-bosomed, wide-hipped way. Very attractive in the particularly Latin manner; with a bottom like two great swelling melons. Gorgeous! But a frigid and acid bitch. Inside that magnificent frame lurked the mind of a horrid little man, a bookkeeper or a tax inspector. It was very annoying. So annoying that he decided on the drink after all. The thought of the sweet burn of the hundred proof rum sent a quick rush of saliva to his mouth. He unbuckled and went to the bar in the rear of the plane. To get there he had to pass the fat Czech. A thoroughly repulsive one, this. He had the armrest up and just about filled both seats. He turned his cold black eyes on the Major as he came by.

"Can I get you a drink of some kind, Mr. Chvosta?" de Laiglesia asked in English. If Libor Chvosta spoke Spanish he had kept it a good secret so far.

"Yes. Champagne." His voice was small and high-pitched, strange for a man of his bulk. Like that of a eunuch. Major de Laiglesia doubted, though, if he was one. There was something too frightening about him, repellant. He was in the right business, this one.

The Major took a bottle of Veuve-Cliquet 1973 from the refrigerator and found a tulip glass in the cabinet. He put it on the silver tray, along with the bottle, then filled a tall glass with ice cubes. The fat Czech would just have to wait a few minutes more. He poured rum over the cubes, swished it about for a moment, then drank deep. It was good, very, very good.

With careful coordinated pressure of both his thumbs below the cork he levered it out of the bottle of champagne with a satisfactory bang, pouring the overflow into the glass without losing a drop. Chvosta took the glass with a grunt that could have meant anything, then drained it in a gulp. *Pig,* the Major thought, as he carefully refilled it for him. The door to the flight deck opened and the copilot poked his head through.

"We're about three minutes out, Major," he said. "Would you please look at the belts?"

The Major nodded and drained the glass, then put it back in the rack and latched the cabinet. All three of the plainclothes guards had their belt secure, as did the girl. Chvosta had no waist, so he couldn't get a belt around it, but he had the belt from one seat through the buckle of the other, and this was locked across his legs. Good enough. The Major threw away the now empty bottle of champagne and belted himself into his own seat. Underneath him he could hear the landing gear grinding down and locking into position. Then the runway was flashing past and they were on the ground.

Once the pilot had turned off into the taxiway he gunned his engines again and bumped on past the terminal buildings towards the hangars beyond. This was not going to be a public arrival. The small jet rolled towards the gaping entrance of a large hangar, big enough to service a 707 but now empty. Into the hangar the jet went and the engines whined down to silence. Behind them the great doors were trundled shut and the passengers blinked into the darkness until the hangar lights came on. The plane's door opened and an Air Force Colonel in full uniform looked in and saluted.

"Mr. Chvosta, Señorita Hortiguela, welcome to Paraguay. If you will come with me, please, the car is just outside."

A wave of humid, hot air came in with him and the Major knew that he was home.

The Colonel led the way to the rear of the hangar and opened the small door there; bright sunlight burned in. Aurelia Hortiguela dug into her large purse and took

out a pair of sunglasses and put them on. Then turned
to the Major and pointed back to the plane. "Our
baggage and the cases of samples — what of them?"

"They are being unloaded right now and will go with
us to the Presidential Palace."

"You are not going to force us to stand around in this
heat, are you?"

"Of course not. Through here, if you please, the
limousine is air conditioned. It will only take a few
minutes."

They went through the door into the middle of a
military camp. Fully armed combat troops were on all
sides, guns at the ready. Facing outwards. There were
jeeps with pillar-mounted calibre 50's, B.A.R. and Bren
gunners, even guards on the hangar roof above them.
An immensely long, black Cadillac with dark windows
waited with its rear door open, flanked by four armored
cars and a six-by-six army truck.

"Your security seems tight," Chvosta said.

"Thank you," the Colonel replied. "We wish to
ensure the comfort of our guests. You will be more
comfortable in the car, if you please."

Chvosta went first, grunting and wheezing as he
pulled his bulk into the back seat. The Colonel and the
girl followed and de Laiglesia closed the door after
them, then went back to supervise the unloading. The
sweat was already beginning to soak into his clothes.

"Drop that and I will shoot you," he called out
angrily to the soldier who was pulling a heavy crate
from the plane. The man stopped and looked down,
fearfully, because it was not just an idle threat. The
Major was well known for his short temper and ready
gun. He would shoot his own men as easily as he would
any Red revolutionary. The soldier stood, shivering,
with the crate resting on the doorsill, until another

soldier hurried to help him.

One by one the heavy sealed crates were removed from the jet and loaded into the truck. The two suitcases were put in on top of them and the Sergeant in charge of the squad saluted de Laiglesia.

"All loaded, Major. Will you signal the convoy?"

"Yes. Get your men into the truck."

Motorcycle outriders with screaming sirens led the way, forcing the traffic to the sides of the road. Police were stationed at every crossroad to stop cars from entering, coming to attention and saluting as the convoy tore past. They did a steady sixty miles an hour down the highway and into Asunción, slowing only to maneuver around the sharp turns in the narrow streets. Aurelia looked out of the window at the crowded filthy tenements that flashed past, but said nothing. Chvosta opened the bar set into the back of the seat just before him and poured for himself a large glass of water from the cut glass decanter. Almost as an afterthought he poured a half glass of malt Scotch and drained it as easily as he had the water. The short walk in the sun had sent the perspiration bursting from his pores and even de Laiglesia, never the most sensitive of men, twitched his nostrils at the rank odor.

The convoy tore on through the baking, sun-drenched and filthy streets. Past a park filled with dead trees, then up a drive they raced and through the ornate italianate iron gates of the National Palace, braking to stop before the steps at the entrance. The guard outside did not open the car doors until the heavy gates had slammed shut and one of the armored cars had parked across the entrance.

The Colonel slowly led the way up the impressive marble steps, into the building and down the length of the great hall. He stopped before the high doors there, guarded by two armed soldiers standing stiffly at attention.

"Are you ready to go in?" he asked.

"Of course," Chvosta gasped, patting the perspiration from his face with a handkerchief. "I have not come this far to be left standing in the corridor. Let's get it over with."

"This is a most important and serious moment. . . ."

"Only to you," Aurelia broke in. "For us it is a simple business transaction. So get on with it."

The Colonel turned away to conceal his anger while Major de Laiglesia made every effort to keep a straight face. He snapped his fingers at the soldiers. "Open up," he ordered.

They passed through the doorway into the grand ballroom, an immensely long and ornate room bright with candelabra and hung with impressively bad paintings. At the far end, a group of uniformed men stood talking. One of them turned when they entered, a pudgy, pale-skinned man with numerous ribbons and decorations on his uniform. He smiled and stepped forward.

"You are highly honored," de Laiglesia whispered. "His Excellency is coming forward in person to greet you."

Walking heavily, President General Alfredo Stroessner came over to meet them. He smiled warmly. Yet, despite his full-dress uniform, the gold braid, the self-centered assurance, he looked like a bald-headed and pudgy son of a Bavarian immigrant. Which, of course, he was.

He was also absolute dictator of the country, with the power of life or death over his four million subjects. He seemed quite cheerful as he stepped forward to shake hands. He could afford to be.

"Señor Chvosta, Señorita Hortiguela, bienvenidos al Paraguay," he said.

"He welcomes us to the country," Aurelia translated for her partner. Chvosta nodded but did not bother to grunt this time. He was sweating even more now after climbing the stairs to the palace.

After the few words of welcome, Stroessner turned to the uniformed group of men who were standing behind him and beckoned a gray-haired naval officer forward. His hair was cropped short, his dark skin marked by a fine network of wrinkles. His left arm was missing and the uniform sleeve turned up and secured at the shoulder.

"This is Admiral Marquez of the Uruguayan Navy," Stroessner said. "Regretably, Dr. Mendez was not able to attend, but was kind enough to send the Admiral in his stead."

They all nodded seriously as though no one knew that the ancient lawyer Mendez was only a figurehead for the ruling junta of admirals and generals. After a recent power struggle in Uruguay, Marquez had emerged on top, just as much a ruler in that country as Stroessner was in this one.

This display of absolute power appeared to make very little impression on Libor Chvosta, as though he spent every day of the week in the company of the rulers of two sovereign countries. He mopped at his wet forehead and neck with his large bandanna kerchief, then spoke.

"If we're all here now we can get down to business," he said, with all the grace and charm of a butcher in an abattoir. "If the cases have been opened I'll show you what you are going to get."

"They are ready in the other room," Major de Laiglesia said to him, leaning forward and speaking in a low voice as Aurelia translated for the others what

Chvosta had said.

"Take us there," Chvosta ordered.

Major de Laiglesia whispered a few words in the Air Force Colonel's ear and the Colonel nodded. There were some quick discussions of protocol among the uniformed aides, eventually resolved when Stroessner and Admiral Marquez, bowing politely to each other, decided to lead the way from the room together. The guards at the end of the hall opened the large double doors and stepped back.

The spacious chamber beyond had been specially prepared for the occasion. All of the floor-to-ceiling windows had been sealed with steel plates, concealed now behind floor-length drapes. A long, marble-topped table, supported on ornate gold legs, ran the length of the room. Two armchairs were placed together facing the center of the table. On the other side, away from the chairs, were the crates that had been brought from the jet. All of the metal bands that had sealed them had been cut and their tops had been levered open. Chvosta went to examine the crates as Stroessner and Marquez sat down on the chairs; their staffs arranging themselves in expectant rows behind them. Aurelia stationed herself at the end of the table and took a spiral-bound notebook from her bag. Her sunglasses had been replaced by reading glasses; she turned the pages of the notebook and pursed her lips with concentration. There was a sense of excitement, of tension in the air as Chvosta rose from his examination and dusted off his hands. He began to speak, slowly and clearly in English, pausing often so Aurelia could translate into Spanish.

"What we have here are representative sample cases taken from the shipment. In some cases we have substituted different brands or slightly different items from those selected by you in your original order. You must remember that we are not off-the-shelf suppliers, but are middlemen. We find the product wanted from those willing to sell. However, circumstances sometimes change between the placing of the original order and the time of shipment. But Global Traders has a deserved reputation for substituting equal or better items for those originally chosen. First item on the list.''

Aurelia put her finger under the entry.

''Anti-personnel concussion grenade. Weight five hundred and eighty-six grams. A three-point-five second fuse. Blast area of maximum concentration is six meters . . . . ''

As she spoke, Chvosta took a black, ridged-metal grenade from the crate at his feet. When he raised it in his hand, the aides stirred, some of them resting their hands on their revolvers. But the arms salesman was interested in profit, not assassination. After holding the grenade up for identification, he placed it on the table-top for examination by the two military dictators. They found it highly fascinating and leaned forward together to look at it more closely; like two theological students bending over a Bible.

Aurelia Hortiguela's voice droned on; rate of fire, caliber of ammunition, land-mine destruction area, force of impact, auxiliary bayonet fittings; as item after lethal item was placed on the table.

Armalite rifles, CN gas grenades, Russian machine guns, American sub-machine guns, belts of ammunition, anti-personnel mines. One after another they were laid gently onto the cool marble surface, until the table became a blue-black and olive drab display of death and destruction.

Stroessner and the Admiral nodded approvingly at the more interestingly lethal items and behind them the aides buzzed with low-voiced conversation as they went through their matching lists. When the last sample had been brought out, Chvosta wiped the oil and dust from his hands and threw the soiled kerchief into the nearest crate.

"Questions?" he asked.

After a moment's hesitation one of the aides spoke up.

"The ammunition substitution for the sub-machine guns. It is of different manufacture . . . ."

Chvosta cut him off with a sharp chop of his hand. "It is of the correct caliber and superior to that originally ordered. We discovered that the original had been in store for over two years and could not give guaranteed nonstoppage as specified. You may test-fire the ammunition yourself, there is enough here for that. Since the substitution was made after the order was placed we are absorbing the twenty percent greater price of the new bullets. Next question."

"The armored troop carriers and light tanks," Stroessner said. "They are satisfactory?"

"Perfectly so. Low mileage, completely reconditioned, with crated spares for at least a year's use. Which brings us to the next step in the negotiations. We have fulfilled our part of the agreement to date. With a great deal of financial sacrifice on Global Traders' part. . . ."

"You have millions of dollars," Admiral Marquez broke in angrily. "Three and a half million at least in the last reckoning. That is a great deal of money."

Chvosta did not wait for Aurelia's translation before he answered; his knowledge of Spanish was undoubtedly greater than he cared to admit. "That is not a great deal of money in the international arms trade, Admiral. In fact it is a very small and inconsiderable amount of money. Global Traders has paid out far more than that to obtain the merchandise that your countries need. Had you not been the heads of government of two sovereign powers we would never have extended ourselves as far as we have. The time has now come to finalize all of our arrangements.''

His voice was cold, his tone almost insulting. Admiral Marquez's neck grew red and he shook himself so that the empty arm of his jacket flapped back and forth. Stroessner slammed both his clenched fists down on the table.

''Your impudence must cease at once, Chvosta. When you heard that our countries were seeking arms for mutual defense it was you who approached us with the arrangement.''

If Chvosta was angry or fearful he did not show it. His voice remained calm and cold.

''This is not the time for insults,'' he said. ''In the arms business we are forced to be realists. Neither Uruguay nor Paraguay has anything to fear from attack from outside their borders. You both have what might be called ''internal problems.'' Groups within your countries that are working to overthrow your governments . . . .''

''With communist aid from without!'' the Admiral said warmly.

''Perhaps true, but unimportant. I will be candid and what I say is all a matter of public record. The UNO, Amnesty International and other groups have condemned certain of your practices. . . .''

''Communist propaganda!''

Chvosta stared coldly and quietly at the Admiral until he had grumbled into silence, then went on.

''This international disapproval has dried up the normal sources of arms supply for your countries. It was because of this situation that I approached you with our offer. We suggested that your countries combine for your mutual aid. You each have something unique to offer. Paraguay has the funds needed for the purchase. But it is a land-locked country. Because of international flight controls their needed weapons cannot be supplied by air. Uruguay has the deepwater port of Montevideo that could receive the seaborne shipment. Trans-shipment by air will then be possible between your two countries. This was my proposal — the one that your countries accepted. Token funds were exchanged. We are now prepared to make delivery. Are you now prepared to pay the balance of approximately two hundred and fifty million dollars?''

"Where is the shipment?" Stroessner asked.

"At sea as agreed. Do you have the diamonds?"

"They will be available shortly. Where is your expert?"

"Arriving by commercial airliner sometime today from Holland. Therefore we have fulfilled our part of the bargain. The weapons are now at sea in a freighter, somewhere in the Pacific off the South American coast as you directed. The requested samples are here . . . . ''

"They havn't been tested yet," the Admiral broke in. Chvosta curled his thick lips in disgust and waved this comment aside as being completely irrelevant.

". . . the samples are here and our diamond man is arriving. What arrangements have you made for payment and delivery?"

"These are delicate matters to handle," Stroessner said, steepling his fingers and nodding sagely.

"I beg to differ, Mr. President. These matters are not delicate — but they are dangerous. Some people do not like to pay, others do not like to deliver. Both of these dangers must be avoided. To put it at its simplest, President, Admiral, we trust you just as much as you trust us. Now what arrangements have been made?"

"Admiral, will you join me for some wine?" Stroessner said pushing back his chair and standing. Aides rushed to pull the Admiral's chair out for him and the two dictators, followed by their entourage, left without saying another word to the arms dealer.

"The insulting bastards!" Aurelia said, throwing her notebook onto the table among the weapons of destruction. Chvosta was smiling coldly at the retreating backs of the military.

"I cannot be insulted," he said. "Only paid. And they need this shipment. You take things too personally."

Only one man remained behind; Major de Laiglesia.

"I have been involved in all of the negotiations needed to make the exchange," he said. "Let me explain — but not here. I have been three days without sleep arranging your visit and the shipping of the crates. Let us find a place to sit down and have some drinks and I will tell you what has been done."

"Have some food there, too," Chvosta said. "But I will need to know at once. This is a very costly business and if it is protracted any longer the price will have to go up."

"Please, Mr. Chvosta, don't be concerned. I have all the details with me. And you might even enjoy part of it."

"What do you mean?" he asked suspiciously.

"I mean you are going to enjoy a luxury cruise on the *QE2*. Now, if you will come this way."

Sergeant Pradera looked on disgustedly as the guard outside the Presidential Palace was changed. These were a slovenly, disorganized rabble. And these were the élite guard! Boots that needed polishing, undressed lines —

and haircuts all around would be a good idea too. For the officers as well, since they were as big a shower as the men.

Tall, rock solid, dark skinned and grizzle haired, the Sergeant stood just inside the gates and scowled with obvious venom at the troops as they marched by. One week, that's all he would need to get them in hand. One week that they would never forget if they lived to be a hundred. These men were a disgrace to the army. His glare burned into them as they passed and even the officers kept their eyes strictly to the front so that they would not intercept that deadly gaze. Everyone in the army knew Sergeant Pradera. Not one of them was happy in his presence.

The Sergeant was old Army. He must be older than some of the Generals but no one dared ask him his age or check on it in the records. The Sergeant would be in the Army until the day he died. If he ever did. Stories were told about that as well. Most soldiers breathed easier these days since he had been kicked upstairs. Now he was involved with security at the Palace and only those soldiers under his direct command could feel the touch of his wrath. He had organized the convoy from the airport that morning — no matter what officer claimed credit for it. In the Paraguayan Army there were three ways of getting things done; the right way, the wrong way — and Sergeant Pradera's way.

The Sergeant waited until the Guard had been changed, his cold gaze following them every step of the way, until the guardhouse door had slammed and they were safely out of his sight. The new Guard straightened their backs more fiercely as they stood at attention at their posts and prayed to the Virgin and St. Tomaso, Patron Saint of Paraguay, that his basilisk eye would not fall upon them. All those in sight of the square breathed more easily when he had stamped by and let himself into the storehouse on the west side.

Sergeant Pradera climbed the stairs as he did everything else — with grim certainty and heavy tread. If anyone else had been in the building they would have fled at the sound of his advance. But he was alone here, he knew that. He should know it, since he was the one who arranged the work rosters and saw to it that very few people had business in this building, and then only when he was present. Many important Army files were stored here. Security was important. Very important.

The Sergeant was a firm believer in security at all times, belt and braces, read the orders back so often that they were memorized. No one should have been on this floor since the Sergeant had last visited it the night before. A thin black thread across the staircase at ankle level, invisible in the badly lit stairwell, was still intact. So were two others he had placed in equally strategic positions. The Sergeant had expected nothing less; he still took the precaution. He stamped to the end of the hall, to the last door, and unlocked it. Opened all four of the locks that had been set into the frame, on both sides and top and bottom. Belt and suspenders. He locked them all behind him and went on into the next room that faced out onto the Palace Square. A good deal of electronic equipment was set up against the far wall. He looked at it and nodded stern approval.

The most important item was the laser microphone set up by the window. While the window itself had been left open the wooden, slatted blinds outside were closed. One of the slats was broken and hanging down, unhappily not the only one in disrepair in the Palace. However, this one left a gap through which the laser was pointed. The Sergeant sighted along it as he always did, and as always it was set just right. Aimed across the square at the window of the sealed conference room.

The Sergeant himself had supervised the securing of the steel sheets inside these windows, so the job had been done well. But someone had broken one of the windows during the installation. Since the Sergeant had not ordered the soldiers to replace the broken pane nothing had, of course, been done. So now the laser microphone pointed through the broken slat, its invisible beam of coherent light flashed across the Square and through the broken window to strike the steel sheet inside.

The Sergeant was still amazed at these miracle machines that he had been supplied with. He had been told the laser light bounced back and was received by the same instrument. That any voices in the room caused the metal sheet to vibrate, and that these vibrations were picked up by the ray and sent back to the machines in this room. He marvelled at them and had not the slightest idea of how they worked. Nor did he care — as long as they worked. He had set them up just as he had been directed and they worked just as he had been told they would. Good.

He seated himself in the chair before the machines and ran back the tape. Leave it on all the time, they had told him. It is voice operated. When someone speaks in the room the words will be recorded. This in itself seemed a small miracle of human ingenuity. But he did not distrust it. He re-ran the tape to the spot he had marked the previous day and donned the earphones. After all of the elaborate preparations today he was very curious to hear what had been said in the room.

The tape ran and he listened. And while he listened his eyes widened slightly, which any soldier in the Army would have recognized as being the same as a cry of surprise from a normal human being. But, of course, no one ever thought of Sergeant Pradera as being a normal human being; he was all Army, through and through.

Therefore, no one in command had ever stopped to consider that the Sergeant was related to human beings, even if he was not one himself. He had never married, other than to the Army, and had no relations that anyone knew of.

But he had a sister who had married and moved to a remote cattle ranch in the north, in the remote province of Amambay. One Christmas, when he had some leave and was tired of the barracks and men's voices and curses, he had decided to visit her. With presents for the children, she must have had children by this time, he went to see her and her family.

He had returned in the new year without the presents and in his usual humor. Even visiting his only living relation had seemed to make no difference to the Sergeant's normal irascible manner.

Though quite the opposite was true. The Sergeant had returned a very different man.

At first, because of his uniform, no one in the little village would talk to him. But the Sergeant had great experience in convincing people they should pour out their hearts to him and an unfortunate man, alone at night, had no reason to doubt the Sergeant's experience. It was in this manner that the Sergeant had heard about the fact that his sister's husband had joined the farmworkers' union and had even helped to organize it, then had talked to others to convince them that they should join the union as well.

The cavalry had come at night. The house had burned to the ground. His sister, her husband, six children and all their livestock had been found in the ruins.

This was the time when the Sergeant, who had never been a political man, began to think about the politics of his country. He had been aware for many years that they were not of the best. There were special army units that were less than kind to elements out of favor with the government. Terrorist groups they were called, or communists. The Sergeant had nothing to do with these units so he did not bother to think about them. But their activities had suddenly become a concern to him. It was easy enough for him to obtain information, and what he discovered was not very nice at all. That was when he began to think about this sister — and about himself.

His thinking had brought him to his room at this time with the roll of tape that he held in his hand. He made a copy of this large reel-to-reel tape on a small cassette, then played the cassette back to be sure it was a good copy. It was. With the cassette in his pocket, he put a fresh roll of tape on the machine, made sure that the instruments were all functioning, and locked himself out of the building as carefully as he had let himself in.

The *zócalo,* the plaza complete with bandstand and promenaders out for the evening air, was a short walk away. The few soldiers he met saluted him crisply as they passed; those who saw him coming in time avoided him completely. The sun had set and there was a slight cooling touch in the breeze now. The Sergeant bought an evening newspaper and sat on a bench under a light in the *zócalo* to read it. One nervous shoeshine boy, egged on by his friends, made so bold as to approach the Sergeant to see if his boots needed a polish. A single brief glare across the top of the paper sent the boy fleeing for his life.

After the Sergeant had finished the football news he glanced down at his boots. Perhaps there were a few flecks of dust on their mirrored surface; it had been a dry day. He looked around and spotted a boy with a shoebox hung from his shoulder on a length of ragged cord. He pointed at the boy and snapped his fingers. The lad scurried over and went feverishly to work while the Sergeant read his paper. The boy had finished minutes before the Sergeant noticed it. Then he glanced down at his boots and dug a coin out of his pocket and passed it to the boy. Who ran quickly away.

It was impossible in the darkness for anyone to see that the Sergeant had passed on the cassette along with the coin.

8

"You know, Hank, I would feel a lot better about this whole business if you would only tell me exactly what is going on," Frances said. She lay back in the large double bed, the covers drawn up to her chin, a piece of buttered toast held daintily in her long-nailed fingers.

Hank Greenstein, wearing only a thin bathrobe, stood at the window watching the rain course down the pane; he shivered.

"Well, it's a matter of utmost urgency, darling, or we wouldn't be here. Don't forget that our firm is one of the largest groups of international lawyers — solicitors — in the world. And I'm about the most junior member. So when they say be international, why, I'm the one that is sent."

"Two days before our wedding day?" Frances's eyebrows rose in wonderment at the thought. "And our families finally agreeing on a big wedding, all the arrangements made. Then this. On a plane at a moment's notice and halfway around the world to Australia. I'm still not sure how you convinced my father that it was all right — or for that matter how you convinced me. You're not a lawyer, Hank Greenstein, you're a con artist." She bit viciously at the toast and Hank turned to admire her.

Frances was something to look at by anyone's standards. Coppery red hair and the peaches-and-cream complexion that went with it. Green eyes that melted

your heart when you looked into them. A figure — and
the clothes sense to display it to perfection — that made
men turn to look after her in the street. That was what
happened to Hank the first time he had seen her in the
restaurant hallway, her vision pulling him up from his
dark thoughts and whipping his head around as though
pulled by an invisible string. What pleasure to discover a
few minutes later that they were both guests at the same
boring reception, and even greater pleasure to have her
agree to leave the reception to join him in a drink more
civilized than the watery punch they were being served.
Then, what paradisical pleasure some weeks later to
actually have her agree to his proposal of marriage.
Finally, what indescribable pleasure to find himself
making love to her within minutes of the proposal.

"Get that look out of your eyes, you lech, I know
what you're thinking," she said. He smiled and walked
over to sit on the foot of the bed.

"You're a mind reader — and you're absolutely
right."

"Well, you're not going to lay one of your over-sexed
fingers on my fair white body until you've answered my
question. What is so bloody important that we had to
drop everything and come here? And make a dishonest
woman of me — Mr. and Mrs. Greenstein, I saw the
way you signed the hotel register."

"Just getting practice. We'll be married in a few days
and it will all be legal . . . . "

"Answer the question and stop dodging the issue."

"I'll tell you today, I promise." He took her hand up
gently in his and kissed her palm, running the tip of his
tongue lightly over it. She shivered and tried to pull
away, but he held on tightly.

"Now stop that! You still haven't answered the question."

She tugged harder and her struggles dislodged the covers which slipped down exposing one conical and perfectly formed breast. At this Hank let go of her fingers and leaned forward to cup her breast instead, bending to kiss the suddenly upright delicate pink nipple. Frances shivered and wrapped her arms tightly around his head.

"God, you know ways of changing the subject," she whispered hoarsely as he pulled the covers from her. They laughed, together, when the breakfast tray crashed to the floor, but it did not interfere with the intensity of their lovemaking.

They were lying quietly, their bodies touching warmly, when the phone buzzed beside the bed.

"At least they had the courtesy to wait until we were done," Frances said.

Hank leaned out and fetched the phone. "Greenstein," he said. He listened for some time, nodding as he did. "Right," he finally said. "I'll see you there at eleven o'clock."

"Are you going to tell me about it?" Frances asked as he threw the covers back and climbed out of bed.

"That call was about the business I'm here in Australia for. I shouldn't be long. Why don't you do some shopping or something and I'll meet you back in the hotel at . . . ."

"No."

"They say there are really great things to buy here in Sydney. You can get clothes made out of kangaroo skins, or aboriginal craftwork . . . ."

"Shut up. I'm going with you."

"Or toy koala bears, sheepskins, opals . . . ."

"Didn't you hear me, you fiendish seducer of helpless women? You are not going to leave me alone in this beer-swilling, sheep-shearing pest-hole."

"The Chevron is the best hotel in town."

"You know what I mean. Where do we have to be at eleven o'clock?"

"It's business, I told you . . . . "

"No, you didn't tell me. That's why I'm going with you."

Hank had little enough time — and he knew when he was licked. "All right. You can come, but only if you just listen. We're going to meet some people and I have to talk to them. Some arrangements have to be made. If you will let me talk to them quietly, I promise to tell you everything that is going on as soon as the business is finalized. That is right away, now, today. Is it a deal?"

"Then you admit that you have been concealing something from me?"

"I'm a lawyer and have been trained to admit nothing, never to no one."

"Rotter. Where are we going?"

"To an exclusive restaurant named the Rhinecastle Bistro, world-renowned for its fine Australian wine served in a gourmet atmosphere."

"Sure. Pink plonk and tough steaks. I'm going to shower first."

"You Brits are sure hard on your colonials."

"When you taste the food you'll know why we shipped them out in chains."

The taxi driver dropped them off right in front of the restaurant, but the rain was so heavy that they were soaked before they got through the door.

"I thought Australia was the land of perpetual sunshine?" Frances said.

"Not quite this time of year. Their seasons are opposite to ours and it'll be winter soon."

"They'll have to enjoy its brisk pleasures without me.

Darling, I must do something about my hair. Where will I meet you?''

"In the bar. I'll order you the most exotic Australian cocktail they have.''

"I don't drink beer. I'll just be a minute.''

Hank stood in the entrance to the bar, looking around the room, until he saw Uzi rising from a table against the far wall. The Nazi-hunter came over to him, extending his hand.

"Welcome to Australia, Hank. It's good to see you here.'' They shook hands.

"I wish I was as happy about it as you are. In any case I'm here — and ready to go. Where is our target?''

"At that table by the far window, see him? He's the one with the bald head with the fringe of gray around the bottom. The table for four with the two empty seats. I arranged that so he and his wife will be having lunch alone.''

"Okay. Did the letter come through?''

"Right on time. The courier brought it this morning.''

He took a white envelope from his pocket and handed it to Hank who tore it open. There was a single sheet of paper inside; he read it quickly and nodded. "This should do it,'' he said, putting the letter into his own pocket. "I'll take it from here.''

"I'll be waiting here in the bar to see how it goes.''

"A piece of cake. He's going to have to say yes.''

"How can you be sure? I know that we are not. I have an alternate plan just in case . . . .''

"Uzi, please. Save your alternate plan for some other time. I know what I'm doing. I've talked to New York and worked it out with some people there. Don't worry. This thing is in the bag and all you have to do is sit back and admire the way that I handle it.''

"I hope that you are right, Hank. As you say, this is your ball game and you know how to handle it best."

Uzi went back to his table as Hank hurried to the bar and ordered two extra-dry martini cocktails, American style. The bartender permitted him to add the traditional drops of vermouth himself. They were just set up on the bar when Frances appeared, and she nodded respectfully after tasting hers.

"I take back everything I said about Foster's lager," she said.

"That's a bribe for good conduct," Hank told her. "We're going to meet some people now and you will undoubtedly open your eyes wide at some of the things that you will hear, but I beg of you, say naught. All will be revealed soon. And, listen, darling," he leaned forward and kissed her cheek, "I am really incredibly glad that you are here with me. There are one or two things I have been waiting for a good time to tell you about. This looks like the time."

"That sounds ominous."

"It's not meant to be. You'll see." Hank led the way across the restaurant towards the paunchy man in the light blue sports jacket. The jacket was almost the same color, he realized, as the blue-rinsed gray hair of the woman who sat across from him, sipping white wine.

"The restaurant is crowded," Hank said, "is it all right if we sit here?"

"Be my guest," the man said in a deep voice with a decided New York accent. "Always glad to help a countryman. And we've been eating with limeys for the last week."

Frances frowned and started to speak — then thought better of it. Hank gave her an appreciative wink, then pulled the chair out for her.

"My wife's a limey," he said, smiling.

"Great news. They're wonderful people, though none of the others are as good looking as her." Frances smiled at this, flattery will always get you somewhere; and sat down gracefully. Hank joined them and got right to work.

"My name is Hank Greenstein, this is my wife, Frances. And you are Mr. and Mrs. Wunderbaum."

"We got mutual friends in the *shmotta* business or something?" Wunderbaum asked.

"No, sorry. You were pointed out to me. You've just arrived in Sydney aboard the *QE2*?"

"A day tour of the city," Mrs. Wunderbaum said. "Everything included in the price of the cruise, including lunch in this restaurant. They didn't tell us it was going to rain."

"They rarely do in cruise brochures," Hank said. "Are you enjoying the voyage so far?"

"It's very nice . . . . "

"The food is *drek*," Wunderbaum said.

"But in such big portions," she admonished him. "The doctor said a cruise, so you got a cruise."

"I'm going to get a new doctor who tells me Miami. At least when I make a business call from there it's in the same time zone."

"I have a reason for asking," Hank said. "This may sound strange, but please think about it carefully before answering. It's this — would you possibly be willing to cancel this cruise if you had all of your money refunded and were flown back to the States? First Class, of course."

"Something wrong with my business that they're not telling me about!" Wunderbaum cried. "I knew it. Go away for a week and the *youlds* lose me business. Go on a world cruise and I'm out of business . . . . "

"No, please," Hank said. "This has nothing to do

with your affairs. It's another matter completely. It's just that I and my wife would like to use your suite for the balance of the cruise.''

Hank was aware of Frances's dropping jaw and staring eyes; however, he did not let his gaze meet hers. Wunderbaum had his own eyes half closed in a most suspicious squint.

"What are you up to? What's this all about?"

"Are you personally acquainted with Mr. David Rabino?"

"Show me someone in the garment center that isn't. All of us together, we personally support the State of Israel."

"Would you know his signature?"

"He knows mine better. I give him enough checks."

"Seriously. Would you recognize his signature and letterhead?"

"Know it? I could forge it. Dave and I, we worked together for years before he got into fund-raising full time. It beats retiring, he said."

Hank took the envelope from his pocket and extracted the letter and passed it over. Wunderbaum opened it and spread it flat on the table before him. Then he took his reading glasses out of his breast pocket and perched them on the end of his nose. He read slowly, and at one point said *Vey!* under his breath and looked up at Hank. Then he finished the letter and handed it back.

"When I think about it, Rabino's signature, it's maybe easy to forge."

"Maybe. And I don't want you to make your mind up on the letter alone. Do you have his phone number? He's waiting for a call from you."

"Sure I know his number. But, mister, here in Australia it's like twenty-one hours behind New York.

So it's early tomorrow of a Sunday there and could be he wants to sleep?''

"He said you're to call him at any time, day or night. It's that important.''

"I'll give him a call now,'' Wunderbaum said, climbing heavily to his feet.

"The food, it'll get cold,'' his wife called after him.

"Tell them to put it back into the oven. If it's like what we eat on the boat it won't do no harm.''

"You shouldn't ask him things like this,'' she said, unhappily, looking after his vanishing back.

"I'm really very sorry,'' Hank said. "If there were any other way, believe me, I would have done that. But this is it.''

"But why? What's going on?''

"I'm sure your husband will tell you.''

"Not if he's like my husband,'' Frances broke in, unable to remain quiet any longer. "Mount Rushmore tells me more than he does.''

"And so!'' Mrs. Wunderbaum reached out and patted her hand consolingly. "They're all the same. The business worries them all the time and they never tell you why, so you worry too, and so what do you get. Trouble. It's that kind of world.''

The waiter made a fortunate interruption and Hank bent over the menu with deep concentration. After they had ordered, the two women had a heart-to-heart talk about the perfidiousness of men, nodding in complete agreement. Hank was greatly relieved when Wunderbaum returned, pulled out his chair, and dropped heavily into it.

"Young man,'' he said, "you got yourself a deal.''

"But . . . why?'' his wife wailed.

"I'll tell you later.''

"I knew it,'' she said, nodding with resignation.

"Later meaning never. Around the world, a trip we're going to take you said. Some trip. When you're not *kvetching* about the food you're on the phone to New York. Maybe we better go home, if only to cure your heartburn."

"Mr. Greenstein," he said, suddenly smiling happily. "I think maybe you saved my life from dying from indigestion and maybe even you saved my business because I know what they do as soon as my back is turned. Have some wine."

The rest of the luncheon was spent in amiable conversation. Wunderbaum knew Hank's firm, had even done business with it and had met his father a few times. When they had finished he squinted at his watch and pushed back his chair.

"Come on, Momma, we got some packing to do."

"A room has been reserved for you at the Wentworth Hotel," Hank said. "You can stay there a few days if you like, or return to the States whenever you want to. And I'd like to thank you for doing what you are doing. It's really great."

"My pleasure. You enjoy the rest of the trip for us. Only watch out for the steak and kidney thing. It'll kill you."

Frances said goodbye to the couple, and watched them as they left the restaurant, waving back when they did. Then she sipped her wine, tapped her fingernails on the glass and smiled very sweetly at Hank.

"Now," she said, "you free-wheeling son of a bitch. You are going to tell me everything, and I mean everything, about whatever the hell is going on around here. The *QE2* indeed!"

"Can I tell you about it after we get aboard? We only have a couple of hours to pack and everything . . . ."

"No! Speak. What was in that letter?"

"Here," he said resignedly. "Read it for yourself."

She did, with growing astonishment, slowly from beginning to end — and then once again before she handed it back.

"There are things about you I really don't know," she said.

"I'm sorry. But don't hate me for not telling you before. When I first met you, why, telling you was, of course, out of the question. By the time we decided to get married it was too late. I couldn't just blurt it out. I mean, you know, sweetest, your husband-to-be is a part-time agent for quasi-legal Jewish organizations. Perhaps, you maybe wouldn't have thought much of the idea. Or of marriage to someone . . . . "

"You can't think very much of me if you believe that."

"I do think very much of you, that's the trouble, I love you so much I couldn't think if possibly losing you. Maybe I was just afraid. Maybe it's good it came out this way, before we actually marry. In case you might want to change your mind."

He looked absolutely demolished and Frances's heart went out to him. "You're absolutely the most foolish man I know. If anything I want to marry you even more. Perhaps the Captain of the ship will perform the ceremony. Very romantic. Do they still do that sort of thing . . . ? "

"Darling! Listen. And think before you answer. Be sensible and think about the fact that your family might not look on me as a prime example of a husband as much as you do."

"I'm marrying you and my family isn't. My father is an anti-Semitic, anti-American old Tory who will change his mind the instant he sees his first grandchild."

"You're wonderful and I'll make an honest woman

of you yet! But this could be dangerous . . . . "

"Aboard the *QE2* in the middle of a luxury cruise? Don't be silly."

"There are some very strange and possibly tough customers aboard."

"There will also be some pretty strange and tough British sailors and sergeants-at-arms or whatever they call them, if I know my Cunard. They won't let anything happen. Will you be carrying a gun? What will you be doing?"

"Nothing quite as adventurous or dangerous as that. Just keeping an eye on these people to try to find out what they are up to. If there is going to be any trouble it won't be my department. I hope."

"I hope so, too — but I don't think we need worry. If I remember that little raid on Entebbe, the Israelis can take very good care of themselves indeed. Now pay the bill and let's go for a cruise."

9

As always, Leandro Diaz had mixed feelings about Mexico City, possibly because he had been living in London for such a long time. London is a fine city when you have money, perhaps the best in the world, but the Paraguayan refugees were poor and always short of funds. And then there was the English weather, always a burden to someone born in the tropics. Mexico had a far more favorable climate, familiar food — and the pleasure of talking Spanish all the time.

The drawbacks were the smog. And the crowds. Mexico's population had doubled in less than seventeen years and it was killing the country. He would never get used to the perpetual, grinding, inescapable poverty that squeezed in upon him. Beggars were on all sides; ragged and filthy children pressed forward with their palms outstretched. Diaz tried to ignore them. He would never have come to this slum street if the voice on the phone had not instructed him to do so. For a lot of reasons the meeting had to be arranged in a very roundabout and cautious way. He pushed through the crowds and finally saw his goal ahead, just as it had been described to him.

In the middle of the row of mean shops, pale green and garish pink, stood the *Pulqueria La Providencia*. Even from here he could smell the rank odor of the *pulque*. Fermented juice of the *agave,* the century plant, sweet and cloying, with a smell so sickening that he always wondered how people could drink it. But it was

107

cheap and it contained alcohol, and if you mixed it with pineapple juice it was almost bearable.

Diaz pushed through the rickety screen door, which seemed to function only as a trap to keep the buzzing hordes of flies locked inside. There was one customer asleep, drunk, his head pillowed on his arms. Otherwise the bar was empty, with just the owner rinsing out glasses in an enamelled basin. He had a three-day growth of beard and a wall-eye and he watched coldly as Diaz approached.

"Good evening," Diaz said. A slight movement of the man's head was his only response. "I was told to come here. For a message."

"You got a name?"

"Leandro Diaz."

"That'll be twenty pesos."

Diaz knew that no payment was needed, that this was pure graft. But it was easier to pay than argue. It had been hard enough to set this meeting up in any case. He passed over the money. It vanished and the barman jerked his head towards the door.

"Outside turn left. Go three blocks straight then turn the corner and there is a restaurant called the *Parador*."

"Do I turn right or left at the corner?"

A disgusted grunt was his only answer; he had had his twenty pesos worth. The restaurant should not be hard to find.

While he walked, there was a marked improvement in the neighborhood, with the slums giving way to a factory block, then a street with small shops. It was easy enough to locate the restaurant, a two-meter-wide neon-bordered sombrero hung over the doorway, emblazoned with the name. He went in, blinking in the near darkness after the full sunlight outside. It was too early for dinner and only an ancient pair of American tourists sat near the front window sharing a *Turkey Molé*. A waiter came towards him bearing a wide menu.

"Good evening, sir," he said, pushing the sheet of cardboard forward hopefully. Diaz waved it away.

"I'm meeting someone here. Are there any messages?"

"No, none at all."

"He may be late. Bring me a beer, a Moctezuma."

Diaz seated himself at a table by the back wall where he could see the entrance clearly. He would just have to wait. Josep was a wanted man. The police of a number of countries — and particularly the CIA — would be happy to pay large sums to lay their hands on him. Therefore, this roundabout way of meeting, to make sure that Diaz was alone. He was pretty sure that he had been followed, positive of it in fact. It didn't matter. He had to see Josep. They had met once, briefly, years earlier, and Josep would know all about his organization and the work he was doing. Yet this would be no assurance to him that Diaz had not turned police informer since then. Therefore, the precautions. He sipped at the chill beer — then jumped, startled, as someone sat down next to him.

"Back entrance. That's why we meet here," the man said. "What do you want, Diaz?"

"To see you about something important to both of us. You got my message . . . . "

He broke off as the waiter approached. Josep ordered a beer as well. He had changed since Diaz had last seen him, lost weight, fined down. His nose was even more hawklike and the skin was stretched tight over his prominent cheekbones. He no longer wore the familiar eyepatch, that would have been too recognizable; but when you looked close it was obvious that his right eye was false. They sat in silence until the waiter had brought the beer and moved away out of earshot.

"Do you still have an organization we could work with?" Diaz asked.

Josep nodded. "Still in operation. We don't have as many as we did before the murders in 1974, but the Tupamaros will fight on as long as there is one of us left."

And they would too, Diaz thought to himself. The Tupamaros in Uruguay had been the toughest urban guerillas in the entire world. Terror had been only one of their weapons. The movement had been crushed by the government, but only after years of struggle. While the organization was dead inside the country, it existed in exile just as Diaz's organization did. They had that much in common, forced to flee from their own countries by military dictatorships at home. Otherwise they were very different. Diaz was working for peaceful liberation by democratic means. The Tupamaros believed in violent revolution. Their common bond was exile — and hatred.

"We must cooperate," Diaz said.

"Why?"

"Because my organization has uncovered an operation launched in common by the rulers of our two countries."

"What do you mean operation? What do those pieces of dung have in common?"

"The need for repression — and the fact that they are loathed by every nation in the civilized world. They must have guns and weapons for this repression and they are running out of sources. But not any longer. They have made a deal with an organization called Global Traders. Have you heard of them?"

"Yes. A really big-time operation. They'll sell anything to anyone — as long as you have the price. They were the ones supposed to have supplied the plutonium to the Israelis to make their atom bomb.''

''They're selling to Uruguay and Paraguay now. An operation worth over two hundred and fifty million dollars. I have a transcript here of a recent conference they had with Global. The weapons and their quantities are all listed. They are going to have a meeting very soon to pay for the shipment. In diamonds, I don't know if we can intercept the shipment — but if we can interfere with the payment the deal won't be completed.''

Josep's good eye glared fiercely. ''Interfered with,'' he said in a low voice, ''And perhaps intercepted?''

''That's what I was thinking about. We are working on the intelligence end — ''

''But you will need people to carry through the interception operation. People who know how to handle weapons and how to fight. Right?''

''My thoughts exactly. If we can stop them, we will have done something important. If we can possibly lay our hands on the payment, or even part of it, there will be funds enough for all our needs.''

''I agree,'' Josep put out his hand. ''Now let me see the transcript.''

''One more thing first. Or rather two things. No indiscriminate bloodshed. Your organization has killed a lot of people who had nothing to do with the military.''

''You can't make an omelette without scrambling eggs.''

''You can this time — or there is no deal. Agreed?''

''Agreed,'' Josep said with disgust in his voice. ''What other conditions are there?''

''The split. Whatever we get out of this is fifty-fifty. Right down the middle.''

''Yes, of course, no trouble with that one. You set

them up and we'll knock them down. Now give me the papers.''

Diaz passed the sheaf of typescript across the table and sipped at his beer while the Tupamaro leader read through the transcript of the tape that had been secretly recorded of the meeting in the Palace in Asunción a few days earlier.

When Josep had finished he let the papers drop from his fingers onto the table as he sat, buried in thought. ''Diamonds,'' he finally said. ''Diamonds. As good as gold — better than gold — anywhere in the world. Untraceable. What is this mention in the end about the *QE2*? Do you have any more details on the connection with the ship?''

''Some. That is the lead we are working on now, in fact that is the lead that started this whole operation. And we have outside aid, people you have worked with before. They will help a lot and they will not ask for any cuts. They just want some Nazis who are involved.''

''The Israelis,'' Josep said, smiling coldly. ''I love them. My country is riddled with Nazi vermin, inside the government and out. We've given information to the underground Jewish groups in the past, and they have put their hands on some of the big fish through us. Each one they get rid of is one less to aid the military government. How are they helping?''

''They've identified some of the passengers aboard the *QE2* as Nazis on their very-wanted list. They have agents aboard the ship now and others at every port of call. We don't know yet what connection the *QE2* has with the payment arrangements, but we'll know as soon as they do.''

''Good — but not good enough. We must get our own people aboard as soon as possible. We can't wait until we hear what is happening. If the deal takes place aboard the ship we must be there. If they leave the ship — then we leave with them and nothing has been wasted.''

''I feel the same way,'' Diaz said, draining his beer and signalling the waiter for two more bottles. ''My first thought was to contact you for help with this operation, since it means a good deal to both of us. Then, when I found out where you were, I had a feeling that a beneficial God was smiling on both of us . . . . ''

''Please. Leave religion to the priests and old women and tell me just what in hell you are talking about.''

''Mexico, of course. The *QE2* is now on its way from Australia to Hawaii. There is nothing we can do in Hawaii, it is too far away and we don't have enough time. And the Americans would love to have you visit their islands. No, it is the port of call after that that is of the greatest interest to us. Acapulco.''

''*Cargata!*'' Josep said, banging the table so hard in his excitement that the empty beer bottle fell over and crashed to the floor. He sat there, thudding one tight fist slowly and steadily into the palm of his other hand while the waiter cleaned up the mess and brought new beers. As soon as they were alone again he leaned forward and spoke in a low and intense voice.

''We've got them. We can do what we want with them. I have my own people in the port there, good, reliable people. There are others already in the country whom I can use.''

''Do you have weapons?''

''Do we! I almost believe in your Providence. We knocked over an Army fort in the mountains just a week ago. We were after explosives — but we hit the jackpot. Grenades, guns, machine-pistols, even a flame-thrower. I have the people and they have the arms and the will. It is up to you now to find out what we can do with them.''

''Leave that part to me. I'll have another report later today. What we need next is an operational base in Acapulco. Can you arrange that as well?''

''There is a large house just down the coast. Empty now. The watchman is reliable when bribed. I'll leave today to set it up. Can you follow tomorrow?''

''Yes. As soon as I set up another communication link.''

''Good. Then we should both look forward to an exciting cruise.''

''We should indeed. And to the success of our mutual ventures. We will drink to that. Tequila. Success!''

Diaz drank the toast, yet at the same time could not help but think of another toast, the slogan of the Tupamaros that they used to roar out at their meetings.

Habra patria para todos, o no habra patria para nadie.

''We will have a homeland for everyone, or we will have a homeland for no one.''

Death and destruction. He had lain down with the lion by choice — because he had no other choice.

Would he be able to rise up again?

10

"Most unhappy to see your uncle leave so suddenly, and only just partway through the cruise," the bedroom steward said, putting the suitcases into the rack. "But every cloud has a silver lining, doesn't it, sir? Here you are going on in his place, and I hope that you do enjoy it as well."

The steward went out into the alleyway again to get the rest of their luggage, then into the bathroom where he turned the light on to see if everything was shipshape, going next to the door to the verandah where he pulled the curtains wide and secured them into place. Hank Greenstein watched the routine closely and marvelled at the efficiency of the shipboard grapevine. It had been Uzi in Sydney who had suggested this course of action.

"You just can't step aboard a ship like this and go into luxury quarters without some kind of cover story. There will be plenty of interest, plenty of gossip. So give them something to talk about. Here is what I told them when we changed the bookings. Wunderbaum is your uncle. He had been called home suddenly for urgent business reasons — no one who has ever talked to him will doubt that story for a second. Therefore, he has given you the rest of the cruise as a wedding present since, completely by chance, you have been honeymooning in Australia, visiting your wife's relatives. That's the basic story, nice and simple, so stick to it."

Hank had definitely decided to stick to it and was

more than thankful for the agent's foresight. The bedroom steward now straightened the flowers in the vase and checked the carafe to see that it had been filled with ice-water.

"Would you like me to unpack for you, sir?" he asked.

"No, that will be fine." Hank gave a quick and worried look in the direction of the heavy leather suitcase. "I have no idea where my wife wants her things. Better let her decide."

"Women always know best, sir, absolutely right. My name is Robert, sir, and that button will get me any time you may need something."

"Thank you, Robert. That's good to know."

As soon as the steward had left, Hank locked the cabin door behind him. And wondered where Frances had got to. They had barely boarded the ship when they had come upon the row of shops, carefully and centrally placed.

"Check us in, darling, or find our cabin or whatever they call it. I'll join you in half a tick."

She had vanished before he could lodge a word of protest. He didn't quite know how long half a tick, or even a whole tick, was, but it was certainly a measure of time in excess of half an hour. He looked at his watch; that's how long it had been now. No point in waiting any longer.

The suitcase was ancient, made of thick, heavy leather and plastered with stickers from hotels long closed, ships long scrapped. It was a survivor from an earlier age when weight did not matter, an extinct species in the jet age, and Hank wondered where on earth they had found it. Why they had found it was obvious; it would take an electric saw to get through the metal fittings and impervious cowhide. The double locks opened easily to his key, but they were far more sturdy and secure than normal baggage locks. He threw the case wide and looked at the electronic equipment nesting among the foam packing inside.

He hoped that he would remember how to work it. He had to remember! It had appeared simple enough when it had been demonstrated to him, and he had been able to assemble it himself after the first try. Hopefully he still could.

The first thing he took out of the case was a diagram of the sports deck of the *QE2*. Two adjoining areas had been ringed in red. One was labelled Yours, the other Theirs. The wall between his cabin and the adjoining suite had been scrubbed over heavily with red ink. Hank turned the diagram to orientate it with the cabin and found the correct wall. It looked just like a wall. There was a framed painting in the center of it, with a settee just below it. Good enough for a start. He poked behind the painting and saw it was secured to the bulkhead by screws. No problem there.

In addition to the electronic equipment, the suitcase also contained a complete tool-kit. Hank used a screwdriver to loosen the two screws on one side so the picture could be levered away from the wall. The tiny microphone could then be put into position behind it and held in place with the sticky tape. He moved it up before securing it so that the wire lead that dangled below came even with the bottom of the frame. He put the screws back into place and was satisfied that there was no evidence visible of his work. The tiny connector on the wire was just seen as a metal dot, and then only if one bent down and looked up under the frame.

Next came the portable radio and cassette player. It was Japanese and large and expensive, with the cassette drive set into the front below the many-banded dials and controls for the radio. It looked very much like every other one of the millions of sets sold. Yet it was very different from all of the others, as much as it resembled them. Hank pressed two of the controls at the same time and the entire front dropped open. Behind it was a deck for six inch, reel-to-reel tape recording. He checked that the tape was in position and closed it up again. Then he opened the back and took out the power cord which he plugged into the points on the wall, after unplugging a lamp. There was another, smaller, cord in the same compartment which he connected to the microphone behind the lamp. Good. All in place, all ready to go. But did it work?

As he turned the set on, Hank had the feeling that he was really not cut out for this kind of work. His heart thudded heavily and warningly and his fingers were shaking. He had never studied this sort of thing in Columbia Law School. There was a rustle of static from the speaker, but nothing else. In a panic he turned the volume higher — and a booming voice flooded the room.

"Was ist los? Was tust du da . . . . "

In a panic he switched it off and stood, shaking, aware of how much his hands were sweating. Had they heard it next door? There was no way of telling. The walls seemed sound-proofed well enough. Could he be sure? As he was reaching down to turn it on again there was a loud knocking on the door.

Trying not to rush and injure the delicate wiring, he disconnected the lead to the microphone and stowed it into the back of the machine.

"Hank? Are you there?" Frances called through the door.

He opened it and let her in — then dropped into the nearest chair.

"Seen a ghost or something?" she asked, concerned.

"No. Just getting used to this secret agent job. I'm not sure that I'm really cut out for this kind of work. I have been setting up the equipment they gave me — and frightening the bejezus out of myself at the same time. Where have you been?"

"Spending money," she said happily. "They are really wonderful in the shops here so they let me sign for it — even though I didn't know our cabin number or anything."

"Captive consumers," he said, sighing wearily. "The only way they can lose out is if you jump overboard. What did you buy that was so important?"

"This — and it is important."

Frances held her left hand out to him and wiggled her fingers. It took him a long moment to realize that she was referring to the wide gold band on her third finger. "Very nice," he said, with a certain lack of conviction.

"At least try to sound as though you meant it! I have been getting by up until now with my engagement ring turned backward to hide the stone, but that can't go on forever, you know. I now at least look like an honest woman, though you have compromised me forever. When do we get married?"

"My God," Hank said, quietly and to himself. This was getting to be one of those days. He remembered that the steward had pointed to a cabinet and had said "bar" and he went to it. It opened to reveal not only glasses and a filled ice-bucket, but filled bottles of booze. Good old Cunard! He poured a large Scotch whisky and remembered in time, before he drank it, to call back over his shoulder.

"Look, darling, a complete bar. How about a little drink to celebrate?"

"Celebrate what — my career as a ruined woman

living a lie? Large pink gin. Come on Greenstein, fix a date for the wedding!''

''Tomorrow. Aboard the ship,'' he said desperately.

''No, they all think that we're already married. Try again. Thanks. Cheers.''

They raised their glasses and drank and the door opened.

Hank's heart started hammering fiercely again. Christ — he had forgot to lock it! And there was all the stuff spread out on the bed!

''Hope I'm not disturbing you,'' the young man said, knocking as he poked his head through the door.

''Just having a drink,'' Frances said with more presence of mind than Hank could rustle up. He took a despairing glance at the leather suitcase: at least it was closed. The man came into the room. He wasn't as young as he had looked at first sight, blond and tall. Although he was smiling his face was hard and stiff.

''Welcome aboard.'' It sounded more like ''velcome'' when he said it. ''My name is Fritz and I'm right next door. We heard that your uncle had to leave suddenly. Hope that it wasn't bad or anything. What a nice big cabin you have here.''

He walked into the room, the smile fixed and unmoving, looking about at everything. Hank's eyes were pulled to the picture on the wall. Could the wire be seen? Had he stowed the lead back all the way into the machine?

''How nice of you to ask,'' Frances said in her most practiced cut-them-dead, colder-than-ice voice. ''We are Mr. and Mrs. Greenstein, Fritz. Mr. Wunderbaum is my husband's uncle. Everything is fine. We will tell him you asked after him. Will that be all?''

Fritz was impervious to insult. He stood before the settee looking down. ''That's a nice tape player you got there. Got good tone, I bet.''

Anger at the man's presence drove away all of Hank's early fears. The son of a bitch was just here to snoop.

"If you can see the tape player, Fritz," he said, "you can see the door. Use it."

"Not very friendly," the man said. The smile was gone now. "Aboard a ship, everyone close, you should be friendly."

"Out!" Hank took a step towards the man — whose hands suddenly closed into fists. Then he thought better of it, straightening up and letting his fingers open wide.

"You enjoy your trip," he said, going to the door. He looked back and winked, then left. Hank slammed the door behind him — and locked it this time. He let his breath out in a whoosh, and realized he was still carrying the drink. He took a big gulp.

"What on earth did that terrible man want?" Frances asked.

"To take a look at us," Hank said, putting down his glass and going over to the tape player. He reconnected the microphone lead as he talked. "There is something big going on and these boys are suspicious of everyone. They are particularly suspicious when the occupancy of the cabin adjoining theirs is changed. And their suspicions just happen to be right."

He turned the sound up just in time to hear a door close in the suite next door. As the voices began in fast German he switched on the recorder. "It'll be very interesting to hear what they think about us," he said.

Frances raised her glass in a salute. "It works. My husband-to-be is a genius. Does he also speak German?"

"School German, just enough to get by. But you can be sure that there are people who will get these tapes and be able to understand every word of that."

"Can you follow it?"

"A little. Whoever's closest to the mike is asking where the other bottle of schnapps is. Our friend Fritz is in the background — that's him — yes it must be him. That voice, with the *"scheissdreck juden"*. That would be him." Hank was angry again and Frances looked up sharply.

"Meaning?" she asked.

"Freely translated as "dirty jews." Those are our Nazis all right. You know, I am beginning to enjoy this job."

"I can see that. But we were talking about our wedding."

He put his glass down and came over to her, took her in his arms and kissed her warmly.

"You'll have the biggest and best wedding in the world as soon as this is over. I promise. Only I have to finish this job first. I'm sorry to see you mixed up in it, and I'm sorry the wedding had to be postponed — really! But I am just glad as hell that there is something I can do to help out the boot to these people. This is no longer abstract. That's the enemy in there. They are up to no good and I am going to help find out what it is and watch while something is done about it."

"My hero," she said, and kissed him. She had meant it to sound funny, light, and it was. But there was more than a tone of seriousness in her voice and Hank heard it and understood it. He kissed her back with warmth and passion.

"I hope that I don't have to be a hero, but after meeting that kraut creep and hearing his frank opinion of us, I am ready for it if I must." There was suddenly anger as well as passion in his embrace and Frances gasped.

"Easy, caveman darling, save that for Nazis like Fritz."

"He's no Nazi, except by training and desire. The second generation. He's too young, wasn't even born until after the Second World War. He must be one of the three men in the suite who could not be identified. At least now we know what he is — if not who he is. But it is the two old ones whom I am really interested in. Hartig and Eitmann. I hope they'll let something drop about the big fish we are after, Dr. Joachim Wielgus."

"Is he the one you told me about? The paymaster-general for all the Nazis in hiding?"

"He's the one. If the anti-Nazi underground in Vienna can lay their hands on him he could lead them to any number of others. Or to their source of funds. Though they say that he is a very hard man. Still, his capture alone would make this entire operation worthwhile."

Hank reluctantly withdrew from the warm embrace to reach for his drink, which he drained. "I wonder where he is now?" he said, frowning at the wall as though he could see through it and into the minds of the men on the other side. "They know all right. Where is Wielgus?"

11

"The hairdresser is here now, Herr Doktor," Starke said, coming out onto the balcony where Joachim Wielgus was sprawled out comfortably on the lounge.

"Is it the same poofter as before?"

"The same. But always a good party member, and a major in the Waffen SS on the Eastern Front."

"All things in his favor, my good General. But a homosexual still, both before and after the war."

"And a hairdresser before and after the war as well — so we must make allowances. He is a valuable man."

"Of course he is, Starke! But you must permit an old friend a grumble now and then. We must make do with what we have, of course. Here, let us have another Schinkenhager so I can prepare myself for the ordeal."

"A fine idea."

Stark took the chilled schnapps from the ice-bucket and poured full two of the thimble-sized glasses and passed one over to Wielgus. They raised their glasses in a small salute and drained them, smacking their lips in satisfaction. Two old men warming in the afternoon sun of Cuernavaca, staring abstractly at the expansive view of Mexican mountains and sky. Wielgus took a deep breath and rubbed his hands together with resolution.

"Duty calls," he heaved himself up out of the comfortable lounge. "Just see that you keep the schnapps cold and I'll be back as soon as I can."

He still walked like a Prussian; age would never

change that. His shoulders were back, erect, and his feet slammed heavily onto the tiled floor with every step. When he opened the door to the hall Klaus was waiting there, snapping to attention, waiting for orders as patiently as he had done for the past thirty-six years.

"Take me to him," Wielgus said and Klaus led the way, opening the door for him, then closing it after he had gone in. Sonderbar was waiting, looking young, slim and relaxed. Until one got closer and saw the dyed hair and rouged cheeks. There was no trace at all of the former SS major in his stance or attitude. He waved Wielgus to the chair he had set before the large mirror.

"Lovely afternoon, Herr Doktor, but, of course, it's always lovely in Mexico. Now let's get this cloth around you — so. Do you have that photograph we took last time? It would make things easier. Thank you."

Wielgus pushed the cloth down while he dug the wallet from his jacket pocket and took out the polaroid picture. Sonderbar tucked the sheet back into position, then examined the photograph.

"Yes, indeed, a very nice job, if I can be so bold as to say so myself. Everything done to alter your normal features as much as possible. You have been losing your hair for years, not that it doesn't suit you, of course — you have a nobly shaped skull and displaying it is all for the best. A shame to cover it, but still . . . and I do believe I have here the wig I made for you last time, how very nice and, see, a perfect fit . . . . "

Sonderbar babbled on like this and Wielgus tuned him out of his attention. The man must be suffered in silence; he was too valuable to them all. In the mirror he watched the transformation take place. A pepper-and-salt wig to cover the baldness. Subtle darkening around the eyes to increase the apparent depth of the sockets. Some bits of molded plastic inside his mouth to change the shape of his cheeks; foul-tasting but necessary. A moustache glued into position; he had never worn one; and finally the eyeglasses. A stranger looked back at him from the mirror. Close friends might still recognize him, but there was no resemblance to the man in the 1941 photograph his enemies possessed.

"Very good, Major Sonderbar, very good indeed. May I have the photograph back?"

"Of course. How nice of you to say so. I rarely do this sort of thing these days, but it is nice to know one's hand has never lost its skill. Shall I remain here — or return tomorrow?"

Wielgus looked at his watch. I'll be back by late afternoon, positively. Is that all right?"

"Absolutely perfect. The good General Starke has an incredible cook and I shall glut myself with luncheon and wine and doze and be fit as a fiddle for your return."

Wielgus grunted something noncommittal and left. A little of Sonderbar went a long way. Klaus jumped up from the chair in the hall where he had been waiting and snuffed out his cigarette. "What do you think?" Wielgus asked.

"A very good job, sir. Changes your appearance completely."

"That's all that is required. Let's go now. The bank closes at one and I want to get there as close to twelve-thirty as I can. Can you do it?"

"The traffic will be heavy, but there should be no problem as long as Juan stays close."

"He will — if he knows what is good for him."

Juan, and the other bodyguard, were leaning against the wall in the shade of the jacaranda, but they got into the Volkswagen as soon as Wielgus appeared. Klaus held the door open in the black Mercedes while he climbed in. Usually they both sat in the front, but today they had different roles to play. Klaus put on his chauffeur's hat, then started the engine.

From Cuernavaca to Mexico City is close to a hundred kilometers. It took three hours on the old, winding road, but no longer. The toll highway now climbs the hills and dives through tunnels in the mountains, then connects with the freeways through the city itself. Here the traffic jams began and Wielgus ignored them, turning up the air conditioner and reading the Wall Street Journal. When they pulled up in front of the Banco de Commercio it was twenty-five minutes to one. The Mercedes stayed in the no-parking zone in front of the bank, while the Volkswagen parked at a fire hydrant across the street. Wielgus took up the large briefcase and went into the bank.

Inside the bank he went to one of the high desks, placed the briefcase between his feet and filled out an application form for access to a safe deposit box. He wrote the form quickly, he knew the box number by heart, but hesitated before signing the card. Instead he took another card and practiced signing "Hermann Klimt" on the back of it a number of times until it flowed smoothly and he was satisfied. He put his card carefully into his pocket before walking slowly to the barred entrance to the safe deposit boxes and ringing the bell there. It took a moment before the old guard shuffled out of the back.

"Buenos dias, señor."

Wielgus answered him in fluent, though accented, Spanish, and passed the card through the bars. The guard examined it at arm's length, nodded and unlocked the gate.

"Would you please sign here — then here, sir. Thank you. This way please."

The guard was a poor man and this was an important job. Rubbing shoulders with the rich day after day. He strutted importantly and produced his key with a flourish and turned it in the left-hand lock on box 457903. Wielgus inserted his key in the right-hand lock and turned it as well. With both locks open the guard pulled out the large box and lifted it in both arms, breathing heavily.

"Heavy, sir . . . but I'll manage. In here, please."

He dropped the box on the table in the small room. Wielgus waited until the door was closed before he moved. Then he locked the door, opened his briefcase and put it on the table and took out a typed list from it which he placed on the table as well. Only then did he open the box and look in at the interior.

It was tightly packed with small chamois bags. Each one was secured with a leather thong which also bore a numbered metal tag. Without wasting any time Wielgus began taking the bags from the box one by one and checking their numbers against the list. When the number matched the list he put the bag to one side. This did not take long. When the task was complete he took out his pen and checked each bag off until he was satisfied that he had all the listed numbers. Only then did he put the large quantity of remaining bags back into the safe deposit box and carefully close the lid. The bags he had removed filled the briefcase two layers deep.

He was about to lock the case when he hesitated. It had been many years since he had last been here, had opened any of the bags. He looked at his watch; there was still time. Carefully he removed the top bag from the briefcase, unknotted the cord, and poured the contents out into the palm of his hand.

Beautiful. First class, all of them. He turned his hand back and forth so the facets of the diamonds caught the light from the fluorescents overhead and sparkled with every color of the rainbow. Compact, costly, attractive. All of the things that wealth should be.

Wielgus never smiled; people made jokes about this, though, of course, not in his hearing. But he smiled now. These stones, they were something worth smiling at.

The smile vanished as quickly as it had come and he was businesslike again. Putting the gems back into the bag, tying it and restoring it to the briefcase, closing and locking this. Then pressing the button for the guard. It took only a few seconds before the door opened.

"Finished already, Señor Klimt? Yes, I remember, you were always an efficient gentleman. Last time you were in — let me see — five years ago, you came and went just as fast. You wouldn't believe how long some people dawdle about in here. With others waiting, too."

The guard picked up the box and left, unaware of Wielgus's eyes burning into his back. The box was returned and locked into place to the satisfaction of them both. As they walked back to the entrance the guard was still talking; he had found that people liked to be chatted with. It made for better tips.

He was right, too. Wielgus passed over a hundred peso note and waved away the effusive thanks. He walked across the bank, nodded at the guard who opened the outer gate for him. Klaus had the door of the car opened and waiting and he climbed in with the briefcase.

"Around the corner and stop," he ordered when Klaus had started the engine.

Klaus never asked questions. He turned at the first cross street and went on until he found a spot at the curb where both cars could pull in.

"Is Juan reliable?" Wielgus asked. "Have you

worked with him?''

"Yes, sir. A good man. Not fast, but he doesn't get rattled or nervous. Good backup.''

"All right then, he'll help you with a job. Tell him there'll be a bonus. For you, too. This must be done quickly. The guard back there in the bank, the one in the safe deposit room. Go back and take a look at him so you will recognize him. Then go with Juan in the Volkswagen, the other one can drive me back. The guard recognized me from my last visit, he even remembered when the visit was.''

"That wasn't very wise of him.''

"It wasn't. Fix him now, when he goes home for his siesta, so he won't tell anyone else about my movements.''

"A wise precaution, sir. It will be taken care of.''

Klaus got out of the car and walked back to the Volks. He was hot in his black jacket but he never unbuttoned it, never took it off. He leaned in the window and spoke briefly to the driver.''

"Drive the Doctor back to Cuernavaca,'' he ordered. "Juan and I will return in this car.'' He waited until the Mercedes had pulled away before he explained to Juan. "We have some work to do. Extra money in it.''

"Good. I am at your orders.''

Juan put the car into the nearest garage and Klaus waited for him on the corner by the bank. He had made the make on the guard. It would be so easy. And a change from everyday events which, while not boring, could use a bit of livening up. This would be lively enough. He hummed as he thought about it. Nice to work again. Nice to be able to do something to help his employer. He would always be grateful to the man. Probably alive because of him. Recovering from a wound and ready to return to the eastern front. And probable death at the hands of the Russians who rarely took prisoners. Never made prisoners of corporals from the Death's Head regiments. Corporal Klaus had little hope of survival. But the temporary assignment of guarding the important civilian had been extended and then made permanent. It was a relationship that they both enjoyed.

There was only a short wait after Juan returned before the guard emerged from the bank. He passed the two men closely, unaware of the predatory eyes upon him.

"I'll make the move," Klaus said. "You just hold him from the back." Juan nodded in agreement.

The time came a few minutes later when the old man took a shortcut down a filthy alley between two streets. There was no one else in sight.

"Now," Klaus said.

Juan ran down the alley as Klaus unbuttoned his coat. The grey scabbard hung down under his armpit to below his waist. The bayonet was long and sharp as a razor. A clumsy weapon to carry about, but one he was secure with. A faithful companion in the east. It slipped free easily as he stepped forward.

"What . . . . " was all the old man said as he was seized from behind and spun about. That was all that he had time for.

Klaus slammed his large hand over the man's mouth and drove his head back against Juan's chest. With his other hand he brought the bayonet up in a hard, precise motion, placed exactly. To slide through clothes and skin, up across the man's stomach, through his diaphragm, inside his rib cage and directly into his heart.

The guard heaved up once and was dead.

Juan tore the guard's watch from his wrist, ripped his

pocket away to get at his wallet. Klaus pulled the bayonet free and stopped to wipe the blood off on the old man's clothing before they left. One more robbery with murder. It wouldn't be investigated. There were five or six like this every day in the city. These things happen.

Once it was free of the traffic the Mercedes picked up speed. Dr. Joachim Wielgus hummed a bit of *lieder* as he bit the end off his cigar. Yes, the doctor had said only one a day after dinner, but today was something special. One little extra cigar could not do much harm.

12

"It's been just like a honeymoon," Frances said, touching up her nails with nail polish, then blowing on them. "Two weeks at sea in this floating hotel. Long days in the sunshine, glorious nights in bed. A real honeymoon. Too bad we're not married."

"We can do it today in Honolulu," Hank said. He was threading a new tape through the heads in the recorder. "Hawaii is part of the States. We can go to a Justice of the Peace, get the knot tied while we wait."

"I don't know. Sounds more like getting your hair done than getting married. I think it would be far better to wait until we get back to London. I'm compromised already, so a few more weeks won't make any difference."

"Your choice, my love. There!"

Hank was getting more adept at the spying job. The reels turned and the new tape ran through. He snapped shut the front of the set, put it into position on the settee and plugged in the lead to the microphone. When the earphone jack was inserted it switched off the loudspeaker and he could listen with the volume turned up. Nothing. Music playing dimly in the background, something being banged down on a table. No voices. He switched on the voice-operated switch and put the earphones back into the case.

"Are the natives restless this morning?" Frances asked.

"Nothing happening at all. Maybe they're all out on the deck admiring the view."

"We should be there, too. All I can see from our exclusive and expensive verandah are the roofs of warehouses."

"Why don't you go on deck then? I have some things to do here first."

"I'll wait for you. I might run into our neighbors who give me the shivers. It's a good thing they cut us dead because that's easy enough to do in return. I'm sure if I had to talk to one of them that I would say something terribly insulting."

"That's only because of what's on these tapes."

"I can understand little or nothing of what's on those tapes. It's just that they radiate a feeling of intense evil. Now don't laugh. I'm sure I would feel that way even if I didn't know who they were."

Hank came over, carefully avoiding her widespread and drying finger nails, to plant a warm kiss on her forehead. "I imagine you would. And I'm not laughing. Nothing about those sons of bitches is humorous. Not that I can understand much of what is on the tapes, my schoolboy German isn't up to it. There is a plan of some kind, they keep referring to that, and when they do it is always associated with the Herr Doktor. We can be pretty sure who that is, though they have never mentioned him by name in my hearing. Anyway, there are I don't know how many hours of guttural kraut conversation on these tapes and I wish I could get rid of them."

Hank was packing the reels of tape into a plastic carrier bag when there was a knock on the door. They moved together, in a familiar routine now. While Hank closed the bag of electronic equipment and put it into the closet with the tapes, Frances unplugged the microphone lead, stowed it out of sight, and pressed the play button on the portable. The soft, nasal rhythms of Dolly Parton warbled out.

"Just a minute," she called in the direction of the door. "But I don't really like country music," she whispered.

"Pretend you do. This ship has six radio channels, but country and western is the one thing they don't program, OK?"

"All clear."

He opened the door and Robert, the steward, was waiting there. "Post has just come aboard, sir. Letter for you."

"Thanks."

Hank took it inside and stared at the featureless white envelope, mailed just the day before in Honolulu.

"For goodness sake — open it! The message is inside, not on the outside, my love," Frances said, leaning over his shoulder. He tore it open and they both read the brief message. There was a single sheet of hotel stationery from the Royal Hawaiian on Waikiki Beach. In the middle of the page, in small letters, was printed "ROOM 1125."

"Not what you would call long-winded," Frances said.

"It's all I wanted to know. The last I heard was that I would be contacted here and told where to take the tapes. Now what can I take them ashore in?"

"You can't. Men don't carry anything off the ship — other than cameras. It's women who always do the world's work and carry around back-spraining parcels. Let me find that nice hessian shoulderbag with the picture of Sydney Opera House on it. Put the sack of them in there."

"Shut up," he hinted. "Get your sunglasses and let's go."

They got their boarding cards at the head of the

gangway. At the foot the wahinis were waiting to drape flower leis about their necks.

"Isn't this exciting?" Frances said, smelling the fragrant blossoms.

"No. Let's find a garbage can to dump these so we won't look like tourists — easy marks for every hustler in town."

"You're being beastly. I'll wear yours as well."

There were cabs waiting to take the travellers and their bulging wallets to the waiting and hungry merchants. They took one of them to the Royal Hawaiian Hotel. There were plenty of cars and other cabs about and Hank had no idea if they were being followed or not.

"Our neighbors on the ship are the suspicious type. They may be tailing us to see where we go," he said.

"What can you do about it? Dart down alleys and such the way they do in the movies?"

"Not my style. We have to lose them — if they are there — without letting them know we even think we are being followed. Going to the hotel is innocent enough, we could be meeting friends there, anything. So here's what we do. Get into the elevator and press one of the top floors, or any floor where no one else is getting out. Once we are sure we have shaken off our tail . . . . "

"You sound so professional!"

" . . . . we separate. You keep the bag but I take the reels. Do some shopping, buy some things to put in the bag, and we'll meet in the bar on the ground floor an hour later. How does that sound?"

"Is there a bar on the ground floor?"

"Is there a hotel in the world without a bar on the ground floor?"

"You're right, of course. If there is more than one

bar in the hotel, I'll be waiting for you in the one nearest
the front entrance.''

''I can see that you're an old hand at this game. Here
we are.''

They pushed through the lobby to the big bank of
elevators at the rear. A fat woman in a floral print mu-
mu was just getting into one of the elevators and they
followed her in just as the doors closed. She pushed the
button for the third floor and turned to them.

''Can ah help with your floor?''

''Very kind. Fourteen please.''

When the door closed behind her on the third they
were alone.

''Should we press for the eleventh and get off there?''
Frances asked.

''No. Someone might be watching the floor indicator.
We'll carry on as planned. You go on to the top.'' He
took out the plastic bag of tapes and gave her a quick
kiss as the doors opened on the fourteenth floor. The
hallway was empty. She smiled at him as the doors
closed, but there was worry behind the smile.

Hank walked down the hallway until he came to the
fire exit. He opened it and checked to see that it was not
the kind that locked automatically behind you when it
closed. He really didn't feel like walking down fourteen
flights. No, thirteen flights he saw, when the number on
the door below proved to be twelve. Superstition rules
the world. He listened carefully before he pushed open
the door on the eleventh floor; he was not being
followed. When he knocked on 1125, Uzi Drezner
opened the door for him, then locked it quickly behind
him when he entered.

''Here are the tapes,'' Hank said.

''Wonderful. Any problems?''

''Not in the taping. Plenty of conversation here. But

our neighbors were suspicious of us at first and looked us over closely. We haven't talked to them since."

"That's fine. I want you to meet Mr. Ginzberg."

A short, gray-haired man rose from the couch and shook his hand. "My pleasure," he said in slightly accented English. His eyes were on the bag, not on Hank, as he spoke.

"Mr. Ginzberg was a professor of German," Uzi said. "But that was before his stay in Buchenwald. He works with us now. Knows every dialect and regional accent in German and can even place the speaker's home town within a couple of miles." They watched Ginzberg leave the room.

"Would you like a drink?" Uzi asked. Hank looked at his watch.

"I suppose so. Sun's over the yardarm. Bourbon on the rocks, please."

Uzi poured out the drinks — an orange juice for himself, Hank noticed. *"Shalom,"* Uzi said. "Make yourself comfortable and tell me what has happened since I saw you last."

"To me, nothing. Anything of value will be on those tapes. It is you who should have some news."

"We have some. We know more of the people who are involved in the affair, we know what they are planning, and we know the sum involved. A small fortune in diamonds . . . . "

"Well, you know a good deal more than I do!"

"We do. But we don't know just when and where the final transaction will take place."

"My curiosity about that can wait. But I want to know the rest now."

"Of course." Uzi took a large sip of the orange juice. "It appears that the Paraguayan underground has an agent very close to the top in the government, or someone with access to their meeting rooms. Whoever it is made a recording of a meeting between General Stroessner and a certain Admiral Marquez who is the present leader of the governing junta in Uruguay. This government, if you don't know, is just about as loathsome as the other. They also have something else in common — they provide safe refuge for escaped Nazis. Other than this they have little else in common nor have they been at all interested in working together in the past. But they are doing so now because they are involved in a very large arms deal. The diamonds will be turned over as payment for the arms which will be landed in Uruguay, after which some percentage of the weapons will be trans-shipped to Paraguay. We know this much and no more. We don't know where the arms ship is now, or even its name. Nor do we know where and when the meeting will take place to pay for the arms."

"But you have suspicions?"

"We certainly have. The *QE2* must be involved somehow. The diamonds may be aboard right now, with those thugs in the cabins next to you. Did you ever hear the word *Diamant* used when you listened to the tapes?"

"Never. Though I could have missed it."

"Not to worry. Mr. Ginzberg will find it if it is there."

"Do you know where the diamonds are coming from?"

"No. But this must be the Nazi involvement. Certainly these tinpot fascists don't have gems in amounts like that. But we need more information, since the source in Paraguay seems to have dried up for the time being. Here are the names we are interested in. Memorize the list and burn it before you leave this room. These two, the Czech and the woman, appear to represent the arms people. The others are on the military staffs of both governments involved.''

Hank took the paper and studied it, thinking aloud at the same time. ''The two suites next to mine, we know the people in there are connected with this affair. But are there any more of them aboard the ship?''

''A good question — and one that is keeping us up nights. A certain amount of breaking and entering has been done and we now have the complete passenger list of the ship. But it tells us little or nothing. Just names. Any number of them could be fakes. It also only tells us who booked and paid for the cabins — not how many might be aboard or still coming aboard. Also, the ship is surprisingly full for so expensive a cruise. We had trouble obtaining cabins for some of our people, but that has been taken care of. They are boarding here in Hawaii.''

''There's a relief to know. How do I contact them?''

''You don't. They'll be in touch with you. This must all be done with a very low profile. Particularly since our Paraguayan associates have taken on some partners. The Tupamaros.''

''I've heard of them. The urban guerillas, terrorists, in Uruguay. But I thought they had been wiped out?''

''Most were. But there are enough in exile to cause trouble. We are still cooperating, but our role is getting smaller and smaller. The resistance movements want the diamonds, and the arms if possible. Or at least to stop them from reaching the two countries. They have promised to throw any Nazis our way, glad to get rid of them, but little else.''

''If only we knew more . . . . ''

''We do,'' Ginzberg said from the doorway. He came into the room, a wad of notes clutched in his hand.

"Those tapes are wonderful, Mr. Greenstein, excellently done. I will prepare a complete transcript later of all the valuable material. But I wanted to share a little discovery with you right now."

They leaned forward, tensely, as Ginzberg smiled grimly and shook the notes in their direction.

"Something very big is going to happen in Acapulco. That is where the action will begin. Also, it appears that Wielgus will be joining the party there, and he personally will be bringing the diamonds with him."

"Aboard this ship?" Uzi asked.

"That I don't know, they were not clear. But they were clear about one thing. The diamonds are Nazi loot, their mutual savings account you might call it. So a number of them will be involved in this exercise in order to keep an eye on their fortune. This is big, very big. It could be the key to the entire underground Nazi organization and all of their finances."

Ginzberg smiled benignly at the wide-eyed expressions on their faces, shock that turned to glee. He accepted the offer of a small glass of whisky and Uzi poured it for him.

"Let us hope," Uzi said. "Let us pray that we get it right. This could be the big one that we have been working for all these years."

They raised their glasses and drank.

13

The city of Acapulco baked in the tropical sun, burning down out of the Pacific blue of the sky. However, out to sea, heavy dark clouds banked up higher and higher, hung with gray sheets of rain that trailed down to the ocean below. Their threatening blackness was lit occasionally by bolts of lightning, but they were still too far away from the sound of thunder to be heard on land. The occupants of the two cars drawn up on the shore road, Costera Aleman, looked at the approaching storm with uncertain speculation. For the guards baking in the Volkswagen, the rain might bring a welcome relief from the stifling heat. They had all of the windows in the car rolled down but there was no escape. However, in the Mercedes the engine and air conditioning were running, so it was cool and comfortable.

"I would like to drive soon, Herr Doktor," Klaus said, leaning back and sliding open the glass partition behind the driver's seat so he could be heard.

"We are still eating," Wielgus said, a cold leg of chicken in his hand, specks of meat and grease on his lips.

"I'm very sorry, sir, but the engine is beginning to overheat, standing like this. If we could drive, the moving air would cool it down and then we could stop again after a bit."

"All right. In a few minutes." He held out his glass

and General Starke filled it with chilled Brauneberger-Jusser-Sonnenuhr. "I don't like the look of those clouds, Starke. That could be a bad storm, a hurricane perhaps."

"I don't think so. The weather report on the radio this morning just mentioned heavy tropical storms, rain, some wind."

"And wind means waves and, *verdamte,* I can't stand being at sea. I am prone to seasickness. And there comes the ship now. I can feel my stomach heave at the sight. Please put the food away . . . . "

He wiped his lips with the linen napkin and dropped it into the basket on the seat between them. Out to sea the *QE2* had appeared suddenly out of a sheet of rain, headed for the harbor, seemingly running before the storm.

"No need to worry on a ship this size," Starke said, closing the basket and putting it onto the floor. He took a cigar case from his pocket. "I read the propaganda that came in the envelope with the tickets. Over sixty-seven thousand tons. Computerized stabilizers. Twin propellers. One hundred and ten thousand horsepower and a cruising speed of twenty-eight and a half knots. This ship will ride out any storm, then quickly leave it behind. Don't be concerned, old friend." He had read through the brochure once; the figures would be remembered forever. Starke had the precise memory needed for military planning, and had been on the General Staff before being relieved and given a Waffen SS division as punishment for being so bold as to differ with one of Hitler's more stupid tactical decisions. History had proven that Starke had been right; it was too late to prevent him from being classified as a war criminal for certain orders he had given to his men.

"It is nice of you to reassure me — but I know my stomach. I know what the sea does for me." He drained his glass and put it into the basket with the rest of the debris. With a nod of thanks he accepted one of Starke's Havanas and neatly cut a V in the end with the gold clipper from his waistcoat pocket. After blowing out the first pungent cloud of smoke he relaxed slightly; leaning forward, he opened the partition. "All right. A little ride now to cool down the engine. Then to the docks. I want to board as soon as possible without waiting around."

Libor Chvosta, though born in Plzen in Czechoslovakia, had long since deserted that socialist country for the more profitable capitalist world. He believed only in money, and more money, and did not care in the slightest how it was earned. It was not by chance that he carried a Swiss passport.

Aurelia Maria Hortiguela was as Spanish as her name, but since Franco's death she had found herself rather unwelcome in that country. It did not matter. She was now an Argentinian citizen and needed all the time she could find for the thriving business she did in South and Central America for the arms corporation she represented. Unlike Chvosta she enjoyed weapons for their own sakes, and indeed had an indoor firing range at her home outside Santiago del Estero, close to the foothills of the Andes. To her, a pleasant evening was a few hundred rounds of ammunition and the holes punched neatly in and around the bull's-eye on the paper target. Then, ears ringing, relaxed and happy, she would climb the stairs to bed with a bottle of good wine. Clara would be waiting for her, soft arms and full breasts, and the night would be perfect. She owed her tastes in weapons to her father, an artillery captain, who had raised her on a succession of Spanish Army bases after her mother had died at childbirth. She owed her tastes in sex to him as well, once she was old enough to discover that all of the other fathers went with the *putas* near the Army bases, not with their own daughters. Aurelia hated men; with very good reason.

As soon as the customs officer had passed Chvosta's passport back, Aurelia pushed hers across the counter. The bored Mexican official flipped through the pages, found the stamp that had been put in at the airport the day before, then banged his own stamp next to it and slid the passport back. Aurelia went through and stood beside Chvosta while they waited for De Groot to join them.

Hendrik De Groot was a cool, apparently indifferent man who maintained an air of calm at all times. He had trained himself to be stolid and unmoving in public, an image that fitted his work, and saved all of his emotions for private display. The customs officer frowned and muttered over the Dutch passport, but could find nothing wrong. De Groot apparently ignored him. The passport was duly stamped and passed back and De Groot took it without as much as a nod or a smile.

De Groot put the passport away in his attaché case and locked it, calmly and efficiently as with any other task. He was better when he worked, whatever he did, for he put all of his attention to it. Growing up in one of the oldest diamond-cutting firms in Amsterdam meant that he rarely thought of anything except diamonds. Though he was young, not yet thirty, he had the eye of an expert and knew cut, quality and value almost by reflex. He travelled a lot since he was an independent valuer who exacted high fees, but never asked his clients' business or discussed it later with anyone. His price bought quality, accuracy — and silence.

"Welcome aboard," the steward said as they stepped off the gangway onto the deck. He examined their tickets and directed them to the nearby lift. Chvosta and Aurelia were both on the first deck, in First Class, with single-bedded outside cabins. While De Groot also had a single cabin, the accounting officials of Global Traders had seen no reason to waste money on his accommodation, so he had an inside room on the fifth deck, deep within the ship. He had made no protest when he had checked the cabin on the deck plan. His fee would more than make up for any discomfort.

From where he stood on the dockside, the Tupamaro leader Josep could see the passengers boarding. His eyes had moved unseeingly over the fat man puffing and sweating in the heat, stopped for a moment by reflex on the magnificent behind of the girl next to him, then moved on. They were unknown to him.

"Are you the one Chuchu sent?" a voice asked from behind him. He turned to see a dark figure in the shadows, a sweating longshoreman with a baling hook over his shoulder. Josep nodded and moved over to join the man.

"Yes, I'm the one who contacted him. Are all of the arrangements made?"

"Just about. Getting your men into my gang was easy. I go to the shape-up, pick whoever I want. There are no questions asked here. But the bags, that's different, that's hard . . . . "

"No, the bags are easy. They are stacked around the corner. Just see that they are picked up and loaded aboard with the rest of the luggage."

"Please señor, you don't understand. The other bags have cleared customs, they've been checked. Yours are just there where the truck put them during the night. I don't know what's in them — I don't care — but if I'm caught. That means smuggling, jail . . . . "

"Just don't get caught. I was told you were the best

foreman on the docks. That you could get away with anything. You're getting paid good money. All you asked, plus a bonus. And something else. You live in Colonia del Flores, don't you?''

"What does that mean?"

"It means you have that nice little house with Bougainvillaea all around it. It was pointed out to me. You have a wife and two daughters there. They are alive and healthy. Now."

"You son of a whore — what are you saying!"

The longshoreman moved forward angrily, the shining hook ready in his hand, swinging. Josep did not move — but his words cut like razors.

"You're a stupid fool. I am not alone in this. Touch me — or don't get those bags aboard — and they'll all be found in bed tomorrow with their throats cut from ear to ear. And you will be sitting there, tied into a chair with your eyelids sewn open so you will have watched it happen. Do you believe me, yes? Yes? Yes?"

With each repetition of the word *yes*, Josep's hand lashed out to slap the muscular longshoreman's face. Not light slaps, but hard ones that rocked the man's head from side to side and drove him back. But the cruel hook was never raised and the humiliation was taken, swallowed, understood.

"I believe, yes, I do," he said hoarsely, rubbing away the blood from his nose with the back of his hand. "Everything will be done, just as you ask."

"Now you show your intelligence. Go do it."

The man stumbled away, humiliated and defeated; Josep nodded with satisfaction. The point had been made. The job would be done just as he wanted it. He strolled along the dockside to see if the rest of the operation was going as planned.

Perfectly. Not too many people were boarding the

ship here, so things were proceeding at a pace very much in keeping with the tropical climate. Most of the passengers had gone ashore for the day so there was really no rush to finish in a hurry, since they would not sail until the following day. Tourists, even world cruise tourists, always enjoyed an evening out in the nightspots and fleshpots of Acapulco. The powers that ordered the arrivals and departures of the *QE2* were only too happy to oblige their cash customers.

One of the cargo booms had been swung out from the foredeck of the *QE2*, high above, and the line now hung down from the block at the end of the boom to dangle, hook swaying, over the cargo net spread out on the cracked concrete below. Some suitcases and trunks had been placed in the center of the net, and while Josep watched, a longshoreman pushed out a handtruck with more suitcases on it. He talked to the policeman who watched the operation with bored disinterest. When he had finished, the two men walked back into the shade of the building together.

From the next bay, a forklift emerged with a number of large suitcases before it on a pallet. It took only a moment to drop the pallet down onto the wharfside. Two other longshoremen appeared and leisurely added these to the pile already in the net while the forklift blatted its exhaust and drove away. The longshoremen strolled after it and, when the policeman returned, nothing had apparently changed. He looked up at the ship, then continued slowly down the length of the wharf. One of the longshoremen reappeared and picked up each corner of the net in turn and slipped the rings of each over the dangling hook. When the job was done he waved to a man on the deck above. The man waved in return and signalled to someone out of sight.

The line tightened and the corners of the cargo net

lifted clear, hesitated for an instant, then continued upward. The net, and its contents, swung up high, twisting
slowly, then over the ship and out of sight. Josep
nodded approval and walked the length of the ship to
the stern where fresh food was being loaded aboard.

Everything was progressing smoothly here as well. A
continuous stream of longshoremen was moving between the ship and the dockside warehouse. They sweat-
ed heavily in the humid, cloying heat, carrying aboard
stalks of bananas, boxes, sacks and crates of fresh fruit
and vegetables. It was heavy, exhausting work, and
Josep smiled wryly as one of the men stopped close by
and mopped at his streaming face with a large and filthy
handkerchief. The man was looking in Josep's direction, but he made no sign that might indicate to an on-
looker that they had known each other for many years.
Josep was looking at the *QE2*, not at the longshoreman,
as he took out a cigarette and lit it. He took only a single
puff before he dropped it to the ground and crushed it
with his heel. The longshoreman turned away and went
into the shed. When he came out again he was carrying a
basket of guavas balanced on one shoulder. He joined
the line of men going up the gangplank into the ship.

No one, other than Josep, appeared to notice that he
did not come out again. Nor did three other men who
were also working in the gang. If the remaining longshoremen were aware of what was happening, they gave
no sign.

When Josep was sure that the men were safely
aboard, and that there was no sign of any disturbance
from the ship, he walked slowly back along the wharf
and into the loading shed. The exit on the far side was
guarded by an armed soldier and a civilian guard. The
soldier eyed him coldly as he approached, leaning on his
heavy Mauser rifle. Josep ignored him and took the pass

from his pocket and handed it to the guard, who glanced at it, nodded, then handed it back. Josep walked on, out into the sunlit street.

He was very happy in Mexico where the universal motto was *No hay reglas fijas*. There are no fixed rules — meaning anything could be done by bribery. The *mordida,* the "little bite," the bribe, was a way of life of which he greatly approved. It really did make all things possible for him.

The battered truck was parked two blocks away, in the shade, he was happy to notice, as he pulled the creaking door open and climbed into the cab. Concepcion Valverde was sitting there, patiently waiting, inhaling gently on a joint. She passed it over to him and he sucked in a deep lungful, holding it for long seconds before he let the fragrant smoke trickle out through his nose.

"No trouble at all. Went like clockwork," he said. She nodded in understanding, but did not speak. A dark, silent, beautiful girl, no more than twenty-five years of age. Wanted for murder in three countries.

"There was a little bit of resistance from one of the longshoremen, but nothing important. I saw the bags safely aboard and our men as well. It's our turn now. Papers."

She took the envelope out of her purse and handed it to him. He checked the tickets and the Mexican passports, then gave hers back. There was a jacket on the ledge behind the seat and he took that with him when he climbed down, and pulled it on. The sun was gone now, hidden by thick clouds, the air even more heavy and oppressive than it had been all day. He looked up at the sky as she joined him.

"Better hurry," he said. "The storm is almost here."

At first there were a few large drops that splatted

heavily onto the dusty street. Then more and more — until suddenly the sky opened up in a deluge, a cataract of water that roared down upon them. They ran the last few feet to the entrance to the dock, yet were still soaked to the skin. But they were indifferent to it, just nodding at the Cunard official's commiseration as he took their tickets. The Paraguayan Leandro Diaz was waiting on the other side of the customs barrier, sitting alone on a bench against the far wall. Josep and Concepcion joined him. Leandro looked at the Tupamaros and raised his eyebrows in an unspoken question.

"Our part has been done," Josep said. "My people are all aboard. What about your Paraguayans?"

"Aboard as well. And we have finally had a report through from our agent. The news is incredible, almost unbelievable."

"Nothing is unbelievable," Josep said.

"This is. As we suspected, the final arrangements for the arms purchase will be made aboard the *QE2*. So we are in the right position to act when the time comes."

"The diamonds?"

"They must be aboard by now, because the Global Traders representatives are here, along with their diamond expert. He can have only one function — to make sure of the diamonds' authenticity and value. But more important than that is the identity of the Paraguayan agent who will close the deal. None other than Stroessner himself!"

"I can see why you said unbelievable! Your scabrous little general actually leaving the country. You must find some way to see that he doesn't return."

Leandro nodded. "My thought exactly. But that isn't all of the news. We have also found out that the Uruguayan representative will be of the same calibre . . . ."

"Not that swine Marquez himself?" Concepcion

asked, leaning forward with eager anticipation. Leandro nodded slowly and she clapped her hands with glee. "This is wonderful, wonderful. Could I cut his throat myself? Could I please?"

"I'm sure something decent like that can be arranged," Josep said, smiling quickly. "This is an opportunity that will be taken. This is a chance to free our country."

"Both our countries," Leandro Diaz corrected. "Now let's get aboard."

14

Hank Greenstein had been standing on the deck near the top of the gangway, watching people come aboard, until he realized that he was highly conspicuous there — as well as also having not the slightest idea who he was looking for. He had retreated then to the open rear of the Quarter Deck where he leaned over the rail to watch the loading. Far forwards, towards the bow, luggage was being swung aboard, while just below him men were carrying food up a gangway and through an open door in the ship's hull. He wondered how they could work in the heat; he was hot just watching them. But thick clouds were blowing up which should have cooled things down — although it was so humid that the absence of the sun seemed to make no difference at all.

"Found you at last," Frances said coming up the ladder from the first deck below.

"I thought you were taking a nap?"

"I was. But I woke up feeling all trapped and claustrophobic with the curtains closed and the air-conditioning puffing away. Had some ghastly dreams."

"You should have retired earlier. No one said you had to stay up until four watching me lose at blackjack."

"But you were winning! You were over two hundred quid ahead. My hero!"

"That's when your moronic hero should have called it quits. I ended up over thirty pounds down."

"Never mind, lover, it was a wonderful experience. And I could also enjoy myself watching those slimy Nazis losing money at the roulette table. It was like something out of a bad movie, all that nattering in German, slamming the table when they lost — even that one who kept twisting his monocle around and around. Is that a drop of rain I felt?"

"It was. And that was one of his friends — and here comes a lot more."

They hurried to the door and pulled it open, were barely inside when the heavens opened up and the rain thundered onto the wooden deck behind them. The Lido Bar was deserted, with just the barman, Sean, carefully polishing a glass. All but a few of the passengers had gone ashore.

"Raining stair rods," Sean said. "Would you people like a drink, perhaps, to put some joy into your life?"

"And alcohol to soothe the system," Hank said. "Why not."

After the Pacific crossing, they were regulars here and had no need to specify their drinks. Sean poured a large measure of tax-free Gordon's gin into a glass, lemon and no ice, with Schweppes tonic on top of that, then put it down in front of Frances at the bar. Hank watched intently, nibbling at the peanuts before him, as the barman poured a much larger measure of Bombay gin into a cocktail-pitcher, added ice and a few drops of Noilly-Pratt, then stirred and decanted it through the strainer into a chilled glass from the fridge. A bit of lemon peel, squeezed over the drink so that the drops of oil could float on the surface, then rubbed on the rim and dropped in, completed the drink.

"Good," Hank said, sipping from it. "First of the day."

"But far from the last, sir, far from the last."

"Thanks a lot, Sean, I appreciate the observation."

"Always happy to oblige, sir."

They finished their drinks in silence, idly watching the barman first slice lemons, then prepare a large container of his own formula Bloody Mary mix. He had worked in New York for a number of years, to the pleasure of the Americans aboard who did not want warm white wine when they ordered a Martini, or beer served at blood heat. Sean reserved these pleasures for his British customers, and what you were served depended upon your accent.

"Do you know how I feel now?" Frances said, holding onto her drink with both hands and staring into the depths. "I have the horrible sensation that someone is walking on my grave." Hank put his hand on hers and held tight. "I know that I'm sounding stupid, and I have never been much of a one for the vapors and female intuition and all that. But just now, at this very moment, I felt a wave of black depression wash over me — completely without reason."

"Completely with reason. With those Nazis aboard and more on the way, with trouble of some kind coming up — I don't blame you in the slightest. I blame myself for letting you come with me."

She shook her head. "No. I would be feeling infinitely worse if I were just sitting at home and worrying myself sick about you. It's better this way and I'm over my fit — so let's go down to the cabin and have a matinée."

"My, but we are being forward today. I bet you think that I'm an easy lay . . . . "

"I know you are."

"You're right. I don't deny it." He looked at his watch. "I have to meet Ginzberg in three hours to give him the latest tapes . . . . "

"That should be just about enough time for what I have in mind for you. Let's go."

They stood and Hank left some money on the bar; Sean waved goodbye. The nearest elevator was just beyond the adjoining lounge so they would not have to go out on deck again.

"Have you been to Ginzberg's cabin yet?" Frances asked. Hank shook his head *no*.

"We meet at the same place every time — the men's room on the boat deck. I know it sounds like every other spy movie, but it really works. No one's ever there, I give him the tape and we leave separately. He'll tell me if there has been anything new on the old tape, but we've heard about all there is by now. That should change now that we're in Acapulco."

Hank had his key ready and unlocked the door to their cabin as they came up to it. He pushed it open and stood aside to let Frances in first.

"Robert's been here making the bed or something," she said. "He's closed the curtains and turned the lights off."

She switched on the lights and gasped. Leandro Diaz stood up from the chair where he had been sitting.

"Please don't be alarmed," he said. "I am an associate of your husband."

"That's true," Hank said, closing and locking the door. "But I wish to hell you would knock or something before you came in. I don't like Frances being startled like this."

"I am sorry, I apologize most strongly. But it was necessary not to be seen. I waited until this cabin was not being observed . . . . "

"You have a key to our room!" Frances said angrily.

"No. Just a certain skill with locks."

While he was talking the door to the bedroom opened

and Josep and Concepcion came out. "Better and better," Frances said in her iciest voice. "Are there any more in there, or is two enough to do whatever little things you do with each other in my bedroom?"

"Frances, please. How these people came here is not important . . . . "

"Oh, isn't it? Not to you, perhaps, but I'm afraid that I'm used to a little more in the way of privacy — or politeness."

She stopped then, realizing that these strangers were completely unconcerned with her feelings; the girl scarcely noticing her. Frances stalked across the room and took out her temper on the curtains, throwing them wide, then looking out at the lashing rain, tapping her fingers angrily on the glass.

"All right, Diaz. What are you doing here and who are these people?" Hank spoke in a low voice, controlling his anger.

"These are my Uruguayan associates . . . . "

"Tupamaros?" Hank said.

"Yes," Josep said, crossing the room and picking up the phone. "May I use your telephone?" He was dialling well before he asked; Hank remained silent. Josep spoke a few words in quick Spanish and hung the phone up again. "I am glad we all have the chance to meet at last. And exchange information. You have something to tell us?"

"That depends what you know already. Do you have a transcript of the material delivered in Hawaii?"

"I had one from your people," Josep said. "I passed a copy on."

"Then you know almost all that we do. These tapes since then go over the old ground with nothing really new."

"All right, then I have information for you. The

meeting will be aboard this ship. The diamonds will change hands here — and the principals involved will be General Stroessner and Admiral Marquez.''

"The national leaders themselves?''

''Exactly. This provides a rich opportunity for us, as you might imagine . . . . ''

He was interrupted by a knock on the door. "Let them in,'' Josep ordered. "Those are my associates.''

Frances was furious — but silent. Hank unlocked and opened the door and four men slipped in. They appeared to be cultivated and well-dressed Latins. But with the same grim hardness about them that Josep had. ''These people will be staying in this cabin,'' Josep said. "They have come aboard the ship illegally and have no quarters of their own.''

''That tears it,'' Frances said, stalking across the room and standing before the arrogant Tupamaro. "For all of the brass-bound nerve you take the prize. So take your friends out of here and . . . . ''

Concepcion stepped close and seized Frances by the shoulders, spinning her about and slapping her viciously across the face. Frances moaned with pain and Hank jumped forward, this tiny sound driving all reason from his brain. He seized Concepcion and hurled her to the floor, clenched and raised his fist.

"Enough,'' Josep said, seizing Hank's arm to pull him away. Still possessed by anger Hank spun about and drove his fist hard against the man's jaw.

Josep fell and rolled and, like a cat, was on his feet in an instant. With a long knife in his hand thrust out before him. His face filled with cold fury; no one struck him and lived. Hank saw this, but would not retreat. He crouched, hands extended and ready, his only chance would be to grab the knife arm. Josep tensed to leap — when Leandro Diaz's voice called out sharply.

"This is a .45 calibre Webley I am holding," he said, moving the barrel of the large revolver back and forth to cover them all. "You will put that knife away, Josep. The violence among us will end here. You will put that knife away, Josep. The violence among us will end here. You will tell that little bitch with you that I will kill her, instantly, if she as much as touches Mrs. Greenstein again. You all understand this language, don't you? Or should I shoot one of you just to make the point clearer? We must work together on this thing, without internal wrangling. Agree now — or get out of here."

"Agreed," Josep said in a toneless voice, folding the large clasp knife and putting it away. His hand lashed out, hitting Concepcion so hard that she gasped and fell to the floor. "There. All even now, Mrs. Greenstein. You have had your revenge. Now we will stop these stupid games and go to work. We need each other. We don't have to like each other. But we will work together for our common goal."

Leandro looked at Josep, at the other Tupamaros, and knew that he had to make his mind up now. Was Josep telling the truth? Probably. He was correct when he said they needed each other. The tape-recorded information added to what his Paraguayan informants passed on to him, had made this entire operation possible. They all knew that. And the Tupamaros had been brought in as a heavy squad, a job they knew how to do and could do well. For the time being they would all work together for their mutual benefit. But afterward — when the others were no longer needed — what would the Tupamaros do then? That was obvious too; they would do just what they wanted to do, irrespective of anyone else's needs or desires. So be it. That particular bridge would have to be crossed when they came to it. For now, they would act in alliance.

"All right then. We get on with the job," he said, putting the revolver back into his belt. He did it calmly and surely — but it was the same calm as that of an animal trainer entering a cage of tigers. If he showed fear he would be ripped to shreds.

Frances went numb with something more than shock. She was aware of Hank's arm around her as he helped her to a chair. She appreciated it and loved him, was immensely glad that he was there. But his presence could not alter the sudden awareness that the world, as she had always known it, was no longer there. She was now living in another and more terrible reality where none of her old values appeared to apply. A world she had read about in the newspapers yet really, truthfully had never thought existed, or rather its existence, for her, was on a par with the reality of the latest novel. Imaginary people, far away, doing imaginary things. As she dropped into the chair, she realized that she had had her first lesson in living in this new world. Keep her mouth shut and forget the social order of things she had always lived in and believed in. She found that she wasn't humiliated by the discovery, quite the opposite. It was a lesson in survival that she had learned. And she wanted to survive.

Hank had learned the lesson too. But as he leaned on the side of the chair, his arm around Frances, he worked very hard to keep his expression blank and set. Because he was filled with a burning fury that had no outlet. Not yet. So he did not wish anyone here to know his feelings. They would, he promised himself that, they would one day. He knew a good deal more about this other world than Frances did, which was one of the reasons he had been so loathe to expose her to it. He knew that some little bit of happiness had died inside of her, died forever, and he detested these people for doing that to her. Nothing could be done about it at the present time.

He would help them in their plans to shake down their vicious little dictators. He would do this in order to assure that the Nazi war criminals were brought to justice. But when that part of the job was done there would be a personal sorting out. He had no idea yet what form it would take. But it would happen, yes, it would, and he was looking forward to that time with immense pleasure.

The atmosphere was still tense, taut, and no one seemed willing to break the silence. The sudden knocking on the door startled them all since it was a new factor, an outside one that none of them were expecting. But the Tupamaros were survivors of countless sudden interruptions, and moved together without a word, crossing silently to the end of the room where they would be unseen when the door opened. After a moment's hesitation, Leandro joined them. Josep silently waved Hank forward.

"See what it is," he whispered. "Get rid of them." He stood behind the door and put his foot just a few inches from it, so it could be opened no wider than a crack.

Hank unlocked the door and looked out.

"Let me in, quickly," Uzi Drezner said, "I can't be seen out here."

Hank signalled to Josep who stepped back, at the same time slipping a pistol mounted with a cylindrical silencer from his shoulder holster. Uzi came in and looked around at the people in the room with no hint of surprise. He waited until Hank had locked the door again before he spoke.

"I see that we are all here now. Good. What I have to say concerns everybody involved in this affair. You can put the gun away, Josep . . . that's right. You do remember me, don't you?"

The Tupamaro nodded. "That was years ago. You

were well introduced and came to me with an interesting offer. Someone you wanted, someone we were happy to be rid of . . . . ''

"Butcher Schultz."

"That was the man. A fat, red-faced butcher who went to work for the government. In the same line of trade. Only butchering people this time."

"He had done that sort of thing years before. In the camps. We wanted him to go on trial. He did. With your help."

"You paid well for that help. And promptly."

"We always pay well for value received. We have cooperated amicably in the past; let us do so in the future. Now I suggest that we all sit down and relax. Would anyone like a drink? Hank, would you be so kind as to oblige?"

It wasn't so much that Uzi took control of the situation, it was more that he ordered their relationships. Started them working together again. Hank was glad to physically do something, pouring out drinks for the few that wanted anything. "I didn't know that you were aboard ship, Uzi," he said, sloshing Scotch over the rocks.

"I came aboard in Hawaii but have been keeping to my cabin. I am sure that some of those Germans know me — they have their intelligence sources, too. But I have not been idle. One of the stewards is Maltese and has a large hungry family at home. He has been supplying me with information. Which is why I came here. I want to hear today's tape. It appears that the Germans are no longer in the suite next to you."

"They've left the ship?" Hank asked, worried.

"No, they are still aboard, they didn't even go ashore here in port. It seems that as soon as the other passengers were out of the way this morning they changed cabins, moving to smaller ones on this same deck that have been vacant since the cruise began. Of course the stewards transferred their luggage which is how I found out about it. So now the two large suites are empty.''

''There is no need to listen to the tape,'' Leandro Diaz said, accepting a drink from Hank with a nod of thanks. ''A report reached me earlier today that General Stroessner left Asunción this morning by plane, bound for the military airbase at Maldonado in Uruguay. He will join Admiral Marquez there and they will be coming here. Those suites are for them.''

''Where will they board? Do you know that? I don't think that the Mexican government would exactly welcome their presence.''

Leandro Diaz shook his head and sipped at the drink. ''They would not enter Mexico in any case. They don't want it known that they are out of their countries. They certainly don't want it known that they are negotiating a large arms deal. Our sources did not know when or how they were boarding, just that they were coming to the QE2.''

''We'll find out soon enough how it will be arranged,'' Uzi said. ''Since they are not here yet we can use the time to make arrangements. What kind of force do we have aboard the ship? Leandro, how many of your Paraguayans?''

''Three, including myself. We could not book cabin space for any more. Nor would it have made any difference. None of the others are good with weapons.''

''Josep — what about you?''

The Tupamaro leader pointed about the room. ''The six of us you see here, and three more in a cabin. There was no more space available, as Leandro says, so these four came aboard as longshoremen and changed their clothes in the crew's bathroom. All four are sailors, they know their way about ships. Most important of all is Esteban Valverde there.'' The serious looking, dark-haired man nodded when they glanced in his direction.

"Esteban is Concepcion's brother, and what might be called a sleeper for our organization. He has never taken place in an operation before, not directly, but he has been invaluable in many other ways. He is Captain of a deep-sea fishing boat. Now he joins us to put his expertise at our command. He and the other three sailors make any operations aboard this ship possible."

"And you want all four of them to stay here in my cabin, don't you Josep?" Hank said, looking first at the Tupamaro leader, then turning to face Uzi.

"Indeed?" Uzi did not seem shocked by the information. "That will be possible for a short period. We will come back to the point after we have discussed our mutual plans." He turned to look at Hank as he said it, as though to reassure him that something would be done about it. Hank shrugged and drank his whisky.

"We have weapons of all kinds. They are also aboard," Josep told them. "We are prepared for any eventuality."

"Well, which eventuality are you exactly planning for?" Uzi asked.

"We have a simple uncomplex plan. We have a deep-sea fishing boat, purchased further down the coast, and it is already at sea. The Captain knows the course of the *QE2* after she leaves Acapulco, and will be standing by at approximately one day's sailing from here. They also have a good radio and are listening for contact or any change of plans. So we simply wait until the diamonds are produced and the exchange is made. When that is done we will know also where the munitions ship is and what details have been arranged for turning it over in exchange for the gems. Then we act. We take the radio room, send out our message where contact will be made, then silence all of the radios. No member of the British crew will be hurt as long as they obey orders. Then we take the Nazis and Stroessner, Marquez and their guards. This time people will be hurt. But I am sure that no one here cares about that. We will have the stones, you, Uzi will have your war criminals, so then we will leave the *QE2* in their fastest launch and rendezvous with our ship out of sight. Sink the launch and that is the end of it. We will all have what we want.''

Uzi made up his mind very quickly. ''I like it. We will cooperate with you in every way. I will discuss plans with you for a meeting at sea to take the prisoners off your hands. What about the munitions ship?''

''That will depend on the situation at the time. If we cannot arrange to take it for our own use, we can certainly inform Global Traders that they will not be paid. So the deal will be off. Do you agree, Diaz?''

The two revolutionary leaders eyed each other coldly. ''Of course,'' Diaz said. ''My people will leave with yours in the escape ship. We will divide up the diamonds before we separate. Isn't that right?''

''Of course it is. Then it appears we are all of a mind. Our task is now to sit and wait quietly to see what their next move will be.''

Quietly! Frances thought to herself. She did not know whether to laugh or to cry, but was so shocked that instead she said nothing. It was hard to take in, to believe. That these people sit about the room, sipping at their drinks and nodding seriously, while they discussed piracy and murder and theft. And her Hank just as serious and agreeable as the others.

She knew now why he had been so reluctant to tell her about his involvement with these people in the first place. The real world of spies bore little resemblance to the clean-cut, game-playing and escapist fictional one. These people played dirty and they played for keeps.

''I'll have a drink, too,'' she told Hank. ''A strong one, if you don't mind.''

15

From the bridge of the *QE2*, a good hundred feet above the water, Captain David Rapley had a clear and unhampered view of the sea ahead, and to port and starboard as well. Off to port, the jungles and mountains of Mexico were slipping away, dimly visible through the tropical showers that were sweeping down upon them. Ahead was the open sea, slate gray and speckled by rain. The arching bow cut cleanly into the surface, sending out a frothing white wave to either side. It was good to be at sea again; Captain Rapley never felt completely comfortable ashore.

"Coffee, sir," the steward said, setting the silver tray before him. Rapley leaned back in the Captain's chair and nodded. Poured from a silver pot into a china cup. A far cry from the poisonous brew served in a heavy chipped mug that had passed for a beverage in the Navy. For a moment, as he stirred in a spoonful of sugar and sipped at the hot and delicious liquid, he had a fleeting touch of nostalgia for those days now vanished. Mugs of tea and large gins in the Wardroom and the pleasures of comrades together doing a job that had to be done. A very different existence from this, the air-conditioned comfort of the world's most luxurious liner. Over sixty-seven thousand tons of ship; one hundred and ten thousand horsepower at his command. A far cry from the five-stack destroyers he had first served in. The hell with nostalgia. They were good days but they were gone. He drank deep of the coffee. Their problems were gone too — and they wouldn't be missed. Life was a good deal easier now.

The Staff Captain came up and saluted, a large yellow envelope in his hand. Captain Rapley returned the salute and scowled at the envelope. There were still problems commanding a ship, but they were of a totally different order.

"We're outside of Mexican territorial waters now," Staff Captain Flint said.

"I suppose we are — or you wouldn't be bringing me that damn thing."

"Temper, Dave, temper. Ours is but to serve, not reason why. Shall I open it?"

The job of the Staff Captain was to shoulder whatever of the Captain's burdens that he could. He was an accredited Ship's Master as well and commanded the *QE2* when the Captain was on leave. While at sea he was very much concerned with staff matters and worked closely with the Hotel Manager whose four gold bands matched his own four stripes. Most of the day-to-day matters concerning the passengers they worked out between them. Only when the problem became too important was the Captain bothered. And he was very much bothered this time.

"See that this is entered into the log," the Captain said, glaring at the envelope as though it contained a poisonous serpent. "I don't like the front office interfering with the running of this ship."

"I agree," the Staff Captain said amicably. "But you must admit that the passengers are what pay to keep the old girl going — so some concessions must be made." He took out a single sheet of paper and passed it over without glancing at it. Captain Rapley read it quickly, his eyebrows drawing together in a scowl as he did so. In the end he snorted loudly and turned to look out at the ocean before he passed the paper back to the Staff Captain.

"Bloody lunacy," he said. "Whatever can they be thinking of?"

"Making money," Flint said, reading the orders. "This is a diplomatic affair of some kind, plenty of extra charges being paid for the extra service. Good headlines eventually and in the long run plenty of good publicity." As soon as he had finished reading he looked out at the sea just as the Captain had done a few moments earlier.

"It's a preposterous jumble of cloak-and-dagger nonsense," the Captain said. "High ranking government officials with diplomatic passports . . . all possible aid . . . a seaplane now in the air and waiting for a prearranged signal to land in order to board these passengers! I've never heard of anything like it."

"All the better. The passengers will love it, they'll take pictures and show their friends at home. You couldn't have arranged a better diversion if you tried."

"Nonsense. It's a dangerous stunt, that's all it is. And what if there is an accident? It's not safe to put a plane down on that ocean out there. Unsafe."

The Staff Captain smiled.

"Come on, Dave, you're letting all the responsibility-to-the-passengers stuff go to your head. During the war you wouldn't have thought twice about seeing a seaplane land on an ocean like that. Wind seven knots, long rollers, easy enough to put the thing down in the trough between them, visibility still over a mile at the worst. A piece of cake. What do you say?"

Captain Rapley thought for a long moment — then smiled. "Send the signal. Until they are aboard the ship they are not my responsibility. If some screwball pilot wants to wreck his craft landing near me it's not my problem at all.''

"Spoken like a sporting man! Let's bring them in and see what we're getting in the surprise package.''

"But see that every bit of this goes into the log! Time of signal, time of arrival, weather conditions, everything. And be sure you describe the sea conditions exactly and be absolutely sure that Sparks makes a recording of everything said. Be this on their own heads. And stop all engines. By the time they arrive I want us dead in the water.''

He sat drumming his fingers on the arm of his chair until the Staff Captain returned.

"They're on the way," he said.

"All right. Lower the boarding ladder and the number one cruise launch. Better go with it yourself to see that the transfer goes off without a hitch.''

The matter was out of the Captain's hands now; he was just as much a spectator as the excited passengers staring out of the windows or braving the rain for a better view from the decks. He watched with the rest of them as the big four-engined flying boat appeared out of the low-hanging clouds. It swept low over the ship — probably to check the wind direction from their flags — the engines roaring mightily, stains on the white skin showing clearly. Then it was past and banking into a wide turn. Dropping lower.

Finally setting down lazily with a splash of foam. The launch rushed out to meet the plane. With his high-power binoculars, the Captain could see the launch swing up to the open door, watch as six men climbed carefully down into the launch. As soon as they started back he issued orders that the deck below, and the forward lift, be sealed off so the new arrivals could go directly to their suites without being seen or disturbed

by the other passengers. He had no idea at all who the
people were who had just come aboard, but considering
the delicacy of the matter this seemed a wise precaution.
In any case, whoever they were, they were politicians of
some kind, Central or South American politicians. This
had to mean trouble. Everything here, or in the Near
East, meant trouble when politicians were involved. In
addition to this, the Captain, as an ex-Navy man, had
always entertained a deep suspicion of politicians whose
prime function in life seemed to him to be that of
cutting Naval appropriations.

Their table for two was set by the window, so Hank and
Frances had a perfect view of the seaplane when it
landed. They could see the ship's launch when it picked
up the new passengers, then returned, disappearing
from sight below them.

"No prizes for guessing who just came aboard,"
Hank said. Frances nodded agreement.

"The top twisters themselves. The principals finally
on stage. I still find it a little hard to believe that I'm
really involved in this. A few weeks ago I thought that
Paraguay and Uruguay were a pair of stand-up comics
— and Nazis were creatures you saw late at night on the
box in old black and white films. I've just had an education."

"Can I tell you how bad I feel about this? How sorry
I am that I ever let you get involved . . . . "

"No, please," she said, leaning forward and taking
his hand in hers. "I don't mean to complain. It's just
that it's all so new for me and it takes some getting used
to. I'm just beginning to realize what a sheltered life I
have always led. I'm not ready yet to thank you for
taking me out of it — I still get a chill down my back
when I think of those Tupamaros . . . . "

"I'll kill them myself. With my bare hands."

The cold, the calmness of Hank's voice, was even worse than anger would have been. He meant it, she knew that. She shivered and held his hand even tighter.

"Please, darling, that's not what I mean. There's enough going on without your getting into more trouble because of me. As I said, I'm not thankful yet that I have been forced to grow up so quickly and face reality. The sudden onslaught of maturity can be a painful thing. But I can handle it — as long as you are there. I have a feeling that I may enjoy life a bit more. Afternoon tea at Fortnum's will do a lot to take the taste of those people out of my mouth."

"Are you finished, madam?" the waiter asked, appearing at her elbow. Hank had enthusiastically consumed his portion of Mexican avocado vinaigrette stuffed with fresh cooked prawns, but she had only pushed hers around on the plate.

"Yes, thank you. I'm not too hungry today. In fact you had better cancel the next course and bring me a green salad instead."

"You'll starve yourself, it's not right," Hank said as the waiter took the dishes away.

"Little chance of that, my love, after the way we have been eating on this voyage." She patted her rounded flank. "I'm afraid to guess how many pounds I have put on."

"And I love every avoirdupois ounce of it!"

"Only from a distance, pet, until Roger the lodger and his companions vacate our suite. Must we let those villains stay with us?"

"I'm afraid they have to. But it should not be for long. We can stay in the bedroom and lock the connecting door and let them make do with the couch and carpet or whatever. I'm not too concerned about their comfort."

"Just mention them and they appear. Isn't that my

girl friend oozing slimily between the tables?''

Concepcion Valverde had entered the Queen's Grill and had seen them, was coming towards them. Stopping as she passed to smile and nod as though to say hello. Her message was more important.

"You're wanted in the cabin. Come now." The coldness of her words was in direct contrast to the warmth of her expression. Frances smiled in return and gave as well as she received.

"Leave us alone you acid bitch . . . you *puta*."

"They are talking of a meeting in the next cabin. You are needed for the listening equipment." She spoke to Hank, completely ignoring Frances, turning and leaving as soon as she was finished.

"What was that you called her?" Hank asked.

"*Puta*. It means whore. It was the worst word I could think of quickly. I must get a Spanish dictionary out of the ship's library and bone up for our next encounter."

"I have to go . . . ."

"Of course. And you'll understand if I linger over my salad and don't hurry back?"

"Yes, I'm sorry about this. I'll be as fast as I can in the cabin. Wait for me here, or if you finish I'll see you in the bar."

"Not in the Queen's Grill Bar. Too stuffy. I'll be in the Lido Bar watching the beach boys showing off in the pool."

"Good. I'll be as fast as I can."

There's just no way out of it now, Hank thought, as he walked slowly back to their quarters. No way. I don't mind for myself, I knew what I was getting into. But I was kidding myself when I thought I could bring Frances on this trip and not have her get involved. It must have been the old subconscious at work; wanting to tell her but afraid to tell her. So unconsciously I set up a situation where she would have to find out what I have been doing. Or am I being too Freudian? Oh the hell with it — what's done is done. He rapped loudly on the door of their suite, then again angrily when it wasn't answered at once. It opened a crack and a suspicious dark eye looked at him before it was swung wide.

Josep was sitting next to the tape recorder with earphones on, listening. Uzi and the girl were watching him, as was Leandro Diaz. The other four Tupamaros were sprawled in the chairs or sitting against the wall. The room was crowded, the air thick with strong tobacco. Uzi looked up as Hank came in, then waved him over.

"They all seem to be meeting in there," he said. "This tape is almost finished. Get another, quickly."

"Just as soon as you get some of these people out of here. Those four, they're not needed. Nor is the girl. Out."

Josep lifted one earphone and nodded solemn agreement, taking no notice of the anger in Hank's voice. He spoke quickly and curtly and the Tupamaros got up and filed into the next room. Discipline. As soon as the bedroom door had closed behind them Hank went to the dresser and found the fresh tape under the clothing in the bottom drawer.

"Shall I change it now? Before things warm up in there?"

"Yes, good idea," Uzi said. "Stroessner and two of his aides are in this suite next to you. Admiral Marquez and his people are across the passageway. All of the conversation has been in Spanish so far. Mostly complaints about the flight down here. A big tropical storm brewing and they had to drop down through it to land. Stroessner was airsick and is feeling very sorry for himself. He is now drinking neat gin to cure the condition."

"That's a remedy I never heard of before."

"He is washing it down with Bavarian beer. A Teutonic boilermaker. The phone rang once and he spoke in German when answering it. He was almost polite when he talked, referring to the other party always as Herr Doktor . . . ."

"Could it be Wielgus!?"

"My fingers are crossed — and yours should be as well. We've had people watching the boarding in every port, but he could easily have slipped through. Our only photo of him is thirty years old. But if Doctor Joachim Wielgus is aboard, why then we are getting close, very close indeed . . . ."

"Silence," Josep said. "He is making another phone call, this one in English. Talking to the weapons people. Telling them to bring the diamond expert at once. Now."

"This is it!" Hank said. "We have them."

Even the stolid Josep permitted a small smile to touch his lips as he nodded agreement.

The meeting was taking place.

16

"Another beer, José, instantly, another beer for the love of God!" Stroessner patted his rounded stomach and groaned, then belched deeply. Major de Laiglesia snapped his fingers in the direction of Sergeant Pradera who was standing stolidly near the bar.

"At your orders, General," the Major said, keeping the chain of command intact.

Pradera opened a bottle, took a chilled mug from the freezer and carefully poured it full, then brought it over on a tray to Stroessner. The General clutched at it, drained half of the contents, then groaned.

"First airsick, then next it will be seasick, I know."

Major de Laiglesia did his best to reassure his suffering commander. "The storm will undoubtedly end soon. And this ship, so big with tremendous stabilizers, you'll feel nothing . . . ."

"Shut up. Pour the gin."

There was a sudden sharp knocking on the door. Sergeant Pradera stepped to one side where he had a clear view of the door, at the same time drawing his U.S. Army issue .45 calibre automatic. An old and treasured weapon with which he had twice won the Paraguayan National Championship.

"Who is it?" de Laiglesia called out, his hand on the doorknob.

"Chvosta."

Stroessner nodded and de Laiglesia opened the door.

Sergeant Pradera waited until he was sure of the visitor's identity before he holstered his gun. The fat weapons merchant had to turn sideways to pass through the door. Aurelia Hortiguela came after him followed by Hendrik De Groot. Chvosta waited until the door was closed before he spoke.

"This is our diamond man, De Groot. Where are the stones?"

General Stroessner groaned again as he stood and turned his back on Chvosta and walked to the bedroom door. He stopped with his hand on the knob and spoke to de Laiglesia.

"Tell them what has to be done." He went into the bedroom and slammed the door behind him.

"Your General is a pig," Aurelia said. Chvosta waved her to silence.

"The diamonds?" he asked again.

"There are certain conditions," de Laiglesia said. "Your expert is to stay here, you are not. He will examine the stones and make an evaluation of their worth at current market prices. Then he will leave. You will all be summoned when we are ready to finalize the arrangements."

"There can be no more delays. We have waited long enough already."

"We will finish this as soon as we can. You must understand that there are complicated international arrangements to be made when dealing with sums of money this size . . . ."

"I care nothing for your arrangements," Chvosta broke in, coldly angry. "You have had almost a year to play your games. You have no more time. Tell your principals that you have a maximum of twenty-four hours to finish your business and complete this transaction. After that there will be a five percent additional charge, that is five percent of the total sum, levied for every day's delay. Understand?''

"You can't do that!''

"I've just done it. You know my cabin number. De Groot, bring me the final figure when you have done your sums. I'll be waiting for you.''

"Yes, Mr. Chvosta.'' The diamond expert remained calm. He was used to this kind of emotional scene when large sums of money were involved. It was of no importance to him; his fee would remain the same. He sat on a chair against the wall and put his heavy briefcase on the floor beside him.

As soon as the armament merchants had gone, de Laiglesia hurried to report to the General, closing the bedroom door behind him so their conversation would not be heard. Sergeant Pradera stared as calmly into space as did the Dutchman. They were both used to waiting. Neither moved until de Laiglesia returned.

"The diamonds, they'll be here in a moment,'' he said. He was trembling slightly, rubbing his hands together. The General had not received the news graciously. A large rum was very much in order at the moment. But he dare not drink alone.

"Mr. De Groot, can I offer you a drink?''

"I never trink alcoholic beverages ven I am vorking.'' His English was perfect, his accent thick. "However, a mineral water, iv you please.''

Sergeant Pradera knew very well what de Laiglesia was after so made no offer of help. The Major opened the bar and found a split of Perrier which he poured out. And the rum for himself, which he drained in a single gulp, putting the glass hurriedly out of sight when the bedroom door suddenly opened and the General poked his head out.

"They are on the way,'' he said. "Unlock the door and

leave it open. And no questions when they come. Just do as they say. I'll wait in here, so let me know when they have gone." He popped back out of sight and closed the door.

The Major forgot the mineral water as he hurried to the door and opened it. De Groot did not mention the oversight. What happened next happened fast; de Laiglesia had just turned around when Fritz appeared behind him, stepping in from the hall. His hand was in his jacket pocket and something hard pressed into de Laiglesia's back. The young German had been living in this suite since they had left Cape Town and knew it well. He looked swiftly around.

"You there, Sergeant," he ordered. "Take out that gun with your fingertips and put it on the floor."

"He doesn't speak English," de Laiglesia stammered, then repeated the order rapidly in Spanish.

The Sergeant looked at the newcomer for a long moment before obeying. Moving slowly, drawing the gun and putting it carefully down on the carpet. When Fritz was satisfied, he pushed de Laiglesia further into the room and called back over his shoulder.

"O.K."

Dr. Wielgus came in followed closely by his bodyguard, Klaus, and the other two young Germans who had also been staying in this suite. He was carrying a black leather bag. He looked coldly at De Groot and waited until the door had been closed before he spoke.

"Are you the one to do the evaluation?"

"I am."

"Then begin."

The five other men watched in silence as De Groot went to the desk and placed his bag upon it. He was calm, ordered, all trace of any nervousness gone. He was at work now. First he took off his jacket and hung it carefully on the back of the chair. Before he opened his bag he took the blotter, ash tray, everything from the top of the desk, and placed them on the floor beside it. Then he snapped the locks open on his bag and took out a number of items. A sensitive quartz balance scale with a digital readout, a powerful lamp with focussing lens, a white cloth which he carefully unfolded, jeweller's loupe, tweezers, a printing calculator, one item after another to be arranged in a careful pattern before him. Only when everything had been done to his satisfaction did he turn around to face the others.

"I will see the stones now," he said.

Wielgus stepped forward and spoke for the first time.

"They are in here. In separate bags. We have records of the diamonds in each bag. You will examine and evaluate each stone, and keep your record by the bag number. Yes?"

"Of course. If you please."

Fritz was the only one not fascinated by the operation. He had picked up Sergeant Pradera's gun and now held it in his lap as he sat against the wall, watching the doors and everyone in the room.

De Groot put the open satchel on the floor beside him and reached down to take out the first chamois bag. Their eyes followed his every movement. He put it in the center of the cloth and examined the tag.

"Number 178-J," he said. Wielgus took a small looseleaf notebook from his pocket and opened it; then made a mark with his gold-barrelled pen.

"Very well. Proceed."

De Groot carefully shook the stones out upon the cloth. Their facets twinkled with every color of the rainbow under the glare of the spotlight as he pushed them around with his tweezers.

"Seventeen stones," he said. Wielgus nodded agreement and made another mark in his book.

It was slow, careful, precise work. Each stone was first wiped clean, then carefully weighed and an entry made. Then De Groot would hold the stone before the light and bend forward, the magnifying jeweller's loupe screwed into his eye, turning the diamond over and over, again and again. Only after careful examination of color, quality and cut would he come to a decision and make an entry into the calculator. He would then place the stone back in the bag and proceed to the next one.

The process went slowly. The only change from routine occurred when he found one stone that bothered him. He put it down on the cloth and took a low-power microscope from his capacious bag and used it to examine the diamond. This resolved whatever doubts he had and he nodded and entered a figure into the machine.

"What is wrong?" Wielgus asked.

"Nothing is wrong. It is chust that this particular stone happens to haf a flaw. A small one, but still a flaw."

"Show it to me on this list," Wielgus said, putting the notebook down on the desktop, then tapping the page with his finger. De Groot looked down the page slowly, then pointed out an entry.

"This one," he said.

Wielgus looked at the record. "How much is the stone worth?" he asked.

"The best price, sold individually, would be three thousand dollars. No more."

"That cannot be. I paid over ten thousand for this, some years ago, from a very reputable dealer."

"You vere cheated." De Groot picked up the next stone and held it to the light. "I do not make mistakes. That is vy my fee is so high."

One hour, then two hours went by, and De Groot never faltered. Only Wielgus remained interested, as stolid and careful as the Dutchman. Watching every movement, marking off the stones and sacks one by one. At the end of the third hour De Groot laid the loupe down on the cloth and stood up.''

''I will now take fife minute rest. I vould appreciate a cold mineral water.''

He stood and stretched, then walked about the room while he sipped at the water. Wielgus did not move from his chair. At the end of the five minute period De Groot returned to his work.

It was evening before the job was done. The last stone was examined in the same methodical manner, no slower and no faster than the others had been, then put into the final bag. This was sealed and placed with the others; a last entry made into the calculator.

''You will now add these up and give me a total,'' Wielgus said. ''You will not speak the sum aloud but will give me the piece of paper. You will then clear your machine and give me all of the printed records. Is this understood?''

''Uf course.''

De Groot did as he had been instructed. He did not bother to mention that as soon as he went to his stateroom he would make a record of the total and of the value of each of the little bags. He had a remarkable memory for money and for diamonds. He would also record the description of the unusual stones. It would be interesting if he ran across any of them again some time.

Wielgus put his notebook away and examined the printouts closely. ''This total,'' he said. ''How accurate is it?''

''It is what I vould get if I sold the stones on the open market. But only an aferage, mind you. If I sold them one at a time, taking months to do it, the price vould be higher. If I sold them quickly, in bulk lots, it vould be lower. An aferage, as I said.''

This satisfied Wielgus who nodded agreement. ''All right. Go now. Tell your principals what you have told me. I assume you can describe the stones and prices to them.'' He had been involved in buying diamonds for a long time and knew the abilities of experts in this field.

De Groot nodded and restored his equipment to the bag with the same meticulous care that he had used in taking everything out in the first place. He even put the items from the floor back onto the desk before donning his jacket. He left without a word. Wielgus waited until the man had gone and the door was locked before he spoke again.

''Major, get the General,'' he ordered. ''You, soldier, open some champagne.''

The Paraguayans hurried to obey. Stroessner appeared some minutes later, bleary eyed, he must have been asleep; but at least he was over the effects of his motion sickness.

''Herr Doktor Wielgus, what a pleasure to see you again,'' he said in thick Bavarian-accented German. He hurried over to take the other's hand in both of his. ''I see the champagne is open, wonderful idea. Do I·assume that we have something to celebrate?''

''A business deal, General, not a celebration. I was thirsty. Here is the total.''

Stroessner set down his glass and fumbled a pair of spectacles from his breast pocket and held them up to read the figure.

''So! It is larger than agreed.''

''Now it is. The market value has risen faster than I calculated. I'll remove enough stones so the value will be correct.''

''Then everything will go through as arranged?''

''It will, if we can agree on the final terms. Up until now we have been dealing through representatives. The time has now come to settle all the details, to be sure that we are in complete agreement and that there will be no slipups in putting the arrangements into effect. Remember, this is a long-term affair that will cover a number of years and there will be a great number of people involved. We must be specific about everything. And in writing.''

''Of course, understood. I will send for Admiral Marquez. The papers are ready? Good. We will agree and then we will sign and then we will drink champagne in celebration of the brilliant future of our countries.''

''Send for him. It has been a long day.''

17

Dr. Joachim Wielgus looked around at the men gathered in the suite as he sipped his champagne and felt, for the first time in a very long time, the indescribable sensation of unlimited power that he enjoyed so much. To him it was the ultimate sensation. He still sent for women occasionally, but they were pleasures to be consumed quickly like food and drink. None of these had the lasting, lifting excitement that his work gave him, making him immune to fatigue. He needed little rest, scarcely any food when he was working like this. Twenty hours had passed since he had last eaten yet he was unaware of it. Not since the good times during the war had he felt this way. Then he had hundreds of factories and camps under his direct administration; the destinies of hundreds of thousands of workers were controlled by his decisions. The factories had kept working and the great German war machine had kept functioning and Joachim Wielgus had made that all possible.

And now he was working another economic and military miracle. The destinies of his comrades were at stake, not to mention the fate and future of two sovereign countries and all of their millions of inhabitants. It had taken over a year to make all of the arrangements, a year of hard work that he had enjoyed immensely. And now it was to be finalized, the crowning achievement of his career.

They waited for him to begin, waiting silently, knowing that he was the one in charge. He stretched the moment out, luxuriated in it. First sipping again from his glass of champagne, then taking a long Havana cigar from the silver case in his pocket. The clipper was on his key chain and he carefully cut off the end. The Major hurried forward to light it. What was his name? De Laiglesia, that was right. The only servant present. A creature who could be controlled absolutely.

There were four more men present at the meeting. His associates Eitmann and Hartig. Good, trustworthy, unimaginative men who could be counted on to obey orders without question. They had assisted him for years and would continue to do so into the indefinite future.

And then the two tinpot dictators. What miserable creatures he had to work with! Stroessner, the brewer's offspring, sweating and drinking neat gin like the peasant he was. But he was also absolute ruler of Paraguay. But poor material still. But what was it that Jew President Rosenfeld had once said about one of these South American dictators, when he had been told that the man was a son of a bitch? Yes, but he's our son of a bitch. Too true. Probably President Rosenfeld had heard someone else say it first.

Next to Stroessner another son of a bitch that he owned. Sadistic, ulcerous, one-armed Admiral Marquez, leader of the military junta that ruled Uruguay with an iron fist. Not much to look at — but he knew how to take orders.

It was time to issue some orders, yes, it was. Wielgus blew out a large cloud of aromatic smoke and spoke suddenly and loudly. "This meeting will begin." The others braced themselves, almost sitting to attention when he spoke. As well they might.

"This is a momentous day, gentlemen, a momentous day indeed. A day that will not only initiate the continued military security of both Uruguay and Paraguay for the foreseeable future, but will guarantee the personal security and happiness of my comrades in the Brunderbund. I want to make it absolutely clear to both national leaders where the finances are coming from for this major operation.

"You know me as an international financier with interests around the world — and so I am. But it is not my money alone that I handle, far from it. The large amount of funds that I invest and control was entrusted to me by my comrades in Germany. Betrayed by Jews at home and abroad, stabbed in the back by the treacherous communists, the Third Reich was brought low. Never humbled, never defeated, hopefully to rise again some day, it nevertheless suffered a severe setback. Despite this, there were people who clearly read the handwriting on the wall, who knew that the only hope for the future of Germany was to save something from the debacle. I am happy to say that I was instrumental in preserving the large part of that national wealth for the future. It was difficult, but I did it, for that was my task. I won't bore you with details, but it suffices to say that the task was an immense one, an impossible one had I not been aided by my two good friends here. We had valuable paintings to dispose of discreetly, jewelry and gold, rare books, everything. It was a labor, but in the end it was done. Some of it was invested to provide day to day funds for the movement. Again I refrain from going into details. But a good part of this money was used to purchase diamonds. A commodity that only appreciates in value as the years go by. This foresight has proven its value by what I have with me now here, by my side."

Every eye in the room was on the case with the diamonds. Wielgus drew deeply on his cigar before he spoke again.

"This case contains diamonds, millions and millions

of dollars worth of diamonds. Enough to purchase the entire shipload of military equipment that will give your two countries security for the next decade. It is yours. An interest-free loan to be repaid over the next ten years. You both know the conditions attached to this loan but I would like to spell them out aloud to you, to then entertain any remarks or reservations that you may have. When this is done we will sign the agreement that I have drawn up and the negotiations with the arms dealers will be finalized.

"The terms are these. One tenth of the total amount due will be repaid by your governments each year. It will be repaid in your national currency at the then current rate of exchange, guarani in Paraguay, pesos in Uruguay. You realize that this face alone is of immense value to your economies since not only is the loan interest free but you are paying back a hard currency loan with your own softer currency." He nodded benevolently as he said this, a bestower of gifts, then drank some champagne. The national leaders were appropriately grateful and murmured their thanks.

"Now, that is what your countries will receive. For our part, it will give a number of our comrades a greater degree of security. It has been agreed that anyone we recommend will be instantly given citizenship and a passport, in whatever name he wishes, in either of your countries. All of the living expenses and whatever funds these new citizens will need will be paid to them from your national treasury to repay the military loan. A simple and mutually satisfactory procedure. These citizens will also benefit their new homelands by being of immense aid in government administration. They are men of great experience. Uruguay, where a number of our associates are already involved in government, knows full well their value. Also, being involved in administration, these good Germans will take the burdens off your hands of administering the repáyment of the loan. They will handle all of the details. To supervise the repayments I am putting my top people at your disposal. Colonel Manfred Hartig here will be liaising with you, Admiral, in Uruguay. As you have agreed, he will become Assistant Minister of Finance and will be in charge of repayments. Herr Karl-Heinz Eitman will have the equivalent position in Paraguay. That is it, simply stated. Now are there any questions?''

Admiral Marquez was unhappy with the terms, but could think of no way of improving them. ''Your people, in our government offices. There will be difficulties. The language, for instance . . . . ''

''That is not a problem, Admiral.'' Wielgus dismissed the objection with a wave of his hand. ''The men chosen for this liaison will all have lived in Central or South America for the past thirty years. I assure you that their Spanish is excellent.''

''Then if not the language, tenure of position. There will be complaints from the civil service if there are dismissals.''

''You are being tiresome, Admiral. These new operations will be created in parallel with your normal departments and paid for out of separate funds. This has all been mentioned in the agreement we drew up.''

''Bring me a drink. Wine.'' Admiral Marquez ordered de Laiglesia. He knew all of these things already. What was sticking in his craw was turning over more of the administration of his country to these Nazis. It kept him in power — but it was hard to take. He drank deeply as though trying to wash a bad taste from his mouth.

None of this bothered General Stroessner. Of German origin himself, he welcomed blood brothers. They would assure that his rule continued in the future as it had in the past. Half of the total annual budget of

Paraguay already went to the military who controlled every aspect of government. His prisons were full, the rebels dead or outside the country, trade unions abolished, the press controlled absolutely. He had no threats — as long as the military was well armed and well paid. This present arrangement would take care of that. His euphoric mood was interrupted by a sudden lurch of the ship, a shuddering motion that passed through him leaving a marked queasy sensation in its wake.

"Did you feel that?" he said. "There are supposed to be things on this ship to stop that. I thought we couldn't feel the waves."

"Stabilizers," Colonel Hartig said. "Fins that extend just below the sea. Effective only in moderate seas. The weather report was for severe tropical storms."

"More comments?" Wielgus asked.

There was really nothing more to talk about. All the details of the agreement had been hammered out during the past months and the parties concerned were in complete agreement about all of the basic principles. Stroessner shrugged while Marquez drank his wine and said nothing.

"Then, if we are in agreement, the time has come to sign. Colonel Hartig, if you please."

Hartig took up the thin briefcase that was beneath his chair and unlocked it. He produced three manila folders. "These three agreements are identical," he said. "Therefore, I shall give you one, General Stroessner, and you one as well, Admiral. If you will be so kind as to open them to the first page I will read mine aloud so as we can be absolutely sure that there is no disagreement on any point. I begin . . . . "

They nodded their heads over the documents as point after point was checked off. This did not take long. Hartig looked up when he had finished, but there were no dissenting voices.

"I take it we agree then, gentlemen. If you would be so kind as to bring your copies to the desk, we can sign. As you can see, I have taken the liberty of entering today's date in every document. Doctor Wielgus — would you do us the favor of signing first?"

"Of course."

His pen scratched once, twice, thrice, and he stepped back. Then the others signed and were each handed a copy of the document. Stroessner shook his head and chuckled aloud.

"Capital! Capital!" he said. "Now all that remains is the transaction with the diamonds and the turning over of the ship."

"Yes. But tomorrow," Wielgus said. "It is after midnight and communication with shore stations will be hard to do by radio. We will begin again in the morning. I will have the Czech informed that we meet here at ten a.m. to finish the operation." He picked up the phone and called a cabin number, issued a quick command and hung up. Within a minute there was a knocking on the door. "My men are here. I bid you all a goodnight."

He picked up the bag of diamonds, opened the door and left.

The slam of the closing door in the suite next door was the only sound that penetrated the hushed silence of the room. All four of the men there had been leaning close to the loudspeaker, turned low so there could be no possibility of audible feedback, listening with intense concentration to every word spoken. Now the sound of the door acted as a release of tension, an end to the meeting, a stopping point. The Israeli, Uzi Drezner, shook himself as though he had just stepped out from under a cold shower. Hank Greenstein leaned forward and turned off the speaker but left the recording tape running.

"The dirty, dirty bastards," he said in a low voice, scarcely aware that he had spoken aloud.

"Amen to that," Leandro Diaz said, wearily, rubbing his hand over the fresh bristles on his face. "Like that. Just like that — they give away my country to those swine. If I had not heard it with my own ears, if I had been told about this, I would not have believed it."

Only the Tupamaro leader, Josep, seemed unmoved by what they had heard. His expression and his manner did not change as he took out a cigarette and lit it. Yet his actions were just as much a statement as theirs. His life was already dedicated to overthrowing the corrupt régime in his country by any means. This disclosure added nothing new to that resolve. You cannot paint the devil blacker than he already is; you can only obliterate him.

"They have put themselves in our hands," he said, exhaling a lungful of smoke. "They have destroyed themselves."

"Josep is right," Uzi said, standing and stretching, then walking about the room to ease his cramped muscles. "We have always known what these creatures are like. Read Hitler's *Mein Kampf* — written over fifty years ago — and you'll find the same anti-Semitic fascist filth that Wielgus was spouting in there. But we have them now, all of them. They have gone too far. You do realize that there is a plan behind this Nazi move that was not mentioned in there, a far bigger plan than buying arms for your two-bit dictators?"

He had their attention now. Even Josep looked up. For him and for Diaz the liberation of their homelands was all that counted. They considered nothing beyond that. Hank was only confused.

"What plan?" he asked. "This looks like a straight-forward deal to trade money for a safe hideout. Isn't that all it is?''

"Far from it," Uzi said. "What we were listening to a
few minutes ago was nothing more than an attempt to
establish a firm base for the Fourth Reich."

"That's insane," Hank gasped.

"Probably. But that doesn't mean that it won't be
tried anyway. Old age is the only real enemy that these
concentration camp commanders and SS men face.
They have all the money that they need, all of the
security; Wielgus and the Brunderbund see to that. But
they are slowly dying off, one by one. Senility, death
and boredom are their only enemies. Over thirty years
has passed since their days of glory. If those days are
ever to come again they must establish a physical base
right now for the glorious Fourth Reich that they are
always talking about. Now they have that base.
Uruguay and Paraguay. They will come to these countries as advisors — but in ten years' time they will
control them outright. A homeland at last. They are
rich, intelligent, vicious — and we live in the world of
the atomic bomb. If they succeed in what they are trying
to do, there will be a Fourth Reich in South America at
the end of that ten-year period. One that will hold the
world up to atomic blackmail to get its way. And we will
have to knuckle under to their demands — whatever
they may be — or face the possibility of a nuclear holo-
caust.''

Hank and Leandro Diaz sat in silent horror at the
thought, but Josep nodded his head understandingly.

"I believe that you are right. And if you are, it makes
it even more imperative that we work together to eliminate this threat. To stop this plan before it is even
started. We will take the diamonds from them and we
will attempt to take the arms ship as well. Are we agreed
upon that?''

He looked around at the silent men who nodded,

slowly, one by one.

"Very good. We will then meet here in the morning to listen to details of the arms deal. Then we will strike. Any of them who resist will be killed. I hope that none of you still have any bourgeois qualms on that score . . . . "

The door opened and Frances came in, swaying as she clutched at the frame.

"Jesus. I've been waiting in that damned bar all night. I suppose you forgot little me?"

Hank jumped to his feet and closed the door and reached for her, but she pushed him away.

"I couldn't do anything else," he said. "I had to stay . . . . "

"Forget it," she said, walking towards the bedroom and leaning against the wall for support. "Found a nice man. Bought me drinks. Nicer than you, my beauty. Had things to talk about other than killing, guns, crap like that." She opened the bedroom door and looked in. "Jesus! It's like a goddamn South American YMCA in here! Will somebody throw these bums out and fumigate the bed so I can get some sleep?"

"Your men will stay in this sitting room," Hank told Josep.

"I would beat her to teach her sense about drinking and speaking to her husband in that manner," the Tupamaro said.

"Would you kindly mind your own fucking business and get them out of that room, then get yourself out of here until tomorrow? It has been a long day."

He stood before Josep, fists clenched, angry and hoping the other man would try something. Josep just turned and left. The others followed and Hank looked at their retreating backs and regretted the day he had ever become involved.

18

From the bridge of the *QE2*, the view of the Pacific Ocean forward was anything but pacific. Mountainous waves rolled in ponderously from starboard in continuous succession, slamming into the side of the great liner, breaking over her bows. Green water rushed across the foredeck and piled up against the rails, pouring through the scuppers back into the sea. Tropical rain lashed down and mixed with the sea water, while the force eight winds blew the tops from the waves and sent them whistling away in sprays of scud. As each wave passed along the hull, the ship rose up to meet it, rolled, shuddered then sank down again. The stabilizers fought an unequal battle but were overwhelmed.

Captain Rapley looked out at the savage spectacle and took no cheer from the sight. The coffee in his cup was ice cold, but he took no notice of this as he sipped it. Up here, on the uppermost deck of the ship, all of the pitching and rolling was more pronounced. He never noticed this either. He was one of the few sailors who, after a lifetime at sea, could truthfully say that he had never been seasick. Intellectually he sympathized with people who suffered this malady, but he had no real understanding of the torture they went through. No, the storm didn't bother him, nor did it threaten his ship in any way. Some pots might be carried away in the galley, dishes and glasses would be broken, but the storm, no matter how menacing it looked, posed no physical problem at all for this vessel. It had weathered worse.

But it was the passengers who would be suffering. The Captain had been out of the Navy and in the Merchant Marines long enough to know that some of his traditional values had to be turned on their heads. In the Navy, the complex fighting machine that he had commanded always came first and foremost. All of her technical facilities were always at peak performance. The engines, electronic gear, guns, torpedoes, mines, all must function faultlessly. Unhappily, they were serviced by imperfect humans who got sick, got drunk, overstayed leave and committed other indecencies that interfered with the perfect functioning of his command. That was the way it had been and he had adjusted to it.

Now, on the *QE2*, his accepted values had been stood on their head. Yes, his crew still followed his commands and could be counted upon to do their part in the successful operation of the ship. But his mission now was not to fight battles and win wars — but to make some one thousand six hundred passengers happy. Perhaps not as noble a cause as the destruction of the enemy, but one just as important to his success in his chosen profession. Nor could he blame his charges. They had paid out a lot of folding green banknotes for the pleasure of a world luxury cruise. Well, they were still cruising — but there was very little luxury in the voyage until this storm blew itself out.

Below decks, the unhappiness was so thick that you could almost detect it in the air. The restaurants were almost empty at breakfast time, with only a few hearty and healthy trenchermen digging into the rich and nourishing full breakfast so bountifully supplied. Most of the passengers remained in their cabins and, if they cared for any breakfast at all, the stewards brought around trays of tea and dry toast.

Hank and Frances were the only diners in the Queen's Grill, alone at their table by the window. Hank drank his orange juice in a gulp, then sipped his coffee. And wondered just what to say. It had been a silent morning so far. Neither of them had slept well because of the motion of the ship, and when the first light had filtered around the drapes over the windows they had found themselves awake and unable to sleep anymore. Without saying a word about it, they were both painfully aware of the Tupamaros in the adjoining room of the suite. Frances had finally kicked off the covers in disgust, then had pulled clothing from the drawers and closet with far more banging than was needed. With her arms filled with clothing she had stamped into the bathroom and had slammed the door. When she emerged, dressed in slacks and a light sweater, her hair bound in place by a scarf, she had nothing to say to Hank, in fact had acted as though he didn't exist. He had gone to the bathroom himself and had enjoyed the luxury of a hot shower — followed by a bracing cold one — but when he had emerged she was gone.

He had dressed quickly and followed her. In the adjoining sitting room, three of the Tupamaros were asleep, one snoring loudly. But the fourth one was wide awake, sitting on the couch and watching him. A large pistol ready on his lap. Hank said nothing, just opened the door and slipped out.

The *QE2* was a big ship, but not big enough to get lost on, and he had found her right away, at their table in the dining room. Making a breakfast of a large glass of Citrocarbonate.

His cheerful good morning had produced no response other than a twitch of her nostrils, as though she had suddenly detected the smell of something very rotten and decayed. Knowing he was never at his best before breakfast, he had enough sense not to make any attempts at conversation until he had eaten something. A knot of hunger had growled in his stomach and only then had he realized how many meals he had missed the previous day. The waiter had scribbled the order, then hurried away.

After that, they had sat in a cold silence that was broken only by the rattling of dishes and cutlery as the ship heaved beneath them. He was glad when his food arrived and he tucked with pleasure into the fried eggs, double rashers of bacon, a small breakfast steak, hominy grits, toast and hot rolls. Frances drained the dregs of her Citrocarbonate, glanced at his plate and turned pale. Hank shovelled and munched happily. It was too much for her and it fractured even her iron reserve not to say a word to him ever again.

"My God — how can you do it? The ship is sinking, all those about you are collapsed on their deathbeds or heaving their cookies into the lavatory pan. While you, ignorant and unfeeling, are eating enough food to feed a Vietnamese family for a year. How is that possible?"

"I was hungry," Hank said, very seriously.

Her jaw dropped — and her anger evaporated as she burst out laughing. She reached and held his hand in hers. The free one; he kept shovelling food seriously with the other.

"I really feel terrible," she said. "And I've not been nice to you."

"You should eat something."

"Yes. And die instantly. I'll have another large Citrocarbonate on the rocks. It's not the sea, really. I've been messing around with boats since as long as I can remember and I'm not bothered. It was those sodding Brandy Alexanders, if you must know. Never chat with a Swede who buys you Brandy Alexanders. He can have only one thing in mind. He is a big wheel in publishing, or at least he said so, but what he wanted to really be was a big wheel in the sack with me. This he suggested with a light pinch on my bottom, but he had claws like a lobster or didn't know his own strength or something because that one grab left black and blue marks. Sobered me up instantly, though. That's when I staggered back to our cabin and made the grand entrance. Sorry.''

"Don't be. You're right to feel as you do. And I want you to point out your Scandinavian masher so I can beat him to a pulp, then push him over the rail.''

"My hero! No, it was my fault for letting him buy me the drinks. I was trying to get away from this whole thing. And I really know that I can't. I'm sorry — no, we're going to have to stop telling each other how sorry we are. You're sorry you got me involved, I'm sorry we are involved. End of sorry time. Did anything important happen?''

Hank wiped his lips and settled back and looked at his empty plate with a happy sigh. ''Not only important but practically unbelievable.''

"Try me. After the last few days I'll believe anything.''

Frances was silent as Hank told her what they had overheard, the details of the unholy alliance that was being forged. Her eyes widened as she listened and at one point she gasped aloud at the enormity of what had been revealed. Slowly and carefully he spelled out the details of the conspiracy and what Uzi thought might be the ultimate aim of the Nazis. When he had finished she shook her head as though dazed; these words struck as physically as blows that stunned her mind.

"You're in no doubt about this?'' she asked, finally. Hank shook his head in a reluctant no.

"I wish I were. But we all heard it — and the facts are

on tape. This cruise of ours that began as a simple job of tracing some war criminals has escalated into something like major warfare. These people must be stopped, now, before their palms get rolling. If we fail and the munitions get through, we might very well be seeing an atomic war in ten years' time.''

''It's not possible.''

''It certainly is. We read about the Nazis in our history books and they seem gone and past, as unimportant to our lives today as Genghis Khan and his Mongol hordes. But we're wrong. My father fought in the war — and so did yours. And it was a close-run thing. If a few decisions and battles had gone differently the Germans might have won. They had the reserves and the forces and the will. We might be sailing now on the *Adolph Hitler* instead of the *QE2* . . . . ''

''Now you're being foolish!''

''No, believe me, I'm not. Luckily history did not turn out that way. But far too many of the German organizers of their war machine, and the concentration camp commanders, are still alive and still as vicious and ambitious as they ever were. They are not a bunch of silly old men, but are dedicated, perverted evil men. They killed millions with their ambitions. Not only those who died in the war but the millions whom they methodically murdered in the camps. Gassed, tortured, poisoned, drowned. And after these helpless victims, including women and children, were dead, they knocked out their teeth for the gold fillings and sold their hair to fill mattresses. If you don't believe me ask the man who was there — he's right aboard this ship. Herr Doktor Joachim Wielgus. He'll know. He's the one who arranged the sale of the gold and the hair . . . . ''

Hank stopped suddenly, aware that he had almost gone too far. Frances's face was white and drawn, her eyes brimming with tears. He took both her hands in his, raised them and kissed them.

"I didn't mean to make it sound so utterly disgusting. But that's the way it is. These are the kind of men that we are dealing with."

"Killing is too good for people like this . . . ."

"No," he said grimly. "Killing is good enough. They must be stopped and they must be killed. The world will be well rid of vermin like this. Sorry, I shouldn't say it that way. I'm beginning to sound like them. Simply — they must be stopped." He looked at his watch and quickly drained his cup of coffee. "I'll have to go back now. Things will start moving fast once the diamonds change hands and we have the details about the arms ship. So one more thing. You must promise me now that you won't go near our room today."

"Isn't that asking an awful lot?"

"Not if you think of it as a battleground instead of a cabin. How are you with a pistol? Have you killed many people with one?"

"If you think for an instant that you are being hysterically funny, you are not." Frances was angry now, trying to pull her hand away from his, but he would not let go.

"I'm not making jokes. I'm deadly serious. If you are there when any trouble starts I'll be worrying about you instead of the job that has to be done. Do you understand?"

"Yes, I do. But can't you get out of there as well?"

"I could — but I don't want to. There are too many Tupamaros involved, and not enough of us. I'm just afraid if they run things their way, well, the situation might get out of hand. I can take care of myself. Just as long as I know that you are safe. Will you do as I ask?"

Frances smiled. "The lady gives a reluctant yes. I'll

go to the sauna and sweat the dregs of the alcohol out of my system, then have my hair done, see a film this afternoon. There is plenty to do.''

''Good. Look into the Lido Bar once in a while. I'll either be there or I'll leave a message with the barman, Sean. Is it a deal?''

''Fine. Good luck, my love.''

She stood up suddenly as he started to leave and embraced him, kissing him soundly and warmly, to the great pleasure of the dining room staff who had had a boring morning so far.

It was still before nine a.m. when Hank returned to his cabin, yet the others were already there. They had ordered coffee — Hank wondered what the room steward, Robert, made of all this — and the air was thick with the smoke of dark Latin tobacco. The same three men were present as the night before; the other Tupamaros were gone.

''We have a first plan of action,'' Uzi said. ''Some of the Paraguayans and the Tupamaros have been assigned to cover any of the opposition who don't show up in the suite next door. Including Wielgus, there are six Germans in all. Their cabins are being watched. Stroessner and the Admiral each have two aides with them as bodyguards, but since they are all close by we are organizing our main forces here. The fat man, Chvosta, might be a threat, as well as his female assistant. We think that the diamond expert can be discounted as a threat. So our forces have been deployed accordingly.''

Leandro Diaz chose this moment to interrupt.

''There is one other factor that you should all know. I think it will be a great help in the hours ahead. I waited until now to tell you, since if the knowledge leaks out the man is dead. You know the Sergeant with

Stroessner's party, Sergeant Pradera? Well — he's our undercover agent.''

"You are sure of this?" Josep asked.

"There is not the slightest doubt. He is the inside man who has supplied us with all the details of the conspiracy. They have no suspicion of him or they would not have assigned him to this mission."

"This is very good news," Uzi said.

"Better than good, remarkable." Josep paced the room, ticking off on his fingers his points as he made them. "Firstly — is he a fighting man?"

"The best in the Army."

"Good. Then his presence there, on the inside, is worth ten men outside in any attack. Secondly — he must be contacted and instructed when to act."

"No," Diaz said firmly. "We cannot risk compromising him. If there is the slightest hint of suspicion he will be killed at once. We will just have to count upon him to act correctly when the time comes. But all of your men must be informed of his identity, that is why I told you about him now. We cannot have him killed by some stupid accident."

"I don't like it." Josep was angry. "There can be no free agents in an operation like this. If he is not contacted my men will treat him like anyone else in the opposition . . . ."

"That's enough," Uzi broke in. "You will tell your people about him, Josep. We each control our own troops in our own way. Is that clearly understood? And, Leandro, does this Sergeant know that we are here?"

"Yes. I made it a point to let him see me when none of the other Paraguayans was present. He nodded, which is enough. If there is any action he will fight on our side, you can be sure of that. But he will not reveal himself until it is absolutely necessary."

"If we could get a message to him to take concerted inside action on our behalf, would he do that?"

"He would — if he were certain the message was genuine. I would have to make the contact myself."

"All right. We'll hold that possibility in reserve. Are you satisfied, Josep? Will you inform your men not to fire upon Sergeant Pradera?"

Josep lit a cigarette, then nodded abruptly. "If that's the way it has to be. But I do not like it. If there are any slipups, if any of my people are hurt, he is not the only one who will die."

"Is that a threat?" Diaz was angry now.

"No. Simply a statement of fact. We are not used to working with others. We have been betrayed too often, too many of us have been murdered in this fashion. We have learned to destroy any threats to the organization before they destroy us."

"That's settled then," Uzi told them calmly, working to make peace. "You are both right. We will compromise. The Sergeant will be treated as one of our party — as of now. But Diaz will make every effort to contact him at the earliest possible moment to put him into the picture and pass along any instructions we may have. Agreed."

Hank watched in silence as Uzi took charge, making peace between the uneasy allies, keeping them under control. The undercover agent must have had a world of experience because here he was, a single man, holding everything together. Hank was glad of his presence. There was a sudden knocking on the door.

"See who it is," Josep ordered, already standing to one side with his gun ready.

Hank opened the door and admitted Concepcion Valerde and three other Tupamaros. She was carrying a large hat box; one of the others had a suitcase while the other two each carried a violin case. It was cornball, Hank thought, like something out of an old gangster movie, but it worked. He had no doubt what was in the cases. Concepcion removed any doubts he might have had by opening the hat box and dumping its contents out onto the couch. Sub-machine gun clips.

They could never have risked smuggling weapons and ammunitions in this quantity aboard in their luggage. Only by forcing the Acapulco longshoremen to smuggle it aboard with the other luggage that had cleared customs had they been able to arm themselves so well. The bags had been marked as cabin baggage and brought there by the unsuspecting ship's porters.

"Any activity?" Josep asked.

"Not much," she said. "The Germans have been stirring about some, a lot of traffic back and forth between their rooms, mostly by Fritz and the other young ones. The Hortiguela girl went to Chvosta's room a few minutes ago."

"They'll be meeting soon," Uzi said. "Are we ready?"

The Tupamaros certainly were. The violin cases were open and the Chinese sub-machine guns passed around. They each had a pistol as well, while Josep stuffed his pockets full of handgrenades. "They'll be pretty lethal inside this ship."

"I know. That is why I have them. We may not need them. But if we do they will be available." He turned to look at Hank. "Are you armed?"

"No."

"Here is a pistol . . . ."

"No." Hank knew that this point would be raised eventually and had thought long and hard about what his answer would be. "I don't want one."

"Whose side are you on!" Josep snapped, striding

forward. Uzi moved between them.

"Sit down, Josep," he said. "I've told you — we cannot fight with each other. Hank's on my team, so I'll talk to him. Hank?" He turned and raised his eyebrows questioningly.

"Everyone here knows which side I'm on. I'm not saying that my personal sacrifices in this matter have been greater than yours, but I've done my part. A long time ago I volunteered to help the Israelis in gathering intelligence. I'll continue to do that. But this present matter has snowballed and my entire life and career will be destroyed if it is discovered that I had a hand in this matter. If one passenger sees me waving a gun around for one second I'll get just what Patty Hearst got. I'm with you all the way and I'll give you all the aid I can. Short of getting involved in any shootouts. That is, unless Uzi feels that he wants to order me to have a weapon."

Hank turned to face Uzi, who looked back with an ironic grin. "You should have been a rabbi," he said. "You make a moral point, then transfer the burden of responsibility to another to prove that point. It's proven. If it is a matter of life and death — well, then I may ask you for aid. Until that time you are our intelligence wing and no more. Do you gentlemen agree?"

Both Diaz and Josep shrugged in real or pretended indifference. This was the way it would have to be. Hank looked at their unreadable expressions and wondered, not for the first time since he made the reluctant decision, if he were doing the right thing. This was not his battle. When he had first gone to London he had been approached for some small assistance by a friend he had been to law school with, who was now living and working in Israel. At no time in his life had Hank ever joined any Jewish associations, he had never been Bar-

Mitzvahed or been religious in any way. As far as the world was concerned the only thing Jewish about him was his name. As far as he was concerned, there was an unforgettable heritage, thousands of years old, that made him instantly accept when asked to perform some simple liaison tasks for the Israelis. That was how this whole business had started.

Very early in the relationship he had been assured that he would not be asked to do anything illegal, or anything that might jeopardize his American citizenship. This promise had been kept and the relationship had been a good one. Never very demanding, but satisfying in that he felt he was doing something more positive in life than marking time in the family law firm until one of the elderly partners croaked and he could be lifted up to that lofty position himself.

The Paraguayan photographs had changed all that. What had begun as a simple liaison, a contact with an outside party who might be trying to compromise the Israeli delegation in London, had grown out of all proportion to his original commitment. He had finally realized that he must draw the line someplace. He had. If he took part in an armed and violent attack against representatives of two sovereign nations, no matter how corrupt these countries were, he was putting not only his life in jeopardy but his entire future. He just couldn't do it, that was all. He had never wanted to be a G-man, a combat marine, a black belt judo champ, never. And he did not want to be a gun-toting international agent. He believed in law and the rule of law and he intended to devote his life to that. He had bent his personal rules of behavior by working outside international law to aid the threatened state Israel. And certainly helping to apprehend criminals like the Nazis was about as moral as you could get. But now he had gone just as far as he could possibly go.

The sudden loud knocking drew their attention. It was not in this room, but was the one in the suite next door; the sound was coming from the speaker of their eavesdropping apparatus. Instinctively they all leaned close to listen.

"Sergeant, get the door," Stroessner ordered, weakly. He sipped the neat gin and stifled a groan. Would this ship ever stop heaving and rolling so? He was keeping seasickness barely at bay with a mixture of dramamine and gin. It worked, but was ruining his digestive tract.

One by one the principals entered; the final meeting had begun.

Dr. Wielgus was first, bringing the bag of diamonds — and the hulking form of his bodyguard, Klaus, to keep watch over them. Admiral Marquez was with him, they had met in the corridor, and Aurelia Hortiguela arrived just moments later. She was alone.

"Where is Chvosta?" Wielgus said, frowning with displeasure. "This meeting must begin on time."

Aurelia looked him up and down coldly and waited an insultingly long time before she answered. "Mr. Chvosta is discomposed. He regrets that he won't be able to attend at the present time."

"What!" Wielgus exploded with rage. "Tell that fat Czech swine that I want him here at once, you hear me? Now!"

Aurelia's smile had no trace of warmth in it. "Why don't you tell him yourself, Doctor Wielgus? The last time I talked to the fat Czech he was heaving his guts out. Seasick. *Mareado*. Or what is the quaint word you Germans have? *Seekrank*. He wouldn't even open the door. Shouted through it that he was dying and I should go away and leave him in peace."

"I want him here, now, even if he has to be dragged."

Admiral Marquez broke in. "May I make a suggestion? A seasick Chvosta will be of no use to us. But my personal physician, Dr. Llusera, is in my cabin. He not only uses pills but has a powerful injection that dispenses with all of the symptoms as well."

"A capital suggestion, Admiral," Stroessner said. "I could use that injection myself. Does the doctor speak English?"

"Of course not."

"Then my aide, Major de Laiglesia, will accompany him and translate. Call first, Major, and have the steward there to unlock the cabin for you." His voice hardened. "And Sergeant Pradera will go as well in case Chvosta has to be carried. Because he will be here. This meeting must begin."

Aurelia Hortiguela tried to leave with the two men, but Wielgus seized her by the arm and pulled her back. "You are staying here," he said and turned away. Ignoring or indifferent to her look of cold fury.

Dr. Llusera was a round and pompous little man. He followed de Laiglesia down the corridor in a mincing waddle, shoulders back and chin held high so that his little black beard appeared to point the way for him. Sergeant Pradera followed behind, bulky and slightly uneasy in his unaccustomed civilian suit. The room steward was waiting by the cabin door in response to de Laiglesia's telephone message that they were on their way.

"I contacted the hospital after your call, sir. They have what you might call a plague of seasickness, both doctors and even the three nursing sisters busy at it."

"I know, I talked to them myself," de Laiglesia lied smoothly. "Luckily there is a physician accompanying our party who volunteered to make himself available. Now if you would be so kind . . . ."

The room steward unlocked the door and wrinkled

his nose at the pungent odor of vomit that washed over them when he opened it. "A bit of the old pong there, sir. I'll leave you at it. Just close the door when you leave — it locks itself." He hurried away as they let themselves in.

Only the weakest illumination filtered in through the closed curtains, so de Laiglesia groped for the light switch and turned it on. The room was a shambles, with clothes and towels strewn about, some of them sitting in splatters of vomit. Chvosta himself lay on the crumpled covers of the bed, the bed linen and his tent-like pajamas also sprayed and befouled. He turned his head painfully to look at them as they approached; his skin was ashen grey and dotted with perspiration.

"I am dying . . . leave me. . . ." he groaned weakly. *"Nemocný . . . bolest . . . smrt. . . ."*

Dr. Llusera treaded his way daintily around the repulsive splatterings and seized up a gross, limp wrist and felt for the pulse. He pursed his lips and nodded, then peeled open the lids to look into a bloodshot eye.

"He will be fine once we control the nausea, get some liquids into him, plus a few cc's of an opiate to control the pain and improve his disposition." The doctor was an old fashioned physician who was unconcerned about possible drug addiction among his patients as long as the symptoms were controlled. "Give some aid, Sergeant, in rolling him over and stripping off some of these befouled garments."

The Sergeant, who in his day had sewn up lacerated horses, disinterred corpses and aided many a drunken comrade back to barracks, had accepted this situation as completely normal and had already removed his jacket and was rolling up his sleeves. But de Laiglesia's skin was changing color to match that of the Czech's. Seasickness had not touched him until this moment, but

the close and foul atmosphere of the cabin seized him
and he felt the nausea rise in his throat.

"I'm going to report to the . . . others what is
happening. I'll return to help you."

He opened the door and fled, without waiting for an
answer. Some fresh air on deck, yes, that first. Then
report what was occurring and come reluctantly back
here. He hurried away.

The naked body of the fat Czech was like that of a
pallid, beached whale. The buttocks rose up like
shivering mountains; the great belly oozed out on both
sides as he lay face down. The Sergeant washed his skin
with damp towels and marvelled because he had never
seen a man that obese before.

"This is really an incredibly fat one, Doctor," he
said.

The doctor nodded as he filled a disposable hypodermic needle through the rubber top of a small flask.
"I imagine his arteries are as clogged with fat as his arse
is."

"I'll bet if you put a wick in that arse and lit it he
would burn for a year."

The doctor smiled, like all medical men he appreciated a good, coarse joke, then jabbed the needle
deep into the quivering flesh. Chvosta groaned and
shivered and all of the fat quivered and shook as well.
The telephone rang.

"Take that," Doctor Llusera said, squeezing slowly
down on the hypodermic needle. "I'm busy."

The Sergeant wiped his hands on a towel and picked
up the phone.

"The room of Mr. Chvosta, Sergeant Pradera
speaking."

The man on the other end of the line also spoke in
Spanish. "Leandro Diaz here. We last met in the Bar

Tampico and your sister's name was Maria. Act as though I am talking to you in English."

"I am sorry, I do not speak English."

"We are aided by the Tupamaros and are close by. We can hear everything. We are going to seize the diamonds. No one will fire at you. Will you aid us when the time comes?"

"Yes. I know you are speaking English, but I am sorry I can understand nothing you say."

"Good. We can count on you. Report this call, tell them you think it was the Dutch diamond expert." The line went dead.

"Look, I'm busy. I can't help you." He hung the receiver up.

"Hold this," the Doctor said, taking a plastic bag and tube from his bag. "I'll give him a drip of 500 cc's of saline and glucose. Hang it from the light here. By the time that's inside him he should be feeling human enough to dress himself. That is a task I do not wish to attempt."

"I'm in complete agreement, doctor. Is this high enough?"

By the time de Laiglesia returned, the room had been aired and Chvosta was sitting in the armchair. Partially dressed, still the color of death, but relatively recovered.

"I'll be ready in a few moments, Major," he said in a hoarse and angry voice. "And I want you to know that I know enough Spanish to understand some of the insulting remarks these two criminals made while they were manhandling me."

"Mr. Chvosta, I'm sure you were mistaken. Perhaps slightly delirious. You were seriously ill, they worked hard to help you."

"Don't make light of this, Major. I know what the word *gordo* means, and some of the others!"

The Major fought to keep his face straight. "I will investigate. If the charges are true in any way strong measures will be taken."

"I'll want to know about them." He pulled himself to his feet and reached for his jacket. The Sergeant moved forward to help him.

"There was a phone call while you were out, Major," the Sergeant said. "I answered because Mr. Chvosta was very weak at the time. Will you tell him about it? The caller only spoke English, but I think it was the Dutchman."

"Yes, I'll tell him."

There was an air of cold hatred permeating the suite when Chvosta finally arrived. He felt it as he came through the door. Though he was weak he was no longer ill, and emotionally he was ready to take on the world. Doctor Llusera's injection of morphine was doing him a great deal of good. It was Wielgus and the Admiral who were the angriest; they were not used to being kept waiting. Stroessner wasn't bothered at all since he was also enjoying the beneficial effects of the good doctor's needle. Aurelia was grimly quiet, seated in one corner.

"Well, I hope that we are ready to begin at last," Chvosta said as he entered, quickly, before anyone else could speak. Seeking some small revenge for the humilities he had suffered. Admiral Marquez's face grew red and he began to splutter, but Wielgus cut him off with a gesture of his hand.

"Yes, we will begin," Wielgus said. This business was too important to permit himself to be irritated. "You have received a report on the diamonds?"

"Yes. The total value of the stones is in excess of the agreed price. I assume you have no intention of being generous to that degree?"

"You are correct. Removal of two of the bags will correct the total."

"I will agree only after De Groot has verified their value against the list in your possession, then has done a random check of five of the other bags. Is this satisfactory?"

"Yes, of course. Bring him up here."

"Go get him," Chvosta ordered Aurelia. She left the room.

"We will get on with the business," Wielgus said, taking the notebook and gold pencil from his pocket and laying them out on the desk before him. "You stated that the munitions ship would be in the harbor of Valparaiso today?"

Chvosta nodded, then dropped heavily into an armchair. "Either tied up at a dock or in the roadstead."

"We have a complete crew standing by ready to board as soon as we have finalized arrangements here. What is the name of the ship?"

Chvosta stared silently at the German, unmoving and unspeaking, his ashen face cold and expressionless. The seconds stretched on and Wielgus barely restrained his impatience.

"Come now, Mr. Chvosta, we have lost a great deal of time today because of your little bout of *mal de mer*. It will be safe enough to tell me the name of this ship, you can trust me . . . . "

"I trust no one, Dr. Wielgus. Without exceptions everyone tries to cheat, sooner or later, in the arms business. It is always simpler to steal arms than to pay money for them. I owe my present position with Global Traders to the fact that I have never been taken advantage of. Never. When the diamonds are here the exchange will take place."

"Are you accusing me of attempting to cheat you,

Czech?'' Wielgus's voice was frigid with suppressed rage. "I could have you killed, like that, in an instant.''

Chvosta's voice was equally cold. "Yes, Doctor, I know your record for killing Czechs and Jews and others of the non-Aryan races. Nevertheless, we will wait for the diamonds. I think you would prefer the arms to the death of one fat Czech.''

The impasse was broken by the return of Aurelia with the Dutch expert. Wielgus waved him towards the bags of diamonds.

"Put that on the desk,'' he said. "Here is your original list. I have removed these two bags, this one and this one. You will check the contents of five other bags at random. Begin.''

De Groot did as he was ordered. This time he needed no equipment and worked much faster. Under the watchful eye of all present he took the bags of diamonds out, one by one, and laid them on the desk. He then counted the bags and swiftly checked the numbers of the remaining bags against the master list. Then he put five of the chamois bags aside and replaced the others. One at a time he opened the bags and let their contents spill out onto the blotter. He did not appear to count or examine them but simply stirred them back into the bag. The job was swiftly done. He straightened up and brushed dust from his fingertips, then handed the list back to Wielgus.

"All correct,'' he said. "The contents of the examined bags is the same.''

Chvosta nodded. "Get the key to the case. Lock it. Bring me the key. Then leave.''

Wielgus passed over the key and De Groot did as he had been ordered. They all waited in silence until the door closed and he was gone. Chvosta held the key in the palm of one large hand and looked at it speculatively.

"I am very thirsty," he said, "and would like a beer."

The silence continued as de Laiglesia hurried to open and pour the beer. Chvosta drank it in a single swallow, belched and sighed. "Now begins the difficult part," he said, looking around at the others. "I wish to keep these diamonds and stay alive. You want the ship in exchange for the diamonds. Here is what we will do. The name of the vessel is the *Lyngby Kro,* formerly a Danish freighter now sailing under the Liberian flag. She is riding at anchor in Valparaiso harbor, having arrived there during the night. The Captain has instructions that two men — and two men only — will be permitted aboard to examine the manifests and the cargo. When you are satisfied that the shipment is as agreed we will proceed to the next step. Your men are already in Valparaiso as we agreed?"

"Yes."

"Then call the operator and have a cable sent at once."

On the other side of the wall that separated the two suites, not twenty feet away from the speakers, Josep stood up and looked around at the others who had listened as intently as he had to the payoff arrangements.

"That's all we needed to know," he said. "We can get the diamonds — and the munitions as well! While they play their stupid little games, afraid of each other, we will be getting ready to sweep the board of them!"

19

"No," Uzi said, speaking firmly and slowly so there would be no possibility of a misunderstanding. "We cannot do that. Any attempt to capture the arms ship would be grand larceny in port, or piracy if on the high seas. I cannot be part of it."

"You cannot betray us now," Josep said. His gun was in his hand and pointing unswervingly at the Israeli's midriff. "If you are not with us you are against us and you are betraying the revolution. There is only one penalty for that."

The other Tupamaros moved slightly as they listened, so that, with scarcely any effort, all of the weapons in the room were pointed in Uzi's direction. Diaz and Hank were also being faced by the muzzles of these same guns. It was a time for taking sides.

"Don't appear so surprised," Uzi said. "I made my attitudes quite clear when we first talked about this. I have only one aim in this matter — to apprehend the Nazi war criminals and see that they are brought to trial. I believe in justice, not in the rule of the gun. But I also understand your position and will do nothing to stand in your way. I will do nothing to interfere with any actions you may take and I will not inform on you now or ever. I reserve the right to express my opinion, however, to attempt to prevent a tragedy happening. But I will not try to stop you. So you see, Josep, you are wrong. It is possible to be neutral in this matter and neither for you nor against you.

Uzi was calm, his voice firm and steady as though the ready guns did not exist. Hank could appreciate it but not understand how he could do it. His own palms were damp and he had the feeling that his voice would crack if he tried to talk.

"Not good enough," Joseph snapped. "If you are in this you are in it all the way." He swung his pistol quickly to cover Leandro Diaz who stepped forward.

"More than good enough," Diaz said. "You are here only because of us. Between us we uncovered this plot, brought you in and mind this chance to get the diamonds. If we can secure the diamonds and capture Marquez and Stroessner as planned, we will have succeeded in accomplishing everything that we set out to do. We won't need arms shipments. That is asking too much. We can overthrow these people without resorting to more piracy. I will do what has to be done aboard this ship because it is the only way. We will capture this ship for a short period to take off these two criminals. We will not injure the *QE2* or steal anything. I am a man of law, too. I will commit this crime to destroy the worst criminals in my country. That is enough. Taking them will stop the arms deal and remove their financing. Then we will have every opportunity to rise up and overthrow these oppressive régimes. I and my people will do this much — and no more."

"More traitors!" Josep was snarling the words as he moved his gun back and forth between them. No one else moved. Hank was just as surprised as the rest of them when he found himself stepping forwards towards the waiting guns.

"I think we need a legal opinion here," he said, as calmly as he could. "And I would like to speak on behalf of Josep and the Tupamaros. Will you listen?"

His words were followed by a stunned silence, broken only by the rapid whispering as one of the Tupamaros translated his words to the others whose English was not so good.

"We need no help," Josep said. But the barrel of his gun was lowered and the tension was drained out of the situation for the moment.

"I'm not offering help. You said we must either be for you or against you. Well, I'm for you. We are on the same side. Now, if we can put the guns away for a moment we can settle the situation once and for all. This cannot happen again. We must stand together and not waste time bickering." He turned to face Uzi and Diaz. "Do you understand this?"

Hank hoped the ploy had worked, hoped he had defused the situation at least for the moment. And at the same time wondered where he had got the nerve to turn his back on the guns. Particularly since he hadn't the slightest idea where this was going. He had spoken on impulse, a trick he had learned in court, to make time for a witness to pull himself together or throw the other lawyer off his stride. And apparently the same technique worked here.

"We'll listen to what you have to say," Uzi said, stiffly. Hank had the feeling that Uzi knew just what he had done and was playing along with him. Diaz nodded agreement as well. Hank turned around again and tried not to show his relief when he saw that the guns had been lowered after all.

"I'm going back to basics. The Tupamaros were brought in with certain promises, Diaz — what were these?"

"We needed their help. We could not proceed with this kind of operation alone. We were to provide all of the intelligence, with the aid of your people, to find out just what was going on. We knew a large payment would be made and the general agreement was that we could cooperate to seize this payment and divide it equally. We would also attempt to capture those two swine. We would also aid in the capture of the Nazis.''

"That is all?"

"Yes."

"Are you sure? No mention was made at any time of seizing the weapons shipment?''

"It was discussed, but no decision could be made until we had more information."

"Josep — is this true?" Hank asked.

"Approximately."

"All right then. Be specific, Diaz. Will your people help to capture the arms shipment?''

"I don't know. We will just have to see what the plan is. But that is not important. Getting the diamonds is. We will cooperate in every way in that operation."

"Is that a promise?"

"Yes."

"I'll sum up then. My group will supply all the intelligence information in exchange for the war criminals. They will aid in this if they can — and will also do nothing to interfere with any action concerning the arms ship. Uzi, do you agree to these terms?''

"I do."

"Then you, Diaz, will work to take the diamonds and the prisoners and will aid in any future operation against the arms ship if you are able?''

"Agreed."

"There can be no turning back now. You will be bound by your word — or you will suffer the consequences." Hank turned to Josep and spread his hands out. "There it is. You have won. They will do as you say and follow instructions. They will not interfere. My people have no interest in the arms shipment so they will neither help nor hinder in any way. The Paraguayans will do whatever they can to help when the time comes. So now we come back to the next step. Getting the diamonds. What is to be done next?''

Josep slid his gun back into his belt and turned and walked to the window. He stood, hands behind his back, looking out at the heaving seas, the heavy rain coursing down the glass. For almost a minute he stood this way, wrapped in thought. It was obvious that this situation was a novel one, for he was not used to having others on his side, separate groups who intended to cooperate with the Tupamaros. For many years every man's hand and every gun had been turned against them. He had to struggle to assimilate these totally new factors. When he turned back to the others his mind was made up.

''We will all work together now to take the diamonds and make prisoners of the others. The division will be as agreed. Anyone who does not help in this will be killed instantly. As to the arms ship, the Tupamaros need no feeble aid or indifferent cooperation. We will do the operation ourselves. Do I hear any disagreement?'' He waited a moment, then nodded. ''Good. Now to the urgent business at hand. I put it to you that we should attack at once, waste no more time. We know the name and location of the arms ship, so no more intelligence is needed on that score. All of the people we wish to capture — and the diamonds — are in the next suite. I suggest we hit them now and hit them hard.''

The other Tupamaros murmured in agreement, but Uzi shook his head.

''Hear me, before you make any rash decisions. You are wrong on two counts. It will be easier to first take the diamonds, and then go after the men if the various groups are separated. That way we can concentrate our strength on the operations one after another. Also — I don't relish attacking a group of armed and desperate men through a single floor. Do you agree?''

Josep thought deeply — then nodded. ''You are correct. I appreciate your skills as a military planner. What do you suggest?''

''Patience. Then divide and conquer. Final arrangements for the arms deal are being made in there right now. They obviously want to finalize their deal while they are all together. Perfect for us, since we can listen to everything they have to say. As soon as the arms ship is turned over to the purchasers, Chvosta will be given the diamonds. And will leave the suite. That is when we hit him with everything we have, a concentrated effort just to get the stones. That way we only have to deal with him and the girl, possibly the Dutchman. The Germans will be out of it. Are we in agreement so far?''

Uzi waited until both Josep and Diaz had nodded agreement before he went on.

''We have the diamonds and we put them in a safe place under guard. Even if they discover what has happened and want to get them back they have no way of knowing which staterooms we occupy. Then, with our flank safely held, we pick them up one by one since they will have separated by that time. First Stroessner, the easiest since we can time our attack by listening to events in the suite. Plus the fact that we have an inside man there. With Stroessner in our hands, the Admiral is next. His physician, Dr. Llusera, won't bother us, so it will be just the Admiral and his aide we have to deal with. The Nazis come next . . . . ''

''No,'' Josep interrupted. ''We save them for last. Before we grab them we must take control of the ship. Our boat is about a day's steaming ahead of the *QE2*. Or was when we started. Her speed is only half that of the *QE2*'s. So we take this ship, send the message to rendezvous. Then seize the Germans. By that time we will be close enough to make contact. We take our prisoners and leave and that is the end of this operation.''

Uzi thought about it, then nodded agreement. ''Yes, you're right. That's the way to do it. Do you have a plan to take the ship?''

''Look at this.'' Josep spread a deck plan of the *QE2* out on the desk and they bent over it. He tapped his finger on three areas ringed in red. ''This is where we hit and where we hold. Take these and we have control of the ship. First, of course, the bridge, and at the same time the Captain's quarters here, close by. As we hit them we hit hard here, the radio room on the Boat deck. That will essentially give us control of the ship, since all orders and commands must go through the bridge or the Captain and his officers. Once we have the officers on duty we'll round up the others and take them to the Captain's quarters.''

''There is one other target,'' Uzi said, pointing. ''The cashier's office here on Two deck, just behind stairway G. There are cable and telegram facilities here and our intelligence seems to indicate that some of them are automatic and can bypass the radio room. You must be sure that this cannot be done.''

''We knew nothing of this!'' Josep was put out; his information was incomplete. He turned to Concepcion. ''You were in charge of intelligence on this project. What happened?''

She shrugged. ''We did our best. I couldn't do it myself and the people we sent did not dig deep enough.''

''That is no excuse . . . . ''

Uzi interrupted before Josep's temper flared again. ''You shouldn't blame your intelligence people, Josep.

Remember our agents are professionals with years of experience. We have files and access to information not normally available. So take advantage of it. Do you have enough men to spare to take the cashier's office?''

"Yes — I'll just rearrange the assignments." He thought for a moment. "We'll divide into three strike groups. I will head the attack on the bridge while you, Diaz, will take out the radio room. Concepcion, you will stand by with one man as a reserve. If you are not needed, then you will hit the cashier. Now when we go we strike hard and suddenly. No shooting, but knock down anyone who resists or tries to spread the alarm. We'll go into exact details before the attack. Later. The diamonds first, then those two sons of pigs. Then the ship. One step at a time. The first step is — waiting."

They waited, first with impatience, then with growing concern at the increased rolling of the ship. As the slow hours passed the fury of the tropical storm steadily increased. By mid-afternoon Hank, normally a good sailor, was beginning to feel some discomfort. Everyone felt the effects to some degree and they were eating dramamine pills like candy. Hank had placed a number of calls to the Lido Bar and was finally rewarded when the barman put Frances on.

"Order me a drink and I'll be right there," he said, then hung up. The others were watching him. "You don't need me now," he told them, "and I want to see my wife. Phone the Lido Bar and I'll be back in two minutes."

"All right," Uzi said, speaking before there were any protests. "Don't be too long."

"I won't be."

As he made his way down the corridor towards the stern, Hank became aware just how rough the seas were. Lines had been rigged and he had to grab for them for support as the ship heaved beneath him. Then he had to stand aside as Robert, their room steward, staggered towards him with a covered tray.

"Thank you, sir. Desperate weather indeed."

"Do you get this sort of thing often?"

"Only twice before, thank God, in my seven years aboard. These seas can't trouble the ship, but you can't tell some of the passengers that. Think we're sinking. Some of them in bed, fully dressed, with life vests on, would you believe it. And sick! Excuse the expression, sir, but you being a far tougher individual eating your three squares and everything, wouldn't know the amount of puking going on. Don't want to complain, but you know who has to clean it up. And no one going up for meals, I been on the trot for twenty hours with tea and toast and soup until my feet have given out. Two more years I retire, sir, if I live that long."

He heaved a deep sigh, reshouldered his tray and went weaving back down the corridor. Hank worked his way aft and had enough sense not to try the stairs but waited for the elevator to take him down to One deck. Frances was alone in the bar, looking out with some dismay at the ocean. When he touched her she gasped, then grabbed him hard and kissed him when she realized who it was.

"What an ocean!" she said, then kissed him again. "I've been sitting here looking at it and working myself into a black depression. Every time we go down like that I'm sure we're going to sink."

The view across the empty swimming pool and the stern of the ship was certainly impressive enough. As a giant wave surged down the length of the ship, its crest reached almost up to the height of the deck, in fact the strong wind tore spray from the top of the wave and spread it across the decks. Since the *QE2* was so long, it did not ride up and down on the individual waves, but rather stretched between two and three waves at one time. Which meant once the wave had passed and the trough came behind it, the stern rose higher and higher above the sea. It was like looking down into a watery valley hundreds of feet deep, as high as from the top of a tall building. Then the next wave appeared and the stern went crashing down and down again, as though it would never stop. The ocean surged up and over the rails again and Frances clutched at Hank's arm.

"It looks worse than it is," he said, turning towards the bar and holding her so she turned with him. "I see that you have a lovely big drink — but are drinking alone. And no barman?"

"Poor Sean was definitely green when he sloped off a few minutes ago. Told me to help myself since Cunard owed me anything I wanted for riding out this storm. Then he vanished."

"As the good gray Robert, our steward, said, you wouldn't know the amount of puking going on! I'll help myself."

"Oh yes, I would. I tread the light fantastic up here from the cinema, around all the neat little piles of damp sawdust."

"Enjoy the film?" he asked, looking at the ranks of bottles, and decided what he really needed was a large tequila and a wedge of fresh lime.

"I don't know if enjoy is the exact word. It was some sort of science fiction space thriller with robots and stolen spaceships and a villain who was really the hero or something. Very amusing, but the theater was equally amusing since it was going up and down and around and around all the time. Unusual, to say the least. Is that enough small talk now? So you can tell me what is happening."

Hank licked a bit of salt off his hand, drained the tequila and bit deep into the lime. "Wonderful. Very little is happening other than waiting, so that nerves are getting rubbed a little raw. Can you possibly hold out up here for a few more hours?"

"I'm going to have to, aren't I? And that's all you are going to tell me, isn't it? Oh, darling, don't look so miserable! I'll be all right. I finally have some appetite, so I'll get me to the Queen's Grill for a solid steak lunch, then back here after a bit. That'll take a few more hours at least."

"You're my dreamboat." He kissed her soundly, with plenty of cooperation. "It could happen any time now . . . . "

The telephone rang suddenly and he looked at her, then leaned over to pick it up and answer it.

"Right," he said. "Two minutes." Then hung up.

He hurried away, without a word, not knowing what he could possibly say.

20

"Yes, thank you for phoning through the information. I would like a printed copy of the cable for my records. To my cabin, that is correct."

Wielgus hung up the phone and could not resist rubbing his hands together as he turned back to face the others who waited silently, expectantly.

"That was from our cargo master in Valparaiso. He informs us that the cargo aboard the ship is as listed in the manifests. The vehicles are as specified and samples taken at random from various cases fit the manifest information. It looks as though your people have delivered as promised, Chvosta."

"Global Traders is a legitimate business enterprise with a sound reputation. It is only our customers who are hard to please."

"Yes, perhaps, but water over the dam now in any case." Wielgus was actually humming as he snapped shut his briefcase. "The Captain of the *Lyngby Kro* has been instructed to disembark his present crew and take our own aboard?"

"That is correct. He is our employee and we have leased the ship from the owners. He will work the ship under the instructions of your Captain, who will function as First Officer. The ship will go to the port of your choosing. After the cargo is off-loaded, the original crew will return. The Captain will disembark his present crew now and accept yours upon receipt of my instructions."

"Then, if you will, cable the instructions."

"As soon as I have the diamonds in my possession."

"What's stopping you from keeping the diamonds without releasing the ship?" Stroessner cried out. "You would be a thief!"

"Only one who is a born thief himself accuses others," Chvosta said coldly, then turned his back on the outraged dictator. He appeared not to notice that Stroessner was spluttering with rage and trying to draw his pistol. Wielgus watched this disgustedly for a moment before speaking.

"General — control yourself! These matters are too important for you to act like an imbecile."

Stroessner gaped in consternation, then let his hand fall away from the holster. It was obvious who was the master here. Chvosta nodded and turned to face Wielgus.

"I have a suggestion for the exchange that I hope will satisfy you. Send for two of your gunmen. When they are here I'll give you the coded message for the Captain. While we are waiting for the answer I will go to my cabin with the diamonds and your two men will accompany me. I trust you and your Germans more than this South American trash you do business with. I wish to be away from them and in your hands. When your representatives cable back that they are in charge of the ship you will have your men leave. I will have the payment for the shipment and you will have the shipment. Do you agree?"

Wielgus steepled his fingers and nodded approvingly.

"Chvosta, perhaps I underestimated your intelligence. Yes, we are Germans, not thieves, and we wish only to conclude a legitimate business deal. I'll have my men come here at once to guard you upon your return to your own quarters. They will stay with you, as you insist, until we have clearance. Now, the message."

"The Captain's name is Bartovska. Simply tell him that all of the arrangements have been successfully concluded and he is now to turn command of the ship over to you. You need not use my exact words, anything resembling that will do."

"Is that all? It does not sound secure."

"It is not all. He will ask your man for a number. The number you will tell him is 93121-91087. When this is done the ship is yours." Chvosta smiled. "He knows the number well. It is the number of his Swiss bank account."

"Very good, excellent in fact. It shall be done in just this manner."

"We take them when they reach the other deck," Josep said, drawing his revolver and spinning the chamber. "If the Germans protest, that is two less to worry about later."

"No!" Uzi was very positive. "There is too much risk there — and no real need for it. Diaz can open any lock. Go now with him, a hit crew. Get into Chvosta's cabin before he does. Into the bathroom. Take them by surprise after they are in the room and the door is locked. If they offer resistance no one outside will know what has happened."

"Yes. You are right again. I'll take him myself, with two men to back me. Let's go!"

"Fritz, Heinrich, come in," Wielgus said. "You are armed?" The two young men nodded and Fritz smiled and patted the bulge at his waist.

"Not all fat, Herr Doktor. But a good P-38 in perfect condition."

"Excellent. Mr. Chvosta here is taking this valuable

bag to his cabin. You two will act as bodyguards and protect him all of the way there. You will also enter his cabin and continue to guard him until I telephone to you that all is well. Is that understood?''

"Yes, Herr Doktor.''

Chvosta heaved his bulk out of the chair and picked up the bag, then nodded to Aurelia Hortiguela. She bent far over to pick up her capacious handbag and every eye in the room. Latin and Teutonic, appreciated the taut dress over the ample expanse of her buttocks.

''I will await your call,'' Chvosta said, then waved the Germans ahead of him into the corridor. He left with Aurelia right behind him. The door closed and General Stroessner burst out laughing.

''I am pleased he trusts you, Herr Doktor Wielgus. Will you take the diamonds back from him?''

''Perhaps. It requires some thought. We may need Global Traders again in the future.''

''With this kind of money, there are plenty who will sell to us and fuck these leeches,'' the Admiral said. ''When we have control of the ship, take the money back and eliminate those two. They know entirely too much about the internal affairs of our countries.''

''I was thinking something along the same lines myself,'' Wielgus agreed. ''I am, of course, an honorable man and wish to adhere to all business agreements. Unless, of course, it is a matter of security.''

''This is security,'' Stroessner said, laughing out loud. ''Kill the bastards.''

Chvosta walked slowly down the swaying corridor, seemingly unaware of the position he had placed himself in. The two young Nazis walked on either side of him and Aurelia followed behind, finding the going difficult in her high heels.

Chvosta came to the lift and pressed the button. Aurelia, who was trailing by a few yards was caught offguard by a sudden heave of the ship and fell, sprawling on the carpet. Fritz looked back at her and laughed, then turned away and moved even closer to the bag of diamonds.

"Step back!" Aurelia called out loudly, in perfect German. "Stay clear and stand where you are and no one is going to be hurt."

Both men snapped their heads about and gaped. She was sitting on the floor facing them with her knees up and her legs spread, her skirt hiked up to her waist displaying the length of her creamy thighs and lacy black panties. However, this attractive view was obstructed by her arms, for her elbows were braced inside her knees, while clasped in both hands was a heavy magnum pistol with a long silencer fitted to it. Her open purse lay tossed to one side.

Heinrich just gaped but Fritz was fast, jumping behind Chvosta as he pulled his own pistol from his waistband.

The big gun jumped in her grip and made a quiet coughing sound. Fritz screamed and spun about as the large bullet caught him in the arm, where it projected slightly from behind Chvosta's broad back. The impact broke the arm, almost severing it, and knocked him to the deck. Heinrich had his own gun half drawn when he realized that the smoking muzzle was pointing directly at his eye.

"You'll never live to raise it," Aurelia said, and he knew it was the truth. He was barely aware of the elevator doors opening behind him, of Chvosta moving forward and the doors closing again. All he knew was that he was looking at certain death. He slowly drew out the pistol and let it drop from his fingers.

"Very good," Aurelia said. "Now kick it over here and look after your friend. I would suggest using his belt as a tourniquet on that arm. With a hole that size he could bleed to death rather quickly."

The gun never wavered as Aurelia climbed slowly to her feet and smoothed her dress back into place with her free hand. Heinrich would cause no trouble now, not with Chvosta safely away. She was still taking no chances, watching closely as he tore the belt from the trousers of the moaning Fritz, then tightened it tightly around the bloodsoaked arm. The wounded man was only half conscious when Heinrich pulled him to his feet and dragged him back down the corridor towards the suite. Aurelia nodded approvingly and looked in both directions; no one in sight. The entire action had taken less than sixty seconds. As soon as the two men were gone she put the gun back into her purse and went quickly to fetch the nearest bucket of sawdust. She dumped this over the blood on the carpet and stirred it about with her foot. Perfect. Just one more case of sea sickness and the vomit covered up. By the time it was cleared away the chances were it would never be recognized for what it was. She knew that the Germans would have their own doctor take care of Fritz; neither party wanted to draw attention to the bloodshed. Humming cheerfully to herself she pressed the button for the elevator.

These Germans were such fools, so prone to flattery. The master race indeed! Had they really convinced themselves that they were honest — but betrayed — men, not mass murderers? They must have, or they would not have believed Chvosta's lies for an instant. And they thought everyone else was a fool. How did they think Global Traders stayed in business when all of their customers were illegals of some kind? The fat man and the stupid girl. They made a good team. And it was so much more interesting to fire at a real target rather than the sheets of paper in the shooting range at home. Everything was working exactly as planned. There would be a large bonus on this one.

She emerged on the upper deck and, while she walked, dug Chvosta's duplicate key out from under the gun that filled her purse, staggering as she did so and falling against the wall. The storm showed no signs of easing up at all. Two sailors hurried by with mops and buckets and she had no doubt at all what they were for. One gray-faced passenger passed her and she walked slower until he was out of sight. Only then did she turn the key in the lock on Chvosta's cabin door and go in. It was dark with the curtains drawn. She made sure that the door was locked behind her — the Nazis were going to be most unhappy about this! Then turned on the lights.

Chvosta made himself free with everyone else's expensive liquors, but was not a big spender when it came to his own supply. An inferior grade of Polish slivovitz that tasted like rancid furniture polish. She needed a drink, so it would have to do. She put down her purse and sloshed a glass half full, and then picked up the water jug. Empty, of course. Chvosta made a good business partner, but basically he was a pig. Glass in hand, she went towards the bathroom when the door swung open.

A tall, dark-skinned man stepped out and pointed a pistol at her. There were two others behind him.

"Where's Chvosta?" Josep said. "Speak quickly."

"Obviously not here," she said as calmly as she could. She had not expected this reception. Walking slowly, she put the glass back on the tray and reached for her purse.

"Move your hand one centimeter more, Aurelia Hortiguela, and you get a bullet right in the middle of your back. I know your reputation well."

She let her hand drop carefully to her side. This must be one of the Admiral's men, with his Uruguayan accent. Which was very puzzling. If he knew about her unusual skills — why hadn't he told the Germans about her ability as a marksman?

"Now turn around slowly. That's better. Where's the fat Czech?"

"I'm sure I don't know. I'm not his keeper . . . ."

"Quickly woman, and no lies, because I will hurt you and hurt you very badly. A few minutes ago you started down here with Chvosta and two Germans. You will tell me right now where they are or I will knock your teeth down your throat with his gun barrel. Speak . . . ."

The telephone rang loudly, then again. Josep looked at it, then waved her forward and ground his gun once more into her flesh.

"Answer it. If you care about your life, be careful what you say."

She nodded and picked up the phone. "Aurelia Hortiguela . . . ." Her eyes widened. "Yes there is — I'll put him on." She held out the phone. "Someone asking if there is a man pointing a gun at me. He wants to talk to you."

Josep grabbed the phone from her and pushed her back with the gun barrel. "Who is this?"

"Uzi. What has happened down there? The two young Germans just came back, one of them has been shot. Where are the diamonds?"

"I don't know. The girl just came back alone. Wait . . . ."

A key rattled in the door and Josep dropped the phone and reached out and grabbed Aurelia cruelly about the mouth and pulled her tight up against his chest, at the same time grinding the gun hard into her side. The pain was terrible and she did not move or resist as he dragged her to one side, out of direct view of the door. At the same time the men in the bathroom stepped back silently out of sight.

Chvosta came in and only saw Josep and Aurelia when he turned to close the door. His eyes widened.

"Close the door carefully and lock it," Josep said, twisting Aurelia's face even more painfully against his chest as he pointed the gun over her shoulder. Chvosta did as he had been directed. Other than the key his hands were empty.

Josep threw Aurelia onto the bed, then tossed her purse to the others as they emerged from the bathroom. "Where is the bag?" he said.

Chvosta looked at Aurelia, who was holding her hand to her blood-stained mouth where Josep had crushed her lips against her teeth. Then he smiled broadly, almost laughed out loud.

"Not here as you can clearly see, Josep, not here at all. I'm surprised to see you here, though I should have realized our Uruguayan friends would have lax security. I am glad that I prepared for all exigencies."

"The bag with the diamonds — you have exactly ten seconds to tell me."

"But I *am* trying to tell you. I was sure these people would attempt to renege on payment so I arranged that as soon as I had the diamonds — and sooner than they had imagined — I would put them in a safe place."

"What safe place?"

"The ship's vault, of course. What could be safer than that?"

21

Josep's face went white with rage and his hand tightened about the gun, his finger trembling against the trigger.

"Don't do it," Chvosta said softly. "The diamonds are in the safe, the receipt for the bag is in my pocket. If you shoot me you gain nothing and perhaps lose the diamonds. Think about that, Josep. You have always killed with a reason in the past. Don't change that now."

"Keep both of them covered," Josep ordered his men, then picked up the phone again. "The Czech is here now — but without the diamonds. He says that they are in the ship's vault."

"I don't doubt that for a second. He's a shrewd operator. All right, we'll work this out. Stay there until I call you back. And have Chvosta call the Germans at once before they send a raiding party down there."

Josep pressed down on the disconnect, then handed the telephone to Chvosta. "Call Wielgus. Tell him where the diamonds are and hang up. Not a word about us, understand?"

"Understood, obviously. And I had planned to make that call now in any case before they do something foolish." He took the phone and dialled a number. "Dr. Wielgus please, Libor Chvosta calling. Yes, I'll hold on. Is that you, Doctor? Of course. The diamonds? In the ship's vault where they will be safe. Such language, Doctor! Goodbye." He hung up, smiling. "They are very upset, Aurelia, about what you did to that pretty boy. There is a chance he may lose his arm."

"Good," she said, holding a tissue to her bleeding lip. "Next time I'll shoot him between the legs and see if he loses that, too. Who are these people? You seem to know this one."

"I do. This gentleman is known as Josep. He is with the Tupamaros. We have had some business dealings with them. But this was before you joined the organization."

"Shut up and go sit beside her on the bed," Josep ordered. "I must think."

"We think before we act," Uzi said. "But we think fast. This is, as the Americans say, a whole new ball game. How do we get the diamonds from the vault?"

"Seems simple enough," Hank said. "Chvosta must have a receipt, we could use that. Or force him to take them out for us."

"It can't be that simple or the Germans would do the same thing with him. He would have planned better than that. Hank, call the cashier's office, it's number eight-four-two, tell them you have something you would like to put in the vault."

Hank dialed the number and spoke to one of the cashiers. He listened closely, thanked the man, then hung up.

"You're right. Chvosta planned this very well. This is Saturday night and the day shift is gone. The vault is closed with a time lock and won't open again until Monday morning."

"Then we must seize the cashier's office," Concepcion said, and they all turned to look at her. "Seize it and burn our way into the vault. It will not be hard.

There will be acetylene torches in the engine room.''

"You're half right," Uzi said. "But to take and hold the cashier's office you are going to have to take the entire ship. Priorities must be reversed. Take the ship first so the vault can be burned open. Once you have the diamonds you can go after your prisoners." He smiled crookedly. "After all — they aren't going to go any place, are they? But the first thing to be done is to get Chvosta and the girl out of sight. They must not let the Germans or the others know that we are aboard. Diaz, call Josep and tell him that I'm on the way down there. My cabin is not far from the one that they are in now. We'll move them there, leave them under guard, then come back here. Our plans must be accelerated and we must move fast."

Diaz had just made the call and hung up when the phone rang, loudly and clearly. Everyone watched closely as Hank crossed the room and picked it up.

"Hello?" He smiled and held his hand over the mouthpiece. "It's my wife," he said, then took his hand away. "How's it going?"

"Funny you should ask. I was sure you had forgotten all about me."

"Never! You are constantly in my thoughts — if not in my arms. Where are you?"

"Lido Bar. Getting Sean smashed. It seems to cure his seasickness. We've had the bar to ourselves all day, but my Swedish friend is prowling around and I imagine he'll join us soon."

"Good. Hold him there so I can come beat up on him. Be there in two minutes."

"My caveman hero! I'll be here."

"You must not leave," Concepcion said as Hank pulled on his jacket and headed for the door.

"Get lost, lady," he told her pleasantly. "And save

the orders for your own troops. Tell them where I am when they get back.''

Moving down the corridor was not easy as the ship gyrated and rolled. The elevator creaked and rattled as it moved down the shaft. It stopped on the upper deck and an elderly couple got on. The man was half supporting the woman, whose skin was a delicate shade of green.

''First time out of bed and out of the cabin all day. And Mama upchucks the second she gets a whiff of food from the dining room. Luxury cruise, my ass. We fly from now on.''

''You can't blame the *QE2* for the storm,'' Hank said.

''I goddamn well can. Every picture of this damn ship, it's sailing on a damn flat sea. Stabilizers my ass!''

''I wish I was dead . . . . '' Mama wailed as the door opened and they staggered out. Hank made his way through the empty lounge to the Lido Bar. Frances was seated at the bar and a tall, blond man was standing next to her, talking.

''Hi, Hank,'' she called out and waved.

The effect on the blond man was dramatic. He staggered back and dropped the book he was holding under his arm. Started to pick it up, then changed his mind and fled the bar by way of the door at the far end.

''Let me guess,'' Hank said. ''That's your Swedish friend and he thinks I have leprosy?''

''Better than that. He heard that you just came out of jail after serving five years for manslaughter. Seems you killed a man in a brawl who made a pass at me.''

''Where did he get an idea like that?''

''From Sean here.''

The bar man smiled and tottered a bit. His eyes had a definite glazed look about them. ''Read it in the paper, I did. New York *Daily News*. Told him all about it. Har!" He snorted approval of himself, neatly poured three fingers of Paddy Irish Whiskey into a glass and downed it with a single motion.

"The poor man was trying to apologize when you appeared," Frances said. "We'll have to see that he gets his book back."

Hank bent and picked it up and looked at the spine. "*Crime and Punishment*. I suppose he thinks I'll come after him with an axe. Well done, Sean. Will you look after the book for him?"

"Wheesht!" the bar man said and poured himself another drink. Then slid slowly down onto the stool in the corner. Hank left the book on the bar. "Have a good lunch?" he asked.

"Not really. My appetite ran out and depression set in. Anything to report from the front?"

"Nothing I dare talk about now." He glanced at his watch. "My God, it's seven o'clock already. And I haven't eaten since breakfast."

"I remember that breakfast. It should last you two or three days."

"Let's go have dinner. I'll fill you in on what has been going on." Hank reached across Sean, who was humming happily to himself and polishing the same glass over and over, and picked up the phone. When he dialled his room Uzi answered.

"Hank here. I'm taking my wife to dinner now. The Queen's Grill if you want me. Anything wrong with that?"

"It's a very good idea. I have taken the liberty of ordering coffee and sandwiches here. Enjoy your meal — and could you be back here by nine at the latest?"

"No problem. Can you tell me what's going on?"

"Not now. Just be here."

As they walked towards the dining room, Hank told

her about the affairs of the day. He did not mention their intention to take over the ship. Frances was not at all disturbed by the news of the shooting.

"When thieves fall out. And it couldn't have happened to a better man than Fritz. I remember some of the nice things he said about the Jews."

They reached the entrance to the Grill, candlelit and attractive. If you didn't mind the fact that the deck was heaving up and dropping away. A solitary diner sat at a distant table, spooning up soup and holding the bowl with his free hand so it didn't slide into his lap. The headwaiter hurried up, smiling enthusiastically.

"Mrs. Greenstein, Mr. Greenstein — what a pleasure to see you. What courage on a night like this! If you please."

He escorted them to their table with a flourish. No mention was made of slacks and sports jackets instead of evening wear. It was enough that they had put in an appearance. Two waiters held their chairs for them, while the sommelier grinned expectantly in the background. He came forward even as they were putting their serviettes on their laps.

"Madame, Monsieur, good evening. Courtesy of the Captain, all brave souls who appear for dinner tonight a bottle of wine." He bent close, conspiratorialy. "Since the Captain is so busy a man, affairs of the ship and the weather, he neglected to say what kind of wine. Might I suggest the Chateau Margaux '69, the best vintage in twenty years. Just now coming into its own. Incredible! I will not show you the wine card in case, by chance, your eyes might stray to the right hand column and you discover what a loss Cunard is making on this generous gesture."

"Sounds like a winner," Hank said. "What about it, Frances?"

"Well . . . only if there isn't any Spanish rioja."

The sommelier's eyes bulged and he gasped — and finally laughed. "A joke, of course! Madame is so wonderful, in weather like this jokes too!"

He started away, grabbing a chair back for support, to be replaced by the headwaiter. "Tonight, I am sorry, but for physical reasons the menu is limited. But the chef has prepared for the first course *ecrevisse* in a special sauce. You are interested?"

"We are," Frances said, liberally spreading butter on a half roll. "Or at least I am."

"Sure, I'll go along with that."

"With your wine a Beef Wellington done to perfection, perfect with this wine."

"We are as putty in your hands."

The headwaiter hurried away and was instantly replaced by the wine waiter, who presented a dusty bottle with all the exuberance of a mother with her first born.

"Admire the color! Prepare yourself for the bouquet. I shall open it instantly to breathe and perhaps, with your fish a pretentious little moselle, just at this moment reaching the chill of perfection."

"Sure. As long as it's pretentious." Hank shook his head in wonder as he left. "The service this evening is something else again."

"More of a tribute to the stoutness of our stomachs than our character, my love."

They enjoyed the attention and their meal. The wine was superb, as was the food. Hank wanted to finish with some Stilton but the headwaiter was so enthusiastic about the *crêpes suzette* that they gave in. With much stirring over the flame, pouring of brandy from on high, then a final burst of fire for the *flambé,* the preparation of the dish was quite spectacular. Later, feeling the tightness of his belt and sipping at his five star Armagnac, Hank was very much at peace with the world. Until he happened to glance at his watch. A quarter to nine.

"Your face fell as though you had seen a ghost," Frances said.

"I didn't mean to do that. But dinner has been so good and everything that I just forgot about our visitors in the cabin. I must be there in a few minutes."

"And you have nothing more to tell me about them?"

"Not yet, that is what they are discussing now. I think I know what they plan to do, but if I said it aloud I wouldn't believe it myself. What are you going to do?"

"Not come back to my own cabin, obviously. I think I'll do the Casino and lose some money at blackjack."

"An hour, no more," Hank said, suddenly making his mind up. "I'm tossing them all out by ten at the latest. Enough is enough."

"I hope you can. But I'll phone first in any case. Please take care of yourself."

"Never fear." He bent and kissed her warmly, then left. Feeling like four kinds of heel, yet not knowing why he felt that way.

When he entered the suite he was surprised to find that only Uzi was there, sipping a cup of cold coffee. All of the ash trays were full and the remains of the sandwich meal littered the room. But the others were gone.

"I can't bear the loneliness," Hank said. "What happened?"

"We've firmed up the plans. Sit and I'll tell you about them."

"They're taking over the ship?"

"Yes."

"Then let me pour a strong drink before you continue."

Hank took a deep swallow of the bourbon and water and dropped into the deep armchair. "When is it going to happen?" he asked.

"Midnight tonight. In a few hours. The ship will be quiet then and there will be two hours to secure things before the next watch comes on. As soon as they have control a message will be sent to the fishing boat for a rendezvous. They should be no more than eight hours away, maybe less. So they will have the night to burn into the safe and get the diamonds. By breakfast time the boat should be close by. Then they will take the prisoners, one group at a time, in the guise of the breakfast waiters.

"I suppose it can work."

Uzi snorted and climbed to his feet, going to the bar himself. Hank had never seen him take a drink before. He sloshed a large measure of cognac into a glass and brought it back with him.

"It's dangerous, almost suicidal. A dozen men to take over and control a ship this size? There are over twenty-six hundred people aboard, passengers and crew. Only one of them has to get wind of what is happening and spread the alarm — just one. Maybe a dozen men can capture the control centers of this ship — but can they hold them?"

"You tell me. Can they do it?"

Uzi thought for a moment — then grinned. "Well, they can certainly try. I remember when the British pulled out and there we were in Israel with invading Arabs coming in from all sides. It was close run, but we won."

"If it happened once it can happen again. Will you be in on the action?"

"Please don't ask. What you do not know can never be used as evidence; as a lawyer you can appreciate that."

"Yes, I do. Thank you. Is there anything you want me to do?"

"Yes. Give me your key, find your wife and retire. If there are people coming and going out here do not take notice of it. If the phone rings let someone else answer it. Get a good night's sleep."

Hank laughed. "Indeed! I don't know how easy that will be to do with piracy going on all round me."

"That's a bad word to use."

"It's the right word. Because that's what these people are going to do. All right, it's in a good cause, but it is still piracy."

Uzi nodded soberly. "I agree and I wish it were possible some other way. There could be terrible repercussions. I have taken what precautions I can. I am travelling under a Paraguayan passport, a very good real one. So if things go wrong they will take me for just another one of the resistance people."

"They can make you talk, though."

"Very hard to talk if you are dead. If this goes wrong that is the only way I can protect our people."

Hank drank in silence, not knowing what to say, knowing at the same time the Israeli was not being dramatic. Just telling the truth. What had started as an attempt to apprehend some Nazi war criminals had snowballed into a major crime that they were both inextricably involved with.

"Give them credit for nerve," Uzi said. "Taking over the QE2 is an ambition that few men would consider."

"Do we drink to their success?"

"I'm not sure. Better drink to the capture and trial of Dr. Wielgus and his associates."

"Absolutely!" They drained their glasses and Hank stood and passed his room key over. "I'm going to play a little blackjack and retire. "It's been a long day. I'm looking forward to the ship's newspaper on my breakfast tray."

22

"It's hard to decide which is worse," the Second Mate said. "The weather or the passengers."

"Not for me to say, sir." After nearly forty years at sea the helmsman still sounded as Cockney as the day he had boarded his first ship. "I never see them at all."

"Lucky man. Occasionally there is a young one you can chat up over dinner, stare down the cleavage and all that in the classic shipboard romance manner. But usually they're old, repulsive, boring and American."

"Good lot, the Yanks. Sailed with them during the war. Yank destroyer pulled me out of the drink after a torpedoing."

"Heaven preserve me! I cast no aspersions on our noble allies. In fact, they are probably the healthiest people in the world, for they seem to live forever and save their money, then go for a cruise on this ship."

The wheel clicked three times as the helmsman brought the ship back on course. The heavy seas kept pounding against her starboard side and it took skill to steer a good course without overcorrecting. The helmsman was the best. He could feel the waves as they swept down upon the ship, and many times he turned into the large ones to keep her bow from dropping off. The waves roared in out of the darkness, burst into foam and vanished again. It was a job that he knew how to do. Though it would have been a lot easier if the twit of an officer would shut up. Bored, that's all. Watch-keeping these days, even in the middle of a gale like this, was mostly a matter of watching electronic readouts.

The Second Mate was indeed bored. In reality he liked chatting up the birds, and even the old folks from time to time. Behind him the door opened and he was glad of the welcome interruption. Unless it was the Captain looking in on his charge. He turned and gaped at the man in the rubber ape mask standing close behind him, at the other two men walking quickly across the bridge.

"You there, stop! You can't come in here . . . . "

Bright light and pain mixed together, sudden and confusing. He had no memory of falling but he was sitting on the deck holding his face with one hand. When he pulled his hand away he saw that it was sticky with blood.

"Stand up, you," the stranger said, waggling a pistol barrel under his nose. He must have been struck with it. He stood and saw that all the men on watch were grouped together, arms raised.

"Very good," one of the attackers said. "Now just stand that way." His English was good, but he had a pronounced accent. Sounded Spanish, maybe Cuban. What on earth were armed Cubans doing — hijacking the ship? It sounded impossible, but it was happening. He looked at the phone on the bulkhead out of the corners of his eyes and wondered if he could reach it. He had to warn the Captain.

"Are you out of your mind, walking in here like that?"

Captain Rapley had jerked awake as his cabin light came on, in a foul humor, looking at his steward standing beside the bed, gaping and apparently shivering.

"What's going on here? Speak up man . . . . "

Then the Captain saw the man who stood behind the steward and held a submachine gun pressed hard against his back. A man in cheap civilian clothes wearing a Frankenstein mask.

"Get up and get dressed," the man said. "Quickly."

"Plenty of traffic tonight," the third radio operator said, watching the hammering of the telex. "You'd think with the stock market closed for the weekend that the passengers' brokers would take a rest."

The clacking machine had a soporific effect. He nodded, then pulled his head up with a jerk. He almost yearned for the bad old days again, when you worked the bug for hours on end, then transcribed code. Hard work but fun in a way. Now, with the communications satellites, cables and phone calls were just bounced down to them through a computer and transcribed automatically. Over the sound of the machine he heard a thudding sound and what sounded like a small groan.

"Not falling asleep on the job," he said, turning. And stopping.

The other operator was lying on the deck with a masked man bent over him. Another man stood beside him pointing a wicked looking machine pistol of some kind at his stomach.

"Well, I'll be God-damned," the third radio operator said and slowly raised his hands over his head.

"The bridge, the captain's quarters and the radio room are all secured," Josep said. "So we won't need you and Jorge as reserves. Take out the cashier's office."

Concepcion had been waiting by the telephone in the alcove under stairway G for twenty long minutes. Since there was just a single night clerk in the cashier's office it had been decided to save this target for last; Con-

cepcion and another Tupamaro had stood by at the
phone in case there was an emergency and they were
needed. But everything had gone smoothly.

"That is good," she said. "Jorge and I will take care
of that other matter now."

"Will you need more aid?"

"Two to one. The odds are very good." She hung up
and signalled Jorge, who rose hesitantly from the chair
and bent to pick up the violin case. The dramamine had
his seasickness under control but he still felt less than
human.

They climbed the stairs in silence and stopped outside
the cashier's office. The corridor was empty. Everything
had been meticulously planned and they had carried out
this kind of operation many times before. Nothing more
need be said. Jorge opened the violin case and took out
the two submachine guns and dropped the case on the
floor. They faced each other as they flicked off the
safeties and pumped the slides to put a cartridge in each
chamber. When this had been done Jorge pulled a
rubber vampire mask from his pocket and slipped it on.
Concepcion seized the door handle and nodded. Jorge
raised his gun.

"Now," she said and threw the door open.

Jorge went in at a rush, shouting as he did.

"Hands up you! In the air!"

What happened then happened fast. The man behind
the desk was white haired with great flowing silver
mustachios. He was reading a magazine and he looked
up as Jorge charged in at him levelling the sub-machine
gun. In addition to the magazine he had a pistol in the
open drawer close to his hand.

It happened so quickly that Jorge never knew what hit
him. The barrel of a pistol appeared beneath the
magazine and fired once, the slug hitting him square in

the heart. He kept on going, face first, and was dead
before he hit the deck.

Concepcion had no time to remember the order
against shooting and only her own reflexes saved her
life. She had entered the office an instant after Jorge, so
that deadly gun muzzle had to swing back to cover her.
In that fraction of a second she clamped down her own
trigger and put a two-second burst of fire into the man.

He went over and back down and she rushed over and
had to kick the gun away from his scrabbling fingers.
Then she stamped on his hand. He made no response
other than flopping over onto his back and glaring up at
her. The burst of bullets had climbed across his body
and torn up the bulkhead behind him. Two of the
bullets had hit him. One in the upper chest and the other
in his midriff. Blood seeped into his clothing but he
ignored it just as he ignored his crushed hand.

"I don't know what bloody stupid game you're
playing at," he growled. "But you're not getting away
with it."

Concepcion kept the gun pointed down at him as she
pulled the phone towards her and quickly dialled a
number.

"Yes?" Josep said.

"Cashier's office secured. One man, a fat fool, he
resisted. Jorge is dead. I had to shoot this one."

"Is he dead too?"

"No. Wounded. Badly I hope. Should I finish him
off?"

"Not yet. Watch him. Lock the door. I'll send help."

Josep came himself, tapping on the door a few
minutes later. Concepcion unlocked it and he came in
with one other man who was pushing a wheelchair. The
Tupamaro was masked but Josep, like Concepcion, was
not. He looked stolidly down at the wounded man.

"A war hero," he said. "Look at those ribbons on his jacket. He even has the Victoria Cross. Bad luck. All right, Jorge first. Is he dead?"

"Very."

"Another martyr. You'll take care of him. Put him in the wheelchair, covered with blankets. I'll stay on guard here while you two dump him over the rail."

The wounded man followed them with his eyes until they were gone. "Going to give me the deep six too?" he asked.

"You speak Spanish?"

"Enough. Thirty years in the Guards you see some strange places. RSM. Crack shot as your gunman found out. Do I follow him?"

"No. We are not criminals. I'll take you to a doctor."

"That's good. Just pick up the phone and dial 0. The operator will send some orderlies with a stretcher."

"I was thinking of a different doctor."

"I thought you might be." The RSM's voice never changed, though the blood was soaking through his clothing and spreading out on the tiled floor. "You are not going to get away with this, not piracy on the high seas."

"Save your strength and shut up," Josep said. This accident would cause a small hitch in their plans, but not a major one. He had to get the man out of here, the blood and damage cleared up, one of his own people left behind as a guard. Then on to the next step. It wasn't even twelve thirty yet. Things were going well. You had to expect casualties in war.

When they returned with the now empty wheelchair, Josep left them on guard while he found a first aid box in the other office and took the bandages from it. The RSM did not protest when he tore the man's clothes open and applied the pressure bandages.

"You're a samaritan, that's what you are," he said, and his face turned chalky as the bandages were tightened.

"No," Josep said. "I just do not wish any traces of blood in the corridors." He straightened up and looked around. "Get this mess cleaned up, Concepcion. Wipe up the blood, move some charts or books to cover those bullet holes. Stay here with the door locked until relieved. I don't think you'll be bothered by any passengers, not tonight."

Despite himself, the wounded man groaned when they picked him up and put him into the wheelchair. The corridors were empty, as was the elevator, and they reached Josep's own cabin without being seen. It was deep in the ship, on Three deck, without a window or porthole and situated in the stern of the ship. The cabin was efficient but small, like a tiny sea-going motel room, and was about as close to steerage as accommodation could be aboard the *QE2*. About the only thing that could be said for it was that they were so deep in the ship that the rolling was less pronounced. This advantage was made up for by the powerful vibration of the engines that throbbed and shook the room and set the wall panels to buzzing.

"He is injured but he is dangerous," Josep warned. "Be on your guard. And he understands Spanish."

Josep hurried now, moving fast to the elevator and taking it high up to the boat deck, then walking up to the Captain's quarters. He could feel the tension in the air when he entered the room. Captain Rapley sat on the couch, dressed now and glowering in his direction. The frightened steward was on the other side of the room next to a young ship's officer, who had a bloody scalp and a rapidly developing black eye.

"Third Officer," one of the armed and masked men

reported. "Came to the bridge unexpectedly. They brought him down here as you ordered."

"Good, we can use him." Josep turned to the Captain.

"I want you to issue some orders by telephone, normal orders without trickery."

"Go to hell."

"Now, I will not attempt to use force on you, Captain, since I know your military record and I know that you are a very strong man. And I also know that you care about your subordinates. Do you recognize me?"

"Only that you are so ugly you don't need an ape mask like these creatures."

"Don't push me too far, Captain. I am beginning to lose my patience." He turned to the other two crew members. "Do either of you know who I am? Speak up, I want the information."

The steward looked towards him fearfully, then at the Captain and quickly away. Josep saw the motion. "You," he pointed. "Do you recognize me?"

"Maybe, sir, I can't be sure. Would your picture have been in the *News of the World?* And an article about you?"

"Very possibly. The name?"

"Josep, sir, something like that. Something to do with the Tupper-marrows."

"You are correct. I am Josep. We are Tupamaros. Did the article say anything more about us?"

"Lots, sir, begging your pardon, just saying what I read. You're guerrillas, only you fight in the cities, Communists. And you kill, bomb, rob banks, that sort of thing . . . . "

"Close enough. Shorn of the propaganda it is close enough. Do you understand now, Captain? Would you like to see me live up to my reputation? I won't injure you — but I will cheerfully maim, perhaps kill your crew members. Do you believe that?''

"I do," the Captain said coldly. "I have access to journals other than *News of the World,* so I know a good deal about you. What do you want?''

"Very good. I wish you to call the engine room or the engineer, or whoever it is you talk to about this sort of thing, and I want you to invent a small situation on Two deck that will require them sending up one man with an oxyacetylene torch. You will say nothing to arouse their suspicions. You will order this man to meet this officer here and we will take it from there. Understood?''

"Very clear."

"Good. You will make the phone call from here and I will listen on the extension in your bedroom. Please do not make any foolish mistakes, Captain."

It worked out very smoothly. The Captain was not a stupid man. Josep went with the ship's officer to meet the engine room rating, who trundled the cutting torch out of the elevator on Two deck ten minutes later. Both crew members were horrified at the thought of cutting into the vault, but were soon convinced by the guns. The sailor pulled on his mask, popped his spark and lit the torch, then set to work next to the lock mechanism. Josep left Concepcion in charge of the situation and took the officer back to the Captain's quarters. It was all working like clockwork and he was very pleased with himself. From the Captain's suite it was not too far to the radio room where Diaz and his men were alert and on guard. Diaz signalled him out to the alleyway, then pulled off his mask after he had closed the door behind them.

"This thing not only stinks but I'm sweating inside of it."

"You're wearing them for a good reason. We change

guards and change masks and they will never know how few of us there are. For propaganda reasons it is best that Concepcion and I show our faces. They respect our reputation.''

''I know all that — but it is still damned uncomfortable. Are we doing all right?''

''Could not be better. One casualty only, and the ship is ours. We can get in touch with the fishing boat now and arrange a rendezvous. I have a contact in Acapulco where the cable office is open all night. He will contact the boat by ship to shore radio. We have a simple code — and the message is already done.''

''Then let us send it and get this business finished with as quickly as possible.''

The operator was more than willing to send the cablegram. It took him a few minutes to contact Acapulco and to transmit the coded message. The contact must have been waiting in the cable office, because the answer came almost as soon as the first message had been received. He tore it off the machine and handed it to Josep, who went into the adjoining compartment to decode it. He worked quickly as well. Less than two minutes later he threw the door open and waved Diaz to him. His features were pale and drawn as though he had just looked death squarely in the face.

''God damn it, God damn it to hell!'' he said and banged his fist again and again on the table.

''What's wrong?'' Diaz asked.

''What's wrong — this is wrong!'' He seized up the cable and crumpled it in his hand. ''Trouble. Because of the storm. The boat that should be waiting for us has had trouble.''

''They aren't out there at all! They've already headed for the nearest port to make repairs.''

23

Hank had fallen asleep easily, as had Frances. At first they had not even considered making love, not with the coming and going in the outer room of the suite. But proximity and warmth had dictated otherwise and the mere touch of his hand on her bare breast had sent an uncontrollable shiver through her body, a motion that had awakened the same desire in himself. They had come together, warmly and passionately surprised at the rising tide of emotion, yet enjoying it at the same time. After that, they had slept, and Frances was still asleep, but the voices in the adjoining room had woken Hank from a deep, yet troubled, sleep. He could not remember the dreams he had had, except that they were violent, destructive. He was almost glad that he was awake now and through with them.

The voices in the other room were angry, arguing. Hank could not make out the words but the tones were obvious. Something was happening, there was some trouble. He tried to ignore them, to go to sleep again, but it was impossible. Eventually he recognized the inescapable conclusion that he was not going to go back to sleep, not now. He rose quietly so as not to awaken Frances, gathered up his clothes and dressed in the bathroom. It was after three in the morning. He had to find out what had happened.

There were just three of them in the room, two men and a woman; Concepcion swung her gun his way when the door opened. Hank ignored her, as well as he could, and looked towards Uzi and Josep.

"What's the trouble?" he asked.

Josep spat a bit of tobacco leaf from his lips and turned to the table to take another of his black cigars. Uzi answered the question.

"It has been a momentous evening. The resistance forces of Uruguay and Paraguay have succeeded in taking control of the *QE2*. Very few of the crew are aware of this, and none of the passengers. At the present time the vault in the cashier's office is being cut into to retrieve the Nazi diamonds. The two representatives of Global Traders are tied side by side in one bed, to their mutual discomfort, and the last time that they were checked they were uneasily asleep. All of the conspirators appear to be asleep, including the injured Fritz, who is loaded to the eyeballs with opiates and feeling nothing at all. Doctor Llusera was heard to say he will not lose the arm. After much rationalization, the Nazis have resigned themselves to the loss of the diamonds since they have the arms ship."

"Then what's the problem?"

"A small hitch in the plans. All of this operation hinges on striking hard and fast, seizing the diamonds and the captives and transferring them to a Mexican fishing boat named the *Tigre Amarillo*. Unhappily for us, the *Yellow Tiger* has turned tail. It has been damaged in the storm and has headed to port for repairs."

"My God! What are you going to do?"

Uzi smiled wryly. "As you might imagine, that has been the subject of our discussion. We do not have many choices since the *Tigre Amarillo* will not be ready for sea for another twenty-four to thirty hours. A broken rudder and bent mainshaft."

"Is there any chance of getting another boat?"

"Absolutely negative. This is a very dangerous business and it was hard enough to arrange for this one. We must use the *Yellow Tiger* or nothing. But can we keep control of this ship long enough for the repairs to be made? And even if we do hold out — how many more hours after that will it be before we can rendezvous with the fishing boat?"

"The answer to that one is obvious," Hank said. "You meet the boat a few hours after it is required."

"What do you mean? How can they catch up with us that quickly?" Josep said.

"Let me ask you a question first. What course is this ship following?"

Josep shrugged. "I don't see the importance of the question. The plotted course, naturally. We are making no changes in the ship's operation. We do not have enough men to control these factors . . . ."

"Of course!" Uzi interrupted. "Hank has pointed out to us that we are being incredibly stupid. The *QE2* must vanish."

"What are you babbling about?" Josep was tired and exasperated.

"Look at this." Hank rooted through the papers in the top of the desk until he found the one that he wanted. "Here is the brochure with all the details about this cruise. Just look at this map — it's diagrammatic but it's clear enough. After leaving Acapulco we are heading south along the Mexican coast, then past Central America. Right in the middle of all the heavy coastal shipping all the way. But why? Each minute we are leaving our contact boat further and further behind. They'll never catch up."

"Of course," Josep said. "We must turn back."

"No," Hank said. "There is no reason to, yet. And

you don't want the ship to be observed. What you must do is head away from land for half of the time it takes for the repairs, then turn back for the second half. So when the boat comes out the contact can be quickly made.''

''Even better,'' Uzi said, stabbing his finger onto the map. ''We turn in the one direction that no one would ever expect, a reciprocal of the course that brought the *Queen* to Acapulco. We head back the way we came — into the Pacific. And we shut down the radios at once. No reports, no cables, no contacts. Just one last coded message to your Mexican contact to make arrangements for communication later, as though the cable originated from another ship. As long as this storm keeps up no one will be able to find us. It will be as though the *QE2* vanished from the face of the earth.''

''That won't be too easy,'' Hank said. ''The weather satellites and American military satellites will easily spot a ship this big.''

''Not as long as this storm holds out,'' Uzi was jubilant. ''They can't see through the muck up there and as long as all the radios and satellite navigation aids are turned off we will be invisible. And nothing is to be marked on the navigation charts, either. There must be no record of where we are and where we are going.''

''Now we are beginning to think,'' Josep said, signalling to Concepcion. ''Get up to the bridge. Esteban is on guard there. He is a sailor, a ship's officer, he will know about the course thing. Have him make these course changes as we have said. Go!''

''Can you hold the ship for another twenty-four hours?'' Uzi asked, the sudden excitement drained away.

''I don't see why not. As the new crew members come on duty we make them prisoners and put the ones going off watch in with the Captain and the others. We can't do this forever, but hopefully we can hold out for a day. The Chief Engineer Officer was getting suspicious that something wasn't right, so the Captain sent for him and he is our prisoner, too, and issuing the right orders. Yes, we can hold out for a while yet.''

"What about the passengers?" Hank asked.

Josep laughed. "Not a clue. Most of them are too sick to care in any case."

"All right, then," Uzi said. "We have the matter of our course under control, and if we don't make any slips we should be able to hold the ship until we rendezvous with the fishing boat. Which brings us back to the matter we were discussing when Hank came in."

"I no longer care to talk about it."

"You're going to have to. You agreed there would be no unwarranted violence or killing. You gave Diaz your word."

"I did. It has nothing to do with the situation."

"It does. Unless you do something soon, the man will die and that will be deliberate murder."

"What's happening?" Hank broke in. It was Uzi who answered him.

"One of the ship's crew was injured when the cashier's office was captured. Shot. Unless he sees a doctor he'll be dead. Josep doesn't want to take him to a ship's doctor. A gunshot wound would be too suspicious. He wants to wait until morning when we capture the Uruguayans. Then we can use their doctor. I want them taken now, without any more delay."

"No. We will adhere to the schedule. We cannot risk a slipup."

There was a rattle of a key in the lock and Diaz came in while they were talking. "Concepcion has taken my post on the bridge," he said. "I have come to see what you are doing about the doctor for the injured man.''

"The plans are unchanged," Josep said with grim determination. "They will not be altered for the sake of this fast shot who killed one of my people."

"We made an agreement. There was to be no unnecessary bloodshed."

"The situation has changed."

"It has not. If you will not act I will get one of my men and we will take over the Uruguayan suite now. We must have that doctor."

"You will risk everything for a stranger's life?" Josep was puzzled, not angry. An attitude like this was beyond his comprehension."

"Of course. I am a politician, and I hope an honest man. What I do I do to free my country from Stroessner and his thugs. If I lose my humanity doing it I am no better than they are."

"He's right," Uzi said. "We need that doctor now."

Grim faced, Josep looked back and forth between them. "Outvoted two to one. I assume you will no longer cooperate in this action if I don't agree?"

"That's correct," Diaz said.

"Then we do it. But not the Germans. They will be too suspicious if we try to hit them during the night. They get guns in their guts for breakfast as we originally planned. You and I, Diaz, we do this together. First Admiral Marquez, then Stroessner. I'm looking forward to this. Uzi — stay here and man the phone. This should not take long."

The alleyway was empty when they emerged from the room. It was just a few feet across to the other suite. Josep knocked on the door, then again. A muffled voice spoke from inside. He answered in Spanish.

"The doctor is needed, quickly. The German with the bullet hole, he has taken a turn for the worse."

The lock turned and the door started to open. As soon as it did Josep hurled himself against it, striking with all his weight. Forcing it wide and hurling himself into the room.

"I know you, Captain," he said to the man in the dressing gown, just as he struck him hard across the side of his head with the long barrel of his revolver. He did not watch the man fall but ran over to Doctor Llusera who was standing, yawning, in the open door of the bedroom. Josep pushed the doctor aside and went into the room, turning on the light. Behind him he could hear Diaz closing and locking the door and he knew that his rear was secure. Admiral Marquez was sitting up in bed, blinking in his direction.

"Who is that? What the hell is going on?" he growled. His contact lenses were in their holder by the bed, but he groped for a pair of old fashioned wire-rim glasses next to them. Josep slid his pistol back into his belt and waited patiently while the Admiral put the glasses on.

"Remember me?" Josep said.

The Admiral did indeed. Josep smiled at the horrified expression on the man's face, the way the color drained from his cheeks.

"Yes, you do remember me. Afraid that I will kill you, Admiral? I could in an instant, I might yet. So just do what I say, don't cross me and don't ask any questions. Better drink some of the water in that glass, take some pills if you have them. I don't want you dying of a heart attack." He turned and called over his shoulder. "Doctor, drag the Captain in here and lay him out next to the Admiral."

"This is outrageous, outrageous," the doctor gasped, pulling the unconscious and heavy form of the aide. "This man is injured, he may have a concussion, I must protest at the manner of this . . . . " For the first time he had a good look at this strange attacker's face — and his own skin paled like that of the Admiral's. "Josep . . . . " he breathed.

"I'm pleased to see that I am not without recognition among my countrymen. Get dressed, doctor, and get your little black bag. You are going with this man on an errand of mercy."

Diaz went out with the doctor, and it was almost half an hour before he returned alone. All of that time Josep just sat in the chair, his gun in his lap, looking at the Admiral and relishing the occasion.

"I left the doctor there," Diaz said. "The guard is watching both of them. He says that the wounded man's condition is stable, but that he must be operated on soon. The bullet penetrated the intestines, luckily missed any vital organs, but peritonitis is a certainty."

"It won't strike that quickly. Call the special bridge number and tell Concepcion to get a man down here at once. It will leave her shorthanded, but not for long. We'll get them all together soon and your man can guard them. Lead the way, Diaz, Stroessner is your target."

"He certainly is. This is wonderful, simply wonderful. I am not normally a vengeful man. But this is different."

They stopped at Hank's suite first, to check the tape and the eavesdropping equipment. Everything was quiet in Stroessner's quarters. They were asleep. Josep stood to one side out of sight while Diaz knocked.

"Who is there?" a voice finally asked.

"Telegram."

The door opened a crack and Diaz found himself staring Sergeant Pradera in the face. He shaped the word *now* with his lips. The Sergeant nodded slightly but did not change expression. He turned and called over his shoulder.

"A steward here with a telegram for you, Major."

The Sergeant stepped aside and Major de Laiglesia took his place. Diaz said nothing. He just watched the expression of disbelief and horror spreading over the Major's face. He opened his mouth to shout — then slumped downwards. The Sergeant had hit a cruel blow on the side of the neck with the edge of his rock-hard hand.

Between them they moved the Major's limp body silently aside and Josep followed them into the room. The Sergeant jerked his thumb wordlessly over his shoulder at the bedroom door. Diaz nodded. Josep leaned forward and whispered.

"I'll bring the Admiral and the other one in here. They'll be easier to watch when they are all together. But first go speak to Stroessner — I know that he is looking forward to meeting you."

Diaz opened the door slowly — and found himself shaking violently. It was totally unexpected, not fear, the opposite if anything. An overwhelming hatred consumed him, a detestation of this terrible little man who had murdered and destroyed Paraguay for so many years. His fingers were on his gun, he was prepared to shoot, to destroy this creature; all trace of civilized morals had fled. For the first time he understood the unreasoning hatred, and violence, that motivated the Tupamaros. They had the right answer. He pulled out the pistol and opened the door wider and saw the empty bed.

This was unexpected, unreasonable, and puzzling to his rational mind. But his reflexes had a much more basic attitude towards survival and his muscles tensed and he jumped back. Therefore, the bullet that was aimed at his head hit the metal doorframe instead and ricocheted wildly away.

All traces of the unreasoning hatred were gone in an

instant. Stroessner must have heard something, become suspicious. He was a wise old fox who had lived this long by keeping himself aware of any plots against his person. As long as he held the gun he was dangerous; the whole operation threatened. Something must be done, and quickly.

"Drop the gun, Stroessner," Diaz called out, "and we won't kill you . . . . "

Two more bullets crashed through the open door and the General cursed loudly.

"Chinga' tu madre!"

"You'll never get him this way," Sergeant Pradera whispered in Diaz's ear. "Force me to go in ahead of you and I'll take care of him."

"He'll shoot you too!"

"Perhaps. But certain chances have always to be taken. Let's go."

"I have your own Sergeant in front of me, Stroessner. If you shoot you won't hit me but you'll kill him."

There were no shots when Diaz opened the door this time and walked slowly in, pushing the Sergeant ahead of him at gun point. When they were halfway through the door, Sergeant Pradera struck. Before he knew what was happening Diaz's gun hand was knocked into the air; the pistol fired, sending a slug into the wall. At the same moment pain surged through his leg as the Sergeant kicked backwards, knocking him to the floor. The door slammed in his face.

Diaz sat there, tensely, for long moments, but no more shots were fired in the room. The ruse may have worked. He climbed to his feet — then raised his gun quickly as the door opened. Sergeant Pradera came out, half smiling, pushing a chrome-plated, ivory-handled automatic pistol into his waistband.

"I enjoyed that," he said. "I'll tie him up, but it will

be a few hours at least before he regains consciousness."

"Wonderful!" Diaz said, clasping the Sergeant's hand, then pulling him to his chest in an *abrazo,* the Latin embrace, pounding him in the back with exuberance. "It's all falling into place. This is the big one and we're going to win it."

"I've been in the dark about what is happening," the Sergeant said, looking at Admiral Marquez and his wounded and unconscious aide. The Admiral had finally lost control when faced with the armed Tupamaros and had begun screaming. He was still struggling now, although bound to the chair, and trying to chew the towel with which they had gagged him.

"There is a lot to explain," Diaz said. "We are in this with the Tupamaros — we need their fire power. It is all working out well. We have control of the entire ship and now we have captured these two cabins. The Germans will be hit next, at breakfast time. The diamonds are in a vault, but it is being cut open and we will have them soon. Then it is a matter of waiting to meet a boat that will take us off — along with our prisoners."

"Sounds very dangerous," Pradera said.

"It is. But if we get away with it, we have Marquez and Stroessner as prisoners and the diamonds to finance our campaign. If things go wrong . . . . "

"Then we are in the shit. But this precious pair will be dead as well. I'll enjoy shooting them myself."

"Good. Will you stay here and guard them? We are short of men, just a handful of us controlling the entire ship. We could use your help."

"Help? This is my pleasure. Leave me here with these roaches and don't worry about them. I have taken orders enough from this trash."

"Good. We'll relieve you at dawn. We can use you when we take the Germans. Their turn is next."

24

Klaus did not like to see his comrades shot. He had seen enough of that on the Eastern Front which, slowly and surely as the war went on, had turned into a butcher shop. He did not mind killing the enemy, that was the only thing to do with the Slavic mongrels, and he had done enough of that himself. They did not take prisoners in the East. Either side. But as the quick victory never arrived and the second, then the third winter arrived, the attrition grew. There were only a few men from the original company left, when Klaus had been wounded himself and sent to the rear, to hospital. That was when he had been assigned to Dr. Wielgus, a fact that had undoubtedly saved his life. They had been good years since then, easy and good years.

Klaus still did not like to see his comrades shot. If he had been left alone to get a good night's sleep it might have been different. Everything would have looked better in the morning. But he was stuck here in the little cabin with the wounded Fritz, and had not been able to get to sleep. The injured man was deeply unconscious, but he moaned in his sleep. This, and his deep breathing and the strong smell of drugs on his breath, had kept Klaus awake. He lay now with one arm under his head, smoking yet another cigarette. The ship never stopped heaving up and down and that was disturbing, too. He reached out to pour another schnapps, then changed his mind. That was no solution.

That goddamned fat Czech and the bulging dyke

woman of his. They had shot a good German boy, half severed his arm, and they were going to get away with it. Klaus had seen enough wounds like this one to know that the arm would never be the same again. Maybe they could save it, but it would always be withered and hang there and poor Fritz would be ashamed of it and the girls would laugh at him. A good, strong, happy German. Now destroyed by those two. And nothing could be done. Wielgus had said no. Nothing must be done to jeopardize the arms shipment.

Well, the shipment wasn't in danger. Klaus grubbed out the cigarette and swung his feet to the floor. The diamonds had paid for the shipment. Now he was going to pay a little on Fritz's account. It wouldn't affect the business deal. If the Czech had any sense at all he would never mention it. The woman first, because she had fired the shot. Klaus finished tying his shoes and pulled on his jacket. It would be good to work the bitch over. And it wouldn't show either, not a drop of blood or a bruise. But she would hurt, oh how she would hurt! He grinned widely at the thought and opened his suitcase. Part of the metal frame came away when he tore open the lining. He had made it himself. A spring steel bar with a sharpened end. Came in handy for a lot of things. As a weapon — or a jimmy to open a door. The bitch would get what was coming to her, all right! He slipped the steel under his jacket and opened the cabin door.

"This one is for you, Fritz," he said.

The ship seemed deserted, the passengers locked away in their steel cubicles, the only reminder of their existence was the faint odor of vomit and the masking, perfumed air spray that hung inescapably in the air. Turning a corner in the passageway, he almost ran into the cabin steward, who was carrying a tray.

"Very sorry, sir."

"That is all right."

"I wouldn't go on deck if I were you, sir. Wet and windy out there. Could be dangerous."

"No. I would not do that. I thought, perhaps a drink, it is hard to sleep. Is there perhaps a bar open still?"

"Just possibly the Midships Bar, on the quarter deck. Usually a late crowd there."

"Thank you. I will find my way."

Klaus went to the elevator, which was a long time coming. He waited patiently; he had always been good at waiting. He went down to the next passenger deck, not up to the bar. This was going to be good; he smiled.

Another deserted corridor. He stood before Aurelia Hortiguela's door and eased the steel bar out from under his jacket, glancing both ways. Empty. This would take only a second. Before leaving his cabin he had examined the lock mechanism of the door; they would all be the same aboard the ship. Here was the spot, just three fingers-width below the handle. Slide in — and pull.

With a tiny snap the lock broke. Klaus went through the door quickly and closed it behind him. He remembered what they had said about this girl's ability with the pistol. Hopefully she did not sleep with the thing. Nevertheless, he raised the bar over his head at the same time as his fingers felt for the light switch. If she had a gun, the bar would get her in the face as she pulled the trigger. There was some risk invovled, but Klaus liked risks; life was too easy at times.

The light came on and he hurled himself to one side, his arm swinging towards the bed.

He did not release the bar because the bed was empty. So was the rest of the room — and the bathroom when he looked inside.

Now what did this mean? Could she be in the bar? He

did not think that likely, not at this time of night. Then where else? The Czech's room; that answer was easy. Maybe they were staying together for mutual defense. Or maybe they were in bed together, screwing. That would be something to see! This was getting better all the time.

There was a Bible on the end table by the bed and he took it up and tore the thick cover off it. Finally one of these was good for something! When he closed the door the cover was over the broken lock, jamming the door shut. Now it appeared to be locked; he did not want to draw attention to the empty cabin until he had finished with these two.

It might be tricky if both of them were in Chvosta's cabin. He listened at the door but could hear nothing. Better to break the lock, slam the door open and go through fast, knock on the light switch as he went by, then hit the deck in a roll. And stay there if she had the gun on him. This night's business wasn't worth getting killed for.

Taking a deep breath, he cracked the lock and went through the door with a rush. As he hit the floor he had a quick glimpse of the empty room and the bed, still made up for the day — and empty.

"Now what the hell . . . ?"

It was exceedingly puzzling. He closed the door and prowled through the empty cabin. What was going on? There was a bottle of vodka on the table and he opened it and took a healthy drink, then grimaced. What foul stuff. Where were Chvosta and the girl? Not here and not in her cabin. Something not too good was going on. Klaus sensed it, more of an animal feeling than a rational conclusion. He felt the short hairs stir on the nape of his neck. Something very wrong was happening. Dr. Wielgus must hear of it at once. As he left he jammed the door shut, as he had done in the other cabin, and made his way towards the elevator. He pressed the button and while he waited he decided to make one more stop before reporting to Wielgus. He would get the Uruguayan doctor and have him look at Fritz again. This would disturb all of them in the Admiral's suite which was a good thing. He wanted them all awake and bothered just as he was.

But no one came when Klaus knocked on the door. He knocked a second time and, suddenly, had a gut feeling that something was very wrong. He had not had this sensation in years — but he recognized it well enough. It was the worry you got when everything was quiet before an attack — or before the bombers came in on you. Something was happening on this ship and it was not good. He did not knock again but instead inserted the end of the bar and heaved. The door moved open slowly. The lights were on and the room was empty. He went in, the bar ready in his hand, closing the door and looking around. Nothing. No signs of disturbance or fuss. Just nothing. And all three men were gone. He grabbed for the phone and quickly dialled a number. It rang twice before Wielgus's sleepy voice answered.

"Something is very wrong, Herr Doktor, very wrong indeed. I went to the cabin of the Czech and the girl and they are gone, not in their cabins . . . . "

"What are you saying, Klaus? Do you know what time it is?" Wielgus was annoyed, his night's rest disturbed.

"Yes, sir. It is after four in the morning. But more important — there is no one in the suite of the Uruguayans. Not a soul."

Wielgus was wide awake in an instant. Treachery and deceit were about him at all times. Now that they had passed over the diamonds, and the arms shipment was on the way, were these little tinpot dictators planning to squeeze him out? It was possible. But it wasn't going to happen. They could play their murderous little games with one another — but not with him!

"Stay there!" he ordered. "The Paraguayan suite is right across from that one. Turn off the lights, try to see if anything is going on there. If these swine are trying to pull a fast one they have another guess coming. They must all be in on it, the Czech and all. They have set us up, that's what they have done. Perhaps the munitions ship does not even exist and all of those cables were fakes! *Verdammte!* Stay there, observe, I'll wake the others and get them here. We must plan. We must hit them before they discover that their little ruse has been discovered."

Klaus clicked off the light and smiled into the darkness. The Doctor would appreciate him even more after this night's business was over. He had uncovered a plot of some kind and would help to set things straight. After this had been done there would be gratitude and Klaus would see to it that it was financial gratitude in a large measure. Enough to buy a house, a barn, a few horses, some women. The future was going to be very, very good indeed.

He eased the door open a crack to look out into the empty corridor. Nothing. He held it that way, patiently, for a long time. He would stay on watch until he saw something or the Doctor phoned him back. He was on watch, on guard, defending his comrades. It was like the war again . . . .

There was the sound of approaching footsteps and the mutter of men's voices. He eased the door shut until they had passed, then opened it. There were two of them and they were using a key to let themselves into the Paraguayan suite. They only stayed a few minutes;

Klaus saw their faces clearly when they left. He hurried to the phone; Wielgus picked it up on the first ring.

"Two men," Klaus said. "They went into the other suite, then left again. South Americans. It is very interesting, sir . . . ."

"What do you mean? Speak up."

Klaus smiled, pleased with himself. "One of the men I have never seen before, though I am sure he is not with either government party. The other man, I have seen his picture often in Uruguay. His name is Josep and he is the leader of the revolutionaries, the Tupamaros."

"You are absolutely sure? Positive?"

"Without a doubt. My life upon it."

"Then it can only mean one thing." Seething anger filled Wielgus; his teeth grated together so loudly with uncontrollable rage that Klaus could hear the sound at the other end of the telephone conversation.

"This entire operation has been penetrated, spied upon by the resistance forces — and now they have captured these stupid play-acting politicians! They are after the diamonds, the arms ship, who knows — they must want everything. They shall not get it, Klaus. All they will get is a bullet. Stay there. Do you have a gun with you?"

"No, I'm sorry . . . "

"We'll bring you one. We will hit them now, instantly, before they discover that they have been found out. Wait for us."

Klaus, again at the door, heard his comrades coming down the corridor a few minutes later. He hurried silently to meet them.

"Nothing changed," he reported.

"Good," Wielgus said. He handed Klaus a pistol. His face was grim; the same expression mirrored by the four Nazis who stood behind him. "I have thought about what we must do while we were on the way here. I will knock on the door and say that I must talk to Stroessner about the arms shipment at once. They will open the door. You will take care of whoever opens the door . . . . ''

"It is dangerous," Klaus protested. "One of the others must go in your place."

"No. This is my responsibility. Come! Before we lose the advantage of surprise."

Klaus stood out of sight to one side as Wielgus knocked on the door, again and again. A voice finally asked in Spanish what was going on.

"It is Doctor Wielgus. I must see the General at once."

"I am afraid that he is asleep . . . . ''

"I don't care. Open now, immediately."

After a short hesitation the lock rattled and the door opened a crack. The room was dark beyond. The Army Sergeant from Stroessner's party looked out at them.

"I'm sorry, Doctor, but everyone is asleep. I had specific orders . . . . ''

He stopped as Klaus's gun appeared over Wielgus's shoulder, pointing him straight in the face.

"Hands in sight," Wielgus ordered. "Walk backward. One wrong twitch and you are dead."

They moved into the room. The lights came on and the armed Germans rushed in after them. Admiral Marquez was staring at them, tied to a chair with a gag in his mouth, his wounded aide unconscious on the floor beside him.

"How very interesting," Wielgus said, looking about. "Watch this man closely. Guard the door, no one to enter — no matter what the excuse. Come, Klaus, we will look in the other room. I'm sure we will find something just as interesting in there as we did here!"

25

The roaring of the flame stopped as the engine room rating turned off the acetylene torch.

"That does it," he said. "As neat a job as if I were trained in the profession. Maybe I ought to take it up as a trade after we make port. Robbing safes can't be more dangerous than this blinking voyage . . . . "

"Stand aside," Josep ordered, pulling the sailor's shoulder. The heavy steel door of the vault was still glowing red from the torch, but the entire locking mechanism had been cut away.

Diaz was uncomfortable in his rubber mask, but he was not aware of it at this moment. He dug through the sailor's toolbox and found an oversize screwdriver. "Use this," he said, handing it to Josep.

Josep pushed it into the opening next to the fractured lock and threw his weight against it. Nothing happened. He did it again just as the ship rolled; the vault door creaked and opened a fraction of an inch. Josep stopped and signalled to the armed Tupamaro by the door.

"Take this sailor to the Captain's quarters and put him with the others. Remain there with the others on guard."

Josep waited until the two men had gone and he was alone in the cashier's office with Diaz — who gratefully stripped off his mask.

"We did not need that sailor as a witness," Josep said. "Let's get this open."

He levered harder with the screwdriver until they

could get a grip on the edge of the door with their fingers. They heaved and the heavy steel door moved, wider and wider, until the vault was standing open.

On the burnished metal floor, in front of the rows of locked safe deposit boxes, stood the bag of diamonds.

Diaz bent over and picked it up and placed it on the table. "You have the key taken from the Czech?" he asked. Josep nodded and dug in his pocket. The key turned in the lock and the bag opened.

"An important moment in history," Diaz said, reaching in and taking out a chamois sack. "This could mean freedom for both our countries." He shook the diamonds out into the palm of his hand where they sparkled and gleamed. Josep nodded agreement. Diaz put the stones back, then locked the bag again. "You take the bag, I'll take the key until we can divide these up."

"Good. Now we will open these boxes and see what other funds the capitalists have supplied us with."

"No. We will not do that. We are not thieves."

Josep's laugh was quick and humorless. "You amuse me, my little bourgeois revolutionary. You hijack the world's largest ocean liner, kidnap two heads of state, burn open the ship's safe to steal a fortune in diamonds — and stop short of taking some small change from the parasitical capitalists who squander their stolen money on this voyage. It is preposterous!"

"We have no time to argue, Josep. I do what I must do to obtain my country's freedom. I will die, if I must, for this freedom. But I will not become a petty thief."

"Watch your mouth, little man." Josep was angry, his pistol half drawn. Diaz would not be moved; his hand was on his own gun. Neither man would back down; the tension grew.

They spun about together as the door burst open.

Concepcion was there, wide-eyed and panting for breath. It was the first time that Diaz had ever seen her express any emotion.

"Come . . . at once," she gasped. "Something has gone badly wrong. German voices . . . in the next suite. They must have released the prisoners."

Josep seized up the diamonds and ran. Diaz stayed behind just long enough to see that the CLOSED sign was in place on the cashier's office before he slammed and locked the door and hurried after the others.

They were all grouped around the speaker when he reached Hank's suite, bent close, listening.

Sergeant Pradera's hands were tied behind his back and he had been thrown to the floor. His face was scratched and bleeding where Admiral Marquez had attacked him with his single hand, hitting and clawing at him before the Germans had dragged him away. Other than this, the Sergeant was not hurt. Though he knew this would not last long. They would want information and knew how to extract it from people. He was aware of this and he knew what was coming. This knowledge did not show on his face, which displayed only stoical calm. His eyes flickered slightly as General Stroessner came raging out of the bedroom, still trailing pieces of the curtain cords that he had been tied with.

"Betrayed," he shouted. "By my own men! Humiliated. This one will not get away with it, I trusted him . . . . "

He tried to take Klaus's pistol from him, but the big German held him easily at bay with one hand. Wielgus emerged from the bedroom and walked across the room to stand over the Sergeant. He glared down at him coldly, then became aware of Stroessner's near hysterical shouting. He turned and struck him across the face with the back of his hand, sending him staggering.

"Be quiet, you Bavarian turd!" he ordered. "I will extract some information and then you may kill the man. Not before. Now go sit down."

Stroessner was shocked into obeying. He had never been struck before; it was unthinkable. This entire situation was unthinkable. He regretted ever getting involved. He stumbled to the sofa and dropped onto it, scarcely aware of Admiral Marquez sitting next to him. Major de Laiglesia was at the bar and he called out to him hoarsely.

"Gin. Quickly! A large glass."

"Put him in the chair," Wielgus ordered. Klaus and Colonel Hartig took Sergeant Pradera under the arms and heaved him up. Wielgus came and stood over him, staring down coldly.

"You will now tell me what I want to know. Josep was seen, so we know that the Tupamaros are involved. Who else? There must be Paraguayan filth like you. How many? What are their plans? How much do they know? Is the Czech involved — and our diamonds? Do you understand, Sergeant? I have many questions. I want answers to them. You are a strong man and you mean to resist me so I will now make you weaker."

As he talked he drew his pistol and cocked it, then bent forward. He placed the muzzle against the Sergeant's kneecap and pulled the trigger.

The sound of the shot was loud in the enclosed space of the room. Under the impact of the bullet the leg jumped and the kneecap was splintered and destroyed. Despite his efforts at control a hoarse moan escaped from Pradera's lips, Wielgus smiled.

"You felt that, didn't you, Sergeant? The kneecap, all injuries there are particularly painful. And you have another kneecap, don't you, Sergeant? And many other delicate parts of your body. Perhaps I shall cut your balls off, take away your manhood. Would you like that? Think of all the places where I can hurt you and, believe me, I shall. Perhaps, yet, the other kneecap next. I shall not kill you, not for a long time, and then perhaps only if you beg me for death because the pain will be so great. Now answer my questions, do not delay.''

Pradera looked up at Wielgus, his face expressionless again. But his lower lip was between his teeth and a slow trickle of blood ran down over his chin.

As the two Tupamaros were maneuvering the heavy sack through the door of Hank's suite, the room steward, Robert appeared behind them.

''What's happening here? I'm sorry, this is very extraordinary . . . .'' His words were cut off as Concepcion came up and jabbed her gun into his kidneys, forcing him into the suite behind the others, then closing the door. Robert could only gape around at the armed men. It was Uzi who took in the situation and acted fast; pointing his gun at Hank.

''Who is this man? Do you know him?''

Hank picked up the cue. ''He's the room steward — don't harm him.''

''That's up to you, Mr. Greenstein.'' He waved Robert forward with his gun. ''We have taken over this suite. You are a prisoner, the same as Mr. and Mrs. Greenstein. If you do what you are told you will not be hurt, nor will they. Into the bedroom.''

Like Hank, Frances had been woken by the tumult in the adjoining room. She was tired, it was just dawn, but she knew that more sleep would be impossible. She was dressed and sitting on the edge of the bed when Uzi opened the door and pushed Hank and Robert in before him, waving a pistol.

"If you do exactly as I say you will not be hurt. Lock this steward in the toilet. Your husband's life will be controlled by his good behavior, as well as your own. You will keep absolutely silent." He bent and tore the telephone from the wall and threw it the length of the room, then forced the trembling Robert into the bathroom and closed the door.

"Thanks, Uzi," Hank whispered. Uzi nodded and put the gun away.

"Jesus!" Frances said. "What a way to start the day." She dropped down on the edge of the bed. Uzi spoke loudly.

"Your husband will be with us, Mrs. Greenstein. Be careful."

"Yes, sure. Does anyone mind if I lie down and close my eyes and make believe I'm asleep? I really can't believe that all this is happening."

The sitting room was turning into an armed camp. Ammunition boxes had been broken open and clips distributed, while the sack had been dumped on the floor and a bulky object was being dragged out of it. It had two tanks, a harness of some kind, and a hose leading to a gunlike nozzle. One of the Tupamaros lifted it and held it up so Josep could slip his arms through the straps.

"A flame-thrower!"

Hank gasped the words aloud and Josep glared in his direction.

"I want silence now. You will all listen to me. We are going to take those Germans now before they find out any more about our plans or discover that we are listening to them. Do you understand? If we do it right we won't get hurt and we'll have fought the last action. We have the diamonds, right here in this bag." He pushed the bag in Hank's direction. "Watch these until we get back. Don't do anything foolish."

"I'll try not to," Hank said dryly. "They'll be here when you get back."

"They had better be." He turned back to the others and in that instant's silence the murmur of voices in the adjoining suite, relayed by the eavesdropping circuitry, could be distinctly heard. Also, loudly and clearly, a single shot. Diaz had been bent over, listening, and he straightened up. His face was drawn and pale.

"Sergeant Pradera. They shot him in the other knee."

"We have no time to waste," Josep said. "There are six of us. That's all we can spare from guard duty. It will be enough. They have about the same number of people. But they will not be expecting this attack. Because of the storm we cannot go in through the window from the verandah. Anyone who tried that would be swept away. Therefore, we have to take them through the single door. It can be done. Fortune was on our side when we found this flame-thrower during the Mexican raid. Now we can turn it to good use. Here is what we will do." He raised the black muzzle of the weapon.

"I'll be on the floor outside the door — with this ready. Concepcion and Esteban will stand against the wall to the left. She will shoot the lock away, he will kick the door open. I will then put in a two-second burst. Aimed up and to the left. We have determined that Sergeant Pradera is tied to a chair on the right-hand side of the room. He has bought us time. We must spare him if we can."

"When I turn off the flame you will all go in over me. Shoot anything that moves. If you are close enough to knock them down or knife them, fine. We need

prisoners, but more important — we need to win. Do
you all know what you have to do? Any questions?''

"Just one," Uzi said. "Are you familiar with that
weapon?''

"Very much so. I put in hours with it in the hills after
we captured it. Beautiful. I'll roast those Germans like
the pigs they are. We go.''

They moved out efficiently and silently, spreading
down the corridor. "Lights," Josep whispered. They
moved quickly and pulled loose the fluorescent tube,
unscrewed the light bulbs. Now, the only light was the
glow from the open door of Hank's suite. Josep eased
himself down on the deck in front of the adjoining suite
while his men took their positions. He waved to Hank,
who closed the door.

In the darkness of the corridor there was only expectant silence.

"NOW!" Josep shouted.

The submachine gun hammered echo to his command, the muzzle flare crackling like lightning. A
boot slammed out and the door swung open.

Sight of turned, shocked faces, men . . . .

Gone in an instant behind a wave of rolling flame, a
roaring violence that died away almost as soon as it had
begun. In the silence that followed, a man's shrill
screaming was heard. Drowned out by the shots that
followed as the attackers stormed in.

Through a cloud of water as the automatic sprinklers
came on, activated by the flame.

It was a battle in hell. Clouds of sickening smoke
poured out from the charred walls and carpeting, to be
beaten down by the spray. Figures stumbled through it
and there was the sharp crackle of gunfire.

Uzi was the last one in, stumbling over Josep, who
had wiggled free of the flame-thrower and was trying to

stand. Uzi shoved him aside, and pushed his way along the wall. There, just before him, was Wielgus, firing his pistol over and over. Uzi did not shoot, but instead hurled his own gun at the man, catching him on the jaw and sending him staggering backwards. Before he could right himself Uzi was upon him, chopping at his wrist, seizing the gun, burying his fist deep in the roll of fat over his solar plexus. Wielgus dropped, falling over Sergeant Pradera who was lying sideways on the floor, still tied to his chair. He had hurled it over when the shooting had started.

"What kept you?" the Sergeant said.

The brief battle was over. Above their heads the sprays of water died away to a trickle, then stopped. Most of the lights were out and someone opened the drapes. Gray light of dawn filtered in on the carnage.

"We have them," Josep said happily.

Diaz looked around at the carnage, the charred flesh of the man next to the door, then turned and threw up.

They had indeed won. At a bitter price to both sides. Admiral Marquez was dead, a bullet through his face.

"Small loss," Josep said, pushing the body with his toe, then pointing his gun at General Stroessner who was unharmed. Stroessner let the empty pistol drop from his fingers and backed slowly away.

It was Major de Laiglesia who had caught the full blast of the flame-thrower — he had been standing just in front of the door when it was kicked open. The Major had tortured his last victim, was now the victim of a torture far worse than anything he had ever inflicted himself. Leandro Diaz looked down at the eyeless, faceless, charred and still living object that was moaning in a continuous, breathless, mewling sound. Then he bent and placed his pistol against the side of the black-charred head. A single, muffled shot blasted out.

Wielgus lay writhing on the floor, both hands pressed to his stomach, oblivious to the fact that Colonel Manfred Hartig lay next to him, sightless eyes staring upward. The handful of survivors of the Polish concentration camps that he had supervised would have enjoyed the sight. There would be no need of a trial for the Colonel.

Karl-Heinz Eitmann was alive, cowering against the wall. He had always been afraid of guns and did not really know how to use one; he had thrown his pistol away when the firing had begun.

This was not true of Klaus who stood, head down, obsessed with bitterness and shame. For over thirty years he had been Doktor Wielgus's bodyguard — and he had failed him in his hour of need. He could not hold a gun. By reflex he had raised his hands before his face when the flame rolled towards him. His face was scorched a bit, his hair burnt away, nothing important. But his hands were like raw meat, the skin hanging off them in strips. He had tried to hold the gun, to fire, but his fingers would not obey him.

These were the only German survivors. The attackers had suffered as well. Three men dead, Concepcion on the floor, blood flowing from her throat and mouth.

"Where is the doctor?" Josep called out. It was Sergeant Pradera who answered him.

"In the bedroom with the injured Uruguayan." Pradera levered himself up on an elbow, trying to ignore the waves of pain from his legs, and looked quickly about the room. "All accounted for. No stragglers with the doctor."

"Diaz, get him," Josep ordered. Diaz hurried into the bedroom and returned a moment later pushing out the protesting Dr. Llusera, his black bag clutched to his chest.

"That man on the bed, he is injured, concussion, I
shouldn't leave him . . . my God!" He looked around
at the blackened chaos, the dead and wounded, the
handful of survivors. "This is awful, awful . . . . "

"Here! This woman," Josep ordered.

The doctor knelt beside Concepcion and saw that her
eyes were open, looking up at him. "Don't try to talk,"
he said. "You have been shot in the neck." He felt
beneath her head. "Very lucky. Missed the spine. No
major blood vessels severed. Lie quietly. I'll dress the
wound, give you something for the pain."

Running footsteps sounded from the corridor outside
and three men burst in through the door. They were
dressed in heavy protective clothing with breathing
apparatus, and carried fire extinguishers and axes. At
the sight of the carnage in the room they stopped dead,
staring at the guns that covered them. Josep waved them
into the room.

"Make sure that the fires are out," he ordered. "Do
not try to leave this room." He went to the telephone
and picked it up off the floor. It had apparently
survived the destruction; he quickly dialled a number.
"Put the Captain on. Right . . . yes, I know about the
fire. Shut up and listen. Call whoever is responsible for
fire or damage control or whatever it is called. Report
that everything is under control. Make him believe it.
What do you mean you don't believe me yourself! Your
ship is not at risk. Here, I'll put one of your own men
on."

He waved over the nearest crewman and left him
talking to the irate Captain.

"What the hell is going on here?"

"A handful of passengers stood in the open doorway,
dressed in robes for the most part, some of them wearing life jackets.

"Bring them in here," Josep said, wearily. "We'll have to find a place to put them."

Everything was coming apart, ravelling at the edges, there were too few of them to take care of everything. Now they would have to make prisoners of all the passengers who were close enough to be aware of what was happening.

"Excuse me, is your name Mr. Joseph?" the sailor said. He held out the telephone. "The Captain. For you. He says that it is very urgent that he talks to you now."

Josep listened, started to protest, then was silent. In the end all he said was, "I'll be right there," then hung up. He looked around and pointed to Diaz.

"You'll have to handle this," he said. "I'll try to send you someone. Get them all into this room and the bedroom, close the door. Tear out the telephones. I'll be back here as soon as I can. You, come with me," he said, signalling to Uzi.

"What is it?" Uzi asked, when they were in the corridor.

"Captain says he can't be responsible if his officers there disobey orders. Something about the safety of the ship. I said we would get up there."

There was nothing more to be said as they made their way forward. The scene on the bridge was not good. Only the frightened sailor at the ship's wheel remained in position. The others were huddled at one end with their Tupamaro guard aiming his sub-machine gun at them. The Third Officer called to them as they came through the door.

"Do something. This cretin speaks no English and I can't explain to him about the danger."

"What danger? Come forward. Just you alone."

The ship's officer hurried to the chart table followed

by Joseph and Uzi. He pointed at the Pacific chart in place there, and explained excitedly. As he talked a wide grin began to spread over Uzi's face until he laughed out loud and interrupted the man.

"That's fine," he said, "very good. It will be taken care of, have no fear." Then he turned to the puzzled Josep and tapped the chart with his forefinger.

"See it?" he said. "See that? It's the answer to all of our problems! The solution we were looking for. We are going to win this thing yet and come out of it alive!"

26

When the Peruvian Coast Guard vessel had first arrived, the *QE2* had been floating alone in an empty ocean. Now, twenty-four hours later, the situation had changed incredibly. The *Huascaran* was still there, her commander, Captain Borras, had kept his ship on station so there could be no doubt in anyone's mind as to which man had been first aboard. Not only for the glory but because of maritime law. Since there had been no one on the ship when he arrived it might be called derelict, in which case the first to board her could claim possession. The Captain doubted very much if he would ever be able to lay claim to the giant ship riding close to him, but it was a pleasant thought to have. In any case he was staying on station and he made sure that one of the *Huascaran*'s sailors was aboard the *QE2* at all times.

There were others aboard as well. The United States carrier *Kitty Hawk* stood by less than a quarter of a mile distant and there was a constant traffic in motor launches and helicopters between the two ships.

And, of course, there were sightseers. A Dutch tanker in ballast lay rocking in the long swells a mile distant, and already two seagoing yachts had arrived to add to the growing crowd of visitors. Other ships, freighters and one cruise liner, had left their normal coastal courses to stop by for a look. In some ways the entire affair had certain aspects of a seagoing carnival. But this was the high seas, far outside any coastal waters, so there was no law to prevent the sightseers from crowding round to gawk.

There was activity now aboard the carrier. Her engines had been turning over just enough to keep her in position and headed bow first towards the advancing waves. Now her turbines speeded up and a sudden plume of exhaust shot high into the air from her funnel. The massive form swung around into the wind and picked up speed. A few minutes later a speck on the horizon grew into a dark blue jet, a long-range two-place attack bomber. It roared out of the sky, tilted up on one wing and whistled off towards the horizon again, before turning back with landing flaps extended and its hook down ready to catch the arresting gear.

Commodore Frith looked out at the sea rushing by below, at the seemingly tiny deck of the carrier approaching ahead and, not for the first time in his life, was glad he had served on deep water ships and had stayed out of the air as much as possible. The last day had more than made up for any flying that he might have missed up until now.

It had started in Southampton with the long expected, almost fearfully awaited phone call. The *Queen* had been found. He was Commodore of the line and Cunard had expected him to leave at once. It was his duty, of course. A single small bag, already packed, passport in his wallet, and he was waiting by the terminal in Portsmouth Airport when the company jet touched down. They were no sooner airborne than they were in the circle for landing at Heathrow. He never saw the terminal because Concorde had been held for him, sitting on the runway for over an hour. The jet taxied close and he hurried across the intervening distance. Her Majesty's Immigration Officers were a little more outgoing than usual and one of them was actually standing at the foot of the stairs as he came up, stamp and inkpad ready. With the official approval for departure in his passport, he had been rushed aboard and was still strapping into his seat when the door had closed and the trip begun.

Admittedly Concorde was the pride of British Airlines, for all the millions of pounds it lost every year, but he was profoundly unimpressed. He always had the feeling that every passenger who crossed the ocean by air was one less for Cunard to transport in a civilized and safe manner, so had no love for the national airline because of this. All the sirloin, champagne and caviar could not make up for the fact that the seats were jammed in, the ceiling low, the plane noisy and vibrating. He kept his observations to himself and, after a treble whisky, managed to doze off, only to discover that they were already landing in Washington, D.C. Commodore Frith stayed aboard, tapping his fingers with irritation, until they took off again for Dallas-Fort Worth.

That was where the American Navy took over. There was no messing about with passports or rubber stamps here, just an incredibly long black Cadillac, with an equally black driver, who saluted and opened the door for him, put his foot on the accelerator and hurled the tons of steel around the airport service roads to the waiting Navy jet. The pilot was leaning against the wing, chewing gum, and extended a clipboard as Commodore Frith climbed out of the car.

"Hi, Cap," he said, in a very American and highly indifferent-to-authority way. "I'm your driver, Chuck. If you would just sign this release form, here and here, so your relatives won't sue the Navy if I plough you into the drink, then we can get going. That's it, and initial here, just like you were renting a car from Hertz. Really great."

This ritual completed, Chuck had handed over the clipboard to the driver of the limousine, then helped the Commodore aboard. Chuck had fastened his parachute for him, showed him how to strap in, then boarded the plane himself.

It had been a fast but boring trip and, in the end, the Commodore had dozed off, only to waken with a start as they upended on one wing and the loud growl of mechanisms sounded from the guts of the aircraft below him.

The landing was almost anticlimatic. One moment the carrier was visible directly ahead of them — the next they slammed into the deck, he was tossed forward against the restraining harness — and someone was opening the hatch next to his head.

After all this, the short hop in the helicopter was over almost as soon as it began. They lifted up, buzzed sideways to fly into the wind, then settled down gently on the rear deck of the *QE2*. The Commodore was pleased to see that all the deck chairs, which usually covered this area, had been carefully cleared away.

An American sailor opened the door of the 'copter and the young lieutenant standing behind him saluted, then took the Commodore's bag as he climbed down.

"Welcome aboard, sir. They're waiting for you on the bridge."

Commodore Frith suddenly discovered that he had nothing to say and merely nodded at the officer. He felt choked by conflicting emotions; immensely relieved to have the *QE2* recovered intact, still puzzled over the mystery of her appearance — and burning with anger over the entire affair. That this should have happened to a Cunard ship, and the *Queen* of all of them. While underneath everything he felt a dense knot of fear over the survival of her passengers and crew. Two thousand six hundred people do not vanish into thin air. Unless, horror of unspoken, unthinkable horrors. They were dead. The ocean had acted as a mass grave many times before.

These thoughts tore at him as he rapidly paced the length of the sports deck, the lieutenant trailing after him, then up to the bridge. There were a number of American Navy officers and ratings there who turned as he came in. A gray-haired officer, of his own height and build, came towards him, his hand extended.

"Glad that you are here, Commodore. I'm Admiral Mydland in charge of this operation."

"My pleasure, Admiral. Thank you for all that you and the Navy have done. Can you give me a report of the situation as you found it?"

"Of course. Let's go over here. I've sent for some coffee. Why don't you sit in the Captain's chair . . . ."

"It is not mine to occupy," the Commodore said stiffly. This awkward moment was glossed over by the arrival of the coffee. The Admiral poured out two cups.

"Let me tell you exactly what we found, then you can make an inspection of the ship," he said. "The main engines were shut down but the standby was running to generate the electricity. All instruments on the bridge were functional. The radios are operational. There are no entries in the log or course-markings on the chart since the time of the last radio contact, four days ago. These are what you might call the normal aspects of the ship . . . ."

"Other than the fact that there was no one aboard?"

"Yes, besides that. But we did find that all of the life-boats and launches are gone and there are signs of a rapid abandonment of the ship."

"What sort of evidence?"

"Lifejacket lockers open and the jackets missing. Things strewn about the passenger cabins, suitcases left open, things like that. And the cabin lifejackets all seem to be missing as well. Then there are some inexplicable things, and others a little out of the ordinary.''

''What sort of things, Admiral?''

''Circular burned areas on the carpets — on every one of the passenger decks. As though there had been intense localized fires on these spots.''

''You aren't going to start talking about flying saucers now, are you? They are always leaving mysterious burned patches.''

''No, I am not,'' the Admiral said, keeping his irritation under rein. ''I am simply describing what we found out of the ordinary. In addition to the burned areas there was the somewhat unusual setup in one of the first class dining rooms where all of the tables were laid for dinner, but just a few tables had been used and never cleared. I don't know what it means. I am simply reporting what we have discovered. The worst things were the evidence of destruction, what must have been fighting of some kind.''

''Like what?'' the Commodore asked, draining the last of the coffee and wishing that he had a drink instead.

''One of the luxury suites. Burned out, and I mean really burned, floors, ceilings, walls, everything. Then drenched with water by the sprinkler system. Not only that — but there are bullet holes in the walls, we even dug out a couple of slugs. And stains on the unburned parts of the carpet that could be blood. I had some scraped off and examined by the doctors and pharmacists, who are reasonably certain that it is blood, and probably human blood.''

Fire and blood and bullets. All of the Commodore's worst dreams were coming true. Dead. Could they all be dead? His head dropped with the terror at the thought, his chin resting on his chest. Not realizing it, he spoke aloud.

"I can't believe that they are all dead, murdered, I just can't believe it. It all seems so impossible."

"The whole damn thing is impossible. Where was this ship for three whole days?"

"That, Admiral, is the important question to ask." Commodore Frith jerked his head up, anger washing away the weakness of fear. "And by God, we are going to find them. First, though, I am going to have a drink — it's been a long and tiring trip."

"Sorry, Commodore, but the American Navy is dry . . . . "

"Thank God the British one isn't! Nor is this ship. I know from experience there are plenty of spirits on board."

"All under lock and key now, one of my first orders."

"Very commendable. But since I came aboard, this vessel is once more flying the Cunard flag. We'll go to the Captain's quarters, Rapley always keeps a well-stocked bar there for entertaining."

And what kind of entertaining was it that was last held here, was the Commodore's first thought when they came through the door. Dirty glasses everywhere, ashtrays filled and overflowing, crushed cigarette packets tossed in the corners.

"Was it this way when you found it, Admiral?" he asked. He was looking around and did not catch Mydland's quick scowl.

"I assure you it was exactly as you see it and my personnel have not touched it since. Other than to seal the bar."

The Commodore noticed the metal tape with crimped-on lead seal that had been wrapped around the bar. He nodded. "Very good. Will you now be so kind as to unseal it? Thank you."

There were a few clean glasses left in the bar, as well as a half-full bottle of whisky among all the empties. Some party indeed. He held a glass out towards the Admiral.

"Will you join me?" he asked.

"I am on duty, sir." The chill in Mydland's voice would have frozen the blood of a lesser man; but not the Commodore's. In truth he was scarcely aware of it. He drank deep and sighed.

"Anything else out of the ordinary?" he asked.

"One very important thing. The vault in the cashier's office has been cut open with a torch — it's still lying there. The funny part is that, although the outer door was broken open, apparently nothing inside was touched. All of the safe deposit boxes are still in place and still locked."

"We must find them!" the Commodore said loudly, jumping to his feet and pacing back and forth, goaded on by the strength of his emotions. "I cannot, will not, believe that they are all dead. The concept is too horrible and I will not accept it until there is irrefutable proof. Were there any clues as to what happened? Any notes, written evidence?"

"I thought about that and had my men do a search, as well as they could in the limited time. They came up with only one thing, written on a wall in the crew's quarters, behind one of the bunks, "WOGS," it said."

"Not too surprising. The British seaman tends to look down on all of the races not native to our islands."

"But there was more, hidden by the mattress, a second line right below it. "WITH GUNS" was what it said."

"Wogs with guns. Not very elucidating. We know

that guns were fired and "wogs" could mean anyone from France to China or in between. These clues are meaningless until we find the crew and passengers — and that must be done at once."

"We have been trying to do that for four days now, Commodore. I appreciate your concern, but everything possible has been done . . . ."

"No, it has not. Since the *QE2* has been found we now know where to look for those aboard."

"Do we Commodore? Perhaps I am being dense, but I don't see it that way at all."

Commodore Firth suddenly realized that because of the intensity of his own emotions he had angered this man. A very stupid thing to do in every way. He put down his glass and went up to the American officer.

"Admiral Mydland — will you please accept my apology? I have been rude and overbearing to you. I cannot justify my actions but I can only explain them because of my ever-present fear over the fate of these people who entrusted themselves to our care. You are in command of many men, so you must know how I feel."

"I do, sir — and there is no need to apologize." He put out his hand and the Commodore clutched it tightly.

"We are all tired, for it's been a damn hectic couple of days," the Commodore said, "for which I must thank you and everyone else, of all the nations, who helped in the search. But now I must ask for one last, great effort."

"What do you mean?"

"If we might go through to the bridge I'll show you on the chart."

The Pacific chart was still spread out on the table, the course marked to the final, fateful day. The Commodore tapped this spot. "We know for a fact that the ship was here at this place at that time. She was

sighted an hour earlier by a freighter who logged the
sighting. His observation matches the plotted course.
Now here," he moved his finger down the chart and
tapped a spot in the empty Pacific. "This is where the
QE2 was found. If you would be so kind as to send for
the best navigating officer aboard the carrier I will show
him the simple equations that he must work out."

"I'm afraid that you are ahead of me."

"With what we know we can determine the area
within which we must search. We know the time and the
place of the last sighting of this ship. We know the time
and place where next she was seen. Your officer will
then take the *QE2*'s service speed of twenty-eight and a
half knots and, after making his computations, will
mark out a circular area on this chart within which the
occupants of the ship could possibly be. The outline of
this area will be all the places the ship could have
reached at this speed and then turned about to reach the
arrival point at the appointed time. Or they could have
been transferred to another ship in the area at that time.
Few ships are large enough to hold this number of
people and it will be easy enough to examine all of those
that might be involved."

The Admiral rubbed his chin and ran his finger over
the chart. "I see what you mean. They could have gone
anywhere out to sea here, then stopped and turned
back. Or they could even have been put ashore here in
Baja California, Central America . . . ."

"Or here, in Guatemala. That coast is all jungle,
without communication. It is possible that they are
there, on the shore — or anywhere else. We must search
every square foot, on sea and on land. They have to be
there!"

Admiral Mydland nodded. "You are absolutely right.
They must be there somewhere, I tell you. They have to

be there." He did not add that they could be drowned, murdered, anything. Those kinds of thoughts could wait. "We have mounted a tremendous international effort over the past days, on sea and in the air, to find this ship. That effort will continue now, and on the land as well. No effort will be spared. I tell you, sir — they will be found."

27

Captain Ernie Bush had been with Western Airlines for a long time — and had been flying for a good number of years before that. He clearly remembered B-29's and C-47's, crop dusting and barnstorming after the war, then the commercial airlines and Super Connies and the first jets. And now the pride of the pack, the 747. This was a plane he loved to fly. When Western had first considered buying these birds, he had pushed as hard as he dared to back the idea. He had taken his own holiday time and money to visit the plant where they were being built, to talk to the engineers and designers, and to go up in one of them. Things had worked out just as he had hoped and now he was Captain and pilot of one of these incredible aircraft and he could think of nothing in this world — or the next — that he would rather be doing with his life.

They would be taking off in a few hours. He had put his flight bag aboard, admired the great, empty, cool depths of the plane, and was now going to post his flight plan. The Met reports had been good. The Pacific storms of the last week had blown themselves out and he looked forward to a happy and uneventful flight.

The first hint of trouble came when he was called into the Flight Controller's office. He stood there in the doorway, a tall and solid man with grizzled hair, fists half clenched, though he was not aware of it, ready to tackle anything.

"What's wrong?" he asked.

"Nothing is wrong, Captain. Please come in. I don't know if you gentlemen have met. Captain Bush, Western Airlines, this is Commander Gimelli, USN."

"My pleasure, Captain," Gimelli said, waving him to a chair on the other side of the conference table. Bush's suspicions grew. He had never had much love for the Navy, having been in the Air Force, and was particularly unentranced by sawed-off gyrene brass with New York accents.

"I've been looking at your flight plan," Gimelli said, "and I wonder if you would possibly consider some changes in it?"

"I see no reason to," Bush said coldly.

Gimelli looked up at him through his bushy dark brows. "Perhaps I shouldn't have phrased it so bluntly. Do you know what I am doing here?"

"No." Said in a tone of voice that practically spelled out the unspoken next words — nor do I care.

"I'm area coordinator for the *QE2* search, working with overseas flights . . . . "

"They've found the ship, so you're out of a job. If you don't need me any more I'll just get moving."

"Captain Bush, are you naturally an ornery son of a bitch or just playing at it?" Gimelli's voice cracked out sharply and Bush jumped to his feet, his face red with anger.

"Now just what the hell do you mean!"

"I mean exactly what I said. Don't you know that the ship was found — but that the crew and passengers are still missing?"

"No, I didn't know that." Bush dropped back into his chair. "I've been out of touch." He certainly had been — at a motel in Encinatas in Baja, California, with a stewardess, an old friend. He had heard a short radio announcement in Spanish and had not thought of the matter since. He never paid much attention to the news in any case.

"Then let me fill you in. For the past four days one of the largest air and sea searches ever mounted has been in progress. For very good reason, since the world's largest liner vanished without a trace. The QE2 has been found, but she is empty of all life. A couple of thousand people, gone, and signs of shooting and violence aboard the ship. So the search is going on for all the crew and passengers who were aboard when she left Acapulco. Here, look at this chart, this is the area being searched. We are particularly interested in all ships in this area or just outside of it. We are asking for reports from all planes and ships that might be of help. When I saw your flight plan I thought that you could really be of great help to us."

"What would you like me to do?"

"Very kind of you to offer. I must first tell you that I have cleared this matter with your Company, who approve the suggested changes, even though it means an expenditure of a few thousand more pounds of jet fuel. The whole world is concerned, as you can see, Captain."

Bush nodded and ate his humble pie. He deserved it. But those three days in the motel had been worth it.

"You are taking a charter flight to Bogotá, Columbia, then on to Peru. Is that right?"

"Yes. It's the start of a new service. Only about a fifty percent configuration, that's a half-load of passengers, but it should get better."

"That was one of the considerations we had in mind when we considered this change in flight plans. Would you look here please, at the chart. We would like you to swing further west than you originally planned, to around one hundred and fifteen degrees west latitude.''

Bush ran his finger over the chart. "That's pretty far off course and way the hell out into the Pacific."

"It is. But you will be flying a great circle course, which helps, and, of course, you will catch the westerly jet stream. These changes should add a maximum of an hour to your flying time. With the extra fuel you will still have your normal reserves."

"And you say management approves?"

"They are enthusiastic."

"That's the way it's going to be, then. Can you tell me why this is so important?"

"Absolutely. We have no ships in this area, or any carrier planes that can reach it. If you will mark the position of any large ships you might see here, on the fringe of our search area, it will be of considerable help to us."

"Is that all you want?"

"Yes. Other than asking you to keep your eyes open for anything out of the ordinary. I can't tell you what that might be — but this whole situation is so extraordinary that, well, who knows what the answer is to the disappearance."

"I'll do my best."

"Thank you."

They took off two hours later. Bush himself was at the controls and, heavily loaded with fuel as they were, they used a good deal of the runway, lifting the nose and pulling up the gear as they headed out over the blue Pacific, leaving the gray smog of Los Angeles behind them. As they gained altitude, he began a slow turn to port that would take them down along the southern California coast. The air was clear here, San Diego showing up below with the farms and suburbs south of it marking the border of the United States. After that the mountains and deserts of Baja, with a quick glimpse of the bay at Ensenada on the horizon before thin clouds cut off the view. Ah, motel of fond dreams. He smiled at the memories, then cleansed his mind of everything except flying.

"This is going to take some navigating," Trubey said. As Second Pilot he was responsible for the navigation at this time. He was working out a true compass heading on the chart and listening to the sound of the San Diego beacon vanishing behind them. Abandoning this reference, he reached out and switched frequencies to the one in La Paz. "We won't be able to take bearings on any stations ahead for a long time. At least the inertial navigator will tell us where we are."

"Well, good for you, my boy, we'll make a pilot of you yet. Don't forget that during the war, B-17's and 24's flew the Atlantic to Britain without radio beacons, without navigational aids of any kind — other than the same charts and sextants ships use."

"Spare me the lecture, Pops. I read the history books, too. It's just that I have a feeling of security knowing where I've been and just where I'm going to. Beckoned by a radio beacon in the night. When I leave those friendly reference marks behind I get angry and remember Air New Zealand in the Antarctic . . . . "

"Bite your tongue when you say that! We'll not have that kind of trouble here. This is going to be a day flight, we're staying at thirty-one thousand feet, and once we have made the search sweep you can twist the dials and get the beacon in Bogotá and we're home free."

"Great, thanks."

"You're welcome." Bush switched on the public address speakers, humming happily to himself. This was a bit like the old days, on your own, without all the navigational aids the young flyers were used to now.

"Good morning. This is your Captain speaking. We have now reached our cruising altitude of thirty-one thousand feet. The outside air temperature is fifty degrees below zero, but the weather in Bogotá is better than that. Clear and sunny and the temperature is now twenty degrees, seventy degrees Fahrenheit. Our arrival time there will be slightly later than you were told because this aircraft, like many others, is cooperating in the search for the passengers of the *QE2*. Therefore, we will be going slightly west of our planned route to report on any ships in that area. I will tell you when we are there in case you want to look out the windows yourself. Who knows — one of you may be the person who finds the missing passengers and crew of the Queen. Have a pleasant flight and thank you for flying Western."

"A master of psychology," Trubey said.

"Naturally. If we are getting in late you might as well let them know. And they'll be busy staring out at the ocean."

The cabin attendants were just clearing away after luncheon when the loudspeakers crackled to life once more.

"This is Captain Bush again. We are now passing over the invisible boundary of the area within which we have been asked to make observations. We are logging any ships that we may sight and this information will be relayed to the authorities when we land. Thank you."

"A lot of empty ocean out there," Trubey said. "And not a ship on it that I can see."

"We're away from the normal sea lanes, that's why. But the visibility is still unlimited, so, who knows. Call back and get us some coffee, will you?"

For the next half hour there was nothing below them but empty sea, empty of ships of any kind. A few light clouds appeared which cut their visibility slightly, but did not really interfere with it. Trubey, peering ahead, saw a dark smudge on the horizon.

"Looks like some clouds coming up."

Bush checked the compass heading, then the chart. "Not clouds, an island, Clipperton Island. It's the only land we're going to see until we are over Central America."

"Clipperton? Really?" Trubey ran his finger over the chart. "It certainly is. I read an article about that island in *Crotch*."

"Wonderful. And just what words of geographical wisdom could you possibly find in a girly magazine?"

"It was pretty good, a real serious article. I even remember the title. *The Mad White Queen of Cannibal Island* . . . ."

"Tremendous. That really sounds serious."

"No, listen, it was. Maybe the writer jazzed up the idea to sell it to the magazine but the facts were bright, honest. Because I looked it up in the *Encyclopaedia Britannica*. I had a bet on with this guy in the hotel."

"Oh, sacred font of wisdom, who can doubt your pale white pages!"

"It's true, Ernie, honest. This island used to belong to Mexico and it's just a hunk of rock out here in the ocean with nothing growing on it and no water or anything. Only it used to be covered yards deep in guano . . . ."

"I knew it! It's turning into a shitty story!"

"Not that way at all. They still mine guano in South America for fertilizer. So it seems that the Mexicans had a camp on Clipperton, in the last century, where they used to dig out the bird guano and ship it back home for fertilizer. It wasn't a popular job — "

"You can say that again!"

"But they needed the stuff. They used to bring all of the food and water in by ship, then take the guano out. Which was OK until there was a revolution and during the war and everything, why, they forgot about the people on Clipperton. By the time a ship stopped by there months later a lot of them were dead and the survivors had been reduced to cannibalism to stay alive."

"You mean that?" Bush looked out at the solitary pinnacle of rock growing out of the ocean ahead, and touched the wheel to turn them in its direction. "It must be true. I don't think you have the imagination to make up a story like that. It must have been pretty gruesome."

"You bet it was. Hundreds of miles out in the ocean, alone, no way off, no food — and waiting for a ship that never came."

Clipperton was a mountaintop in the sea ahead, a gray pinnacle of rock jutting up out of the blue sea. Utterly alone. Trubey had the high-power binoculars to his eyes now and was examining the island.

"Now that's what I call a grim place," he said. "No trace of green, trees or plants or anything. The rock is streaked white all over, guano in the making I guess. A sort of natural bay. Lot of rock formations in it, I can just make them out. Rows of rocks along the shore."

He lowered the glasses and rubbed his sore eyes. The 747 tore on through the empty sky and past the island at a steady six hundred and fifty miles an hour. It began to shrink into the sea behind them.

"It couldn't be," Bush said. "It just couldn't be — but it could be as well."

"Going to let me in on this?" Trubey said.

"A wild idea, that's all. Really wild. Those rocks you saw. Could they be boats?"

"Looked a lot like rocks to me . .-. ."

"Listen. They say the *QE2* could have been in this area. All of the ship's boats and launches are gone. I know it sounds crazy — this whole thing is crazy — but could they be down there, on this deserted island, drawn up on the shore?"

"Jesus . . . ." Trubey breathed the word out quietly, realizing what it could mean.

Captain Bush switched off the autopilot and seized the controls and started a slow turn, throttling back at the same time. "Get on the radio to Mexico City and give them our position. Tell them that I am dropping down to six thousand feet to take a closer look at the island. Keep the frequency open and let them know that we'll be giving them a running report. Then tell the passengers what is happening."

Turning and dropping steadily, the great aircraft headed for the island. Coming in lower now, from the west with the sun behind them, they could see the dark clusters on the beach clearly, watch them as they grew larger and larger.

"Boats! By God, they're boats!" Trubey shouted as they tore over the sparkling bay. "The whole shore down there is covered with lifeboats!"

As they hurtled by they could clearly see the flares that were now bursting in the air above the crowded beach.

As they swung out to sea again even the passengers, crowded at the windows, could see the hundreds and hundreds of people on the strip of shore, waving and waving and waving . . . .

28

"Be quick," Josep said. "I have no time for any games. What do you mean that this little speck on the chart is the answer to our problems? That is as foolish as these officers saying we are going to crash into it."

"They're right," Uzi said. "Our present course will take us unpleasantly close to Clipperton Island. In a storm like this we need all the sea room we can get. But what I propose is that we don't alter course, that we sail at top speed to this island. How long before we reach it?"

The Third Officer used the dividers on the chart. "We'll be there in about six hours. That is why I want to discuss a course correction now . . . ."

"You'll do nothing of the sort," Uzi said. "You have radar, don't you? You can see it when it is miles away?"

"Yes, but . . . ."

"No buts. Stay on this course. I will have the Captain verify this. Now, cause no more trouble, do you hear?"

Uzi drew the puzzled Josep out into the corridor. "This is our chance to finish this operation and come out of it all in one piece. What we must do is hold the ship for a few hours more."

"Then?"

"Then we will be off Clipperton Island. We will have the fire alarms sounded again, and the abandon ship order given as well. We'll have the Captain make an announcement to everyone. They must take to the boats.

The ship must be abandoned.''

"Of course! We'll unload them all on the island! Brilliant! The *QE2* is completely computerized, practically automatic. Even with our few men we can sail this ship to our rendezvous. We'll just leave the ship there, empty. Let them figure that one out. By the time they do we'll be long gone. But what about the people on this island? They'll have radios, they can report us . . . . ''

"No worry. I was talking to one of the officers when we passed the island on the way to Acapulco. Empty, uninhabited, nothing there except some birds. The life-boats are well provisioned with food and water. The people won't come to any harm . . . . ''

"In here. Something bad is happening!''

It was one of the Tupamaro guards who came through the door from the Captain's quarters and saw them. Josep took a deep breath and led the way.

Captain Rapley was on the phone, listening. "Yes, I'll tell them,'' he said, then hung up. He saw Josep coming through the door. "There has been a development you should know about. The First Engineer Officer has discovered that the ship has been seized by your people. He has taken over the engine room with all the ratings there and has sealed the door. He has delivered an ultimatum. You have just half an hour to return the ship to my command. If you do not, or you attempt to break into the engine room, he is closing down the engines and sabotaging them so they won't run again without major repairs. I told him that this would endanger the ship and the lives of everyone aboard — but he was adamant.'' The Captain looked at his watch. "There are now approximately twenty-five minutes left.''

"You fool!'' Josep shouted, pulling his gun and

pushing it close to the Captain's face. "People are going to be hurt because of this man's stupidity. Phone him back, instantly. Tell him that your life is in danger if he persists in this action."

The Captain drew himself up, his expression grim. "I said that he was adamant. There is nothing more that I can do. I suggest you end this business at once. I'll take that gun."

"You have it," Josep said, striking him across the neck with it, leaving a bloody welt. "You people never seem to learn. Get two of your men and come with me — move!"

They moved. There was no doubting the instant menace of the gun in that trembling hand. Shaking with rage, the finger ready on the trigger. He herded them before him to the deck below and into the burned-out suite. The passengers huddled there surged forward, shouting, when they saw the Captain. Josep fired twice into the wall next to them and they fell back screaming.

"You, Captain, and your men. I want you to pick up and carry these three bodies — unless you prefer me to bring your bodies instead. Put a blanket around the burned one so it doesn't come apart. Now move!"

They did not want to, but they obeyed. The sailor carrying the charred body of de Laiglesia was trembling with horror — but he did as he was told. Captain Rapley staggered when the corpse of Admiral Marquez was draped over his shoulder, but he said nothing. Colonel Hartig, as fat in death as in life, could not be lifted and had to be dragged. Josep took one of the submachine guns and herded the laboring men before him to the lift that descended all of the way to the engine room, urging them on with the gun to the locked engine room door.

"Drop the bodies, here," he said. "Then remain

where you are. You, Captain, go to that phone over there. Call your officer in the engine room. Tell him you are out here with two of your men. Tell him about the bodies. Tell him to open the door and look for himself if he wants to. Assure him I won't be here, that I'll be a hundred meters back down the hall. That is the truth. Tell him to look at the bodies. Then I want you to tell him that I will kill you, your two other men here, and every single one of the ship's company if he does not come out at once and cease this madness. That is the truth. Do you doubt it?"

"No," the Captain said.

"Good. Tell him not to bother about what he has read about me in the papers. Tell him to open the door and look now at what I can do. I won't shoot him. I don't have to. Now do this."

Josep turned on his heel and stalked back down the corridor and stopped when he reached the end. He leaned against the wall as he watched the Captain pick up the phone. The fools. He was so tired. His eyes were sore; every muscle hurt. He must take some pills to wake up, as soon as this crisis was over. Could they hold out for six hours more? Yes! They had to.

He saw the Captain put the phone down and turn to the door. After a moment it opened hesitantly and the Engineer Officer looked out. He talked to the Captain, then looked at the corpses — then up at Josep where he stood, gun ready. The man's shoulders slumped and Josep knew that another crisis was past. But how many more would there be?

It held together — barely. With each calamity averted, the whole mad scheme still came closer and closer to disaster.

Passengers were beginning to discover what was going on. Not very many, and they were pushed into the gymnasium with the others and locked away. But each occasion like this demanded a diversion of manpower. If it hadn't been for the storm, the takeover would never have stood a chance of succeeding. But most passengers stayed in their cabins or did not venture any further than the dining rooms. They were too ill or too uncomfortable to wonder why the cashier's office was closed, the gymnasium locked, the Captain's parties cancelled. They just prayed for the storm to stop and went back to bed.

The two ship's doctors discovered at gunpoint what was going on. One guard was left in the hospital as they operated on the wounded cashier, did what they could to repair Sergeant Pradera's shattered kneecaps, sewed up the wound in Concepcion's neck, bandaged Klaus's hands.

In every part of the ship desperate, exhausted men held ten, twenty times their number at bay with the menace of their guns. Most of the sailors knew what was happening now, but respected their orders to do nothing about it. What had happened in the engine room was common knowledge.

Two hours after he had been left alone, Hank got a message through to Diaz to come to his suite at once. Diaz did so, dropping exhausted onto the couch.

"What is it?" he asked.

"I'm tired of watching the baby. This bag of diamonds. My wife is still in the bedroom, getting hungry and letting me know about it, and the poor steward is still locked in the bathroom. What are you going to do about this?"

"I'll get Josep down here. I don't dare go near that bag if he isn't here. I'll use your phone."

Busy as he was, the Tupamaro leader made the time when the diamonds were mentioned. He came in and dropped into a chair just as Diaz had. He listened in silence, then nodded when Hank said he wanted no more responsibility of looking after the bag and its precious contents.

"You are right," Josep said. "It was a temporary expedient." He took the key from his pocket and bent and unlocked the bag and looked inside.

"You're very trusting," Hank told him.

"There is very little trust involved where millions are at stake. They appear not to have been touched. Do you agree, Diaz?"

The Paraguayan shrugged without rising. He was almost too tired to think. Josep was not. His eyes were red with fatigue but his brain did not appear to be affected in any way.

"I have a suggestion," he said. "We can spare no one to watch this bag. And I trust no one — that is no one person."

Diaz nodded. "Agreed."

"We'll take the bag to the hospital. Your Sergeant Pradera is there, as is Concepcion. We'll have them both moved into the same room. See that they have guns. Bring the bag and leave it there. With those two looking after it, it will be safer than any vault."

"Agreed. You are a shrewd man, Josep. And it will be safe for each of us as well, with one person from your party there and one from mine. I agree. The bag will be guarded without sparing anyone for the job."

"Then let us do it now, get it over with, because it is almost time for our radio contact. The last cable said it would only be a matter of a few hours before the fishing boat would be ready to put to sea."

"Wait, before you go," Hank said. "The room steward is still in the toilet. He can't know that I'm involved."

"I'll let him out," Diaz said. "And warn him about the takeover by now. Go in front of me while I hold this gun on you."

The frightened steward was released — and a thoroughly angry Frances as well. She led Hank off to see that he had a late breakfast, as well as a number of well-chosen words that she had been choosing for the past hours. Josep and Diaz took the bag with its precious contents down to the hospital.

There were protests — but the arrangements were made. The only room big enough for two hospital beds was the consulting room on the port side of Two deck. Under the persuasion of the guns the medical orderlies took out the desk and examination table and moved in the beds. The bag itself was put on top of the shelves of medical books and journals that covered one wall. Concepcion sat on the edge of her bed and watched.

"You have a gun?" Josep asked.

"Of course, here," she said. Her voice was hoarse, raw. Heavy bandages were about her throat and neck and she was very pale.

"Good," Josep said. "Lie back, regain your strength. Let no one come near the diamonds."

She only smiled in answer and sank down against the pillows.

Sergeant Pradera was wheeled in on a gurney and it took two orderlies, with the doctor's help to get him onto the bed. Both of his legs were encased in plaster to immobilize his knees. When the medical team had gone Diaz passed a Webley .45 caliber pistol over to him.

"The diamonds are in the bag," Diaz said. "The bag remains there and no one is to go near it." Pradera nodded and put the pistol under the covers by his side.

"Secure. Make sure the lights are left on all the time. When you say no one, you include the girl there?"

"Let me introduce you. Sergeant Pradera, Concepcion Valverde. She is your opposite number in the Tupamaros. You guard the bag together. Neither of you goes near it."

"Not my problem, is it?" the Sergeant said. "It is hers." He turned his expressionless face her way. "Touch the bag and you are dead, woman. Remember that."

Concepcion spat with anger and turned away.

"Enjoy your stay in hospital," Diaz said cheerily as he and Josep left. Concepcion glared after him, then swung her legs off the bed as soon as he was gone, stood and walked over to look down at the Sergeant.

"You were the one on the inside, weren't you? Working with them every day." Pradera nodded. "Took some guts. You didn't talk, either, when they did that to your legs."

"It took some guts for you to walk into the prison of La Libertad and blow away the prison governor and his guards. I know of you, Concepcion."

She smiled, a rare expression on her always stern face and for a moment was a lovely young girl. But only for a moment. "We will get along, Sergeant. If you will watch the bag while I go to the toilet I will not be long."

"If I am disturbed you will only have to step over the body upon your return."

Concepcion and Pradera were the only members of the hijacking party to relax in the next hours. Only by threats of violence, and violence itself, could control of the giant ship be maintained. Tempers were drawn thin and the doctors treated a steady stream of bruised and battered people. It was only by chance that there were no bullet wounds — or deaths — as of yet.

Four hours passed. Four hours of growing tension that could end in only one way. Josep was alone with

Captain Rapley in his bedroom, saying just that.

"I have no control over my crew," the Captain said. "Not while they have guns at their heads."

"You have moral control, Captain. You can issue them orders to cooperate, to cease this subtle resistance. My men are tired, their fingers uneasy on the triggers."

"I'm sorry, but that is the situation. I can do no more."

"Would you do more if I turned your ship back to you?"

"What do you mean?" the Captain snapped. "You are surrendering?"

"I did not say that. We are leaving the ship soon. We have done what we had to do." He held up a sheet of paper. "Your radio room is shut down and guarded, but I have had your Chief Radio Officer in there and we have been exchanging cables with a shore station, though, of course not identifying this end as the *QE2*. I have had the answer that I have been waiting for. Another ship will rendezvous with us at this location. If you agree to set the correct course to get us to the appointed place at the correct time, and also agree to hold your crew in check until we get there, if you do that, why then the violence will be at an end."

"Do I have any choice?"

"No. And someone will be dead very soon if you don't make your mind up rather quickly."

"I'll do it, of course. But I promise you that I will make every effort to see that you are apprehended as soon as possible when I am once more in command of this ship."

"Of course. I expect no less."

"Then it is agreed. I want to issue orders to the crew at once, then we'll go to the bridge and I'll set the course."

The telephone rang, and the Captain answered it after Josep nodded permission.

"What does this mean?" he asked Josep, covering the phone with his hand. "Radar reports that we are within range of Clipperton Island."

"Hang up. We'll go to the bridge. Clipperton is simply the reference point where we stop and turn around. Let us go up there so you can take charge."

Captain Rapley walked in front of Josep, so he did not see the smile of victory on Josep's face, the outward sign that with this one last bit of trickery and deceit the entire operation would finally be able to fall into place.

29

The abrupt, piercing scream of the ship's siren jerked
Angus Macrahanish out of a half-doze. He was lying on
his bed, reading *Greenmantle,* not for the first time, and
sipping some good Campbletown malt now and again.
This was the easiest way to pass the time until the storm
died down. His wife, in the next bed, snored lightly in
her sleep, rendered unconscious by a combination of
lunch and large doses of dramamine. The shrill siren did
not disturb her in the slightest.

"Now what the bloody hell is it?" Angus said,
throwing the book down and jumping to his feet. When
he stood up he realized that the ship was barely rocking,
the first time in days, and that the engines had slowed,
almost stopped. He went to the window and wiped off
the condensation; a large rocky cliff was visible not too
distant, only partially obscured by the driving rain.

"Wake up," he said, giving Martha a shake. "Something's happening. This bloody cruise." Not for the
first time did he wish he was still back behind his desk in
Aberdeen getting a decent day's work done and not piss-
ing about all over the seven seas on a so-called holiday.
The speaker in the wall rustled and crackled and came to
life.

"This is Captain Rapley speaking. You will all have
heard the alarm sounded for abandon ship. Everyone
aboard has an assigned station and you will remember
from boat drill that you are to proceed to your stations

wearing your life jackets. Now I wish to be very frank with you. The ship is in no danger of sinking, no danger at all. But there has been a fire aboard which is being contained. Until it is absolutely secure I wish you to proceed to your boat stations. Will you kindly proceed now to your assigned stations. If you are in any doubt about this please ask your room steward who will give you specific instructions. I repeat — the ship is in no danger, no danger at all. However, noxious fumes from a small fire are creating an annoying hazard and it would be better if you left your cabins and proceeded to your stations at once.''

''Bloody hell!'' Angus said, shaking his bleary-eyed wife awake again. ''Wake up, that's a good girl, wakey wakey. They're having a bit of the old lifeboat drill just to keep us amused.''

He dug the life jackets out, then opened the door to the corridor — slammed it at once. ''Bloody hell,'' he muttered again to himself, and choked back a cough. Filled with acrid smoke. They had better get on deck.

''My jewels!'' Martha said, knotting the ties of the vest. ''I can't leave them here. Someone will steal them.''

She dug the jewel box out of the dresser drawer and Angus took it from her and threw it into a small suitcase. Along with two bottles of whisky. There was no telling how long this nonsense would last.

Sheila Conrd hoped that what was happening would last forever — or even longer! This was passion, passion that she had never experienced before, a rising all-consuming tide of pleasure that did not stop, a wave that rose up and up and threatened to break and never did. Jesus, it was wonderful . . . wonderful!

She was moaning, then shrieking aloud with the unbearable gorgeousness of it all, wrapping her legs around his back and pressing, squeezing, her arms tight around his back as well, her fingernails digging into his flesh.

Her screams blended with the scream of the siren, a not unpleasant combination that Hendrik enjoyed. But even the best things had to end sometime and with a final slow and powerful thrust of his hips he succeeded in effecting a simultaneous climax. Sheila's voice cracked and she went limp, sobbing, all passion spent, unable to talk. He liked that and he caressed her generous breasts until her quivering stopped.

"Hendrik . . . ." she said, and stopped for breath. "Hendrik, you are something else again. I swear, if I had come one more time I would have exploded. Jesus . . . !"

"That's fery nice. It is good you haf pleasure, that way is my pleasure too."

"Pleasure! Baby, you got a touch that is worth diamonds."

"It is funny you should say that. By profession I am a diamond expert."

"How I envy the diamonds your very lovely fingers gently touch! I could write a book about you — in fact, damn it, I will write a book about you. What research!"

"It is my pleasure. A woman like you, so ample of body, mature and appreciative . . . ."

"That's the right word, Hendrik-baby, appreciative is what I am. In fact, why don't you join me in New York for an all-expenses-paid holiday? Research. I hope I live."

"Most kind. But my vork in Amsterdam . . . ."

"So we'll research in Amsterdam. A bed's a bed any-where . . . say, did you hear that, like a siren?"

"Yes. It is the call to the lifeboats. It has been

sounding some minutes now."

"And I didn't hear it! Out of this world."

"We must leaf."

"Only if you promise to come back. This cruise has finally gotten good."

They dressed quickly and Hendrik De Groot fastened her life jacket for her; her fingers were shaking so. The sirens were sounding even louder now and when he opened the door they could smell pungent smoke. He took her hand in his and led her out, carefully guiding her through the crowded corridors, filled with stumbling, coughing figures. Two stewards were trying to keep them going in the right direction.

"This way, if you please. I'm sorry, do not attempt to use the elevators. The stairway is ahead. That's good, thank you kindly, keep moving, ladies and gentlemen, if you please."

The sirens sounded steadily and the Captain's voice spoke again from the PA system.

"Please do not panic. I know that the smoke is disconcerting, but it presents no danger, none at all. Just proceed to your assigned boat stations and await further instructions. This is Captain Rapley speaking and I will report to you again in a few minutes . . . ."

" . . . in a few minutes," the hotel manager said into the microphone. Josep leaned over and switched it off.

The hotel manager had the same four stripes on his coat sleeve that the Captain did, though his were gold on white instead of gold on blue. He was in charge of all the functions of the ship that did not have to deal with the operation of the *QE2*. He was Captain Rapley's age, he had responsibilities commensurate with the Captain's. His voice was educated and somewhat resembled Captain Rapley's. But he was not the Captain.

He had only said that into the microphone because a man stood next to him with a gun pressed to his side. While the Captain lay unconscious on the deck at his feet — struck down by the barrel of this same gun when he refused to make this announcement. The hotel manager had seen this happen and reckoned that discretion was the better part of valor. He had pretended to be the Captain and had read out the prepared message that the Captain had refused to read.

"Very good," Josep said, straddling the Captain's unconscious body. "The crew may realize that it was not the Captain speaking, but there is nothing they can do. We are under control. Is that right, Diaz?"

Diaz stood on the other side of the bridge, leaning tiredly against the window. He nodded. "All taken care of. We hit them sudden and hard. Everyone cleaned out of the engine room even before they could shut the engines down, much less sabotage them. Radio room, the Bureau, everything. Doors locked and one of our people inside and well armed."

"Perfect. You, hotel manager, call someone and get a report. I want to know the instant that all of the passengers are at their stations." He handed over the phone and stood close while the manager dialled.

Diaz pulled himself awake, suddenly, realizing that he had fallen asleep on his feet and was slumping down the wall. He had a sharp feeling of nausea at drifting off, then waking up like that. And he was dizzy. And why shouldn't he be? He forgot the last time that he had slept. The past days and nights blended into a haze of fatigue and he had the depressed feeling that he would die before it was all over.

"It appears that all of the passengers are at their boat stations, but crewmen are checking the cabins to make absolutely sure," the hotel manager said.

"Good." Josep signalled to Diaz. "Get on the other phone and pass the word to our people to use the fire extinguishers on the smudge-fires we lit on each deck. I want the air cleared before we make our own checks, just to make sure that no one is preparing any surprises."

The lifeboat drill was well-organized and the crew had had years of experience in herding passengers to their correct stations. Short minutes later the call came through that all passengers and crew were standing by at their positions.

"That is just the news I have been waiting to hear," Josep said, taking a folded sheet of paper from his pocket and handing it to the hotel manager. Josep was proud of it; he had originated the idea and explained it to Hank Greenstein who had written it up in the form of a command. The hotel manager read it with growing alarm and he was trembling with despair when he had finished it.

"I can't possibly read this out, no! I refuse. You cannot make me . . . . " He quailed back as Josep pumped the slide on the sub-machine gun and a bullet was ejected onto the floor. He picked it up and held it before the hotel manager's face. A shiny brass case with a dull, grease-coated, leaden bullet at its tip.

"Look at that," Josep said. "See that slug? It tears through flesh and through bone and makes a big exit hole when it goes out because it has a hollow nose. Now if I put this gun to your eye — like this — and pulled the trigger, you would be dead before you heard the shot. A brave man might make the sacrifice. But . . . . "

He pulled the gun muzzle away from the man's horrified face and used the toe of his boot to roll over the Captain's unconscious body. Then placed the gun against his head.

"I'm not going to shoot you if you refuse," he said. "I'm going to kill the Captain instead. Then bring his officers in here and shoot them, one by one, until you agree to make the broadcast. So, how many men must die to convince you that you must do it? You will agree in the end. But how many deaths do you wish to have on your conscience first?"

The hotel manager drew himself up, trying to decide, weighing one evil against another. Diaz's low voice cut through the silence.

"Don't be a fool. He means to do it. He has done it before, right on this ship. Do you want to see the bodies to prove it? Captain David Rapley will be dead meat in ten seconds if you don't do as you have been told."

On the deck, the Captain rolled his head from side to side and, still unconscious, moaned in pain.

"Yes . . . I'll do it," the hotel manager said in a hollow voice. He raised the sheet of paper and Josep reached out and turned the microphone on.

"This is Captain Rapley speaking. It has been reported to me that all passengers are now at their boat stations. However, the crew are still fighting the fire which has been contained, but is still smouldering and giving off dangerous fumes. Therefore, I have decided to remove all passengers from any chance of danger from smoke inhalation. You will notice that we are near Clipperton Island which is breaking the force of the sea so that launching of the boats will present no danger at all. You all have gone ashore many times in the launches for day trips during this cruise, and now we are going to do that again . . . ."

His voice broke off as Captain Rapley rolled over towards him, eyes wide with pain, and tugged at his trouser leg. The hotel manager looked down in horror.

Josep reacted instantly, kicking the Captain viciously in the ribs, and again in the head. Then grinding the gun hard into the hotel manager's side. His actions spoke louder than any words would have. Fighting to control the tremble in his voice, the hotel manager continued reading.

"We are going to have a shore visit. The people on the island have been informed by radio and are willing to welcome you. Since everyone will be going ashore this time we will use the lifeboats as well as the launches so you can all go at once. Enjoy your trip ashore, I wish I were going with you, and I am sure that you will all enjoy setting your feet on solid ground again, if only for a short time. Thank you."

"All crew members. Abandon ship."

These last words sent a shock wave of fear through the waiting passengers. Had the Captain been lying? Were they in danger? Was the fire spreading? Abandon ship, they had heard the words as had the crew. The crew obeyed their orders, herding the passengers forward and into the lifeboats. Unresisting, the passengers moved, holding tightly to the few possessions that they had taken with them. The blocks on the davits creaked as the first lifeboat began its descent, the sailors fending it off from the hull as the slow rollers rocked the ship back and forth.

High above them, out on the bridge wing, Josep looked down at the lifeboats splashing into the sea and moving free of their dropped lines and nodded happily. "Working perfectly," he said to himself. The launches were also in the water and pulled up by the lowered boarding ladders.

Diaz opened the door to the bridge and called out to him. "I have the hospital on the phone, they want to talk to you."

Josep seized the phone, listened, then spoke.

"I do not care what the doctors say. The patients must be moved. All of them. A lot of people have been shot through the guts and have been sewed up and lived. Get him into the launch now with all of the others. The doctors can go with them. Concepcion will help you. Yes. She's staying with us. Sergeant Pradera? Wait — I'll ask Diaz. He turned and raised his eyebrows.

"The Sergeant will have to go. He won't be able to transfer with us, and he needs a skilled operation quickly. I'll get down there now. And bring the bag up here. With Concepcion's help, of course."

"Do that."

The doctors were waiting to move Sergeant Pradera when Diaz got to the hospital. They had been waiting a few minutes because the Sergeant insisted that they wait. The large revolver he held made a convincing argument. Concepcion looked up as Diaz came in.

"We were expecting you. The Sergeant did not wish to leave until you came." She nodded towards the bag of diamonds on the shelf.

"Very wise," Diaz agreed, and turned towards the bed. "All right. I am here, Sergeant. Why did you wish to see me?"

"Take this gun," Pradera said, throwing it over. "I am a loyal Paraguayan and I kept it to defend myself against this revolutionary they put me in this room with. I put you on your honor not to kill me — even though we are on opposite sides. I trust you, but not this piece of Tupamaro garbage. I fought you honorably and was wounded defending General Stroessner, the leader of my country, from you filthy revolutionaries. Long live Paraguay! Long live General Stroessner!"

"Get him out of here," Diaz ordered, looking on silently while the wounded man was taken out, the door closed. "What was that about?" he asked Concepcion.

"A little bit of play-acting. That tall doctor speaks good Spanish. He'll be a witness now that the Sergeant was not involved in seizing the ship."

"I should have thought of that myself. I'm too tired. I should have said goodbye."

"You'll see him again. Now let's get the diamonds up to the bridge."

"I hope we meet again," Uzi Drezner said, taking Hank Greenstein's hand. "We couldn't have done this without you."

"I think you could have," Hank told him. "I feel more like an observer than a participant."

"Just keep on thinking of yourself that way," Frances said, pushing the last of her clothes into the suitcase and slamming it shut. "We're going ashore now with the rest of the passengers because that is just what we are. Passengers. We came along for the ride." She turned on Uzi, glaring at him. "I'll never forgive you for getting Hank involved so deeply in this, making him a part of a criminal activity, a criminal like yourself."

"I am sorry," Uzi said. "Believe me, Mrs. Greenstein, I say that sincerely. We only intended to use him to provide information . . . ."

"But you used him, didn't you. Use is the right word?"

"I'm afraid we did. But I will be frank. I would do it again if I had to. I would use anyone to capture those Nazi criminals. That is my life, and I don't think it is a wasted one. Although I said I was sorry you people became innocently involved in all these insane schemes, I hope you will remember that if these schemes succeed the criminals will be brought to justice. Think about that. It is something to be proud about. Goodbye."

Uzi turned and left abruptly. Hank reached out and took the bag from Frances. "I hope he's right," Hank said. "If Wielgus and Eitmann are brought to trial all of this might very well be worthwhile."

"If killing and kidnap are ever worthwhile," Frances said wearily. Then reached up and kissed him. "Let's go ashore. I'm looking forward to standing on something that doesn't move up and down. Just for a change."

Captain Rapley came painfully and hesitantly back to consciousness. Even before he opened his eyes he knew that he was in a small boat because of the choppy motion, the slapping of the waves. His neck and head hurt, his side was painful. Memory was slow in returning — and when it did, he jerked awake and tried to sit up. Gentle hands held him down. He blinked up at the hotel manager, who was sitting next to him.

"It's all over then?" he said, surprised at the weakness of his own voice. The hotel manager nodded, his face a picture of deep misery.

"We had to abandon the ship. We had no chance."

"They tricked me. Made me cooperate. Let me think that I would have the ship after they left. When all of the time they intended to get us all off, to hijack it." A deep, familiar ship's horn sounded in the distance. "Help me sit up," he said.

There it was. His ship. The mightiest liner ever built, the *QE2*. Hundreds of yards away across the sea. Swinging about, her propellors churning up a froth at the stern as the engines picked up speed. Sailing away from him.

"There was no more shooting, thank God," the hotel manager said. "All the passengers are ashore, unhurt, as well as the crew. We're the last ones. They held us hostage while they searched the ship, kept making announcements that we would be shot if any of the crew tried to remain aboard. They flushed out a few. Beat them up and tossed them in the launch here. The doctor has seen to them. Nothing serious.''

''They'll be caught,'' the Captain said with feeling. ''They won't get away with this. They can't.'' He looked up at the thick clouds already darkening with the approaching night. ''These clouds will have to clear away soon. The storm is blowing itself out. They'll be seen, captured. They are just not going to get away with this.''

The hotel manager did not answer. He just sat and looked at their ship already getting smaller as it picked up speed. Then he shook himself and turned to look towards the bow of the launch, towards the grim island they were approaching. Almost dark, over twenty-five hundred people here. Some of them injured. His responsibility. They would need shelter, food. He would think about that and forget the *QE2* now disappearing in a rainstorm far out to sea.

30

"More champagne?" Josep asked. Uzi nodded and held out his glass. "You too, Diaz. Drink up. This is a celebration of sorts, isn't it? We're going to win. Against all odds, against everything. We're going to win. Even the storm is on our side. Those clouds up there are as solid as they were when we left Acapulco. When was that? It seems a million years ago. Three days. Just three days."

He lolled back in his chair, most of the sirloin steak uneaten on the plate before him. There were greater satisfactions than food and drink, women, anything. The unalterable pleasure of success. They had done it. They had won.

"Success," he said, and drained his glass. Uzi and Diaz did the same. They were alone in the immense dining room, finishing off the salad they had found in the refrigerator, steaks they had fried. There were dirty dishes and soiled tablecloths all around them. None of the hijackers bothered to clean up after eating. Not with all the freshly laid places at the tables.

"When was the last contact?" Uzi asked.

"About an hour ago. I talked to the *Tigre Amarillo*. No more troubles since the repairs. They are using a radio direction-finder on our transmitter, homing in on us. If we are on course they should be in sight soon."

"The course has not been changed," Diaz said. "Let us hope the Captain gave us the correct one."

"Esteban checked it," Josep said. "He has a

captain's ticket. Fishing boats. The theory is the same. He says it was right. All the machinery still running fine. The miracle of modern computerization. If anything should go wrong we couldn't fix it. But as long as the engines are running, the bridge instruments working, why we just sail along merrily. Esteban and the other two are keeping a watch on the engines. That is what really counts.''

"I found another note," Uzi said. "Hidden behind the radios."

"We should have them all now. At least all of the ones that can be easily discovered," Diaz said, pushing his plate away. "When they find this ship there should be no clues, no clues at all as to what happened. We are all agreed on that. We want to be in port and off the fishing boat before they think of looking for us.''

"Equally important," Josep said, "is the revolution. Those agreements that they all signed to let the Nazis take over. Do you realize what political dynamite they are? If we time things carefully they will be the lever that tips these regimes out of office. We must plan it with exact precision. First, rumors will be leaked that Stroessner and Marquez were aboard the *QE2*, and missing along with everyone else aboard the ship. Enough people in Uruguay and Paraguay know that this is the truth, so not only will the rumor not be stopped, but it will prove to be true. Then, at precisely the moment of most unrest and dissent — we release copies of the agreements. All at once, all over the world, at the same time. Every newspaper and television station will have a copy and the wave of reaction and disgust will spread. The unrest and rioting in our countries will turn to a single force of revolt. Unstoppable. That is when we hit the demoralized and leaderless troops and hit them hard. It will be like Iran all over again. No one will dare defend the discredited governments. The army will very possibly join in the revolt. It will all be over in a day. That is what I plan to do, Diaz, and I suggest you think strongly about doing the same in Paraguay. Think, organize, strike. Liberty is very close at hand.''

''Yes,'' Diaz said, ''I agree completely. Liberty is at hand and that is certainly worth drinking to.'' He filled his glass and raised it. ''To the freedom of our countries.'' He drank the toast, emptied the glass, then stood. ''I have to get up to the bridge now to relieve my man there.''

By agreement, the bag of diamonds had been left on the bridge near the wheel, in clear sight of anyone there. Two people at least were always on duty, one Tupamaro and one Paraguayan. If Josep had any plans to capture the arms ship which was now at sea, he had not mentioned them. The diamonds were the prize to be shared. Two hundred and fifty million dollars worth.

Uzi cared nothing about the stones. His prizes were locked in two cabins below. He went into the kitchen to prepare plates of food for them. With the operation nearly over he cared less and less about South American politics as he became more and more engrossed in plans to get the two Nazis safely out of Mexico. It could be done, but it must be done carefully. He put the plates on a tray and took them to the elevator.

There was little chance of violence from the prisoners, but he took no chances. Putting the tray onto the carpet outside the cabin, he drew his gun before unlocking the door. The cabin was silent and dark, the curtains drawn.

''Come and get your food, Eitmann,'' he called out. There was only silence in response. Keeping the gun ready, Uzi carefully reached in and turned on the lights — then jumped back.

There was no need. Karl-Heinz Eitmann was lying on the carpet, gasping for breath. There was blood on his forehead. His own belt was tightened about his neck, with the other end knotted about the lighting fixture — which had been pulled from the wall and was lying next to him. Uzi took it all in and shook his head.

"You are losing your touch, Eitmann. The man who organized all of the slave labor for the Reich should have been able to commit suicide without bungling it." He nudged the man lightly with his toe. "Off the floor, you look very foolish there. And put that belt back in your trousers where it belongs."

Uzi brought in the tray of food while Eitmann stumbled to his feet then dropped into the chair, the belt dangling from his hand.

"I'll pay you very well," he said hoarsely. "I am not without funds, no one would ever know. Please, take the money, let me go. I promise to have nothing to do with the Bruderbund, ever again. It was a mistake . . . ."

"Your entire life was a mistake. Shut up and eat your food."

Uzi slammed the door as he left. He took no pleasure in the man's humiliation, his constant tearful pleadings to be freed, the promises of larger and larger sums of money. He did not seek vengeance upon this pitiful creature. Just to bring him to justice.

Wielgus was a different matter. This was a man who made it very easy to detest him. He had not said a word since he had been captured; the burning hatred in his eyes spoke loudly enough. He ate well and slept well and kept himself prepared for an opportunity to escape. But Uzi was equally prepared and ready to die if he had to before he let that happen. As he was locking the door again, Uzi heard running footsteps and turned to see one of the Tupamaros hurrying towards him, brandishing his gun in the air.

"They are here! We can see them!" he shouted. "The boat has arrived. Come, get your German pigs on deck. I'll help you herd them."

There were shouts of jubilation when they came out on the Boat Deck and one of the Tupamaros let off a burst of automatic fire into the sky.

Coming towards them, just over the horizon, was a dingy and ancient Mexican fishing boat. It was the most beautiful sight that they had ever seen.

"All right," Josep said. "Let us make sure that we have done everything that we can. Esteban, what about this ship?"

"Main engines off. There is a stand-by generator that is turning over to supply power. All radios are turned off, but power is being supplied to them. The same with the instruments on the bridge. The last launch, the one we did not let them take to the island, is in the water and tied to the accommodation ladder. "I'll take care of the ladder as soon as we are all aboard."

"Good. Then we are ready to go. Phone the two men on the bridge and get them down to the launch with the bag. So far everything has worked perfectly. But let's get away from here before our luck runs out." He prodded Wielgus with his gun and herded him towards the elevator.

It all ended that quietly. The handful of Tupamaros and Paraguayans who forced a blubbering General Stroessner before them, Uzi and his Nazi prisoners, all of them went carefully down the steps of the accommodation ladder to the folding platform at the bottom where the launch was tied up. This was one of the two red-painted boats that were normally slung just aft of the bridge. It was designed to be used as an emergency boat at sea, was water-jet propelled and immensely powerful. The engine burbled over quietly as they climbed aboard.

"Pull it around the stern," Esteban said to the Tupamaro sailor at the helm, untying the lines at the same time. He ran quickly back up the accommodation ladder and seconds later the lifeboat falls began to grind upwards, lifting the ladder back into its stowed position.

The launch moved swiftly with the slightest touch of power, around to the high stern of the liner. They waited there until Esteban appeared on the deck above, waved to them, then climbed to the rail and dived neatly into the sea below. As soon as he was aboard, they started towards the fishing boat that had heaved to and was waiting.

Uzi sat in the stern with the two sullen Germans, and watched disinterestedly as Josep bent and picked up the bag of diamonds and carried them forwards towards the bow, kicking the shivering Stroessner to one side as he went.

"Where are you going with that?" Diaz said, rising to follow. And in that instant everything changed.

All of the Tupamaros were in either the waist or the bow of the launch. Josep turned and his sub-machine gun was in his hands. The other Tupamaros had their weapons raised as well.

It had only taken a few moments. Diaz started to reach for his gun — and stopped. Even Concepcion, smiling coldly, had her gun pointed at him. He let his hand drop.

"Don't try anything," he told his two stunned Para-guayan companions. "Keep your hands in sight."

"Very wise," Josep said. "That goes for you as well, Uzi. Just stay neutral, this has nothing to do with you."

"Then I assume it has something to do with me," Diaz said, forcing the words through his tight-clamped teeth, realizing far too late that he should have expected some treachery from the Tupamaros.

"Perfectly correct. I want your guns. You won't be harmed. But you might object at the division of these diamonds."

"We share them fifty-fifty," Diaz said.

"That was the original agreement. However, since then we have taken certain losses and have made expensive arrangements. I am changing the split slightly. We are taking it all!"

Josep smiled when he said this and the Tupamaros burst out laughing, thinking this tremendously funny. Uzi was not laughing.

"I thought you were a man of honor, Josep . . . ."

"Watch your mouth!" Josep said, angrily, raising his gun. "I do what must be done. Be happy that you are alive and have that grunting pig, Stroessner, as a hostage. Feel sorry for us, we lost our Admiral Marquez. The extra diamonds will make up for that loss."

Diaz nodded. "I agree. You have had losses, you have had even higher expenses. Two thirds, one third, I will agree to that split."

"I don't care what you agree or what you want. But I shall be generous even though I do not have to be. I will spare you one of these bags of diamonds. A nice big one. That is if my revolutionary comrades agree?"

The Tupamaros laughed and waved, enjoying the joke. Josep dug the key from his pocket and unlocked the bag, throwing it open. And stopped, staring, paralyzed.

Then he grabbed it up and turned it over, dumping it out.

A rain of books and magazines fell to the deck.

They stood, all of them, unmoving at the sight, until Wielgus's laughter cut through the silence. The nearest Paraguayan cuffed him until he was silent as well. Josep bent and picked up one of the books.

"Dorland's Medical Encyclopaedia," he read. "Medical books, all of them, and doctors' magazines." He spun about and pointed to Concepcion. "You did it. You. Nobody else could. Alone in that room with the Sergeant. All the medical books were there. No one else could have gotten near this bag."

"No!" she screamed. "I swear! I know nothing. How could I?"

"Well, the Sergeant with his legs in casts couldn't have done this!" Josep shouted in wild fury. He grabbed the bag and poked inside it. "Cut open on the bottom. Then sewn up neatly. Beautiful stitches. A woman's touch . . . ."

"NO!"

Her screamed word was cut off by the blast of gunfire that tore into her, drove her over the gunwale of the boat into the sea and beneath the surface. Josep ran over and fired again at the corpse as it floated back out of sight and was gone. He spun about, gun quivering from side to side like a questioning dog's nose, screeching now with madness.

"Who has them? One second to speak, then I fire. Diaz, you arranged it with her, a plot. Where are they? You'll not win this way!"

"I didn't, I swear . . . ."

His words were drowned out by the burst of automatic fire and he shrank back instinctively. But the bullets were not aimed at him. But at General Stroessner.

The fat little man screamed like a girl, writhing as he

rose, staring unbelievedly at the blood bursting from the bullet holes in his body.

"If Josep does not win, no one wins!" the Tupamaro shouted, saliva wet on his lips as he pushed the mortally wounded dictator out of the launch and into the sea. He raised his gun again, but it clicked on an empty chamber when he pulled the trigger.

As he struggled to release the clip and jam in a new one, Uzi stood and stepped forward.

"Search everyone, search this launch," he said. "If the diamonds are aboard you will find them easily enough. But whether you do or not I have an offer for you. These Nazis are worth money to me. Don't harm them. Deliver them alive to my people and we will pay you a hundred thousand dollars for Wielgus, fifty thousand for the other one. That is money you can have for your revolution even if you don't find the diamonds."

Uzi's words calmed Josep, the thought of getting hard cash in exchange for the German prisoners certainly raised a new consideration. By reflex his trained fingers found the release and the empty clip clanged to the deck. He replaced it with another, scarcely aware of the action. "You could pay more than that," he said.

"That will not be necessary," Wielgus called out loudly, drawing their attention to him. "Those diamonds were in my trust. I have more where they came from. Release me, Josep, and you will have all the money you need. We will start with a million dollars. You would like a million dollars wouldn't you . . . ?"

"Be quiet!" Uzi ordered, clenching his fists and moving towards the Nazi. Josep waved him back to his seat with the barrel of his gun. Then smiled.

"Now the conversation is taking a more interesting turn. I am sorry, Uzi, but I think I will do business with the Doctor and his associates. With the diamonds gone, he is my only possible source of profit.''

"We had an agreement," Uzi said. "The Germans are mine."

"Not any more. The bullets in my gun make sure of that. I like the sound of their money."

"Do you like the sound of their politics?" Diaz broke in, his voice cold as death. "I thought that we were fighting to get rid of this kind of vermin. Would you free them, align yourself with them?"

"Of course," Josep said. "Politics make strange bedmates. Uruguay will be liberated — that is all that matters."

"But you have the means to do that. The agreements your government signed with these Nazis. That piece of paper will bring about world revulsion — and the revolution you so desperately desire. If you work with these Nazis you compromise everything you say that you stand for."

"That is enough!" Josep swung up the gun. "We have had enough discussion. I have made my decision. I accept the German's offer. He will supply the funds we need, the whereabouts of the other diamonds does not matter now. Anyone who as much as utters one word of protest now will taste some bullets. I mean that. Come over here, Doctor Wielgus, so we can free your hands."

Wielgus stood and smiled at the silent men in the stern of the boat. "So the Jewish interests have lost in the end as they must always do. We will build our power again and the world will one day discover that the power of the Reich is not dead."

"Well said, Doctor," Josep agreed. "In addition to your money, perhaps we can use your aid in the new Uruguay . . . . "

A single shot sounded and Josep stood rigid, the final

word *Uruguay* on his lips. Then, as though in slow motion, the submachine gun fell from his hands and he leaned forward, falling, faster and faster. Slumping dead on the deck of the launch.

Behind him Esteban sat, quietly, the pistol that had fired the shot was still in his hand. No one moved, the Tupamaros as rigid with shock as all the others.

"He wanted to betray us," Esteban said in a voice so low they could scarcely catch the words. "Betray the revolution. I followed him, believed in him, believed he was the leader who would guide us to victory. I even sat here and did nothing when he murdered my sister. Loyalty, we must have loyalty. But not when we take in this Nazi filth as our partners. If we do that, why then the revolution is well and truly lost and we are no better than those we seek to replace."

He threw the pistol to the deck beside Josep's body.

In the silence that followed, Uzi's voice cracked loud as a whip.

"Put the guns down. We have had enough killing. I don't want to shoot." His gun was levelled at them. "But I will if I must. Let us stop this murder now . . . . "

"Millions!" Wielgus shouted. "Don't listen to this dirty Jew with his kike offer of a few shekelks! I'll give you millions . . . . "

His words choked off in a gasp as the nearest Tupamaro tucked his pistol into his belt and casually leaned out to clamp his hand on Wielgus's throat, to squeeze hard so that the German's face turned scarlet and his eyes bulged. Only then did he release his grip and let the man fall, gasping, onto the deck.

"My offer still strands," Uzi said. "We'll pay cash for these two specimens. With that money and the signed agreements you will have your revolution.

Without having to deal with these scum.''

"We will do it that way," Diaz said.

"It is our only choice," Esteban said, and none of the Tupamaros chose to argue. Some strength had gone out of them with Josep's death. He was their leader, the one who had showed them the way. But now he was gone. He had murdered Concepcion before their eyes and it was perhaps only fair that her brother had exacted retributive justice. Everything was confused and the only thing that was clear was that he was dead.

The time to act had long passed. Their guns were put aside and one of them pulled a canvas tarpaulin over the body. Then the engine died away and voices called down to them and they looked up to see that they were beside the *Tigre Amarillo*. The momentous, world-changing events had taken only a few minutes.

They climbed aboard the fishing boat, pushing the German prisoners up ahead of them. Esteban remained to the last, looking at the body of the man he had killed, the man who had been their movement, their life. He came to a decision and called out to the other Tupamaros.

"We must sink this launch. Bullets through the flotation tanks, then grenades. The corpse of this person will stay aboard for burial at sea. That is what Josep told me before he left. Josep leads our revolution always, in the flesh when he is by our sides, in spirit when he is not.''

The others nodded with understanding. The great leaders never die. Barbarossa sits in his cavern in the rock waiting to be called; Holger Dansk will return; somewhere in the mountains of Morelos, Zapata still rides his white horse, ready for the time when he will be needed.

The machine gun roared and splinters flew from the

side of the launch. Other guns joined in and the launch dropped astern, rocking in the hall of fire, low in the water. Esteban primed two grenades and threw them into the sinking boat. The men aboard the *Tigre Amarillo* fell to the deck as the grenades exploded and bits of shrapnel whirled over their heads.

When they stood again just a swirl in the water and some floating debris marked where the launch had been. Uzi leaned close to the staring Wielgus and spoke softly in German to him.

"Look closely. Your Fourth Reich just sank with that launch. We have you and we will have your blood money some day, but even if we don't, your movement is at an end. And so are you, Herr Doktor Joachim Weilgus."

Wielgus did not protest, or even raise his head. For suddenly he was nothing more than an old man with a past and no future, absolutely no future at all. He lurched forward to hurl himself over the rail but Uzi's strong hand seized him and pulled him back.

"It won't be that easy," Uzi said. "A million dead Jews would like to see some justice done first."

The fishing boat's engine blatted loudly as she ran up to full speed and turned her bow back towards Mexico. Her white wake stretched out longer and longer as she grew small on the horizon, then vanished from sight.

Silent and still, the waves slapping against her high black sides, the *QE2* was alone in the ocean at last.

31

Through a rift in the clouds a bar of sunlight penetrated, striking gold highlights from the waves as they ran up onto the beach, hissing as they ran back through the coarse sand. On the rocky slopes behind the beach the nesting seagulls screamed like lost souls.

Libor Chvosta had spent an uncomfortable night on the unyielding beach, finally falling asleep just before dawn. The sunlight woke him now and he tried to pull up the blanket to shield his eyes — then realized the significance of the light and sat up, yawning.

The last of the clouds were disappearing on the horizon. The storm was over at last. A few people were beginning to stir among the thousands sleeping on the beach, walking towards the area in the scrub that had been cordoned off as toilets. The lifeboats lay in neat rows where they had been beached at high tide. Everything had been efficiently organized by the ship's personnel. He could see that the kitchen staff and stewards were already awake, brewing up something hot to drink from the lifeboats' stores. Chvosta smacked his lips together, aware of the foul taste in his mouth. He had scarcely had anything to eat, just some water to drink, all the time he had been locked in the cabin with Aurelia. Nor had he wanted anything after his seasickness had returned. Now, on dry land again, he felt well — and ravenous. He threw the blankets from his immense body, sat up and stretched. Aurelia was lying asleep next to him, her round, full rump rising up, clearly delineated by the blankets. Chvosta reached slowly out.

"Bitch," he muttered and prodded his large thumb again and again into her flesh. She squealed and was awake. When they had been tied in that bed together, and he had been sick, she had said some unforgettable things. He would make her pay.

"I'm going to get something to eat. For myself. Meanwhile you find some paper and start preparing a message to Captain Bartovska aboard the *Lyngby Kro*. I made provisions in case the payment was misdirected. He knows what to do. Those Uruguayan sailors are never going to reach port with those arms."

"And how am I supposed to send this cable?" Her voice dripped venom; she rubbed her sore buttocks. "The boat and launch radios have all been destroyed, you heard that yourself."

"We won't be on this island forever. If you were listening so closely, then you must have heard them talk about filling the empty water cans with petrol. With the storm over, the launch should be able to reach Mexico. And they'll be searching for us. We'll be off this rock soon. And I want that cable ready. Do it now."

He stalked away, sniffing the air in anticipation, his massive stomach rumbling its need. This deal would have to be written off, what with the two contracted governments tottering, the payment gone — and the German paymasters themselves apprehended. But Global Traders wouldn't lose out, once they had the cargo back from the ship. The nonreturnable dances that had been paid would more than cover their expenses. The arms would be sold elsewhere at a good profit. He might even get a bonus out of it. If he did, after she apologized, he might even let Aurelia keep her job. She was really too efficient to fire.

It would all work out. And at least one good thing had come out of all this already. The Nazis, the guard had told him, half of them killed and the others going back for trial. Wonderful! He would do business with Nazis, he would do it with the devil if he wanted some guns, but that did not mean he had to like them. He knew what they had done in Czechoslovakia during the war. So killing a few and putting the rest away, that was a very good thing. The day would be warm, the food would have to taste good, whatever it was. He was humming as he came to the makeshift kitchen, stepping around a little man in a rumpled steward's uniform who was sipping a cup of tea.

Robert finished his tea and returned the cup. There had been little enough to do since they had come ashore, what with all the kitchen staff and sailors pitching in together. It had been one of the other room stewards who had searched him out this morning, waving the paper.

"'Ere, Robert, ain't this bloke one of yours?"

The message was written on a single folded sheet of heavy paper, sealed shut by heavy string that had been sewed around the edges. MSR. GREENSTEIN — FIRST CLASS — URGENTE was printed on the outside in heavy capital letters.

"Only one Greenstein in First Class," Robert had said. "I'll see if I can find him. Ta'."

Poor Mr. and Mrs. Greenstein, he thought, trudging through the sand, looking at the faces of the people sprawled out there. What a luxurious honeymoon! Happy enough to start, what with the free trip from the uncle and all. But then the hijackers bursting in and using their suite for their shoot-ups, not to mention locking him in the bog most of the night. And then to be

cast away on this island! At least they weren't hurt —
and what a story to tell their grandchildren.

A woman turned towards him, yes, it could be. He
hurried over.

"Mrs. Greenstein? I hope that you are all right this
morning."

"Is that you, Robert? My heavens, you aren't
bringing us a breakfast tray in bed are you? With the
morning paper?"

"I wish I could, madam, I honestly do. In fact, now I
know where you are, I can bring you some tea and those
hard-tack biscuits. And marmalade. Not too bad."

"No, really, I was just joking."

"That I realize, madam. But anyone who can joke in
circumstances like these deserves whatever services I can
render." He started away and then turned back, digging
in his pocket. "These same circumstances will make me
forget my head in a minute. The reason I came looking
for you. A message passed along for your husband, if
you please."

"Thank you, you're very kind."

Frances watched the rumpled, unshaven steward
stamp off firmly across the sand. Doing his duty to the
last. Rule on, bloody Britannia! Service to the very end,
well after the ship had sunk. She turned to look for
Hank, waving.

"Guess what?" she called out. "The morning post is
here and breakfast will be on the way soon."

"You're marvelous! How do you do it?" He kissed
her lightly on the cheek so his whiskers wouldn't scratch
her. Then turned the piece of paper over and over,
examining it.

"Who on earth could have sent this? Does MSR.
mean mister, missus — or monseigneur?"

"Well, you will never know until you open it, will
you, darling?"

"True, true." He dug out his pocketknife and cut the stitches, unfolded the sheet. The message inside was brief and he frowned as he read it a second time. Then handed it over to Frances.

POR FAVOR MUSIT YOU COM ME IN HOS-PITAL — SARGENTO PRADERA.

"What does it mean?" she asked.

"It means that this business isn't over yet. You were in the bedroom and didn't hear it. Unhappily I was there and heard every word. He was the Paraguayan secret agent who was right on the inside, reporting to the resistance. The Nazis caught him. Shot away both knee-caps. It wasn't fun. That was what started the big shoot-up. They went in after him."

Frances's voice was cold as death. "And now he is after you for some reason. They still want you involved. Well, you just aren't going to do it. Throw the note away."

Hank crumpled the piece of paper in his hand, held it tightly in his fist.

"I can't turn my back on him," he said. "It will do no harm to just see him, find out what he wants."

"Well, it will do some harm right here, Hank Greenstein. We aren't married yet no matter what anyone thinks. You go see this red revolutionary and you just don't bother to come back. I have had just about enough of this business to satisfy me for life." She spun about and sat down on the sand, her stiff back to him. He reached out, but did not touch her.

"I'm sorry," he said in a low voice. "But I have to see what it is about. Please, Frances. I love you. Never forget that. But I have no choice."

He left then and never saw that she was crying quietly, the tears running down her face.

The hospital was easy enough to find. Crude as it was, canvas boat covers held up by oars, it was the only

structure of any kind on the beach. Since the rain had
stopped, no one had suffered during the night on the
tropical beach. A white-coated doctor was seated on a
box outside the makeshift tent, sipping a mug of tea.

"Is Sergeant Pradera here?" Hank asked.

"Inside. First bed. Are you the one he sent the note
to?" Hank nodded, not sure how much to say. "Can't
hurt to talk to him a bit. He says he recognized you on
the ship, met you when you were in holiday in
Paraguay."

"Lovely country, Paraguay."

"I wouldn't know. I don't think much of some of the
people they had aboard ship. Right through there."

The Sergeant was still on the stretcher that had been
used to take him from the ship. The handles were
propped on boxes; it made a good enough bed.

"*Señor Greenstein. ¿Habla Ud. Español?*"

"*Si. Poquitito.*"

"Very good. I am glad to see you here. You must
speak very quietly because the doctor outside understands Spanish. He thinks that you are just someone I
know from Paraguay."

"I know. He told me."

"Good. Keep it that way. I really know of you
through Leandro Diaz and your friend, Uzi Drezner.
You were pointed out to me."

"Then do me a favor, please. Don't point me out to
anyone else. No one knows that I was at all involved in
this business."

"I shall keep it that way. As you know, I can keep
secrets." Hank glanced down at the Sergeant's legs,
concealed by the blanket, and nodded grimly.

"I know," he said.

"Good. You must get a message to your friend, Uzi.
To be relayed to Diaz. It is that they must not trust the

Tupamaros. They are a bad lot and treacherous and will betray us the first opportunity that they have.''

''I agree,'' Hank said. ''But isn't it a little late for messages?''

''It is. For messages alone. But I have taken it upon myself to act first.''

He pulled the blanket down, disclosing his bare legs, heavily bandaged and in casts that extended above and below each knee. The bandages below the casts were soaked with dark, dried blood. Between the casts was a pillowcase, the end tied with a knot and filled with something lumpy. The Sergeant grunted as he pulled the bag up and swung it to the ground beside his stretcher.

''Take these when you leave,'' he said. ''I will create a diversion. These are the diamonds that everyone has been after.'' He smiled as he saw the expression of shock on Hank's face. ''That's what they are. Those Tupamaros would never have given us our share, never. That girl thought I couldn't leave the bed because they carried me to it. Stupid! I used my arms, pulled myself across the floor. Not easy, but I did it.''

Not easy! Hank remembered the fresh blood and wondered at the man who could drag himself out of bed with legs in that shape.

''Every time she left the room for a few minutes. Cavalry, that's me, old cavalry. Kept my knife, leather awl on it. Cut the bottom of the bag, put in books from the shelves up there, sewed it up again. Ravelled the blanket to make thread. She never guessed. Now the rest is up to you. Take the diamonds out.''

''I can't!''

''You're the only one. I'm military, wounded, I'll be searched, watched. I can't do it. But you're a refugee when they take you off this island. Your bags will never be opened. Contact Uzi. He'll know what to do. How he shares them is up to him. The diamonds are Nazi money, meaning stolen Jewish money. Let it go back to him. Tell him I did it. Tell him that our movement should get a share. Paraguay must be free.''

Hank looked at the innocent-appearing pillowcase. Millions of dollars. A lot of people had died for this. Now it was his. To keep if he wanted to. He smiled at the thought. The Sergeant knew that much about him. He would get the diamonds to Uzi. This was his own personal victory over the Tupamaros and what they represented.

''All right, Sergeant,'' he said. ''I'll do as you ask. And tell Uzi just what you said. And thank you for trusting me.''

''There are no thanks needed. It is not only the Stroessners and Nazis of this world we must fight. It is the Tupamaros as well. *Vaya Ud. con Dios.*''

''And the same to you, Sergeant.''

Sergeant Pradera's eyes narrowed as he looked over Hank's shoulder and his face grew grim. ''I planned a different diversion,'' he said. ''But this one is far better. Hand me something heavy, ahh, yes, those pieces of rock there. Then take the bag and stand to one side. Leave quickly so you will not be seen.''

Outside the shelter, the doctor stood up and opened the medical box that he had been sitting on.

''You said you wanted to see this one today, doctor,'' the Bo'sun said. He was a big man with even bigger hands, and one of them was clamped hard around Klaus's upper arm. The German's head was lowered and he looked at the bandages around his aching, throbbing hands.

''Thank you, Bo'sun. Those hands will need treatment.''

''Aye, aye, sir. We don't want the Nazi son of a bitch

going septic or whatever before they take him back for trial for shooting up the ship.''

"Let's not prejudge before the trial or whatever."

"Of course, sir," with no slightest trace of contrition in his voice.

Klaus screamed with shock as the rock caught him in the side of the face, spinning him about. The second one thudded against his ribs.

"Murderous swine!" the Sergeant shouted. "They did my knees and you held me. Come close so I can get my hands on your neck!"

No one saw Hank leave.

Frances had made her mind up and had decided exactly what she wanted to do long before she found out what was in the filthy pillowcase that Hank had leaned against their suitcase when he returned.

"You're a bastard, and I love you," she announced firmly, before he had a chance to speak. "You are going to keep on doing these things, I know, and I'm going to keep on not liking it. But I'm not going to live without you. Understand?"

"Understood. Can I kiss you now?"

"No. Not until you have shaved. And you are going to marry me quick before anything else happens. Which I'm sure will be very soon if I know you. Now, what's in the pillowcase? The Sergeant's old laundry?"

"Sort of. Let me put it in the bottom of the suitcase, then I'll tell you."

"Don't worry, all your jewelry is still here, still safe," Angus Macrahanish said, stirring his finger about in the bottom of the bag where rings, necklaces and strings of pearls lay casually between the two bottles of whisky. Why not a quick one for his health's sake? He was sore all over from spending a night on the sand listening to

Martha's snores. He uncapped the half-full bottle and took a healthy drink. Lovely! He lowered the bottle and sighed happily — and his glance fell on the man lying nearby him on the sand.

That was another thing that had kept him awake. That big blowsy woman had been snorting like a steam engine most of the night, not to mention an occasional howl like a cat in the back garden. She might very well comb her hair and sing happily to herself — she had had a good night. Amazing, he was such a small, skinny chap. And looking the worse for wear, as well he might. Angus leaned over and extended the bottle.

"Here. Would you like a wee dram?"

"Yes. Indeed. You are ferry kind."

Hendrik extended a quavering hand and seized the bottle's neck. It burned, but it was very good. Life-restoring. He was beginning to reconsider Sheila's book and her visit to Holland. For the first time in his life he realized that it was really possible to have too much of a good thing. Sheila leaned over and patted his arm warmly. He tried not to twitch when she did it. Too much, really too much.

It was like the Fourth of July, or VE day or a Cup Final with the crowds cheering and jumping around, the flares from the Very pistols going off over their heads, and the roar of sound as the giant 747 tore along parallel with the beach. The words AIR WESTERN very large on its side. A very fine sight indeed.

Hank pointed to the Stars and Stripes painted on the plane's tail, and pulled Frances close and kissed her despite the damage his whiskery embrace did to her skin.

"Look, darling," he said. "It's going to be all right now."

"The cavalry is coming!"